AF412250

JURISDICTION IN MARGINAL SEAS

JURISDICTION IN MARGINAL SEAS

with

Special Reference to Smuggling

BY

WILLIAM E. MASTERSON

KENNIKAT PRESS
Port Washington, N. Y./London

JURISDICTION IN MARGINAL SEAS

First published in 1929
Reissued in 1970 by Kennikat Press
Library of Congress Catalog Card No: 78-110932
SBN 8046-0915-2

Manufactured by Taylor Publishing Company   Dallas. Texas

TO

ELOISE BORDAGES MASTERSON

PREFACE

THE question of jurisdiction in marginal seas has always been a troublesome one; and within quite recent years, it has become an increasingly important and active one. Its codification is now under consideration by the Committee of Experts for the Progressive Codification of International Law appointed by the Council of the League of Nations in 1924; it became the subject of diplomatic correspondence in 1922 when the United States Government began the seizure on the high seas of foreign vessels engaged in introducing or in attempting to introduce into the nation's commerce illicit cargoes in violation of her revenue laws and the National Prohibition Act; during the past four years, it has been the subject matter of treaties between some nineteen States; and several non-official International Law societies and associations have proposed solutions of the question through draft conventions.

The recent exclusion of certain articles of commerce, especially alcoholic liquors, by several countries and the imposition of a heavy duty upon their importation by others have given rise to renewed activities of smugglers operating in foreign vessels off the coasts in several parts of the world. The enforcement on the high seas of the national revenue laws, often spoken of as the "hovering laws," against these vessels centered attention upon the question of the extent of the so-called "territorial waters" and the further question of how far a State may, under International Law, exercise a special jurisdiction beyond such waters over foreign craft engaged in violating or in attempting to violate certain of its laws. This latter question has never been specifically dealt with very fully, though it has been frequently considered incidentally in connection with discussions of the more general question of the so-called "territorial waters." In this volume the method of treatment is reversed—emphasis is laid upon the question of this special jurisdiction, while its relation to the more general question of "territorial waters" is discussed when it seems helpful or necessary to do so. It is believed that a need for such a treatment has arisen, and this need is the justification for this book.

It was found all but impossible fully to understand many of the laws passed to end smuggling from sea without tracing the history of smuggling itself. This history has, therefore, been gone into very thoroughly from the date of the earliest official records obtainable, down to the present time, as a necessary background for the study of the centuries of legislation, court decisions, and diplomatic discussions dealt with in this volume. Legislation on this subject, which began in England as early as 1699, and in the United States in 1789, studied in the light of this history, furnishes an interesting example of how the law undergoes the development necessary for the extermination of the evil against which it is directed.

A great deal of the important materials relating to the subject, including departmental orders and instructions, interdepartmental and diplomatic correspondence, and, in some instances, court decisions, have never been published. It was found necessary, therefore, to carry on the research from original records, not only in the United States, but also in several European countries. The records of several unpublished court decisions and the unpublished correspondence between the Commissioners of Customs at London and the collectors at the several English outports, dating from the seventeenth century, and the correspondence between several departments of the English Government from 1850 were examined in the library of His Majesty's Customs at London. These materials proved to be invaluable in clearing up some of the obscure provisions of the English law, in showing the conditions which made these laws necessary, in establishing the practice of courts and customs authorities in enforcing the laws, and in clearly presenting the views of several departments of the British Government between 1850 and 1875 in regard to the international status of such laws. The author is grateful to the Commissioners of Customs and Excise for permission to examine these materials. He is, also, greatly indebted to Bertram R. Leftwich, M.B.E., F.R.Hist.S., Librarian to His Majesty's Board of Customs and Excise, who has spent a great deal of time from year to year in collecting at the various outports and in organizing and admirably systemizing the two and one-half centuries of correspondence between the Collectors and the Commissioners of Customs, for his assistance in connection with the examination of this correspondence. Mr. Leftwich was good enough to read painstakingly the part of the manuscript dealing with the development of the English law, and thanks are due him for helpful suggestions and discussions.

The records of many unpublished court decisions enforcing the revenue laws on the high seas were found in the old Memoranda Rolls at the Public Record Office, London. These decisions are meagerly reported, but enough of the record is usually given to show that the laws passed by Parliament from time to time were vigorously enforced against foreign vessels. The author is grateful to Hilary Jenkinson, Maitland Memorial Lecturer in the University of Cambridge, and J. J. O'Reilly, Assistant Keepers of the Public Records, for their assistance in connection with the examination of these records.

A great deal of hitherto unpublished diplomatic correspondence and other materials were examined also at several departments of the Government at Washington, D. C. The author is greatly obliged to the following gentlemen for their coöperation in placing before him the materials in their respective departments or for discussions of the views of the United States Government and the practice of the various officials in enforcing the revenue laws against foreign vessels on the high seas: L. C. Andrews, Assistant Secretary of the Treasury; Tyler Dennett, Chief of the Division of Publications, Department of State; William R. Vallance and Frederick M. Diven, Assistant Solicitors, Department of State; and Commander Charles S. Root, United States Coast Guard, Chief Intelligence Officer.

Among other friends and colleagues in this country and abroad to whom thanks are due for information or for helpful criticisms, the following are gratefully mentioned: Arnold D. McNair, C.B.E., LL.D., Fellow Gonville and Caius College and Lecturer in the University of Cambridge, and formerly reader in Public International Law in the University of London; H. C. Gutteridge, M.A., LL.M.; Sir Ernest Cassel, Professor of Commercial and Industrial Law in the University of London; Calvert Magruder, Professor of Law, Harvard Law School; H. A. C. Sturgess, Librarian and Keeper of the Records, Middle Temple, London; Stephen P. Ladas of the Bureau of International Research of Harvard University and Radcliffe College; Stanley W. Schaefer of the New York Bar, New York City; and Howard L. Leroy of the District of Columbia Bar, Washington, D. C.

The author is also very greatly indebted to the Bureau of International Research of Harvard University and

Radcliffe College for its assistance in the preparation and publication of this volume. Very especially has he to thank two members of this Bureau, George Grafton Wilson, Professor of International Law at Harvard University, and Manley O. Hudson, Bemis Professor of International Law at the Harvard Law School, for their helpful advice throughout. These gentlemen were good enough to read the manuscript and to offer many valuable recommendations for improvement.

The author is indebted to his wife for her assistance in examining and transcribing many of the old records in this country and abroad and in the preparation of the manuscript, and for her aid and coöperation in many other ways.

The Introduction is taken largely from a paper read by the author before the Grotius Society in London in May, 1927;[1] while some of the views expressed in the Conclusions are taken from a paper read before that Society in June, 1928.[2]

WILLIAM E. MASTERSON.

Kendall House,
Cambridge, Mass.,
May, 1928.

[1] *The Transactions of the Grotius Society, vol. 13.*
[2] This paper will appear in the *Transactions* of the Grotius Society for 1929.

INTRODUCTION

THE old claims of the maritime powers to dominion in the high seas were abandoned some two hundred years ago. It has always been evident, however, that for some purposes, at least, it is necessary for the state to retain a certain measure of jurisdiction over the waters adjoining its coast: the nation's defense and safety must be secured; navigation must be made safe for vessels visiting its ports; health must be protected, the revenue safeguarded against smuggling craft, and the coast fisheries must be reserved for its nationals. The development of the idea of this jurisdiction in the coastal waters has not been without its difficulties. Especially has the maximum distance seaward to which certain laws may be enforced in these waters been a constant and fruitful source of controversy among nations; and so varied has been the practice and so divergent the views of governments on this point that it may be safely said that there has not, as yet, emerged from the confusion a clearly defined and crystallized principle of International Law, unless it may be said that three miles, or one league, must be allowed as the *minimum* distance.

A thorough treatment of the historical development of the law relating to jurisdiction in the marginal seas with respect to fisheries, neutrality, crime, pilotage, collision, quarantine, salvage, revenue, and customs is beyond the scope of this volume. The laws passed to protect or regulate these various interests, or claims, involve different considerations, and they have, therefore, developed along different lines; laws securing or regulating a particular interest have been evolved from factors peculiar to such interest. They, thus, necessarily present distinct questions, and should, therefore, be dealt with separately in a study of the law pertaining to jurisdiction in the littoral seas. The attempt within recent years, on the part of some writers, judges, and governments, to fix a single zone beyond which the application or enforcement of them all is forbidden, thus treating them as a single problem, has cast this extremely difficult subject into hopeless confusion, and has littered the juristic literature on the subject with careless assertion. Such attempts are often veiled efforts to dodge the accurate solution of a perplexing problem. Assertion and hasty generalization have been handed on, copied, and repeated until repetition has led to their acceptance by some as representing statements of a principle of International Law. They have resulted in the belief by some English and American writers that no national interests may be safeguarded or regulated, under International Law, beyond a single zone of three miles from the shore.

Obviously, however, the littoral state has less concern with a simple assault by a seaman in the hold of a passing foreign vessel one mile from the shore than with a naval engagement ten miles out between belligerent dreadnoughts with their present-day engines of destruction. It has not as high a concern with a collision between foreign vessels 2.9 miles out as it has with an armed and powerfully manned foreign smuggling vessel hovering 12 miles out, seeking an opportunity clandestinely to run ashore or to unlade merchandise whose importation is forbidden. Clearly it has more concern with a foreign vessel fishing near its shores than with a passing vessel only a few hundred yards away. These and many other examples may, perhaps, serve as intimations that the various interests, or claims, must be approached as separate problems, and that some of them, at least, must be and have been given different solutions. It would seem that one way out of the confusion into which the question of the so-called "three-mile limit" or "territorial waters" has been cast, and in which it has been abandoned, is to trace historically and to study analytically the laws and practice of the maritime nations with reference to each interest, as a distinct and separate subject of inquiry.[1]

This volume deals primarily with jurisdiction over foreign smuggling craft to prevent the clandestine introduction of prohibited or dutiable goods into a nation's commerce. This phase of the subject is of ever-increasing importance. It presents a distinct and separate problem. In theory and in practice, it must be and has been, by most nations, at least, disassociated from the questions of jurisdiction for some other purposes, such as neutrality and fisheries. Many recent laws and decrees dealing with other interests are included, when they are helpful in showing the positions of governments on the question of jurisdiction to prevent smuggling.

An accurate and comprehensive understanding of the so-called "hovering laws" of to-day and of their past and present relation to International Law cannot be gained without an analysis of their historical background of 250 years. A thorough study, therefore, has been made of the question since it first arose, from statutes, diplomatic correspondence, parliamentary debates, official reports of legislative committees, court decisions, international arbitral awards, instructions to revenue and coast guard officers, treaties, interdepartmental correspondence, the old English Parchment or Memoranda Rolls, custom-house records, and other materials. Hence, there is found

---

[1] This has been done admirably and with scholarly precision by Thomas Wemyss Fulton with reference to the fishery interests, in his *The Sovereignty of the Sea* (1911).

in this volume a great deal of material hitherto unpublished. In the development and analysis of the law of this subject, reliance has been placed almost altogether upon original sources for statements and conclusions. Reliance upon secondary sources and statements of writers leads to inaccuracy and incompleteness, and such reliance in the past by some writers on International Law has proved to be particularly disastrous in the treatment of this subject.

Because of the great difficulties one encounters in obtaining access to historical records and documents in many foreign countries, it was decided to develop the subject with special emphasis upon the law as evolved in England and the United States, though many of the laws and decrees of many other countries are included. The subject is dealt with in the following order:

1. The Development of the English Law.
2. The Law of the British Empire.
3. The Development of the Law of the United States.
4. Diplomatic Correspondence, Treaties, International Arbitrations, etc.
5. Conclusions.

Some of the diplomatic correspondence, treaties, and arbitral awards antedate some of the municipal laws discussed, but it is believed that a better understanding of the international situation may be had after the municipal law of each country has been presented in its entirety. It would seem better to develop first the general policies and purposes that lie behind municipal legislation, for it is this development which has led naturally and logically to international considerations, and to whatever International Law there is upon the subject.

Many of the details as to the amount of smuggling carried on, the type of the craft employed, and the methods of the smugglers might have been omitted; but extensive use of footnotes has been availed of in order to include some interesting materials, which have not been published before, because they point, in many cases, to the necessity and furnish the *raison d'être* for much of the legislation by Parliament and Congress, which has, in turn, influenced the laws of many other countries.

In tracing the development of smuggling legislation in its application to the marginal seas, it is evident that the distance seaward to which jurisdiction has been exercised has not remained fixed, but that it has been altered from decade to decade as necessity required. Among those factors that have entered into the determination of that distance and into the frequent changes of it found in the laws of some countries, there may be mentioned four in this connection:

1. The distance from which the smuggler hovered, operated, or became a menace to the revenue and legitimate trade.
2. The type and speed of his craft.
3. The extent to which smuggling was carried on.
4. The commodity smuggled.

These factors, and others, will be discussed at length in connection with the analyses of legislation, parliamentary debates and papers, interdepartmental and diplomatic correspondence, and other materials. These changes in legislation were especially frequent in British law. Therefore, one finds, as he would expect to find, that as smuggling became less prevalent after the year 1850 and was almost entirely wiped out after 1870, whether due to the reduction of customs duties and the adoption of the free-trade policy, the strengthening of the naval force, the introduction of steam power, and the increased vigilance of officers, legislation became stabilized, and the great distances of eight and one hundred leagues adopted by Parliament for almost two hundred years as the limits of jurisdiction in the adjacent seas were no longer necessary, and in 1876 they were accordingly reduced to one, three, and four leagues.[2] Again, a certain measure of jurisdiction was exercised through English legislation for many years over foreign vesels approaching the English coast, hailing from ports where prevailed the plague and other diseases believed for a time to be contagious, but this legislation was repealed, also, when the belief that these diseases were contagious was declared to be superstitious.[3] In the case of the United States, four leagues for jurisdiction over smuggling craft was chosen in 1790, and has remained fixed in the law.

When the question of the limit of this jurisdiction is approached historically through centuries of legislation and other sources referred to, that is, through the practice of the several nations, rather than through some theory, one finds that the limits chosen by the various states have not been uniform, and in the case of Great Britain, at least, different limits have been adopted for different periods of history, and for different parts of the coast. In other words, the point to be borne in mind is that the extent of jurisdiction for revenue purposes has been determined with the view to eradicate an evil, without reference to the much-discussed theories of "Territorial Waters," the "Three-mile Limit," or "Cannon Range."

[2] As will be pointed out later, these changes were made in 1876 for several reasons, which are considered in their appropriate places.

[3] See *Parliamentary Debates* (Hansard), 1844, vol. 76, cols. 1292-1310; ibid., 1842, vol. 61, cols. 608-618; 1825, vol. 12, col. 993; 1845, vol. 78, col. 1316; 1893, vol. 16, col. 628, vol. 17, cols, 714-5; 1894, vol. 22, col. 955; 1895, vol. 32, col. 1279; 6 Geo. IV, c. 78, and Piggott, *Nationality,* vol. II, p. 52, et seq.

CONTENTS

INTRODUCTORY CHAPTER

PART I
THE DEVELOPMENT OF THE ENGLISH LAW

CHAPTER I
DURING THE SEVENTEENTH CENTURY

CHAPTER II
FROM 1700 TO 1736

CHAPTER III
FROM 1736 TO 1745

CONTENTS   xxi

PART II

THE LAW OF THE BRITISH EMPIRE

INTRODUCTION

CHAPTER I

LEGISLATION

PART III

DEVELOPMENT OF THE LAW OF THE UNITED STATES

CHAPTER I

FROM 1775 TO 1920

CHAPTER II

FROM 1920 TO 1928

PART IV

DIPLOMATIC CORRESPONDENCE; TREATIES; INTERNATIONAL ARBITRATIONS

INTRODUCTORY REMARKS

CHAPTER I

DIPLOMATIC DISCUSSIONS, 1806-1892

CHAPTER II

THE COQUITLAM (1892-1920); DIPLOMATIC CORRESPONDENCE AND ARBITRATION BETWEEN THE UNITED STATES AND GREAT BRITAIN

CHAPTER III

DISCUSSIONS OF THE RUSSIAN FISHERY AND CUSTOMS LAWS TAKING JURISDICTION FOR FOUR LEAGUES BY THE UNITED STATES, GREAT BRITAIN, RUSSIA, AND JAPAN, 1910-1912

CHAPTER IV

THE SEIZURE OF FOREIGN SMUGGLING VESSELS IN 1922 BY THE UNITED STATES UNDER THE NATIONAL PROHIBITION ACT AND THE FOUR-LEAGUE STATUTES AND OTHER LAWS

CHAPTER V

THE RUM TREATIES, 1924-1928

PART V

CONCLUSIONS

PART I
THE DEVELOPMENT OF THE ENGLISH LAW

JURISDICTION IN MARGINAL SEAS

PART I

THE DEVELOPMENT OF THE ENGLISH LAW

CHAPTER I

DURING THE SEVENTEENTH CENTURY

§ 1. The Rise of Smuggling in England

Smuggling to and from sea was a serious problem in England for many centuries. From the thirteenth century on, growers of wool looked longingly toward France and Holland and Sweden for markets for their surplus produce, whose exportation, however, was forbidden. From the seventeenth century on, the importation of many other articles was either highly taxed or prohibited. Smugglers, as a result, arose in vast hordes both on sea and on land. From the earliest time, drastic action was taken by the English Government to put an end to this illicit trade.

As early as 1678,[1] the Board of Customs wrote to the collector of Customs at Stockton-on-Tees:

[1] January 11. All correspondence between the Board of Customs and the collectors of the outports as well as interdepartmental correspondence found under the English law, was taken from documents in the library of His Majesty's Customs at London, unless otherwise indicated. See the Preface for further explanation.

"Whereas we are informes that great quantities of French Wine of ye growth of this year and other French prohibited goods have been of late and are frequently landed and put on shoar in divers by creeks, bayes and other places of this Kingdom and from thence conveyed in ye night into ye houses, warehouses and cellars of merchts, vintners and other retailers of wine to the defeating of the good intencions of ye late Poll Act and to the great prejudice of His Maj'ties Customs, we doe therefore direct that you doe call together all ye officers of His Ma'ties Customs within your Port . . . and that you give them strictly in charge that they doe use their utmost endeavours for ye prevencion of those frauds and abuses and violation of ye said law and that they bee very vigilant that French wines bee not landed under ye name of other wines and yt none of ye French prohibited goods be landed under any false denominacion or by means of fals package whatsoever."

And in 1680,[2] the Board wrote as follows to the same collector:

"Being informed that 5 or 6 sevl. vessels are now lading wine att Burdeau and other parts of France most part whereof are supposed to bee intended for this Kingdome to bee privately stolen on shoar and being likewise informed that some new wines have already been attempted to bee landed in this Kingdome, Wee desire you to call all ye officers of your Port and admonish them to use all diligence to p'vent ye landing of any French wines, Fr. linen and other French prohibited goods and if they shall discover and meet with any vessels laden in part or in whole *wth* any Fr. Wine, Fr. linen or other Fr. prohibited goods within ye limits of your Port you are to cause them to be stayed till ye have informed us all ye

[2] October 30.

grounds and circumstances of their comeing in, and receive our directions."

In 1699, "for the better preventing the Exportation of Wooll out of this Kingdom or Ireland, into foreign Parts," it was enacted that the Lord High Admiral should appoint certain ships and "8 armed Sloops, constantly to cruize on the Coasts of England and Ireland, particularly between the North of Ireland and Scotland, with Orders to take and seize all Ships, Vessels, and Boats, which shall export any wooll with intent to carry it into foreign parts." [3]

Thus, in the seventeenth century, no limit seaward was fixed for jurisdiction over craft engaged in smuggling certain goods into England or exporting wool therefrom. Orders were issued to one collector to prevent the landing of French wines and other prohibited articles; and Parliament directed vessels "to cruise on the coasts" and seize all vessels found exporting wool. The interpretation of the instructions of 1680, directing the collector at Stockton-on-Tees to "stay" all vessels laden with certain goods within the limits of that port, involves some difficulty. The limits therein named have reference, perhaps, to the lineal extent of the port along the coast line, as well as to the distance seaward in the adjacent waters under the jurisdiction of the collector at that port. The limits seaward of the ports in the early years of the eightecnth century were not uniform—some were measured in fathoms of water, and others in miles. [4] It is unnecessary, however, to determine those limits at this early period; for the English Government was then claiming and maintaining sovereignty over the entire four bodies of water known as the "English Seas," which would

---

[3] 10 and 11 Wm. III, c. X, sec. XVI.
[4] See pp. 9-10, *infra,* where some of the limits are considered.

embrace the limits of all ports. Hence, there was nothing novel or unusual in the exercise of jurisdiction over smuggling craft for an indefinite distance, as provided by the Act of 1699.

There were, doubtless, other such orders issued by the Board of Customs during the seventeenth century. The two extracts quoted are illustrative. England was, thus, in the seventeenth century engaged with the smuggler, but legislation and instructions to the collectors of the outports had not assumed very definite form. Precise definition was not necessary at this period, in view of the old claims of all the maritime nations to jurisdiction over whole seas, which were still lingering in the seventeenth century.[5]

[5] For an excellent history of these claims, see Fulton, *Sovereignty of the Sea*, Introduction.

§ 2. Legislation

*Jurisdiction taken for Two Leagues and within the
Limits of any Port*

The eighteenth century witnessed a great deal of drastic
legislation and many orders and instructions from the
Board of Customs in the warfare against smuggling, which
was ever on the increase, until it eventually produced a
condition of all but anarchy on some parts of the coasts
and in the littoral seas. Legislation during the new century took more definite form; in many instances, it fixed
definite limits of jurisdiction over the smuggling craft of
all nationalities—namely, two, three, and four leagues
from the shore as well as the large areas of the sea known
as the "King's Chambers"; while other laws declared that
certain conduct within the limits of a port or, again,
anywhere "at sea" constituted criminal offenses.

The correspondence between the Board of Customs and
the collectors at the outports and the reports of committees appointed by Parliament to study and report on
the question of smuggling, reflect, in great detail and with
great clarity, the rise and rapid growth of the evil during
the new century, the necessity for new and more drastic
legislation, and the practice in vogue of cruising for and
seizing vessels on the high seas.

During the period under consideration, namely, from
1700 to 1736, legislation penalized the taking in of goods
anywhere "at sea," and certain conduct within the limits
of a port, or, again, within two leagues of the coast.

The first of the British so-called "hovering acts" of the eighteenth century, passed in 1709, provided that "if any pepper, raisins, mace, . . . or any other sort of goods whatsoever, liable to the payment of duties, shall be unshipped, with intention to be laid on land (customs, . . . not being first paid or secured) or if any prohibited goods whatsoever, shall be imported into any part of Great Britain," the persons concerned in the unshipping should forfeit treble the value of the goods unshipped, and the vessels and boats and horses and carriages made use of in the landing, removing, or conveying the goods, as well as the good themselves, should likewise be forfeited.[1]

The provisions of this law are not clear. It is possible that it was aimed at the unshipping of goods upon the coast from a vessel in port, with the view to their introduction into the country without the payment of duties; while, on the other hand, the legislator may have meant to provide for the forfeiture of the goods in case they were unshipped anywhere at sea with the intention to lay them later on land, and of the vessel, wherever found, made use of in conveying the goods to the shore.

The next Act of Parliament dealing with the subject was passed in 1718. This was "An Act against clandestine running of uncustomed goods, and for the more effectual preventing of frauds relating to the customs."[2] It dealt with the taking in of goods "at sea" and with vessels of fifty tons or under hovering on the coasts. The preamble recited that the laws in force for preventing the unlawful importing and clandestine running and landing of customable and prohibited goods had been found to be ineffectual, whereby His Majesty had been greatly defrauded in his duties.

[1] 8 Anne, c. 7, sec. 17, "An Act for granting to Her Majesty new duties of excise and upon several imported commodities. . . ."
[2] 5 Geo. I, c. XI.

Section III provided for the forfeiture of "any foreign goods, wares or merchandise," which should "be taken in at Sea" by any "Collier, Fisher-boat, or other coasting vessel or boat," [3] or "out of any ship or vessel whatsoever, in order to be landed or put into any other ship, vessel or boat, within the limits of any port," without the payment of duties. Also the master or persons in charge of both the in-taking and the unlading vessels "shall forfeit treble the value" of the goods unshipped, unless the unlading was due to necessity. No limit or distance was specified. It is not necessary to determine the limits of the various ports; for the offense defined was an unlading "at sea" with the intention to place the goods on board a vessel in the limits of any port, regardless of what those limits were. Nothing was said as to where the goods could have been seized or the masters arrested; but as already indicated, during this period, seizures and arrests were made anywhere on the "English Seas."

The necessity at this time for legislation prohibiting hovering on the coasts is pointed out in section VIII of this Act, in the observation that divers ships of fifty tons or under, laden with coffee, tea, brandy, spirits, and other goods, "pretending to be bound for foreign parts, do frequently lie hovering on the coasts of this Kingdom, with intention to run the same privately on shore as opportunity offers, to the great . . . loss of the revenue." This

---

[3] It was the practice of these vessels to receive cargoes from French and Dutch vessels, and to transfer them to fishing vessels, or to carry them into port as ship's stores or to secrete them in the sea near the port of destination. The Board of Customs wrote to the collector at Malden on April 15, 1767: "Several Cutters are gone from the coasts of Kent to France and Holland to take in uncustomed goods and from thence to proceed to the tract which the colliers use in going to and from Newcastle to Sunderland in order to dispose thereof, amongst them and other coasting vessels who run the same on shore." The officers were, therefore, charged "to rummage all light and loaded colliers and all other vessels immediately on their arrival at your port."

section then provided for the visitation, by the officers of the customs, of the following vessels:

> Any ship or vessel of the burthen of 50 tons, or under, laden with customable or prohibited goods, . . . found hovering on the coasts of this Kingdom, within the limits of any Port, . . .

not proceeding on her voyage for foreign parts or to some other British port. The officers were permitted to go aboard any such vessel, take an account of the lading, demand a bond in the sum of treble the value of the foreign goods on board, conditioned that such ship would proceed on its voyage and land such goods at some foreign port. If the bond was refused, or if given and the voyage not continued, the foreign goods could be removed and taken ashore; if the goods were customable, the customs had then to be paid; but they were forfeited if they were wool, or any other prohibited goods or other goods liable to forfeiture if found on ships at the time of their unlading. The ship also was subject to prosecution if it was liable to condemnation, but nothing in the Act provided when it was so liable.[4]

[4] Sections II, III, and VIII were renewed from time to time for stated periods and were eventually made perpetual in 1810 by 50 Geo. III, c. X. They were repealed, however, in 1825 by the Act of 6 Geo. IV, c. CV. The Statutes renewing these sections are: 9 Geo. I, c. VIII, sec. VIII; 2 Geo. II, c. XXVIII, sec. III; 8 Geo. II, c. XXI, sec. III; 15 Geo. II, c. XXXIII, sec. III; 20 Geo. II, c. XLVII, sec. V; 27 Geo. II, c. XVIII, sec. IV.

An instance of the enforcement of sec. VIII is found in a report from the Port of Wick, Scotland, to the Board on November 8, 1742, in which it was said that when the "ship John and Margaret of Dunrosness in Zetland . . . came into Scrabster Road," the customs officer told the master that he would have to go to the customs house and give a "hovering bond." The officer went on board the vessel later, as the bond had not been given, only to find that the cargo of spirits and tobacco had disappeared.

It was stated in this Act that small boats under fifteen tons burden were more advantageously used for the practice of smuggling brandy, strong-waters, and spirits; wherefore, it was provided that if any such goods were brought into any port, harbour, haven, or creek in any ship, or boat, under fifteen tons, the ship should be forfeited and broken up.

Section II provided that all rum, imported in any cask not contain-

The correspondence between the collectors at the outports and the Board of Customs during the early years of the eighteenth century gives the limits of some of the ports. The limits of all the ports do not appear in the records available at the library of His Majesty's Customs at London. Those that were found are given below.

The limits of the port of King's Lynn were reported by the collector at that port to the Board on July 8, 1714, to extend "from the corner commonly called Sutton Corner, East into the Sea to 14 fathom of water and from thence in a supposed line till it fall opposite to the sand hill or place commonly called Burnham Meales and so to the Harbour of Burnham Overy to the same depth of water towards the North East and so directly from the said bounds and limits up the River of Lynn Regis, . . ."; while on October 28, 1729, the same officer reported that this port extended fourteen fathoms water into the sea between Ryhope Nooke and Huntcliffe Foot.

The limits of the port of Whitby, according to a report by the collector to the Board on July 30, 1729, extended "into 30 fathom water" between Whitby and "our next adjoining Ports viz. Stockton and Scarbro."

According to letters from the collectors to the Board, the following other limits were reported:

The limits of the port of Newcastle-on-Tyne, on September 6, 1726, extended "from the promontary or point called the Soutar Point, about 3 miles from Tin-

---

ing twenty gallons at least, should be forfeited, unless such importation was without fraud or concealment, in which case it could be entered and the duty paid. This provision, it was stated, was found necessary because of the frequent importation of rum in small casks "with design that the same may more easily, privately, and clandestinely be carried off and conveyed without paying the duties." This is the first of the many acts regulating the size of the casks in which liquors could be imported. The size of the casks containing liquors and other commodities on vessels hovering on the coast was later regulated by legislation. Sec. II is noteworthy in this connection, as showing the reason and necessity for such future legislation.

mouth Barr towards the So. East and by East and so into the sea to sixteen fathom water," directly to Hartley Bates; while the limits of the port of Yarmouth, on October 31, 1728, extended "from Cromer church in the County of Norff, and by an imaginary line bearing north into the sea to the distance of 3 miles from the land and then bearing by an imaginary line at the same distance from the shoar East South East 3 miles and by the same line and same distance bearing South till it falls opposite Lewestoff Ness and from thence from the same line and same distance bearing South and by West till it falls opposite to a place commonly called Covehithe, Cove Kitts or Cothy in the County of Suffolk, 3 miles from the shoar and from the said bounds and limits West in at the Peer commonly called Yarmouth Peer and so north up the River Yarmouth to Yarmouth Bridge."

Thus, under the Act of 1718, vessels could have been visited at varying distances from the coast, according to the port off which they lay. It would be a difficult task to translate into miles the data presented in this early correspondence as the limits of the ports. No attempt has been made to do this; for shortly after this law came into force, new legislation was passed, extending the jurisdiction and defining its limits more precisely, so that, while the Act now under discussion remained in force for many years, it was superseded, in practice, by a new one. Since the new Act, which was passed to force the hovering vessel to stand farther out at sea, fixed this distance at two leagues, it follows that such limits were less than two leagues, at least.

The Acts of 1709 and 1718 mark the beginning of a long list of statutes, extending over a period of nearly two hundred years, designed to end the practice of smuggling from sea. In the beginning, such legislation was necessarily experimental. Consequently, such changes had to be made from time to time as were thought or found to be necessary to put an end to this ever increasing evil, as it was carried on for the time being. Thus, in the hovering law of 1718, vessels were subjected to visitation only when found hovering on the coast within the limits of any port. Ostensibly, the vessels found to be a menace at that time and, therefore, those sought to be reached by section VIII of the Act of that year, were those that hovered on the coast within the limits of a port; therefore, visitation within such limits was thought to be sufficient to cope with smuggling from the hovering vessel. On the other hand, unlading of goods anywhere "at sea," in order to land them or to put them into another vessel within the limits of a port, was made an offense. As will be presently observed, as smuggling increased, and as it became more difficult to detect and abolish the practice because of the employment of more skilfully and deceptively-constructed and swifter and larger craft, and because the vessels stood farther out to sea than the limits of a port, legislation went through great and rapid changes, not only as to the penalties and forfeitures prescribed, but also as to the character of the craft embraced within its terms, and the distance into the neighboring sea to which jurisdiction was extended. In other words, the laws underwent, from time to time, whatever changes became necessary to stem the rising tide of a rapidly growing evil. Eventually, very drastic legislation became necessary, in view of the vast extent of smuggling, the daring and boldness with which it was carried on, and the great distance at sea from which the smuggling vessel operated.

An Act of Parliament passed in the next year, 1719, is a striking illustration of the point just made. It was "An Act for preventing frauds and abuses in the public revenues of excise, customs, stamp-duties, post-office, and

house-money." [5] Section XXXI of this Act, after referring to the Act of 1718, and more particularly to section VIII thereof, providing for the visitation of vessels
found hovering on the coast within the limits of any port,
declared that "such ships or vessels, to elude the intent of
that law, do lie at anchor, or hover on the coast as near
to the said limits as may be, whereby the masters of such
ships or vessels have better opportunities of making their
signals to the exporters of wool, and the runners of uncustomed and prohibited goods, to draw down to the sea-side
(as they frequently do in great numbers of armed men)
and of running the goods on shore, and carrying off the
wool and coin of this kingdom in their boats, which make
more frequent trips to and from the shore than they could
do, if such ships or vessels were obliged to lie at a greater
distance from the shore. . . ." It was then enacted that it
should be lawful to compel the master of the following
vessels to come into port: "any ship or vessel of the
burden of 50 tons or under, being in part or fully laden
with brandy, . . . found at anchor or hovering within 2
leagues from the shore," not proceeding on her voyage. [6]
The master, the ship, and the brandy were declared to be
subject to the same "rules, regulations, penalties, forfeitures" as such cargoes, ships, and masters were subjected to by section VIII of the Act referred to when the
vessel was found hovering within the limits of a port.

The practice just referred to in section XXXI, which
made this law necessary, is well described in a communication from the Board to the collector at Southampton,
dated October 13, 1719:

"There was on your coast [about a fortnight ago] a
vessel, pretended to be Dutch, but an English master,

---

[5] 6 Geo. I, c. XXI.
[6] In English and American law, the league, as employed in the
hovering laws, has been used synonymously with three miles.

out of which there was sold in a few days at least £6,000 worth of callicoes, silks and spices and . . . the ship was during that time like a fair, which goods were clandestinely run ashore and convey'd into the country by a hundred and sometimes 500 horses in a night, and being also informed that the same ship will come again on your coast in order to committ the like practices, we direct you to excite the severall officers under your care to do their utmost to prevent the same."

Large gangs of men, upon receiving the proper signal from the vessel, would assemble at the point upon the shore where the hovering vessel expected to run its goods. They were employed, of course, in unlading the vessel, and in carrying the cargo up the cliffs and thence into the interior of the country. These gangs for many years overawed and overpowered the armed forces of the government. In a communication from the collector at Weymouth to the Board, dated March 4, 1718, it was said that ". . . the smuggling traders in these parts are grown to such a head that they bidd deffiance to all Law and Government. They come very often in gangs of 60 to 100 men to the shoar in disguise armed with swords, pistolls, blunder busses. . . ."[7]

[7] The extent of smuggling from sea, and its rapid increase, and the consequent necessity for this new legislation are reflected in other correspondence that took place at this time between the Board and the collectors at some of the outports. Several interesting communications are as follows:

On March 25, 1715, the collector at Yarmouth wrote the Board as follows:

". . . It has been the frequent practice for French sloops to come upon the coasts of Suffolk and particularly to Dunwich where they land quantities of wine and brandy so that gentlemen and Publick Houses are filled therewith, (as we are told) and the officers at Southwold cannot come thither without rideing 7 miles about so that the Crown hath suffered much thereby.—We humbly propose as a remedy . . . that a boat with 2 able boatmen and under the direction of a proper officer with horse, as att Lewestoft, were fixed at Walderswick which would not only serve Southwold Haven but also Dunwich and the places adjacent."

Section LXII was a similar provision with reference to vessels of the same tonnage "laden with customable or prohibited goods" found at anchor or hovering on the coasts of Ireland within the same distance from the shore. Officers were directed to go on board such vessels, take account of the lading, and demand security as provided in section VIII of the Act of 1718. If security was not given, or, if given, and the vessel did not proceed on its voyage, the same procedure and forfeiture followed as were prescribed in section VIII of that Act.[8]

Thus, legislation was again directed only against the vessel employed in smuggling at this particular period, namely that of fifty tons burden or under; and as the hovering vessel, at this time, stood just beyond, but near the limits within which hovering was penalized by the previous Act, namely, the limits of any port, the new distance to which jurisdiction was extended was enlarged to two leagues in order to embrace the waters in which it now hovered. It will be shown hereafter that as the

---

On September 4, 1716, the Board reported to the collector at Weymouth the presence at "St. Martins in France a Dutch build dogger with French colours, man'd with Scotch, laden with salt underneath which are between 40 and 50 chests of armes bound for North Britain." "You are pursuant to His Royal Highness's pleasure to seize and secure" this ship if it "shall arrive on your coast."

Further communications from that port reflect the extent of the smuggling carried on in that vicinity:

"Mr. Wm. Challoner . . . is engaged in the smuggling trade on this coast and hath lately runed neer this place a considerable quantity of brandy which I hope to get soe full proof of as to charge him therewith in the Exchequer." June 3, 1717.

On March 18, 1716, it was observed that an addition should be made to the officers and boats to assist "in detecting the great running of goods."

[8] This section recited that divers ships of "50 tons or under laden with tobacco, brandy, spirits, and other customable or prohibited goods, pretending to be bound for foreign ports, do frequently lie hovering on the coast of Ireland, with intention to run the same privately on shore as opportunity offers to the great diminution of his Majesty's revenue and ruin of fair traders," and to take in wool destined to England without a license.

larger vessel was employed in the smuggling trade at a later period, it was brought within the terms of the new laws; and as hovering was carried on at an increasingly greater distance from the shore, the limit of jurisdiction seaward was continually extended.

To summarize, the legislation between 1699 and 1736 provided:

1. For the seizure of any vessel which was found exporting wool with the intention to carry it into foreign parts, and for the appointment of sloops to "cruise on the coasts" for the purpose of seizing all such vessels.

2. For the forfeiture of certain commodities, "unshipped, with intention to be laid on land," and the vessel made use of in removing or conveying such commodities, and treble the value of the goods by the persons concerned in the unshipping.

3. *a.* For the forfeiture of any foreign goods "taken in at sea" by certain vessels or "out of any ship or vessel" in order to be landed or put into any other vessel within the limits of any port.

b. For the visitation of any vessel of fifty tons or under laden with forbidden goods, hovering within the limits of any port.

4. For compelling the master of any vessel of fifty tons or under found at anchor or hovering within two leagues of the coast, having brandy on board, to come into port.

§ 3. The Continued Rise of Smuggling from Sea

*(1) Correspondence between the Board of Customs and
the Collectors at the Outports*

In spite of the new legislation, smuggling rose to greater heights than ever between 1719 and 1736, the date of the next Act to be passed. English and French vessels were the chief offenders, especially the English, for foreign vessels did not have the facilities for cooperating with the gangs on shore, usually necessary for a successful run. Many of the collectors at the outports and the Board of Customs repeatedly reported that smuggling was ever on the increase, to the great detriment of the revenue, and that the powerful bands operating on land and at sea steadily grew more determined.

The conditions that prevailed at Southampton, for example, were summarized in a letter from the Board to the collector at that port on November 28, 1719, as follows:

"The officers have often been insulted and obstructed in the execution of their duty within the lymitts of a port by French Vessells, with numbers of armed men, who carry on the smuggling trade to the great loss of the Revenue and ruin of the Fair Traders." Orders were given to apply to commanders of His Majesty's ships for "assistance as occasion may require."

And on November 20, 1733, the Board wrote to the same collector that "there are now at Dunkirk no less than 30 vessells on the smuggling account, taking in goods to run on your coasts . . . give it in strict charge to all the officers belonging to your port to be very diligent in looking out for the said vessells to prevent frauds being committed."

The same conditions prevailed at Aberdeen, Scotland, at this period. On August 28, 1721, the collector at that port informed the Board that ". . . the dangerous smuggling trade carried on at the creeks of this Port . . . is now come to a very great height we have account that 2 other ships besides those we formerly wrote of are arrived upon the North Creeks of this precinct in ballast both which we have good ground to believe are come from Bordeau load wh. wine and brandy which they have run upon this coast. These great frauds are . . . prejudicial to the revenue. . . ."

On December 31 of the next year, the same collector reported:

". . . we labour under the greatest discouragement imaginable in the management of the revenue at this Port from the daily menace of that most pernicious trade of smuggling, which after using all means in our power we have found impossible to curb. . . ."

From Newcastle-on-Tyne, it was reported on June 19, 1725, that ". . . Blythnook is become a place of great trade both for coasting and oversea vessels and that a very great smuggling trade is carried on almost with ye least disturbance, there being only 2 officers."

On June 13, 1729, the collector at the port of Yarmouth wrote the Board that many French vessels were hovering on the coast between that port and Newcastle. These vessels had threatened to sail in such large numbers as to be able to defy the English men-of-war and to afford protection to the English smuggling vessels. They insisted, however, upon reserving for themselves, as against the British and Dutch, the smuggling trade with the colliers. The collector asked for stronger ships with which to resist them.[9]

On August 27, 1733, it was reported from Yarmouth that ". . . considerable quantities of goods are daily run on the coast of Norfolk and . . . great quantities are run in the City of Norwich."

[9] This report is very interesting. It reads in part:

". . . There is a great number of French vessells hovering on the coast between this place and Newcastle." Six sail were seen at Tinmouth Barr. ". . . they was so audacious as to lye close ashore and send their boats up the river and publickly sell their brandy and to those colliers that bought, they would send their men and boats to help them over the barr." One saw "6 sail of Burlington Bay, they also publickly declared they should sayle in such numbers as should enable them to defye all the Men of Warr and Custom Boats on the coast and that they would protect and assist all English smuglers that had a design to land goods but will not suffer the English or Dutch to sell brandy to the Colliers being resolved to have that trade to themselves. We are just now informed that they have engaged one of the Men of Warr and kill'd abundance of men. It could be wished the Publick Officers would admitt the Lord of ye Admiralty to send 2-20 gun ships, they would doe more service than 10 of them appointed, they being too weak and not proper saylers to encounter with the French sloops."

On July 2, 1730, the Board reported that the smugglers had grown "very insolent" on the coast of Swansea and had even obstructed the officers in the performance of their duties, and had refused to allow them to rummage their vessels.[10]

The collector at Whitehaven wrote the Board on October 18, 1723, that he feared that the smugglers at Millham had frequent opportunities to run brandy and tobacco and other goods from the Isle of Man, and he requested the addition of tidesmen during the summer months to "assist the officers there in guarding that coast." [11]

The Board notified the collector at Stockton-on-Tees on February 16, 1731, that ". . . great quantities of prohibited goods are run and offered for sale in severall houses in your Town. . . ."

A report from Yarmouth, dated December 8, 1729, gives a picturesque account of the methods employed by some of the merchants engaged in smuggling across the Channel from Calais. It was said that there were "4 Mechts. in company" at Calais who fitted out every sum-

[10] This report to the collector at Swansea reads, in part:

". . . The smuglers are grown very insolent on your coast and obstruct the officers in the execution of their duty perticularly on ye 24th May last they were obstructed by the Mastr and Mariners of the ship 'Galloway' who came upon deck with pistols and drawn cutlasses and refused them to rummage. . . ."

[11] An extract from this report reads:

"Being apprehensive that ye smugglers had frequent opportunity's at Millham to run brandy and tobacco and other goods from ye Isle of Man, we humbly mov'd your Honrs. on the 23rd May 1722 for leave to send tidesmen thither in the summer season to rowl their months about and assist the officer there in guarding that coast." Tidesmen are called to-day "assistant preventive officers," whose duty it is to remain on board until the incoming vessel is unladen. But in the early part of the eighteenth century it was their duty to accompany every vessel carrying dutiable goods on draw back, bound for a port in the home seas—including Norway, Denmark, Holland, France, and North Germany—to see that no goods were unladen at sea and run back into England.

mer "10 snows from 40 to 60 ton," which were well provided with large numbers of men and ammunition for defensive purposes in case of attack by the officers of the customs. Each snow carried about four hundred casks of brandy, made up from the contribution of various "distillers and other traders." This fleet advanced "on the coast" of England and kept "within 7 or 8 leagues one of another" to be prepared to assist each other in case of danger. When one snow had sold its cargo, it returned to Calais with the money that all the snows had received, and returned with another cargo, so that "they keepe constant round of comeing with brandy and goeing with money." [12]

(2) *Committee Report to the House of Commons, 1733*

The fact that the legislation of 1718 and 1719 did not accomplish the results expected is reflected, also, in an extensive report made by a committee to the House of Commons on June 7, 1733.[13] This report discusses, among other things, the methods employed by the smuggler, the

[12] The report reads, in part, as follows:

"There is at Calais 4 Mechts. in company who fit out every summer 10 snows from 40 to 60 tons. They provide the snows with good number of men and amunition of war to make a vigorous defense in case they are attacked by ye officers of the Customs or any small force. When they are fit for the sea, then the distillers and other traders put in what brandy they please, some 40, some 50, some 100 casks. These snows take one with the other about 400 casks each when laden, then come on the coast and keep within 7 or 8 leagues one of another to be ready to assist each other in case of danger, the first that has sold his cargoes speaks with all ye rest and takes from ym what money have rec'd. and goes for Calais and loads again and comes again on the coast, soe they keepe constant round of comeing with brandy and goeing with money. Their method of accounting with those that put in the brandy is this. If they sell and gett of well, then the severall adventurers allow the merchants soe much p. cask to the men. If the vessels are stopped by the Men of Warr or Custom House Boats and they only take the goods and discharge the vessell, then the men have no pay for the voyage, they always goe no purchase no pay."

[13] *Parliamentary Papers* (First Series), 1733, vol. I, p. 601, et seq.

type of craft used, and the rapid growth of this illicit trade during the first quarter of the eighteenth century. It is included here as a summary of the conditions reflected in the foregoing correspondence between the Board of Customs and the collectors at the outports, and as showing the necessity and demand for new legislation. It also enables one to understand some of the provisions of the new legislation.

This report states that vessels employed in smuggling would take out clearances for the ports of Spain, Portugal, or some other foreign country, in order to produce them if they were found or met with on the coasts of Britain and Ireland, while endeavoring to run their cargoes.[14] It describes the activities of the numerous gangs of smugglers; for example, between 1723 and 1733, two hundred and fifty-six customs officers had been beaten or murdered on board the sloops and boats appointed for the prevention of running goods. During the same period, 251,320 pounds of tea and 652,924 gallons of brandy and a large quantity of wine were seized and condemned; two thousand persons had been prosecuted, and two hundred and twenty-nine boats and other vessels employed in the trade of smuggling had been forfeited.[15] Great quantities of brandy had been run out of colliers, "which they take in at sea out of foreign vessels," according to the testimony of witnesses that appeared before the committee.[16]

The report mentions many instances of the seizure of tobacco run on shore from sloops and other craft,[17] and a few instances where vessels were sighted and chased off

[14] This has been one of the favorite schemes of the smugglers. It was employed by the so-called rum-runners off the American coast after the passage of the prohibition law by the United States in 1919. See p. 213, *infra*.

[15] *Parliamentary Papers* (First Series), 1733, vol. I, p. 610.

[16] Ibid., p. 611. The Act of 5 Geo. I, c. XI (1718), was aimed at this practice. See p. 6, *supra*.

[17] Ibid., pp. 649-51.

the coast, when there was any suspicion that they were attempting to smuggle goods ashore. For example, it is reported that "on . . . the 30th March, last in the morning, the Tryal Man of War, . . . perceiving a cutter towing from the shore near Orfordnes, with her boat ahead, gave chase to her, and boarded the cutter, and seized her with 905 lb. tea and 54½ lb. coffee"; and that the collector at Yarmouth on May 28th, 1733, had stated that it was agreed that certain men of war and their boats "should keep a good look-out at sea, and to endeavour to secure any vessel or boats that appeared on the coast, or endeavoured to run any goods." [18] Officers belonging to a smack in the service of the Commissioners of Customs, "having been out on a cruize at sea," met with a brigantine called the *Constance Jane* of London, which came from Camphere in Zealand, and which had on board large quantities of tobacco, tea, and coffee, for which the master produced bills of lading for North Bergen; "but there is great reason to believe that the whole cargo was designed to be run in some parts of Scotland; for there were several Scotch passengers on board: [19] the master acquainted the officers that he loaded corn for Holland from Cromartie, so it's probable he is really bound for that place." It is added that "it is very common on this coast . . . to meet vessels from Holland and France, laden with prohibited goods, with pretended clearances for Bergen; when we believe their intention is for running their cargoes in some parts of the North of England or Scotland." [20]

[18] Ibid., p. 647.

[19] This practice of having on board nationals of the country to which the illicit cargo was destined gave rise in later years to legislation directed specifically against foreign vessels carrying one or more British subjects or whereof one half the persons on board were such subjects. The presence of such subjects on board certain vessels carrying prohibited cargoes was made conclusive evidence that the vessels were smugglers. Many such acts were passed. See, for example, pp. **77, 88**, and **152**, *infra*.

[20] *Parliamentary Papers* (First Series), 1733, vol. I, pp. 647-8.

A large number of small boats were employed in the trade. The report mentions instances of seizures out of vessels "found hovering on the coast" with forbidden goods on board.

It is impossible fully to understand the enormous extent to which smuggling was carried on from the Continent during the early years of the eighteenth century without reading the report just discussed.

§ 4. Orders Issued by the Board of Customs for Seizing Smugglers

The correspondence between the Board of Customs and the collectors at the outports during this period contains many orders issued by the former, for intercepting, cruising for, and the taking of vessels suspected of being smugglers.

On August 19, 1703, for example, the Board reported to the collector at King's Lynn that the addition of two more watermen had been made "by which means . . . ye yacht may lye more frequently than she does and board most ships in ye channel coming from and going to Wisbeck and other places." Again, it was reported by the Board of Customs to the collector at Southampton on March 26, 1728, that "sloops . . . are appointed to cruize on ye coast of this Kingdom in order to prevent ye exportation of wool and running of goods." On August 6, 1726, the Board instructed the collector at Beaumaris "to hire one vessel . . . for 6 months certain to cruise from Holyhead to St. David's" in order to prevent "frauds from the Isle of Man"; the vessel was to be commanded by an "able sailor and well qualified," who was "to lose no time in getting out to sea." On July 26, 1729, orders were sent to King's Lynn for the Boston Sloop "to keep within the Boston Deeps and only stretch her cruise when suspected vessels are found to hover on the coast." [21]

[21] Many other such instructions are found in this correspondence. The Board wrote the collector at Exeter on March 26, 1726, to send

§ 5. General Instructions to Commanders of Revenue Cruisers, 1732

In 1732, instructions were issued to the "Masters of Smacks," or Revenue Cruisers, as follows:

"The Masters of Smacks, etc. who are appointed to command vessels to cruize on the coasts of Great Britain, are diligently to attend on board, and to keep their vessels in constant motion within their respective Districts or Stations, unless in cases of necessity or pursuit of suspected vessels: and in cruizing they are to speak with all ships or vessels which they shall meet at sea; and if they have reason to suspect they have goods on

---

instructions to "cruize on the coast of this kingdom to prevent the exportation of wool and running of goods."

It was reported from Dundee, Scotland, on November 14, 1735, that "one Grieg of St. Andrews in France has run a whole cargo near that place. . . . The most probable method to put a check to these pernicious practices would be to have one of the sloops returned back to the mouth of this river, who have good men and double crews can go out to Sea with their Boat and be of great service."

The officers seem very diligent in following the movements of vessels suspected of smuggling. The collector at Whitby wrote to the Board on April 7, 1728, "I shall us my indevors to prevent goods coming ashore if any such vessell [a brigantine loden from St. Martins in France] should come on this coast."

On June 19, 1728, the officers at that port were excited by the Board "to be watchful, on ye coast upon a vessel called 'North Berghen,' Cuthbert Cooper, Mastr. who is gone on a voyage towards Hambro to take in goods with intention to run ye same on this coast. . . . She has sham bill of loading as if consigned for North Bergen . . ."

On November 21, 1728, directions were given to the same officers "to be very active and vigilant to prevent wool being sent out of this Kingdom and yt notice from time to time be taken and given to ye Board if any Owlers hover upon the coast especially such as belong to or are bound for Sweden. . . .

"There is a woolen manufacture setting up in Sweden but they cant carry on with success without wool."

(The exporters of wool were called "Owlers," because they worked at night.)

On August 14, 1729, the Board wrote to the collector at Stockton-on-Tees: "Mr. Burchett, Secry to the Lords of the Admiralty having by Ltr. 9th instant transmitting to the Commissioners a list of such of His Majesty's Sloops as are appointed to cruise on the coast of this Kingdom in order to prevent the exportation of wooll and running of goods. . . ."

board designed to be smuggled, they are diligently to watch their motions, and keep them company till they are clear of the coast within their respective districts in order to prevent the fraudulent landing any such goods.

". . . and in case they discover any such goods [goods whose exportation was forbidden] to have been shipped or shipping for foreign ports, they are to seize the same with the vessels, etc." [22]

§ 6. Seizures on the High Seas

There is noted in the correspondence between the Board of Customs and the collectors at the outports many instances of seizures of foreign vessels on the high seas during this period. Very seldom, however, is the exact place of seizure noted. Under the Acts of 1718 and 1719, the seizure of certain hovering vessels was permitted anywhere within two leagues of the coast or within the limits of a port; and under the Act of 1718, any foreign goods taken in "at sea" were subject to forfeiture. The Act of 1699, which was still in force, directed armed sloops to cruise "on the coasts" and to seize all ships engaged in exporting wool to foreign parts, without defining any distance within which seizures might be made. As already pointed out, in the eighteenth century, the nations were not restricted to fixed limits for making seizures.

The collector at Yarmouth reported on March 31, 1730, that "yesterday was brought in . . . a French vessel called St. John the Baptist of Calais with 200 half anchors [ankers] brandy"; [23] and on March 14 of the same year, he reported the capture of the *Aimable* of Calais, which was "met with . . . on the Yorkshire coast." The col-

[22] See p. 1, note (1), *supra*.

[23] An anker was nine gallons—the amount one man could carry, strapped to his back, up the stony beaches when the liquor was run. These casks were strung on cordage, so that they could be thrown overboard and picked up later if the vessel should be chased.

lector at Newcastle-on-Tyne reported to the Board on August 21, 1724, that "a French dogger of about 50 tons burthen" with brandy on board was taken while "hovering on ye Lincolnshire coast with a French snow in company." It was said that proof could be furnished that the dogger had broken bulk on the coast.[24] On September 2, 1729, the same collector wrote that "The Deal Castle, Capt. Mead, Commander, has brought into Shields four French vessels which were smuggling on the coast. The officers have taken out of them and sent to the warehouse 790 half ankers of brandy" and various English coins and other metals.[25]

[24] This interesting report reads in part: "Captain Robinson, Commander of the *Spye* sloop has brought into this Port a French Dogger of about 50 tons burthen called *La Mouche* of Calais, with 56 half ankers of brandy on board which he met with hovering on ye Lincolnshire coast with a French snow in company. When Captain Robinson came up with them they fired several shot at him but at last all ye crew save two boys quitted ye Dogger and made their escape in ye Snow. On ye 17th Mr. Thomas Lambton seized the said dogger and brandy. He has sent the brandy to ye King's Warehouse, says can easily procure proof of ye Dogger's breaking bulk on ye coast."

[25] The following reports were received from the collector at Newcastle-on-Tyne:

February 25, 1733/4. "The Prince of Wales Sloop, . . . hath cruised on this coast and guarded the same between Teesmouth and Berwick for 12 months past. He hath made seizure of 2136 gallons of brandy, 18 pounds tea, 2 pounds 3/4 of coffee, one cable and 3 oars." March 1, 1733. The *Young Daniel*, William Reddouch, Master, came within "10 fathom water off the Tees about a mile from the land in the limits of the Port of Stockton, in order to run the remaining part of her cargo, the master having appointed a great many on that coast to be ready to receive and carry of the same." A chase followed, and she was taken eight leagues from land.

Other reports were received as follows:

From Yarmouth January 28, 1733: a cutter was brought into port laden with tea and brandy; the crew of six persons entreated the capturing officers to take the cargo, and to allow them to depart with their vessel. From Harwich, October 25, 1726: two French vessels were found in Sirewal Bay near Aldeburgh with one of their boats and a great number of horsemen on shore to be used to receive the cargo. They fired upon the officers, but five of the French crew of the French *Cleven,* John Gilbert, Commander, were taken. From Swansea, July 12, 1733: the *Dolphin* of Port Isaac was brought in by the *Milford* Snow.

CHAPTER III

FROM 1736 TO 1745

§ 7. Legislation—Jurisdiction taken for Four Leagues

By 1736, sweeping changes in the law were found necessary. It was stated in the preamble to the Act passed in that year [1] that ". . . notwithstanding the several laws already made to prevent the unlawful importing and clandestine landing and running of prohibited and uncustomed goods, divers wicked and evil disposed persons have of late not only carried on, and do still continue, such pernicious and illegal practices, in open defiance of the laws, to the great diminution of the public revenue, . . . and likewise seduce great numbers . . . to join with them . . . , whereby the evil is become so general, that it is necessary that some further provision should be made for effectually preventing the same. . . ."

It appears that many different kinds of liquors and tea were now being smuggled, and that small casks were being used for this purpose in order to facilitate transshipment at sea. As the correspondence between the collectors and the Board of Customs shows, larger vessels than fifty tons were being employed in the trade at this time. A new law embracing this larger craft and prohibiting this new practice was found necessary.

Section XXII of the Act of 1736 provided that where "any ship or vessel whatsoever coming or arriving from foreign parts," found at anchor or hovering within the limits of any port, or within two leagues of the shore, or

[1] 9 Geo. II, c. XXXV.

discovered to have been within the limits of any port, not proceeding on her voyage, having on board 6 pounds of tea, or any foreign brandy, arack, rum, strong waters, or other spirits in casks under sixty gallons, all such goods and their containers should be "seized and prosecuted" and forfeited, "whether bulk shall then have been broken or not." [2]   Under the language of this section, the forbidden goods could have been seized on any vessel, wherever found, provided it *had been* within the limits of any port with such goods on board. This introduced a new provision, which is found in nearly all subsequent legislation.

Section XXIII observed that "foreign goods are frequently taken out of ships at sea without the limits of any port, with intent to be fraudulently landed in this kingdom." It then provided for the forfeiture of any ship, boat, or vessel whatsoever, not exceeding 100 tons, into which any foreign goods were taken in at sea within four leagues of the coast, "whether the same be within or without the limits" of any port, without payment of duty. All such goods were forfeitable; and the master of any in-taking or unlading vessel and all persons who assisted in the unshipping were subject to a forfeiture of treble their value.

A case of seizure made under this section is referred to in a communication of October 9, 1772, from the collector at Newcastle-on-Tyne to the Board of Customs, which reported that the ship *Smeadmore* was seized "as being under the burthen of 100 tons for taking in at sea several parcels of India Nankins and Handkerchiefs, tea and china ware"; but she was released when found to be above that tonnage.

---

[2] This provision is similar to provisions of the Acts of 1718 and 1719 except that no limitation is placed upon the size of the hovering vessels, and other goods are included.

This was the first English statute extending jurisdiction to four leagues.

§ 8. Court Decisions

The old *Memoranda Rolls* record the seizure and condemnation of many vessels engaged in violating the Act of 1736. For example, a coasting vessel, the *Happy Isabel,* was taken and forfeited for having taken goods on board at sea within four leagues of the coast, in violation of section XXIII.[3] The nationality of the vessel is not given, but since it was a coasting vessel, it was, in all probability, English.

The Spanish lugger, *U. S. Concerio,* was forfeited, because brandy was "unshipped and run into this Kingdom."[4]

The *Endeavor*[5] and the *William*[6] were forfeited for *hovering* within four leagues of the coast. There was no law in force at this time calling for the forfeiture of vessels found hovering within four leagues of the coast. It is, therefore, difficult to understand these two cases, unless the vessels were proceeded against for having taken in goods within four leagues of the shore and found *hovering* within that distance.

La Renard of Boulogne, of 29 31/94 tons, was forfeited for having put off near Dungerness a boat laden with spirits.[7]

[3] Exchequer K. R. *Memoranda Roll,* 29-30 Geo. II, Trinity Term, No. 24.

Goods were often forfeited for having been unshipped within four leagues of the coast. See, ibid., 17 Geo. III, Michaelmas Term, Nos. 498, 507, 532, and 540, for examples.

These *Rolls* are deposited in the Public Records Office, London.

The reports of the cases taken from them are very brief. Very few facts are given, and the pleadings are quite general. Very seldom is the statute given under which the proceeding is had.

[4] Ibid., 50 Geo. III, Michaelmas Term, No. 222.

[5] Ibid., 11 Geo. III, Easter Term, No. 108.

[6] Ibid, 14 Geo. III, Michaelmas Term, No. 338.

[7] Ibid., (1819) 59 Geo. III, Easter Term, No. 234.

§ 9. Discussion in the House of Lords of the Necessity for and the Sanction by International Law of the "Hovering Laws," 1739

The sanction by International Law of the "hovering laws" and their origin and necessity were very clearly explained in the House of Lords on February 22, 1739, by the Earl of Illay,[8] who said:

"The liberty of searching the ships of foreigners upon the high seas, on suspicion of piracy, is a liberty that is established and regulated by the law of nations alone; but the liberty which every nation enjoys, of searching, on suspicion of unlawful trade, the ships of foreigners that approach near to their coast without any necessity, is a liberty that is not only established by the law of nations, but is generally regulated by the particular laws or customs of each respective society. In this country it is established and regulated, not only by immemorial custom, but by several acts of parliament; and it is impossible for us, by any precautions we can take at land, to prevent the exportation of our wool, the importation of prohibited goods, or the clandestine running of goods in upon us without paying the duties, unless we take the liberty of searching such ships, upon our own coasts, as give just cause to suspect their being concerned in, or designed for, some such unlawful trade. This, my Lords, has been found by experience to be true; and therefore by an act of the 10th and the 11th of the late King William, it was provided, 'That our admiralty should appoint two fifth rate, and two sixth rate ships, and eight armed sloops, to cruise on the coasts of England and Ireland, to seize all ships and vessels exporting wool to foreign parts.' Now, my Lords, if any of the men of war, or armed sloops thus employed, should see a French ship hovering, or lying at anchor within a few leagues of our shore, and boats passing and repassing between her and the land, are we to suppose that they are only to visit such ship, according to the rules prescribed by treaty, and to give entire credit to her . passports, or sea-letters? If they did, they would always find her bound from some port of France, to some port in Norway

[8] He was Lord-Justice General, 1710-1761, and Keeper of the great Seal of Scotland, 1733-1761. His title is given in the reference in the next note as the "Earl of Isla."

or the Baltic; or from some port in Norway or the Baltic, to some port of France; yet, nevertheless, she might be half loaded with our wool, and waiting at that place for the rest of her cargo; Therefore, in such cases, it is absolutely necessary to make some sort of search, and we have always done so, without any nations having complained of our making, by such a practice, any encroachment upon the freedom of their navigation and commerce.

"The case, my Lords, is the same with regard to smuggling: it was found by experience, that all the precautions we could take at land, could not prevent that pernicious trade, and therefore we have, by several acts of parliament, enforced and regulated the right we have by the law of nations, of searching, as well as visiting, such foreign ships as approach our coasts, and give just cause for suspecting their being concerned in, or designed for carrying on any contraband trade. For this reason, we ought to be cautious of denying this liberty or privilege to any nation; for if we do, every nation in Europe will say to us, 'With what measure ye mete, it shall be measured to you again': as you will not allow us to search your ships upon our coasts, we will not allow you to search our ships upon your coasts; and if by this means we should be debarred searching any foreign ship upon our own coast, it would be impossible for us to prevent smuggling, or the exportation of our wool. Not only the Dutch and French, but all Nations that had any use for it, would soon fall upon ways and means to steal away from us as much of our wool as they could have occasion for, to the great prejudice, if not the utter ruin of our woolen manufacture." [9]

[9] *The Parliamentary History of England, from the earliest period to the year* 1803 (Hansard), vol. X, col. 1232.

CHAPTER IV

FROM 1745 TO 1783

§ 10. Rapid Rise of Smuggling from Sea: Methods of the Smugglers

*Report and Recommendations of a Committee to the House
of Commons and Correspondence Between the Board
of Customs and the Collectors at the Outports*

The acts passed during the period just considered had the effect of reducing smuggling temporarily on some parts of the coast, at least. At Barnstable, the collector wrote on September 14, 1736, that the evil "seems to be at a stand and which we cannot but ascribe chiefly to ye good effects of the late acts." He reported that the smugglers, learning of the new laws from the pilots or in "other ways," would throw overboard the tobacco near the coast, which was intended to be run. The evil was ever on the increase on many parts of the coast, however. The situation grew steadily more intolerable and unmanageable. The question came before Parliament again in 1745, and a committee was appointed to inquire into "the most infamous practice of smuggling, and consider of the most effectual methods to prevent the said practice." This committee submitted a most exhaustive report together with recommendations for new legislation.[1]

The report states that much smuggling had been going on between England and Ireland; that many cases of tea and brandy had been run at Benacre Warren, in Suffolk, at Kesland Haven, and other places on the coast, and

---

[1] *Journals of House of Commons*, vol. 25, pp. 101-110.

that government vessels had, therefore, been ordered to cruise on the coasts. "Formidable gangs of smugglers," since the late Act of Parliament, had prevented the seizure of "prohibited goods on shore, and on great number of vessels at sea"; and officers, attempting to make seizures "have been beaten, and cruelly wounded." [2]   The

[2] Smuggling was reported on September 19, 1739, to have grown to "an excessive height" at Beaumaris. At Southampton, it was said, on January 11, 1742, to have "greatly increased and is daily increasing." The increase was due to the laying aside of the *Hurst* sloop, which left only two vessels employed on the coast. It was said that the appointment of three vessels for the guard at Southampton, Portsmouth, and Cowes was "absolutely necessary." To the westward of Torr Bay, smuggling was "very much increased," and it was "notoriously practiced between Bourn Bottom and the Isle of Wight by a large gang of smuglers under protection of their guns and small arms, besides a number of men on board their cutters," according to a note from the Board to the collector at Weymouth of August 16, 1744, who was instructed to notify the supervisor of the sloops and other boats employed in the Customs Service if any of the smugglers appeared "on the coast." At Colchester, the Board noted in a letter, dated September 7, 1751, to the collector at that port that "great quantities of goods are almost daily run on your Coast, particularly tobacco stalks." At Barnstaple, the collector reported on October 15, 1748, that the trade had begun again, and it was feared that in view of the "general peace . . . soon expected," "this pernicious trade . . . will again be carried on with great impunity unless a smack is ordered to prevent it and stationed as heretofore." The collector at Cardiff reported on July 21, 1749, that while no attempts had been made to run goods within his district "since the war broke out with France nor since the Peace," the smugglers were daily expected ". . . as they are busy on the South Coast." Ships were requested for use in cruising on owlers and smugglers. The declaration of peace had a decided bearing on the amount of smuggling. It was reported from Stockton-on-Tees on March 5, 1763, that "in consequence of the Peace," it was feared that the practice would greatly increase, and orders were given to officers to be most diligent.

It was reported from Penzance on June 19, 1749, that a great smuggling trade was being carried on there and that more goods were being run than ever. The smugglers had become so daring that the officers could not perform their duties without being "knocked in the head, such are the vast number of smugglers that assemble together."

A similar report was received from Barnstaple on July 26, 1755. This port also reported on June 9, 1763, that goods were unladen and run from French Cartel ships "now lying at Appledore to carry off the French Prisoners." This port had reported on October 13, 1752, that it was feared that the Island of Lundy might become a "magazine for smugglers," for small vessels could hover with safety in Lundy

trade was carried on in "open boats," or "large wherries, that generally outsail any of the custom-house sloops."

Road. It was suggested that this Island be "fixed within the Limits of a port" by an act of Parliament; otherwise, the legality of some seizures might be disputed, as the island was four leagues from any shore. Other reports of similar content were received from Stockton-on-Tees, December 3, 1754, where, it was said, that one or more smuggling cutters or sloops was seen about every three or four weeks, and from Hull, July 23, 1755, where the vigilance of the officers had ended the trade on that part of the coast.

Similar reports were received, as follows:

From Stockton-on-Tees	April 4,	1768,
From Yarmouth	August 21,	1769,
From Weymouth	December 3,	1770,
From Swansea	February 20,	1773,
From Swansea	November 23,	1782,
From Swansea	October 25,	1783,
From Whitby	October 11,	1774,-a
smuggler appeared off the coast nearly every day,		
From Hull	March 10,	1779,
From Stockton-on-Tees	March 11,	1780,
From Colchester	January 5,	1782,
From Beaumaris	October 20,	1783.

A large number of the "privateers and tenders belonging to His Majesty's ships of war" were engaged in the trade. It was reported by the Board to the collector at Dartmouth on July 12, 1747, that these vessels would go over to Holland and other foreign countries and "in the course of their voyage either by meeting ships at sea or otherwise, take on board great quantities of goods . . . and run them on the coasts in the several Ports and Harbours of this Kingdom."

Similar reports were made to the collectors at Colchester and Beaumaris on July 21 of the same year. Vessels pretending to be privateers were running goods on the coast of Poole. (Collector at Poole to the Board, September 9, 1758.)

On September 13, 1737, Dartmouth reported daily runs of "great quantities of tea and other goods."

A great deal of smuggling, especially of tea, was carried on also from East India ships after they arrived in the Channel. The Board of Customs instructed the collector at Dartmouth on April 16, 1750, to keep close watch on these vessels "in the chopps of the Channell," in order "to prevent the running any goods from those ships as they pass the coast." And on August 29, 1744, the Board reported to the collector at Malden that seven of these ships had arrived "in the Downs under convoy of 2 men of war," and that it was feared that great quantities of goods would be attempted to be run from the ships as well as the men of war. The collector was directed to instruct several officers to be very careful in looking out to prevent the running of goods from these vessels as they passed along the coast.

Particular reference was made to smuggling from the Isle of Man to the Scotch coasts, Ireland, Wales, and Lancashire.[3] But large fleets had been stationed on the

[3] During the period under discussion, the Isle of Man became one of the great centers of activity of the smugglers, so that in time a special statute was made necessary, extending jurisdiction over certain smuggling vessels hovering within three leagues of that island or within three leagues of the coast of Great Britain, if coming from that island, with liquor on board. The Board of Customs wrote on October 23, 1736, to the collector at Whitehaven, a port on the English coast northeast of this island, that the "Town and county are still mostly supply'd with brandy, rum, tea, and tobacco, soap and other high duty goods illegally imported and we are apprehensive they are furnished with these commodities from Ireland but chiefly from that warehouse of Frauds, the Isle of Man." It was said that the island was so near that the boats would run their goods over at night, bury them on the shore, and return the same night. Boats from the English coast were employed in this trade; also the merchants in this island employed for this purpose "bum-boats," which lay off that coast about a mile or two in the daytime, awaiting the return of the light colliers or other vessels from Ireland or elsewhere, to which they sold their cargoes and then returned for fresh supplies. If these passing ships purchased more than could be passed as ship stores, they secreted the excess in the sea on the English coast at marked places before going into the harbor; but if it was a small quantity, they would place it in small kegs and hide it on the ship. It was said that vessels belonging to the port of Whitehaven engaged in the coal trade to Ireland numbered about one hundred sail from twenty to one hundred ninety tons burden with crews of from three to eighteen men.

It was reported from the same port on April 7, 1749, that the illicit trade from this island, carried on in wherries and open boats, was "increasing to the unspeakable loss of the Revenue." And on July 27, 1750, the collector again reported that the trade was carried on "to a higher degree than ever in Manx open boats which draw so little water that the Custom House sloop cannot come at them amongst the sand banks and shoals that abound . . . to the northward of this place." It was said that a fleet of ten or eleven sails were seen in one day, all laden with wine, brandy, rum, tea, and tobacco, and East India goods in small casks, trusses, and bags, so that they might easily be carried away after landing. These vessels sailed along about three leagues from the shore "steering for the borders."

And on May 8, 1756, it was reported by the Board to the collector at Beaumaris that "great frauds" were carried on from the island to that part of the coast.

Nor was this trade from the island confined to English vessels. The collector at Whitehaven reported to the Board on May 29, 1764, that since the crew of a customs vessel were cruelly beaten "for seizing a Dutch vessel in Ramsay Bay with tea from Holland," no

coast of Kent and Sussex, whereby smuggling at those points had been almost broken up; but this only resulted in the shifting of the smuggling trade to the coast of Suffolk. Most of the tea smuggled was brought from France, Holland, Sweden, and Denmark, but it was run with greater ease from the French coast.

One witness before the committee testified that he had formerly been engaged in the smuggling business and that most of the vessels employed in smuggling belonged to His Majesty's subjects, and were "generally Folkstone cutters, from fifteen to forty tons burden; and that some are sent by the French and Dutch from Boloign and Middleborough: that these vessels are met, three or four miles from our coasts, by boats, which bring the goods ashore; and before the present act, he believes twenty or thirty cargoes were run in a week," that the principal commodity run was tea, three million pounds of which had been smuggled each year during the last three or four years. He stated that the danger or likelihood of seizure at sea was greater than on land, "yet the smugglers most commonly escape the custom-house sloops, by means of intelligence sent from the inhabitants on the coast, when those sloops sail out of port; . . . smugglers, to escape being seized at sea, frequently make out their clearance from the foreign port, at which they took in

---

one had molested the smugglers. This report stated that goods were run on board "small wherries and boats built on purpose for that wicked trade." It was said that the colliers bound to Ireland and the coasters had "Bum-Boats" to go out from the island and supply with tea, brandy, or anything they wished, any hovering vessel on the coast. Through these and other means, smuggling had risen to great heights since 1751.

On November 24 of the same year, Whitehaven reported that nine laden boats were seen passing by from that island "towards the Border." "Dutch Doggers," also, were venturing in from the island.

Beaumaris reported on May 21, 1767, that four large cargoes had been landed within that port from the Isle of Man within the past six months.

their lading, to some other foreign port; so that if they are not met at sea by the custom-house sloops, within six miles of the coast, they are not liable to seizure; and that he has known several smuggling vessels escape by this contrivance. . . ." [4] Another witness testified that sixty English cutters and five or six vessels of thirty to forty tons, belonging to merchants at Flushing, were constantly employed in running goods; that the likelihood of seizure at sea, especially off Kent and Sussex, was greater than on land, because one person in every ten assisted the smugglers in the coast counties, in getting their cargo ashore. Another witness testified that tea was run in Scotch vessels from Denmark, Sweden, and Holland, on the northeastern coast of England and the eastern coast of Scotland; while smuggling into the southern part of England was carried on from France, Holland, Jersey, and Guernsey by means of "lime vessels."

Others testified that the officers of the customs had not been as diligent as they should have been in "seizing the boats and men employed in smuggling." Others found defects in the present Act, in that when the custom-house sloops met at sea a vessel employed in running goods, they only took out the goods, and let the vessel and men go, who immediately returned for another lading. Another witness noted the defect in the present act relating to the seizure of vessels clandestinely importing brandy, in that if such vessels were under the burden of forty tons, they were liable to be seized and burnt; but if above forty tons, they were not even liable to seizure; but that vessels of any burden, which ran tea, were liable to seizure. The small number of seizures of vessels at sea was accounted for by the fact that they could outsail the custom-house sloops and the King's ships.

The remedies suggested by the committee were reduc-

[4] See p. 20, *supra.*

tion of duty on tea, enforced service in the Navy by persons convicted of smuggling, and the destruction of all vessels taken in the practice of smuggling.

§ 11. Legislation—Jurisdiction for Two Leagues Retained and Three Leagues Introduced

(1) *Jurisdiction for Two Leagues*

These conditions were destined to call for new legislation, for Parliament felt that legislation was the remedy. This accounts for the large number of laws passed in the warfare on this illicit trade. Six of the seven new acts passed between 1736 and 1783 did not extend jurisdiction seaward. They all took jurisdiction for two leagues. They provided for the seizure of new commodities on the hovering vessel, for the forfeiture of the vessel in certain cases, according to the recommendation made by the committee to the House of Commons just considered, for the seizure of hovering vessels on the coasts of the American colonies; and the size of the vessel made forfeitable when found at anchor or hovering within the forbidden distance with the forbidden goods on board was increased. Some of the reasons for the passage of these new laws have already been considered; some of them are found in the preambles to the acts themselves; while others will be considered hereafter.

These six acts are considered briefly.

In 1751, an Act was passed for "the more effectual securing the duties upon tobacco" and to put an end to what was described in the preamble as "great frauds and abuses . . . frequently contrived" by persons engaged in the tobacco trade.[5] It provided for the seizure and forfeiture of tobacco and snuff, or the forfeiture of their value, when found in quantities of one hundred and fifty pounds respectively on any ship or vessel under seventy

[5] 24 Geo. II, c. XLI, sec. XXVI.

tons burthen, coming or arriving from or having cleared outwards for foreign parts, if found at anchor or hovering within the limits of any port or within two leagues of the shore or discovered to have been within the limits of any port, whether bulk had been broken or not. The master was subject to a fine of £100. If the vessel was over seventy tons, he was subject to the same fine, but no provision was made for the forfeiture of the cargo.

In 1763, the Act of 3 Geo. III, c. XXII, section V, provided for the forfeiture of the vessel, if not over fifty tons, if found hovering within two leagues of the coast, if it had on board those goods which had been subjected to forfeiture when found on board within that distance by the two Acts of 9 Geo. II, c. XXXV, section XXII,[6] and 24 Geo. II, c. XLI, section XXVI,[7] already considered.[8] The two older Acts referred to provided only for the seizure and forfeiture of the forbidden goods, but not the vessel that they were found upon; the new Act subjected to forfeiture the vessels upon which the goods were found.

In 1764, by the Act of 4 Geo. III, c. XV, section XXXIII, it was provided that any foreign ship or vessel and all goods on board thereof should be seized and forfeited when such vessel was found hovering within two leagues of the coast of any British colony or territory in America, whether bulk had been broken or not, if such

[6] See p. 26, *supra.*

[7] See p. 37, *supra.*

[8] This was "An act for the further improvement of His Majesty's revenue of customs; . . . and for prevention of the clandestine running of goods into any part of His Majesty's dominions." It was declared that "the laws already made to prevent the clandestine importing and landing of foreign brandy, rum, strong waters, or other spirits, tea, tobacco, tobacco stalks, and snuff, in small vessels, which hover upon the coast of this kingdom, have been found insufficient for that purpose," whereby further provision was made necessary.

vessel did not depart in forty-eight hours after having been required to do so. It also provided for the stopping and seizure of any vessel when bound for such colonies, when it was within two leagues of the shore in order to take from such vessel any goods for which there was no cocket. (Section XXIX.)

In 1765, it was declared by the Act of 5 Geo. III, c. XLIII, section XXVII, that the laws already made to prevent clandestine importing of foreign brandy and other liquors in small vessels which hover upon the coasts had been found "insufficient." Provision was then made for the forfeiture of any ship or vessel of fifty tons or under coming or arriving from foreign parts, having on board twenty pounds of coffee, or any goods liable to forfeiture by any law upon being imported into Great Britain, if found at anchor or hovering within the limits of any port or within two leagues of the shore, whether bulk had been broken or not. All such goods and their containers were forfeitable. (Section XXXVIII.)[9]

In 1779, fourteen years later, the preamble to an act passed for "more effectually preventing the pernicious practices of smuggling in this kingdom . . .," (19 Geo. III, c. LXIX), declared that since the several laws of customs and excise already made had been defied, whereby "great quantities of prohibited and uncustomed goods, and particularly of tea, foreign brandy, and other foreign spirits, continue to be illegally imported into and landed in this kingdom," it had become "highly necessary, for the preservation of the public revenue, . . . and the quiet and good order of the kingdom, that some further pro-

[9] As a further precaution against smuggling, section XXVII provided for the forfeiture of any vessel of one hundred tons or under, and its goods, which imported into Great Britain any foreign brandy from any port of Europe, Asia, Africa, or America. See, also, 7 Geo. III, c. 43, sec. 6, for the adoption of two leagues for all vessels carrying French silks to be smuggled.

visions should be made for the better preventing such illegal practices. . . ." [10]

Section II of this Act provided for the forfeiture of any ship or vessel, if not over two hundred tons burden, coming or arriving from any part of Europe, having on board any tea, coffee, foreign brandy, or other foreign spirituous liquors, or any goods liable to forfeiture for being found on board any ship coming from foreign parts, at anchor or hovering within the limits of any port or within two leagues of the coast.

As already noted, by the Acts of 3 Geo. III, c. XXII, and 5 Geo. III, c. XLIII, vessels of fifty tons or under had been made forfeitable if found hovering within two leagues with certain goods on board, or if coming from foreign parts with certain goods on board and hovering within the same distance. Section II of the present Act supplemented those Acts by making forfeitable all vessels of two hundred tons or under, coming from Europe with certain goods on board, found at anchor or hovering within the same distance.

Section III made forfeitable all boats, wherries, pinnaces, barges, gallies, or any other vessel rowing or made or built to row with more than six oars, found upon the land or water within any part of Great Britain or within two leagues of the coast, without regard to their nationality or their cargo. [11]

[10] It then prohibited the importation into Great Britain, from any part of Europe, of any foreign brandy or other foreign spirituous liquors in any vessel or cask which did not contain sixty gallons at the least, upon penalty of forfeiture of such goods and the ship "of whatever burthen the same may be."

[11] Certain exceptions were named, such as barges or gallies belonging to His Majesty· or boats used in the service of merchant ships, and those which had been licensed by the Lord High Admiral.

In 1721, by 8 Geo. I, c. XVIII, sec. III, it had been provided that "if any boat, wherry, pinnace, barge or galley, rowing or made or built to row with more than four oars," should be found upon the water or within certain named counties or in the limits of certain named ports,

(2) *Jurisdiction for Three Leagues*

In view of the conditions that existed in the Isle of Man,[12] Parliament passed an Act in 1765 which took jurisdiction for three leagues in the marginal seas for the first time in English law.[13] By this Act, it was provided that any ship or vessel arriving from Great Britain with any goods on board prohibited to be imported from Great Britain into the Isle of Man, or any ship or vessel with any goods prohibited to be imported into or exported

---

"such boats, wherry . . . or the value thereof," should be forfeited, and the owner should forfeit £40. Sec. III of the Act of 1779 extended the clauses, penalties, and forfeitures of the Act of 1721 to the various craft named in that section, which should be found in any of the places or within the distance from the shore named therein.

The report of the committee to the House of Commons of 1745 (see p. 31, *supra*), observed that a great deal of smuggling was carried on then in "open boats," or "large wherries, that generally outsail any of the custom-house sloops," and cutters from fifteen to forty tons burden.

In 1731, the trade was carried on at Whitehaven "in open boats with good oars which drew little water," which could "thrust into any place, over any bank," and which could "easily, if it do not blow, out-row the cruiser which is built for sailing and rather too heavy to be managed by oars with any success. . . ." (Collector at Whitehaven to the Board, May 26, 1731.)

And on May 25, 1754, the Board sent instructions to the collector at Dartmouth to be "very watchful" of certain "cutters and boats" that had "gone down as low as the Isle of Wight . . . in order to take goods from on board East India ships in their passage up the Channel . . . and carefully to rummage all boats and gallies they [the officers] meet with particularly those rowing with four or more oars."

The large rowing vessels, equipped with six or more oars, were very swift, and they were employed in rowing illicit cargoes across the English Channel.

[12] See p. 34, *supra*.

[13] The Act of 5 Geo. III, c. XXXIX, sec. VII.

This was "An act for more effectually preventing the mischiefs arising to the revenue and commerce of Great Britain and Ireland, from the illicit and clandestine trade to and from the Isle of Man." According to the preamble, this Act was passed to prevent the importation of certain goods into the Isle of Man, contrary to the provisions of 7 Geo. I, c. XXI, and the subsequent clandestine running of such goods ashore from the Isle of Man to the great prejudice of the trade and revenues thereof, and to render more effectual "several other acts of Parliament relative to the trade and revenues of this Kingdom."

from such island, found at anchor or hovering within three leagues of that island, or discovered so to have been should be seized and forfeited together with such goods.[14] It was also provided that any ship and its goods should be forfeited if found at anchor or hovering, or discovered to have been within three leagues of the coasts of Great Britain or Ireland, when such vessel was coming from the Isle of Man with brandy or other liquors on board, whose importation from that island into Great Britain or Ireland was forbidden.[15]

This Act was the last one passed until 1784.

§ 12. Court Decisions

The old *Memoranda Rolls* record some very interesting cases of forfeiture under section V of the Act of 3 Geo. III, c. XXII.

In *The Uffro Anna*,[16] it was alleged that the vessel was forfeitable for having on board more than six pounds of tea and foreign spirits in casks of less content than sixty gallons, and for having been found within the limits of the port of Ratcliff, and "hovering within 2 leagues of the shore." The nationality of the vessel is not given, but one van Stockheram of Rotterdam was master, and van de Lande and van Oordt appeared in the suit and claimed the vessel as owners. The jury found that the vessel had not been hovering within the limits of a port, but within two leagues of the coast. Judgment was entered for the King, and the vessel and the cargo remained forfeited, and the hull of the vessel was broken up.[17]

[14] See secs. II, IV, V, and VI for a list of the prohibited goods referred to in sec. VII.

[15] Sec. VIII.

[16] Exchequer K. R. *Memoranda Roll,* 4 Geo. III, Hilary Term, No. 99.

[17] The tea and the spirits were forfeitable if found on a vessel hovering within two leagues of the shore under sec. XXII of 9 Geo. II, c.

§ 13. Orders by the Board of Customs for Seizing Smugglers on the High Seas

The usual instructions were issued during this period to cruise for owlers and smugglers. No limitation was placed upon the cruising radius.

The Board of Customs notified the collector at Stockton-on-Tees on May 8, 1750, that application had been made to the Admiralty for a sloop or man-of-war "to extend his cruise upon the Yorkshire coast to Whitby and the Ports adjacent and correspond with the officers of the customs to prevent the practice at present carried on by the smuggling vessels." This letter referred to the frequent appearance of a French lugger on the coast.

In 1751, the Board issued instructions for the commanders to the collector at Dartmouth, as follows:

"Herewith you will receive an Act of Parliament passed the 24th year of His present Majesty's Reign for the more effectual securing the duties on Tobacco.—And for the due execution of the said Act you are to take care to observe the following instructions.—That if any ship or vessel under 70 tons coming from foreign parts or having cleared outwards in Great Britain for Foreign Parts having on board 100 lb. of tobacco or any tobacco stalks or 50 lb. of snuff shall be found at anchor or hovering within 2 leagues of the shore or shall be discovered to have been within port and not proceeding on her voyage (unless in case of necessity and of which notice has been

---

XXXV. P. 26, *supra*. And the hovering vessel was forfeitable under 3 Geo. III, c. XXII, sec. V. P. 38, *supra*.

A vessel from Rotterdam, the *John and Hannah*, and her cargo, were forfeited, because the vessel was hovering on the coast in Symington Crook. Ibid., No. 100.

Other vessels were forfeited for having been found within two leagues of the shore. Ibid., 17 Geo. III, Michaelmas Term, No. 499, and 22 Geo. III, Michaelmas Term, Nos. 255 and 292.

given agreeable to the 26th section of the said Act) you are to seize the said goods and prosecute the master for £100 penalty and if the ship or vessel be above 70 tons the master will be liable to £100 but in that case the goods are not liable to seizure." [18]

On May 25, 1754, the Board sent instructions to Dartmouth "to rummage all boats and gallies they [the officers] meet with particularly those rowing with four or more oars," which had gone out to meet vessels from India in their passage up the Channel.[19]

On May 28, 1756, the Board notified the collector at Beaumaris that a cutter had been ordered "to cruise from Holyhead to Chester Bar and in Carnarvon Bay," for smuggling craft.

On July 3, 1763, it was reported to the collector at Malden that Lieut. Chas. Garencies, commander of the *Hector* Cutter, had been appointed "to cruize from Harwich along the coast of Sussex to Sheerness to prevent the infamous practice of smuggling." [20]

On July 13, 1763, there appeared a list of eleven sloops and cutters at Wick, Scotland, which were ordered "to cruize on the coast of North Britain" against the smugglers. The Board sent instructions to Cardiff in 1766 [21] for the officers "frequently to cruize along the shores in their boats and to board and strictly rummage all ships and vessels they find hovering thereon" in order to put a stop to the great smuggling then going on. On November

[18] This is a reference to the Act of 24 Geo. II, c. XLI. (See p. 37, *supra*.) These instructions are in keeping with the provisions of that Act.

[19] See Act of 19 Geo. III, c. LXIX, sec. 3, and 8 Geo. I, c. 18, sec. 3, pp. 39-40 and note 11, p. 40, *supra*.

[20] Large forces of soldiers had to be stationed on certain parts of the shore to assist the officers of the customs "in preventing owlers and smuglers from running of goods." The Board to the collector at Exeter, November 28, 1747.

[21] June 17.

14, 1776, the Lords of the Treasury issued instructions to Penzance that strict orders be given commanders of custom-house sloops "to go to sea and bring in all smuggling vessels, boats and men they meet with." [22]

§ 14. Seizures on the High Seas

Several cases of seizures on the high seas of vessels engaged in smuggling are spoken of in the communications between the Board of Customs and the collectors at the outports.

Exeter reported on October 23, 1756, that the *Hawke* privateer had taken and brought into that port a French ship, called the *Robuste* from St. Domingo, of three hundred fifty tons burden, mounting twelve guns and carrying thirty men, laden with sugar, indigo, and coffee.

From Penzance it was reported on March 6, 1762, that the *Shaftesbury* had brought in a Dutch sloop of sixteen or eighteen tons, laden with geneva, which was "hover-

[22] Other communications passed as follows:

Beaumaris, June 3, 1775.

Southampton, September 5, 1771,—the Board directed Commander Richard Wallis of the King George Smack "to extend his cruise from Southampton to Portland Westward and round the Isle of Wight to the Looe Eastward."

Swansea, February 20, 1773,—request for a cutter to cruise "from Tenby along this coast and the Bristol Channell and the English coast down as far as Bideford or the Land's End of England." It was reported that many foreign ships arrived in the Bristol Channel, where much smuggling was carried on.

Cardiff, October 23, 1783,—a request for "a great cutter, well manned with a few guns mounted, to sweep the Channel from Lundy up to Bristol."

Colchester, January 10, 1784,—eight cruisers were appointed "to cruize between Yarmouth and Portsmouth to prevent the infamous practice of smuggling."

Beaumaris, September 4, 1783,—the riding surveyor pointed out the necessity of "an armed ship or vessel to cruize in the seas and bays about here" and a cutter "to cruize in this district from Holyhead to St. David's Head."

Dover, May 12, 1788,—a request for additional cruisers to go out to sea for smugglers.

ing within a mile of land at the Eastern Part of Mounts Bay." [23]

On February 18, 1778, a vessel, "lug sail rigged having 3 masts," was brought into Campbeltown after chase had been given. [24]

[23] Swansea reported on February 1, 1745, that the *Charming Nanc* from St. Christophers came to an anchor in Mumble Road a league from and in sight of that port; rum, sugar, and other goods were found on board. Beaumaris on February 28, and March 3, 1763, reported the appearance of a vessel with "sloop sails" in Partmillaen Road with sixteen men on board, carrying twelve swivel and two great guns; she had defied the revenue boats and officers, and it was feared that she intended "to . . . land cargo on this coast."

[24] Orders were given by the Board to Stockton-on-Tees on August 15, 1752, to be "particularly vigilant" in watching all suspicious vessels and all ships arriving from Denmark, as a sale of tea from a China ship was being made at Copenhagen, "which is apprehended will be run into this Kingdom."

On July 3, 1749, the Board instructed the collector at Malden to look out for "a black cutter" then lading at Rotterdam with "tea, muslin, etc."

FROM 1783 TO 1802

§ 15. Smuggling from Sea Rapidly Increases

*Reports and Recommendations of Committee to House of
Commons and Correspondence Between the Board of
Customs and the Collectors at the Outports*

The laws passed between 1699 and 1765 and the orders
issued by the Board of Customs were not effective in
reducing the evil which the English Government was
seeking to end. On the contrary, smuggling was ever on
the increase. Towards the end of the eighteenth century,
it had become so prevalent and the methods of the
smugglers so bold that it became once more a subject of
special inquiry by the House of Commons. In 1783 a
committee was appointed "to inquire into the illicit
practices now used in defrauding the revenue of this
kingdom, and the most effectual methods of preventing
the same." An exhaustive investigation was made by
this committee, and three voluminous reports were laid
before the House of Commons. These reports summarize
the condition of affairs presented in the correspondence
that was carried on continually between the Board of
Customs and the various collectors at the outports. They
show the extent of the practice of smuggling and the new
methods employed by the smugglers, which rendered
inevitable still further legislation.

The first report of December 24, 1783, states that the
"fraudulent importation of many articles of revenue,

. . . has lately increased to a very alarming degree, and is carried on with the most open and daring violence, in every accessible part of the coasts of this kingdom," in vessels "from 30 to 300 tons, mounting from 6 to 24 guns, and navigated by crews from 12 to 100 men," whose cargoes consisted chiefly of spirits, tea, tobacco stalks, snuff, East India goods,[1] wine, drugs, cambriks, laces, and silks. The number of vessels employed was one hundred twenty large armed vessels and two hundred smaller vessels.[2] The largest of these vessels could carry,

[1] The collector at Cowes reported the seizure on June 5, 1784, of several boats at the Isle of Wight, where they were concealed, pending the arrival on the coast of the "East India Fleet." These vessels were of a type whose construction was forbidden. For a fuller discussion of the trade with the East India Fleet, see note, p. 33, *supra,* and p. 52 et seq., *infra.*

[2] The port of Beaumaris reported the presence of "a large Irish smuggling cutter" of one hundred fifty tons on the coast on June 3, 1775.

At Swansea, the vessels employed in the trade were "mostly cutters from about 50 to a hundred tons carrying guns equal to their burthen with a considerable number of men," but it was not known where they were built or to whom they belonged. (The collector to the Board, October 25, 1783.)

At Sunderland, a cutter had been "hovering of the mouth of our harbour for some days past. She is upwards of 70 foot upon the keel, 30 footbeam, . . . mounts 16 six pounders, has 20 swivels, carries 50 or 60 men. . . . So daring and abandonned are the Commander and his piratical crew that when persuasion will not prevail upon the masters of the colliers to purchase of him he threatens to fire into their ships to intimidate and induce them to deal with him." (The collector to the Board, July 9, 1776.)

That collector on October 16, 1783, and the collector at Stockton-on-Tees on October 23, 1783, reported that the craft employed in that trade were chiefly "cutters and luggers of force, are built at Dover, Folkstone and Cowes and belong to Flushing and Dunkirk."

From Hull, the following interesting seizure was reported on July 15, 1777: The schooner *Kent,* "the largest of the smuggling armed vessels which has infested this coast for some years past and which none of His Majesty's cutters . . . have dared to attack," had been taken by four such cutters and brought into port. She had often been seen trading with the shipping within three or four miles of the shore in Bridlington Bay. "She was strongly fortified, had on board when taken 16 four pounders mounted on carriages, and 20 swivels mounted with a very large quantity gun powder, shott and other ammunition. . . ." Thirty-nine members of the crew were taken on board a revenue

in one freight, three thousand half-ankers of spirits, ten or twelve tons of tea, and many other valuable articles.

---

vessel. She had on board 1974 half-ankers of geneva and 554 oil-skin bags of tea.

This port reported again on March 10, 1779, that the vessels employed in the trade on that coast were "upwards of 150 tons, full manned and armed with carriage guns, swivels and small arms," and were so powerful that the revenue cutter was no match for them and other vessels that infested the coast.

The following interesting letters were written from Harwich to the Board:

It was said that there was on October 6, 1777, upwards of thirty sail of small cutters constantly employed in smuggling between the Naze Point and the Mouth of the Thames; they had escaped from the revenue cutters "by running over the sands where on account of their great draft of water, those cutters dare not follow." They thus carried on "a great trade in the rivers and creeks which abound in these parts." On August 4, 1778, there was submitted a list of eight smuggling cutters ranging in tonnage from 75 to 140 tons burden, mounting from 4 to 12 guns, and carrying from 24 to 45 men, which "constantly run their goods upon the coasts of Essex, Suffolk and Norfolk." On November 1, 1778, it was reported that the "Bee" cutter came in "from a cruize and brought . . . the 'Neptune' cutter of about 40 tons, William Dawsett, Master from Flushing," which was taken after an hour's battle, on the shore off West Burrows, to which she had been chased. On March 8, 1779, it was said that a large cutter of 200 tons, mounting 14 four-pounders and carrying 47 men, had lately made it a practice of bringing large cargoes from Flushing. The revenue cutters were no match for her.

Similar reports were received from:

Dartmouth, August 23, 1770;

Cardiff, October 23, 1783;

Beaumaris, September 4, 1783;

Pool, October 31, 1783,—vessels carrying from seventy-five to one hundred men and from twenty-two to twenty-six guns were employed in the trade;

Cowes, on October 23, 1783, reported the presence of a lugger, the *Carnish Ranger*, of 300 tons, mounting 26 guns, which convoyed three other luggers, and the *Wasp* of 270 tons with 22 guns. Each of these vessels carried 3000 casks of liquor and 10 tons of tea, and made a trip every fortnight;

Invernes, November 5, 1784;

Aberdeen, April 6, 1784, and January 14, 1788;

Portsmouth, May 8, and December 17, 1784;

Penzance, December 2, 1785.

The Times (London) also reports the seizure of many smuggling vessels and their cargoes at sea, as well as in port, and the desperate engagements that took place between the armed smugglers and the

They resisted, successfully, attempts at seizure, by firing
upon and beating off or outsailing the revenue cruisers.

———

revenue officers. Only a few of these reports from the year 1795 to
1804, inclusive, are noted here.

On August 21, 1795, it reported that on Wednesday night a smuggling
boat, with 400 casks of foreign spirits on board, was taken by the
revenue officers belonging to Shoreham Custom-House.

Monday an account was received of the *Swallow* revenue cutter,
Captain Smith, having fallen in with a large smuggling ship on the
Sussex coast, which after a smart engagement of about half an hour,
she captured; there were upwards of 5000 gallons of brandy and geneva
on board. One man was killed, and two wounded on board the
smuggler, and three belonging to the *Swallow* were wounded.—Ibid.,
September 16, 1795.

Last week the *Badger Lartar,* and *Lively,* Revenue Cutter boats,
being on the look-out off Folkstone, chased a lugger on shore laden
with spirits which the officers seized; a large gang of smugglers came
down armed, when a battle ensued, and a continual firing was kept up
on both sides for some time; but the smugglers being very numerous,
they got the greater part of the cargo off.—Ibid., December 12, 1796.

Customs' Officers fell in with a very large smuggling cutter about three
miles South West of Penlee Point, lying at anchor and about to put
her cargo into boats then alongside her, for the purpose of landing
it at Cawfand. One officer was killed in the fight that ensued, and the
smugglers escaped.—Ibid., December 31, 1798.

A custom-house boat seized a smuggling lugger off Deal, when in the
act of weighing anchor to proceed to Dover; several boats appeared
and compelled the Officers to forego their prize.—Ibid., January 11,
1802.

For other instances of seizure or encounters with smugglers, see the
issues of December 29, 1795; November 12, 1796; December 3, 1799;
July 2, 1800; and August 24, 1802.

Many of these large, powerfully armed vessels were English vessels
which had been granted permission to arm as privateers during the
wars, but which had not disarmed when peace was established. They
had even increased their complements of men since the peace, for men
had become more plentiful, and their services could be procured very
cheaply. (The collector at Dover to the Board, December 24, 1783;
and the collector at Cowes to the Board, October 23, 1783.)

Many of the vessels used in the trade were fishing craft. (Collector
at Dartsmouth to the Board, October 23, 1783.) Much of the smuggling
was carried on with the aid of the poorer classes of workmen and
fishermen that dwelt in small villages along the coast. They assisted
in unlading the cargoes and carrying them to the shore, where bands
of men were in waiting with their horses—from fifty to a hundred—
to carry the goods inland. (The collector at Dartmouth to the Board,
October 23, 1783; and the collector at Beaumaris to the Board, October
20, 1783.)

They also took under their convoy and protection the small defenceless smuggling craft.[3]

The landing of the cargoes from these vessels was regulated by signals from scouts placed on the shore to

[3] The collector at Dartmouth reported to the Board on August 4, 1772, that a large smuggling cutter "feloniously and piratically plundered and sunk on the coast of Cornwall" the *Prince Ernest* shallop employed in the service of His Majesty's customs. The collector at Beaumaris sent in on May 7, 1770, and June 10, 1773, accounts of encounters with large smuggling vessels, during one of which a revenue cutter was supposed to have been captured and was later employed in the trade. At Stockton-on-Tees, two smuggling cutters chased the revenue cutters from that part of the coast. (The collector to the Board, November 10, 1774.) A cutter of 120 tons burden, carrying 40 men and 14 carriage guns, observed "about 3 miles from the shore," was chased; it gave fight and won the day. (Collector to the Board, Newcastle-on-Tyne, July 31, 1777.)

Similar reports were received from the following ports, which further reflect the helplessness of the defense forces:

From Malden, January 29, 1782, and November 5, 1783;

From Cowes, June 10, 1784.

The smuggling vessel, furthermore, outsailed the revenue cruisers, according to the correspondence that passed between the collectors of the outports and the Board of Customs. The collector at Hull, for example, wrote to the Board on November 19, 1768: ". . . the 'Humber' sloop under my command sails so very dull that notwithstanding upon every cruise I make I see many smuggling vessels which I know to be smugglers and accordingly chase, yet if it blows any wind we never can come up with them. We indeed frequently come upon them near the shore disposing of their cargoes that we often get within half a mile and sometimes within gun-shot of them before they discover or are prepared to get away from us but so soon as they get their sails set they leave us at a considerable distance and are in a short time out of our sight and we have never boarded them but in a dead calm." From Exeter, it was reported on August 4, 1770, that it had become the practice for the smugglers "to carry on their illicit trade in Lug-sail vessels which from their construction gives them a considerable advantage over cutters in point of sailing and we find by experience that the 'Wren' tho as good a sailing cutter as any in England hath, merely on account of the difference in sailing, lost many capital seizures." Permission was asked to build a new vessel to be used in checking the "growing evil, smuggling within our district." The *Charlotte* Cutter came in "from a cruise," upon which it met several lug-sail vessels, which outsailed the Charlotte, as the smuggling vessels usually did. (Newcastle-on-Tyne, collector to the Board, March 17, 1774.) On July 28 of that year, it was reported that smuggling was increasing by reason of the superior sailing ability of smuggling vessels.

the "vessels at sea, which instantly proceed, according to the settled signal, to some other place of rendezvous, at 15 or 20 miles distance, and land the cargo in the night time." [4] An amazingly complex organization and systematic co-operation between the owners of the vessels and the forces assisting on land (gangs of armed men), are described in this report. This organization had grown to be so enormous and so successful that it was entirely beyond the control of the customs officers, who merely remained "quiet spectators" during the running of goods and who had "hardly any powers of exertion upon the coast, beyond the detection of small illicit importations . . . attempted by merchant vessels, or by coastwise trade." [5]

Mention is made of smuggling in other ways, such as that carried on by "coasters, which take goods aboard at sea, or in foreign ports," and by small boats from twenty to fifty tons, which carried spirits and tea from the continent, and received assistance from fishermen. It is stated that in Scotland the crews of the vessels sometimes escorted the goods into the country. This interesting observation is made with reference to the smuggling of tea from India, as carried on at this time: "It is well

[4] This system is described in great detail by a letter from the collector at Whitby to the Board, dated November 12, 1807. It was said that the towns of Robinhoods Bay and Straiths were general rendezvous for large vessels, such as cutters and luggers employed in smuggling. The armed bands of men would assemble when the secret notice was sent around that a vessel had appeared on the coast. The goods were sent ashore by the smuggling vessel's "own boats assisted by the fishing cobles or are taken along the coast by those cobles to some more convenient landing place. . . ."

[5] The port of Stockton-on-Tees wrote to the Board on March 11, 1780, that three or four vessels had been at anchor for a fortnight which had run a large quantity of goods "without having received the least molestation from any of the King's or Custom House Cutters." At Portsmouth, while a cutter was unlading into a boat "off St. Helens," the revenue vessel was forced to remain "at a distance a tame spectator of this fraudulent transaction." The smuggler was of three hundred tons burden. (Collector to the Board, May 8, 1784.)

known that when ships are expected from the East Indies, smuggling vessels, and boats of various sizes and descriptions, and from every part of the coast, cruize for them in the British Channel, and carry on a constant traffic with them, from the entrance of the channel to their arrival in the Thames. As soon as the laden ships arrive at their moorings, the places near which they lie become the resort of smugglers, and resemble a public fair: the officers of the East India ships are induced . . . to this traffic," because they had to pay duties both to the East India Company and to the public. This practice also extended to ships with cargoes from West India. It was reported that eleven million pounds of tea were smuggled into Great Britain annually, at a loss to the revenue of £1,000,000 yearly; and that thirteen million gallons of brandy and other spirits had been smuggled in during the last three years.[6]

A second report was made by the committee on March 1, 1784.[7] It states that "the South West coast of Scotland, from the water of Orr to the Firth of Clyde inclusive, is now, and for some time past, has been, the great scene of smuggling both at sea, and on shore;—that the vessels which bring their cargoes from Flushing, Ostend, Gottenburgh, and even from Copenhagen, are increasing in number and size; exclusive of smaller luggers and wherries, and of large row boats (some of them of a new construction, 40 feet long, and rowing with 12 or 16 oars) which are almost constantly employed in bringing over tea, spirits, tobacco, etc., from Redbay, and the North East part of Ireland; and some Manx Boats, which take in cargoes at sea, or bring them over, in the night, from the Isle of Man." The same practice was carried on

---

[6] *Parliamentary Papers, from 1731 to 1800*, vol. 36, No. 58; or ibid., Second Series, vol. XI, p. 228. For a further discussion of the East Indian trade, see p. 33, note, *supra*.

[7] Ibid., No. 59, or p. 263 of the reference to the Second Series.

upon the southeast coast of Scotland from the same foreign cities. Tobacco was smuggled into Scotland by vessels "arriving directly from Virginia, and landing their cargoes upon the coast." The seizure of seventy-one ships from 1770 to 1782 off the coast of Scotland alone is noted.

The report mentions the following defects in the laws then in force:

1. Only vessels under 200 tons found hovering within the prohibited distance were subject to seizure and forfeiture, while many of the smuggling vessels were larger.

2. Only vessels under 50 tons could be broken up for hovering, and under 100 tons for importation.

3. No punishment was provided by any statute for opposing or hindering, with violence, customs officers in "seizing goods liable to forfeiture, on board of vessels hovering within two leagues of the shore, or at any greater distance."

4. The justices of the peace rendered judgments too favorable to the defendants.

A third report was made by the committee on March 23, 1784.[8] It is based on the facts brought out in the two reports just considered, and it is largely devoted to recommendations for severer laws and for specific changes in legislation thought by the committee to be necessary to end this wholesale fraud on the revenue and the violation of customs laws, to an extent unparalleled in the history of mankind until the smuggling of liquor from sea into the United States arose after the passage of the national prohibition law in 1919. The committee made eight significant observations:

First, the report notes the fact that the hovering acts (9 Geo. II, c. 35; 3 Geo. III, c. 22; 5 Geo. III, c. 43; and 19 Geo. III, c. 69), "limit the forfeiture therein mentioned to two leagues off the coast." It then adds: "It is the opinion of the Revenue Boards, and of well-

[8] Ibid., No. 60; or p. 282 of the reference to the Second Series.

informed persons, that an extension of this distance would distress the illicit traders, by rendering the communication and exchange of signals with their associates on shore less easy; and that it would also give greater scope to the revenue cruisers in the execution of their duty:— They propose, therefore, that this distance should be extended to four leagues, comformable to act 9 Geo. II, c. 35, which forfeits goods taken out of any ship within the distance of four leagues. With regard to the Irish Channel, this distance might perhaps be unlimited."

Second, "In order to prevent the mischiefs resulting from the practice of arming vessels for the Channel trade in time of peace, it is proposed to your Committee, that all vessels be made liable to seizure which are generally called cutters, sloops, luggers, shallops, or schooners, or vessels, of any other description, whose bottoms are clincher—work built, and not employed in his Majesty's service, or under the admiralty of any foreign state, found hovering within 4 leagues of the coast, even though they shall exceed 200 tons, or which shall have on board any carriage or swivel guns, or other arms or ammunition whatever . . .", unless carried as merchandise or as defense under a license. It was also proposed that the master of a vessel found hovering within four leagues of the coast, "armed with any cannon or swivel guns, (except as before excepted) for the purpose of smuggling, and having on board any prohibited goods, shall, upon conviction, be liable to 6 months imprisonment, whether such arms shall have been made use of or not."

It was suggested that the vessels above described, "equipt with a haul-jib, navigated by British subjects, and found at sea with prohibited goods on board, shall be equally liable to seizure, and forfeiture or if found hovering or at anchor within the distance above described;

—and also that no clinch-wood vessel (lighters excepted) should be built of a larger burden than 60 tons."

The report declares that according to the officers of the navy smuggling vessels could be distinguished by:

1. The build of the vessel, and burden;
2. The manner and proportion of rigging;
3. The manner of arming;
4. The proportion of men to the burden.[9]

The large ones outsailed smaller ones of similar construction, and this fact was responsible for the gradual increase in size of the smuggling vessels. The clinch-work mode of building had been adopted, because they outsailed the carvel-built vessels. Hence, the reason for forbidding the use of the former type except as revenue cruisers.[10]

Third, the hulls of all vessels, made liable to forfeiture by 19 Geo. III, c. 69, should be broken up.

Fourth, all vessels seized for hovering or for importation of spirits should be "broken up or used in his Majesty's service, which is at present practiced only with regard to vessels under 50 tons, forfeited for hovering, and to those under 100 tons, forfeited for importation of spirits."

Fifth, the revenue cruisers should be authorized "to fire into any vessel which shall refuse to bring-to, such vessel then being, or having been discovered to have been, hovering or at anchor within 4 leagues of the coast; provided that, previous to such firing, certain signals shall be made, if in the day, and if in the night, both signals and hailing, to denote, that such cruiser was employed in the service of the revenue."

[9] See p. 82, *infra,* for an Act of Parliament passed in pursuance of this observation.

[10] On November 19, 1768, the collector at Hull had written to the Board, recommending for that port a vessel of "clinker work and of a construction calculated intirely for sailing and much the same of [as] that of the vessels used in the smuggling trade on this coast." It was said that such a vessel being in ballast trim would have the advantage of the loaded smuggling vessels.

Sixth, it was recommended that all "penalties in this act be extended to all such offences as shall be committed within 4 leagues of the coasts; as also, that the offenders shall be liable, to the like penalties, whether any officer of the revenue shall be wounded or not." It was stated that the omission to make such a provision with reference to offences on ships, "though within the legal distance for making seizures," by the Act of 19 Geo. II, c. 34 (1774), was due to the fact that at that time only a few outrages had been committed by the smugglers at sea.

Seventh, mention is made of 19 Geo. III, c. 69, by which "boats built to row with more than 6 oars are forfeited," but the forfeiture "is eluded by the smugglers, who now use boats 40 or 50 feet in length, and which occasionally row with 10 or 12 oars; though having only 6 thwarts, and 6 row-locks fixed, as the law now stands it is difficult to prove they are more than 6-oared boats." It was, therefore, proposed "that the forfeiture be extended to all rowing boats that shall be found to exceed 30 feet in length aloft, from stem to stern, except such as are already excepted in the said act." It was suggested "that no boat should be built exceeding the length of 28 feet from the fore part of the stem to the stern, and measuring less than 8 feet at the main thwart, and in a similar proportion for smaller boats, under a penalty to be levied on the builder; excepting only London Wherries, and such as are enumerated" in the act mentioned.

Eighth, "The great and infallible remedy towards the prevention of frauds against the revenue is, undoubtedly, to be sought only in the reduction of duties." This was specially true with reference to the duties on tea, for that article was the most easily smuggled.

§ 16. Legislation

Jurisdiction Extended to Four Leagues and over the "King's Chambers"

The foregoing committee reports point to the necessity for new and more drastic legislation; and Parliament lost no time in passing a new act embodying some of the ideas set forth in the third report. It should be added, even at the expense of repetition, that all new legislation on this increasingly important subject was designed to reach smuggling on the high seas wherever it was carried on. As the smuggling vessels moved farther out to sea, new legislation went out to meet them. As new types of vessels were employed in this practice, they were brought within the forfeiture clauses of the new laws. Legislation followed the evil in an effort to end it wherever and by whatever craft it was practiced. Parliament realized that the law could not remain cast in some mould or frozen within the bounds of a fixed zone, there to remain impotent before the hosts of smugglers who chose to hover just outside this zone. The laws were adjusted and re-adjusted to meet a nation's need. There was no principle of International Law to which they were made to conform. After the three reports were submitted to Parliament, new legislation was speedily passed, extending jurisdiction in the marginal seas, bringing within its terms new craft not hitherto included, and following the other recommendations made by the committee.

It is interesting to note that in the year preceding the passage of the act carrying out the first recommendation of the third report, the Board of Customs reported to the port at Campbeltown that smuggling upon the north coast had been carried on for some time past by "vessels which lye far without the limits and get fishing boats from every part of the coast to go off 20, 30 and even 40 miles and bring their cargoes on shore." The collector at that port was directed to destroy these boats "if it can be effected by Law."[11]

The new law passed in 1784 was "An act for the more effectual prevention of smuggling."[12] The preamble referred in a general way to the conditions described in the correspondence between the Board of Customs and the collectors at the outports and in the reports to the House of Parliament. It declared that the laws passed to prevent clandestine importation had not been sufficient, but that the "pernicious practice" of smuggling had been carried on and had "greatly increased" by "large armed vessels at sea, and by numerous gangs of smugglers upon land," whereby further provisions were made necessary. Following the first recommendation of the third committee report, the Act provided for the forfeiture of the following craft: Any ship or vessel found at anchor or hovering within the limits of any port, or within four leagues of the coast, or discovered to have been within such limits or distance, having on board any brandy, or other spirituous liquors in casks of less content than sixty gallons, or any wine in casks if the ship did not exceed sixty tons, or six pounds of tea, or twenty pounds of coffee, or any goods liable to forfeiture upon being imported into Great Britain. The goods named were also to be forfeited.

The expression "found or discovered to have been" was explained in 1875, in a communication by the Board of Customs to the Treasury, to mean "found in 'flagrante delicto'" or, when not so found, discovered by "ex post facto evidence" to have been guilty of the offense for which the offender would have been amenable to the law if "caught in the fact."[13] That is, a vessel was subject to

[11] Board of Customs to Collector at Campbeltown, September 8, 1783.
[12] 24 Geo. III (2d sess.), c. XLVII.
[13] See note, p. 1, *supra*.

forfeiture under this provision when it came within the limit named, though it may have subsequently steamed outside. If, for example, the vessel was shown to have been within a British port, attempting a clandestine landing, it could have been pursued and captured for having been "discovered to have been" doing that which had rendered it liable to forfeiture.[14] That is, it could have been arrested anywhere found, when discovered to have been previously within four leagues of the coast.[15]

Section IV provided that the following craft, belonging in whole or in part to British subjects, should be forfeited if found within the limits of a port or within four leagues of the coast:

1. All vessels called cutters, luggers, shallops, or wherries, of whatever built;

2. All vessels of any other description, whose bottoms were clench work, unless they were square-rigged or fitted as sloops, with standing boltsprits;

3. All vessels, the length of which was greater than in the proportion of three feet and one-half to one foot in breath;

4. All ships, armed for resistance.

The goods laden on such craft were also made forfeitable.

This provision was made in pursuance of the second recommendation of the third report of the committee. As already noted, vessels named in this section were the type principally employed in the trade.[16]

[14] See *L'Abandance*, p. 134, *infra,* and *Attorney General* v. *Schiers,* p. 121, *infra.*

[15] Sec. II exempted the vessel from forfeiture if the enumerated goods were on board without the knowledge or privity of the master or owner; but by sec. III, the goods were nevertheless forfeitable, and the persons in charge of them were subject to a fine of treble their value.

The distance of four leagues had been adopted in 1736, but only as to the act of unlading. See p. 27, *supra.* The present Act adopted this distance for hovering vessels of whatever size or nationality.

[16] The vessels named in sub-sec. 3 of this sec. were included, because large rowing vessels were being built with concealed or detachable row-locks, so that, while being equipped for the use of more than six

Vessels and/or boats of various types and sizes "belonging in whole or in part to His Majesty's subjects" are the subject of legislation from now on. After 1784, such vessels are made forfeitable at varying distances from the shore, under varying circumstances, by many acts, including those now in force, namely, 39 and 40 Vict., c. 36, and 53 and 54 Vict., c. 56. It is, therefore, necessary to determine the nationality of such craft in order to determine whether this section is applicable to foreign vessels. Under the law of England, a vessel owned only in part by a foreigner has never been admitted to British registry as a British ship; while the laws of some other maritime powers permit part ownership of their vessels in foreigners. Therefore, such vessels could not have been British, but were either foreign or nondescript as to their flags.[17] While the Act under discussion was meant to

---

oars, they were, nevertheless, able to present the appearance of having only six, when captured. The collector at Cowes reported to the Board of Customs on June 5, 1784, that vessels constructed contrary to the provisions of 19 Geo. III, c. 69, p. 39, *supra,* had been seized in the Isle of Wight; one of them measured thirty-nine and one-half feet in length and five feet in breadth and, therefore, was of "greater length than boats rowed with 6 oars are usually built." It had only "6 fixed thwarts but the distance from the stern to the fore thwart is 12 feet and the same distance from aft thwart to the stern, between which are marks that indicate from the paint being rubbed off, that other thwarts as well as row-locks have occasionally been fixed so as to ship and unship at pleasure." See, also, note 11, p. 40, *supra.*

[17] See Piggott, *Nationality,* Part II, p. 40.

The history of the English law on this subject is found in 26 Geo. III, c. 60; 4 Geo. IV, c. 41; 6 Geo. IV, chs. 109 and 110; 8 and 9 Vict., c. 89; 17 and 18 Vict., c. 104; and The Merchant Shipping Act of 1894, 57-58 Vict., c. 60.

As to the status of vessels owned by a British corporation some of whose members are aliens, see an article by McNair, Arnold D., "The National Character and Status of Corporations," *The British Year . Book of International Law,* 1923-4, pp. 44, 50.

The pertinent provisions of these Acts are as follows:

Section X of the Act of 26 Geo. III, c. 60 (1786), required owners applying for registration of their vessels to take an oath that "no foreigner, directly or indirectly, hath any share or part or interest in the said ship or vessel." This section was repeated in substance in

embrace and did embrace all foreign vessels so owned, yet
it was, in all probability, aimed primarily at those that

---

sec. XII of 4 Geo. IV, c. 41; sec. XIV of 6 Geo. IV, c. 110; similar
provisions are found in sec. XIII of 8 and 9 Vict., c. 89 (1845).

Section XII of 6 Geo. IV, c. 109, provided that no ship should be a
British ship unless duly registered and navigated as such. (Certain
exceptions were made by sec. XIII.)

In order to register a ship or vessel, sec. V of 4 Geo. IV, c. 41, and
sec. V of 6 Geo. IV, c. 110, provided that it must be:

1. Wholly of the build of the United Kingdom or of some British
   colony or territory, or
2. Condemned as a prize of war, or as forfeited for breach of the
   slave laws, and "which shall wholly belong and continue wholly
   to belong to His Majesty's subjects, duly entitled to be owners
   of ships or vessels registered by virtue of this act."

Sections XIX and XXI, respectively, of these Acts provided that at
the time of obtaining the certificate of registry, a bond should be given
by the owners, conditioned, among other things, that the certificate
would be delivered up "if any foreigner or any person or persons for
his use and benefit shall purchase or otherwise become entitled to the
whole or any part or share of, or any interest in such ship or vessel."

While these early Acts did not require registration of British-
owned vessels, yet it is clear that no vessel could have been British
unless duly registered, and that it could not have been registered, and,
therefore, could not have been British, if owned wholly or in part by a
foreigner. Thus, any vessel so owned was either a foreign vessel, or
was nondescript as to its flag.

The provisions requiring that all British vessels shall be owned wholly
by British subjects are carried forward in secs. 19, 38, and 56 of 17 and
18 Vict., c. 104, and secs. 1, 2, 3, 9, and 25 of 57 and 58 Vict., c. 60.

Vessels may be owned in part by foreign countries:

Under the Italian law ". . . foreigners, not domiciled nor resident
in the state, may have shares in the ownership of a national vessel
up to one-third part." Also, an Italian vessel may belong to
"foreigners who have become domiciled or resident five years at least."
If foreigners not domiciled or resident in the state acquire more than a
one-third interest, they must transfer the excess over one-third in one
year's time; or such excess will be judicially sold.

A company whether under the name of a firm or with limited liability,
even when its officers are situated abroad, is considered as national
if any one of the partners, who is liable for the whole, and who gives
it its name is a citizen of the state. Such a company, which is com-
posed of foreigners, but is established or has its principal office within
Italy, is treated as a foreigner domiciled in Italy. A joint stock company is considered to be national if its principal office is within Italy
and its general meetings are held there. (Sec. 40, Part I, Title II, c. III
of the Mercantile Marine Code of 1886. F. W. Raikes, *The Maritime
Codes of Italy*, p. 123.)

were then being built by British owners in foreign countries to be used in the smuggling trade. According to Lord Teignmouth and Charles G. Harper,[18] when a heavy bond was required from "all owners of boats on this side of the channel—which bond was forfeited, together with the boat, if found engaged in smuggling—a number of English boat-builders had started business on the French coast to meet the requirements of the trade. . . ." These boats were frequently from thirty-eight to forty feet in length; and they "were navigated under license from the French government on condition that one-third of the crew were Frenchmen." No less than eighteen were under construction at Boulogne in 1821.

Some years later it was provided by section XV of 6 Geo. IV, c. 109, that no ship should be admitted to be a ship of any particular country unless three-fourths of its crew were subjects of such country, or unless it was wholly owned by such subjects usually residing in the country. This provision, however, could not destroy the effect of the laws of foreign countries permitting foreigners to own, in part, vessels flying their flags. Consequently, section IV of the Act under consideration embracing vessels owned in part by British subjects necessarily applied to foreign vessels in some cases.

An unpublished case, reported in *The Smugglers,* just

Under the French law, "the half, at least (of the property in French vessels), must belong to French subjects" (Law of 9th June, 1845.) J. T. B. Sewell (1897), *French Law as Affecting British Subjects.*

There seems to be no limitation on ownership of Spanish vessels under the Spanish law. However, under the Portuguese law, Portuguese ships must be entirely owned by native or naturalized Portuguese. A foreigner not naturalized who obtains a Portuguese vessel by inheritance or gift must transfer it to a Portuguese within thirty days. F. W. Raikes, *The Maritime Codes of Spain and Portugal,* pp. 200-1.

[18] *The Smugglers,* vol. II, p. 73. Lord Tiegnmouth served as a commander on several government vessels and was Inspecting Officer of the Coast Guard from 1881 to 1889.

referred to [19] sustains this view. The *Four Brothers*, hailed off Dieppe, was taken in 1823 after a prolonged fight. Twenty-two men on board were arraigned and charged with feloniously firing into a revenue cutter of His Majesty, the *Badger*, on the high seas, about eight miles off Dungerness. The defense set up was that the vessel was Dutch and her crew Dutchmen. Mr. Justice Park, in summing up to the jury, said that the prisoners should be acquitted if: (1) no part of the vessel belonged to any subject of His Majesty or, (2) one-half of the crew were not British subjects, for if neither of these facts existed, the cutter had no authority to fire at the vessel; but that if the jury believed that any part of the vessel belonged to such subjects, or if one-half the crew were such subjects, the cutter was justified in boarding the vessel, and resistance by the latter would be a capital offense.

The jury found the prisoners not guilty, for they found that the ship and cargo were wholly foreign property, and that more than one-half of the crew were foreigners.

The Act under which this proceeding was brought is not stated; at any rate, the charge to the jury and the jury's finding show that vessels which were owned in part by Englishmen or one-half of whose crew were English might be foreign and that they were so treated by the courts.[20]

[19] Vol. 1, p. 133, et seq., note (18), p. 63, *supra*. The record in this case is not preserved at the Customs House in London.

[20] As a matter of fact, the crew were, in all probability, nearly all Englishmen from Folkstone, but the jury found as they did because of the sentiment in favor of smugglers and smuggling at that time. It is said that the prisoners were liberated in the midst of great popular rejoicing.

Evidence as to the distance from the French coast was given; for it was said that by the law of nations ships of war were not permitted in time of peace to molest any vessel within one league of the coast of any other power. But this would apply to the molestation of a domestic as well as a foreign vessel, and hence this point had no bearing on the question of the nationality of the vessel or the crime charged.

In 1875, these vessels were referred to in a communication by the Board of Customs to the Treasury as possessing the "elements of British ownership."

Section XI of the Act of 1784 made it a felony, punishable with death, for anyone on shore or on any vessel to shoot at any vessel in the service of the customs, within any port or within four leagues of the coast, or to shoot at or to wound a customs officer on board or going or returning from on board any ship in the exercise of his duty, within the same distance.[21]

Section XXIII provided that any vessel liable to seizure or examination by this or any other act of Parliament which did not bring-to when required to do so or upon being chased should be shot at or into.

This provision was made in pursuance of the fifth recommendation of the third report to the House of Commons.[22]

Still further legislation was found necessary only ten years later, in 1794, when a law was passed with special reference to certain parts of the coast, bringing large areas of the high seas within the jurisdiction of the customs.[23] These areas, in some instances, include waters as far as fifty miles from the nearest land.

Richard Bowen sent in from Falmouth his application for his share of the "prize money due to him as marine when on board the 'Badger' cutter at the capture of the 'Four Brothers' smuggling cutter." (Collector at Falmouth to the Board of Customs, July 26, 1827.)

[21] See, also, sec. XV.

[22] P. 56, *supra*. Sec. XXV retained the distance of two leagues prescribed by 19 Geo. III, c. XLIX, sec. III, for boats, wherries, pennaces, barges, and gallies rowing or made to row with four or six oars; and it extended the provisions of that Act to all such craft which exceeded twenty-eight feet in length or whose length was greater than in the proportion of three and one-half feet to one foot in breadth.

Sec. XVII fixed the venue of offenses committed within ports or within four leagues of the coast; and sec. XVIII provided for the giving of information to justices of the peace and certain other officers when any offense had been committed within that distance, and for the issuance of a warrant for the commitment of the offender.

[23] 34 Geo. III, c. 50.

Section VIII of this Act declared that it was expedient to extend the provisions of the laws then in existence, whereby certain vessels found within four leagues of the coast were forfeited; it was then enacted that any ship or vessel, having on board any brandy or other goods in the quantities named and specified in 24 Geo. III (2d sess.), c. XLVII, or one hundred pounds of tobacco or snuff, should be forfeited, together with such goods, if found at anchor or hovering or discovered to have been within a supposed straight line from and to the following points:

1. From Walney Island, in the County of Lancaster, to Great Ormshead, in the County of Denbigh;
2. From Burdsey Island, in the County of Carnarvon, to Strumble Head, in the County of Pembroke;
3. From the Lizard, in the County of Cornwall, to the Prall, in the County of Devon;
4. From the Prall, in the County of Devon, to the Bill of Portland, in the County of Dorset;
5. From the Cromer, in the County of Norfolk, to the Spurn Head, in the County of York;
6. From Flamborough Head, in the County of York, to the Staples in the County of Northumberland;
7. From the Mull of Galloway, in Scotland, to the point of Ayre, in the Isle of Man.[24]

The goods also were forfeitable.

Section VII made further provision for the forfeiture of every cutter, lugger, shallop, wherry, smack, or yawl, belonging in whole or in part to His Majesty's subjects, unless of a certain defined construction, when found within ports or within four leagues of the coast, or within the Chambers defined in section VIII. By the Act of 35 Geo. III, c. 31 (1795), the provisions of this section were extended to such vessels of any build whatsoever.[25]

[24] These waters are sometimes called the "King's Chambers." See Walker, *The Science of International Law* (1893), p. 169, et seq.

[25] It seems, however, that all such craft had been subject to forfeiture for ten years previous to this act; for the Board of Customs wrote to

Section XI provided for the forfeiture of these vessels when found within four leagues or within the Chambers, with arms or ammunition on board, unless they had a license to carry arms.[26]

Section IX provided for the forfeiture of any open boat belonging as aforesaid, built for rowing and/or sailing, and of a certain build and specified dimensions, if found within the same distance or areas; and any vessel named in section VII was subject to forfeiture if found with any open boat on board.

To summarize, legislation from 1783 to 1802 extended jurisdiction over certain smuggling vessels, of whatever nationality, and with no restrictions as to ownership, and over others owned wholly or in part by British subjects, for a distance of four leagues from any part of the coast. Shooting into a customs vessel within the same distance was made a felony, punishable with death. Off certain specified parts of the coast, jurisdiction was extended over all vessels, carrying certain cargoes, and all vessels of certain types and build, anchored or hovering within certain large areas of the sea called the King's Chambers.

None of the laws passed before 1783 were repealed, so that they all were in force at the beginning of the nineteenth century.

---

the collector at Harwich on January 17, 1785: ". . . all vessels that come clearly within the description of cutters, luggers, shallops, or wherries, are subject to forfeiture if they have been made use of since the first of October, let them be rigged, fitted or built in any manner or form whatsoever. We beg leave to observe that the term 'cutter' giving so great a latitude, opinions may vary and the question naturally arising is, what constitutes a cutter?

"A vessel, clench built, sailing fast is usually stiled a cutter. Can a vessel Carvel Built, rig'd in every respect like a supposed cutter, with boltsprit drawing out and in, be termed a cutter?"

[26] See sec. IV, 24 Geo. III (2d sess.), c. XLVII, p. 59, *supra*.

§ 17. Court Decisions

Numerous cases of forfeiture under the Act of 24 Geo. III (2d sess.), c. XLVII, are found in the *Memoranda Rolls* of this period. Sufficient details are given in these old proceedings to show that the laws were being enforced literally against foreign as well as domestic vessels.

The cutter *Grayhound*, H. Mager, master, not being square-rigged, was found within four leagues of the coast and seized, and proceeded against presumably under section IV of the Act. It was alleged that the vessel belonged in whole or in part to His Majesty's subjects; but the Queen of Portugal appeared and claimed the vessel as owner, and entered a denial that the vessel was found within four leagues of the coast. An "inquisition" was ordered, and a jury summoned to try the issues.[27] The verdict of the jury is not given.

The *Two Brothers*, whose nationality is not given, and its cargo were seized and forfeited for having been found hovering within four leagues of the coast with the intention of running tea and spirits. It was alleged that the vessel belonged in whole or in part to His Majesty's subjects. The master was John Pissing, and the vessel was from Ostend.[28]

The brigantine *Holsfarne*, Antonio Niccolicklato, master, one hundred and twenty tons burden, from Sant, last from Guernsey, was seized for hovering within four leagues of the coast.[29]

The lugger *Friendship*, of Saint Ives, 20 32/94 tons burden, square-rigged, without a license from the Admiralty, was seized within four leagues of the coast. A judgment that she remain forfeited was entered.[30] This pro-

---

[27] Exchequer K. R., *Memoranda Roll*, 26 Geo. III, Easter Term, No. 388.

[28] Ibid., Easter Term, No. 394.

[29] Ibid., Trinity Term, No. 644.

[30] Ibid., 35 Geo. III, Trinity Term, No. 19.

ceeding was probably under section XI of the Act of 34 Geo. III, c. 50.[31]

Several cases are reported in 1799. The libel in one case reads, in part, as follows:

"Be it remembered that Mr. Hird, an officer of His Majesty's Customs . . . did seize and arrest . . . as forfeited a certain ship or vessel . . . for that the said ship or vessel was . . . found hovering within four leagues of the coast of this Kingdom towit at Ratcliff . . . in the county aforesaid [Middlesex] and not proceeding on her voyage . . . then having on board several parcels of foreign brandy, . . . foreign spiritous liquors called rum and . . . Geneva, . . . being in vessels or casks which did not contain 50 gallons at least and exceeding the quantity of 2 gallons for each seaman . . . contrary to the form of the statute in that case made and provided. By means whereof the said Ship . . . became forfeited." It was alleged that she was forfeitable "for that the said ship . . . was . . . discovered to have been within 4 leagues of the coast of this Kingdom towit at Ratcliff aforesaid in the county aforesaid," with the said liquors on board.

"And also for that a certain boat belonging to the said ship or vessel being an open boat built for rowing or sailing or for rowing and sailing belonging in the whole or in part to His Majesty's subjects was . . . found within 4 leagues of the coast of this Kingdom towit at Ratcliff . . . in the county aforesaid, such boat being of the length of 18 ft. and under the length of 24 ft. from the forepart of the stern to the aft side of the Transum . . . and the depth . . . being greater than in the proportion of an inch and one quarter . . . to every foot in length . . . contrary to the form of the statute. . . . By means whereof the said ship . . . to which such boat belonged became for-

[31] See p. 67, *supra*.

feited. Wherefore his Majesty . . . prayeth . . . that the said ship . . . may . . . remain forfeited. . . ."

The ship was claimed by "William Carpenter of Hastings in the county of Sussex." An "inquisition" was ordered, and twelve men "free and lawful" were summoned as jurors.[32]

The *Hannah* sloop of Fawney was seized, as forfeited, "for that it . . . was . . . found hovering within 4 leagues of the coast of this Kingdom, towit at Ratcliff. . . ." The point of seizure was "about 2 leagues off the Wolff Rock within the limits of the port of Penzance." She was forfeited for hovering at this distance with certain tobaccos and liquors on board, and because she was of less burden than one hundred and twenty tons, contrary to the statute. The proceeding was against both the vessel and her cargo. Peter Brown claimed the vessel.[33]

There was also a proceeding to condemn, as forfeited, the cargo of this vessel. Three men by the name of Maingy, whose nationality is not given, appeared and claimed the goods. An "inquisition" was ordered.[34]

There is a proceeding against a cutter licensed for a particular trade, found with a cargo not within the terms of its license. Thomas N. Robolliard, of the Island of Alderney, appeared as claimant of both goods and vessel. The jury found that the vessel was hovering within four leagues of the coast, whereby she became forfeited.[35]

The *Happy Go Lucky* was seized about three leagues from the "Start point," hovering with forbidden goods on

[32] Ibid., 39 Geo. III, Eastern Term, No. 220 (1799). For a similar case, see ibid., 40 Geo. III, Mich. Term, No. 35. The vessel was a shallop, belonging in the whole or in part to His Majesty's subjects. Richard Carter claimed the ship and cargo.

[33] Ibid., 39 Geo. III, Easter Term, No. 227.

[34] Ibid., No. 228.

[35] Ibid., 40 Geo. III, No. 499.

board. The goods were claimed by J. Bray, J. Vallack, and Wm. Brown.[36]

The *Ledwell* sloop was forfeited under 34 Geo. III, c. 50, section VIII, for having been found, and discovered to have been hovering within four leagues of the coast with brandy on board. The vessel was "within a supposed straight line from the Lizard in the County of Cornwall to the Prall in the County of Devon." [37]

[36] Ibid., 39 Geo. III, Michaelmas Term, No. 366.

For other cases, see ibid., Nos. 170 and 195, Hilary Term, and No. 50, Trinity Term; 40 Geo. III, Michaelmas Term, No. 509; *The Marie Christine,* 51 Geo. III, Michaelmas Term, No. 78.

[37] Ibid., 40 Geo. III, Michaelmas Term, No. 501. No. 502 is a proceeding against the goods on this vessel. Nos. 505 and 509, and No. 37 of Hilary Term are similar proceedings.

CHAPTER VI

FROM 1802 TO 1825: THE GOLDEN AGE OF SMUGGLING

§ 18. Legislation, Taking Jurisdiction Over the English and Irish Seas, and for Two, Four, Eight, and One Hundred Leagues

In spite of the two Acts passed in 1784 and 1794, smuggling went on unabated on most parts of the coast. The ports of Sunderland,[1] Harwich,[2] and Plymouth,[3] however, reported rapid decline in the trade. The decline at Sunderland was not attributable altogether to the effect of the new laws; the collector at that port reported that the practice had been checked by the outbreak of war. Plymouth reported that the decline there was due to "the heavy losses the smugglers had experienced by captures made by the different cruisers and officers on this and the Western Coast."

Poole reported on December 31, 1787, that eleven vessels of the burden of from twenty to fifty tons, carrying chiefly liquor and tobacco, were employed on that coast. It was said that each vessel made eleven voyages a year and carried from five to twelve men, according to the tonnage. A similar report was received from Campbeltown on March 9, 1789.[4]

[1] Collector to the Board of Customs, October 10, 1795.
[2] Ibid., October 9, 1795.
[3] Ibid., November 5, 1801.
[4] Seizures of, or encounters with, smuggling vessels were reported by the following ports:
  Plymouth, April 22, 1800; June 16, 1804; October 26, 1805. One capture was made five leagues from the Lizard.
  Campbeltown, February 6 and October 18, 1792.

The first Act of the nineteenth century was passed on June 22, 1802. As a result of the increase in the smuggling trade, jurisdiction seaward over foreign as well as domestic vessels was greatly extended, in fact, doubled. The distances of the previous century now gave way to eight leagues; while jurisdiction over the King's Chambers, taken by the Act of 34 Geo. III, c. L, was left undisturbed. This extension of jurisdiction came through "An act to alter, amend, and render more effectual an act, made in the 24th year of the reign of His present Majesty, for the more effectual prevention of smuggling in Great Britain." [5]

This Act referred to the Act of 24 Geo. III, c. 47, and "several other acts" made since the passing of that Act, by which vessels were liable to forfeiture if found hovering within four leagues of the coast, and declared that it was expedient to extend these laws "for the more effectual prevention of the practice of smuggling, and the protection of the public revenue and the fair trader." It then provided for the forfeiture of the following vessels with the goods on board: every ship, vessel, or boat found hovering or discovered to have been within eight leagues of the coast under any of the circumstances described in 24 Geo. III, c. 47, or in any other act passed for extending its provisions, which would, by virtue of these acts, be liable to forfeiture for hovering or discovered to have been within four leagues of the coast. All the clauses, penalties, and forfeitures relating to boats or ships found within four leagues, and those relating to the goods therein, were extended to all such vessels and boats and the goods therein, when found hovering

---

Dartmouth, October 21, 1801. The *Bolt* was taken seven miles out with cargo ready for slinging and with no manifest on board.
Harwich, April 8, 1779.
[5] 42 Geo. III, c. LXXXII.

or discovered to have been within eight leagues of the coast.

Section 2 provided that all pains, forfeitures, and fines provided in the Act referred to, relating to ships or boats hovering or discovered to have been within four leagues of the coast, or to any master, or to any goods, should extend to all such ships and boats, goods, and masters, when the ships and boats were found hovering or discovered to have been within eight leagues of the coast, as if they were "repeated and re-enacted in . . . the present act."

Section 3 retained the distance of four leagues "as to that part of the coast of Great Britain which is between the North Foreland on the coast of Kent and Beachy Head on the coast of Sussex." [6]

This Act changed the older Act of 24 Geo. III, c. 47, by extending jurisdiction over all hovering vessels with certain cargoes on board, from four to eight leagues on all parts of the coast, except that between Beachy Head and the North Foreland. The other Acts of the eighteenth century—those adopting two, three, and four leagues and the one taking jurisdiction over the King's Chambers —were left undisturbed.

Section 4 of the Act under consideration contained a rather singular provision. It provided that it should be lawful for the jury to find for the crown, if at the trial relating to the seizure and forfeiture it should appear that prohibited goods were on board and that the ship was "bound for or hovering on the coast of Great Britain, for

---

[6] It was provided that the distance of eight leagues "shall be measured in any direction between southward and eastward of Beachy Head," and that the Act should extend to "such limits and distance of eight leagues in every direction from Beachy Head although any part of such limits so extended may exceed the distance of four leagues before mentioned, from any part of the coast of Great Britain to the eastward of Beachy Head aforesaid."

the purpose of the clandestine importation or illegal running" of the said goods, even if it were "doubtful whether such ship, vessel, or boat, was within such limits or distances as aforesaid," "in like manner as if it had been fully proved that such ship, vessel or boat, was hovering or found, or had been discovered to have been within any such limits or distances as aforesaid." This provision shows that Parliament chose the four and eight leagues merely as convenient and desirable distances for jurisdiction over the smuggling vessel, and that when a vessel was bent upon smuggling, the fact that it, perhaps, stood beyond such distances would not prevent the forfeiture.

Three years later, in 1805, a new bill came before Parliament. Its purpose and the principle upon which it rested are well stated in the discussions in both Houses of Parliament. On April fifth, "The Chancellor of Exchequer moved, that the House should resolve itself into a committee on the Act of 24th of his present Majesty, for the prevention of smuggling. He stated, that the practice of smuggling had increased to an alarming extent, and he had thought it his duty to submit to the house a bill to remedy so dangerous an evil. The material object he had in view was, to make articles of high duty in packages of certain sizes liable to seizure, if found on board any ship in the narrow seas. The distance within which they should be prohibited should not be less than one hundred leagues from the English coast. We had clearly a right to make any provisions we pleased with regard to the navigation of our own seas by our own subjects, whatever exceptions might be necessary as to neutrals.[7] Another object of the bill referred to the hovering distance with respect to Guernsey and the other Islands

---

[7] The law, as finally passed, however, gave jurisdiction over foreign vessels for one hundred leagues, in some cases. See p. 77, et seq., *infra*.

in the Channel. It was notorious that smuggling from thence had been carried on to an enormous extent. The measure he meant to propose, in order to obviate it in future, was to prohibit packages below a certain size from being on board ships, hovering off those places. . . . The report was received, and leave was given to bring in the bill." [8]

On June 28th, the Attorney General, in supporting the bill, stated, with particular reference to section VI, authorizing seizure and forfeiture of vessels found hovering within two leagues of the islands named in that section, that "the principle of the bill was nothing more than that of the hovering acts, as old almost as the revenue itself: vessels having liquors on board in contraband packages, and found hovering or sailing to and fro, and not proceeding on their voyages, wind and weather permitting." [9]

Lord Hawkesbury, in support of this bill in the House of Lords, said on July 8th: "The islands of Guernsey and Jersey were well known to be a great *entrepôt* for various kinds of merchandise; they, of course, became a great *entrepôt* for smuggling also; and the state of our trade required that smuggling should be suppressed as much and as speedily as possible, particularly in those islands, in and from which it was carried on to an amazing extent. The bill, he allowed, was of the highest importance, and, as such, it had received the fullest and most serious consideration."

On the same day, the Duke of Clarence declared that the officers employed to prevent smuggling "thought that such a measure was certainly necessary." [10]

---

[8] *Parliamentary Debates* (Hansard), 1805, vol. 4, col. 224. For further comment by the Chancellor of the Exchequer on the enormous amount of smuggling into these Islands, see ibid., 1805, vol. 5, col. 631.

[9] Ibid., 1805, vol. 5, col. 647.

[10] Ibid., col. 803.

The Act passed in 1805 represents a new type of legislation.[11]

So widespread and so alarming had the evil of smuggling become by this time that Parliament swept away the old distances, and, for the first time in the history of English legislation, extended jurisdiction, in certain cases, to one hundred leagues. Two leagues were chosen for the Channel Islands. Before 1805, no "hovering laws" had been passed for these islands: for this reason, smugglers could, with safety, land there and run their goods when hard pressed. These islands became such a safe retreat for smugglers that the customs laws were extended at this time to include them, but only as affecting smugglers and the running of goods to and from them.[12]

This Act provided for the seizure and forfeiture of the following vessels, *belonging in whole or in part to His Majesty's subjects*, or whereof *one-half the persons on board were such subjects* (except any ship or other vessel

[11] "An act for the more effectual prevention of smuggling," 45 Geo. III, c. CXXI, July 12, 1805. The preamble of this Act declared that further provisions were "highly necessary" to prevent smuggling because, "in defiance of the several laws of custom and excise, great quantities of goods are illegally imported into, and landed in the United Kingdom, as well by clandestine means as by open force, to the great detriment of the revenue, and the subversion of all civil authority."

The collector at Cowes reported on April 11, 1804:

"Smuggling in the Isle of Wight is now carring on to a very alarming extent and we have no doubt the 'Sea Fencible' system tends much to promote it as every smuggler holds a 'Sea Fencible' certificate and crosses to Guernsey and Alderney fearless of the Impress or Revenue officers." This was a system of licensing persons to use prizes as convoys for the small coasting vessels. The Royal Navy protected the larger merchant craft.

The collector at Cardiff reported to the Board of Customs on December 22, 1804, that brandy, geneva, and salt were brought over from the Islands of Guernsey and Jersey in armed and strongly manned vessels.

The port of Macduff reported on December 26, 1804, and again on August 14, 1811, that the trade was practically nihil.

[12] A. Hyatt Verril, *Smugglers and Smuggling*, p. 118.

square-rigged): any vessel or boat coming from foreign parts, having on board any foreign brandy, or other spirits in casks of less than sixty gallons, or any tea exceeding six pounds, or any tobacco or snuff in any cask containing less than four hundred and fifty pounds, if found or discovered to have been within the British or Irish Channels, or elsewhere on the high seas within one hundred leagues of the coasts of Great Britain or Ireland. The goods also were forfeitable.

It has already been observed that vessels belonging only in part to British subjects could not have been British vessels, and were, therefore, foreign bottoms, or were nondescript as to their flags.[13]

The provision in question introduced a new consideration. It embraced vessels whereof one-half the persons on board were British subjects. The ship's registry determines its nationality, and the nationality of the persons on board has nothing to do with the nationality of

---

[13] See p. 61, *supra.*

It was declared by sec. 2 that any vessel or boat, not coming from foreign parts, should, nevertheless, be deemed to be coming from foreign parts, if on the high seas it had taken on board out of any ship or vessel coming from foreign parts any of the goods named; and such boat or vessel and such goods and their containers were declared forfeited.

Sec. 6 adopted the two leagues for the Channel Islands, as stated above; it provided for the forfeiture of any ship or vessel having on board foreign rum or other spirituous liquors in casks not containing sixty gallons at least, or tobacco or snuff in casks containing less than four hundred and fifty pounds; or any ship or vessel which did not exceed fifty tons burden, having on board wine in casks of less than "a reputed hogshead," found at anchor or hovering or discovered to have been within two leagues of the coasts of the islands of Guernsey, Jersey, or Sark, or within two miles of the coast of Alderney. Such goods and their containers were also forfeited.

Sec. 10 granted like powers and authorities to officers for bringing to and going and remaining on board and searching all vessels made liable to forfeiture by this Act—that is, those found or discovered to have been within two or one hundred leagues or two miles—as were contained in any act or acts that granted to such officers any powers or authorities in relation to any such goods or any ship or boat within the ports, or hovering on the coasts.

the vessel itself.[14] It appears that this provision was inserted, because the smuggling vessel was frequently manned in part by British seamen, and/or had on board British subjects who owned the cargo, or who were serving as pilots; also British longshoremen were frequently on board to assist in running and landing the cargoes. As evidence that the legislator meant to embrace both British and foreign vessels, it should be noted that in an Act of 1819 it was observed that the laws were being defeated by foreign vessels and boats, having on board British subjects, but not amounting to half those on board; that is, if one-half of the persons on board the foreign vessels or boats had been British subjects, such vessels and boats would have come within the terms of the statute. Provision was then made by the Act of 1819 for jurisdiction over foreign craft with *one* or *more* British subjects on board.[15]

The two requirements as to ownership and the persons on board, according to the Solicitor to the Board of Customs in 1859, "identify them [vessels] with English sail," "as being wholly or partly British-owned or manned." The Board in 1875 referred to vessels so owned as possessing "the elements of British ownership."[16]

The Board of Customs in 1859, in explaining to the Treasury the application of those sections of the law in force at that time, calling for the forfeiture of vessels with one-half the persons on board British subjects, found, under certain circumstances, within the distances of four

[14] See Piggott, *Nationality*, Part II, p. 45, and the case of *The Four Brothers*, p. 64, *supra*.

For some limited purposes, a seaman takes the nationality of his vessel, but this principle has no application here; for the question under consideration is one of jurisdiction over the vessel, and not the person.

[15] See p. 88, *infra*, and the case of *The Four Brothers*, p. 64, *supra*.

[16] See p. 1, note, *supra*.

and eight leagues from the shore,[17] said: ". . . if half the persons on board be British subjects, she [the foreign vessel] is then liable to detention if found within" four and eight leagues of those parts of the coast prescribed by the Act.[18] The Board, in explaining in 1875 the application of the same law, said that it applied to foreign vessels if at least one-half of their crews were British subjects.[19]

However, in the same year in explaining the meaning of section 217 of 16-17 Vict., c. 107,[20] calling for the forfeiture of any vessel or boat, found within the *British or Irish Channels or within one hundred leagues of the coast,* with one-half the persons on board British subjects, from which any part of the cargo was thrown overboard or destroyed to prevent seizure when *chase was given,* or when signal was made to bring to, the Board of Customs took the position that such section applied only to "British ships having half their crew British subjects." No reason for this distinction is given. If the Act is applicable to foreign vessels when found within four and eight leagues of the coast, it is difficult to understand why it is not applicable to such vessels within one hundred leagues of the coast. On the other hand, the distance of one hundred leagues, as used in the Act of 16-17 Vict., was employed as sanctioning chase of offending vessels as far out into the high seas as practical; for the Board, in the communication of 1875, noted that the choice of that distance in 16-17 Vict. was merely the choice of "a definite for an indefinite distance," for in the case of a fugitive wrongdoer, no limit of distance could properly be applied to the pursuit on the high seas. In 1864, the Solicitor to the Board explained that section 217 of 16-17 Vict. was

---

[17] Sec. 25 of 18-19 Vict., c. 96; p. 106, note (9), *infra.*
[18] P. 139, *infra.*
[19] P. 146, *infra.*
[20] See p. 106, note (12), *infra.*

intended to cover any distance to which chase of a wrong-doer might reasonably extend. If the foreign vessel with one-half the persons on board British subjects was found within four or eight leagues of the shore under the forbidden circumstances, it could certainly have been chased for one hundred leagues under this section.

In 1807, a new Act was passed broadening the jurisdiction within one hundred leagues. All vessels which had, by any act or acts of Parliament, been made liable to forfeiture if found hovering within four or eight leagues, were now made forfeitable if found hovering within one hundred leagues of the coast, if such vessels belonged in whole or in part to British subjects, or if one-half the persons on board were such subjects. Four and eight leagues were adopted for boats of a certain build and for all vessels found hovering on the coasts with certain articles on board, not hitherto included in any act of Parliament.[21] Some of the sections of the Act are very complicated and require close analysis.

More particularly considered it declared forfeited every vessel exceeding fifty tons, belonging in whole or in part to British subjects, or having one-half of the persons on board such subjects, which was rigged or fitted as a lugger. No distance was named.[22]

The following vessels *belonging in whole or in part to British subjects,* or *having one-half the persons on board such subjects* were declared forfeited when found or discovered to have been within the British or Irish Channels or elsewhere on the high seas within one hundred leagues of Ireland or Great Britain:

[21] 47 Geo. III (2d sess.), c. 66, August 13, 1807. This Act was declared to be expedient for the "more effectual prevention of smuggling, and of the illegal importation of goods, wares, and merchandise."

[22] Certain exceptions were made by sec. 2, such as fishing or licensed vessels.

1. Any boat rowed with or constructed to row with more than six oars.[23]

Such a boat might belong to a foreign ship and be rowed by British subjects toward the shore with the intention of landing the cargo, or of transshipping it to another vessel nearer the shore. The statute would embrace any foreign boat within one hundred leagues of the shore which was owned in part by British subjects or which was rowed entirely by British subjects, or by one-half of such subjects, or which had on board one-half of such subjects to be used, perhaps, in the running, or in the transshipment of the cargo to another vessel, or who were on board for any other purpose.

2. Any ship or boat, not being a lugger, and at the time fitted and rigged as such, having on board or being navigated by a greater number of men than in a specified proportion to the number of tons of her measurement, for examples,

if of thirty tons or under and above five tons, four men;
if of one hundred tons or under and above eighty tons, seven men;
if above one hundred tons, one man for every fifteen tons of such additional tonnage.[24]

It will be recalled that the third report to the House of Commons of 1784 stated that according to the officers of the navy, smuggling vessels could be distinguished by four things, one of which was the proportion of men to the

[23] Sec. 3. Sec. 4 made certain exceptions, such as boats employed in the whale fisheries, and those belonging to merchant ships exceeding two hundred and fifty tons.

By the Act of 19 Geo. III, c. 69, any boat and other named craft, rowed with more than six oars, were made forfeitable if found within two leagues of the coast. Boats were being rowed from the Continent across the British Channel as well as from hovering vessels. Some of them were large—from forty to fifty feet in length—and were rowed with ten or twelve oars. They could move swiftly and carry large cargoes. See the seventh recommendation of the third report to the House of Commons of 1784, p. 57, *supra*.

[24] Sec. 5. The proportions are different if the vessel is a lugger.

burden.[25] If more men were employed in navigating the vessel than specified by this section, it was evidence, which was made conclusive, that the vessel was bent upon smuggling. Such a vessel was, therefore, declared forfeited if found within one hundred leagues of the coast, regardless of its nationality, provided it was owned in whole or in part by British subjects or had one-half of such subjects on board.

3. Any ship, vessel, or boat of whatever size of description, that had or had had on board during the voyage any cordage adapted for slinging small casks, any casks under sixty gallons, or any other articles to be used in smuggling, such as tubes for drawing off liquid, not being part of the cargo and included in the ship's regular official document.[26]

4. Any ship, vessel, or boat that had on board any tobacco or snuff, when such tobacco or snuff, even though in containers of legal size, was separated or divided within such containers into smaller packages, or if any other goods were found in any package of tobacco.[27]

5. All ships, vessels, or boats, which were, under any act or acts of Parliament, liable to forfeiture for hovering, or for having been discovered to have been within four or eight leagues of the coasts of Great Britain or Ireland, respectively, and which were by any such act or acts described and specified as to such distances; and the clauses, provisions, and forfeitures contained in such act or acts were extended to all ships, vessels, or boats and the goods laden thereon, covered by this section.[28]

By this section any vessel, so belonging or having one-half the persons on board British subjects, was forfeitable

[25] P. 56, *supra*. It does not appear why Parliament was so long in passing this measure after the committee submitted its observations and recommendations.

[26] Sec. 8. The articles named were also forfeited.
The cutter *Vectis* of Portsmouth was seized on the high seas within one hundred leagues of the coast for having on board casks of less content than twenty gallons used for smuggling. Exchequer K. R., *Memoranda Roll*, I Vict., Trinity Term, No. 21.

[27] Sec. 10. The tobacco and snuff were also forfeited.

[28] Sec. 17.

if found within the British or Irish Channels or elsewhere within one hundred leagues of the coast, if, for example, it had on board any brandy or other liquors in casks of less content than sixty gallons, or any other goods forbidden by 24 Geo. III (2d sess.), c. 47.[29]

Section 9 provided for the forfeiture of the following vessels: Any ship, vessel, or boat whatsoever, found within or found or discovered to have been hovering within four and eight leagues of such parts of the coasts of Great Britain or Ireland, respectively, as had been in any act passed for the prevention of smuggling described and specified as to such distances, having or having had on board during the voyage any cordage or other articles or goods named in section 8 of this Act.

This section added no new principle; it is similar to the Acts of 24 Geo. III (2d sess.), c. XLVII, and 42 Geo. III, c. LXXXII; it only brought vessels within the terms of those Acts when materials used for smuggling were found on board. It was applicable to all vessels of whatever nationality and regardless of the nationality of the persons on board.

This section provided, also, for the forfeiture of any boat rowed with or constructed for rowing with more than six oars, if found within or discovered to have been hovering within four or eight leagues of the coast, as specified.

This provision was applicable to all boats of whatever nationality. If they were owned in part by British subjects or if one-half the persons on board were such subjects, they were subject to forfeiture if found within one hundred leagues of the coast.

By section 32, a vessel made liable to seizure or examination by this or any other act of Parliament could be brought to for the purpose of examination. The pro-

---

[29] For this Act, see p. 59, *supra*.

visions of 24 Geo. III, c. XLVII, relating to chasing, bringing to, or firing into any vessel liable to seizure and examination were extended to vessels made so liable under this or any other act.[30]

Jurisdiction for one hundred leagues was taken again in 1816, 1817 and 1819. By the Act of 56 Geo. III, c. CIV, section 20, provision was made for the forfeiture of any square-rigged ship or vessel of two hundred tons or upwards, belonging in whole or in part to His Majesty's subjects, whereof one-half the persons on board were such subjects, if found without a license, in the British or Irish Channels, or within one hundred leagues of the coast.[31]

In 1817, by the Act of 57 Geo. III, c. 87, section 15, the following vessels belonging in whole or in part to British subjects, or whereof one-half the persons on board

---

[30] Sec. 11 provided for the forfeiture of the following vessels: any ship, vessel, or boat, belonging or having such persons on board as provided in sec. 3, upon which, after its departure from the Islands of Guernsey, Jersey, Alderney, and Sark, bulk should be broken or any part of the cargo unladen, or any alteration be made in the form or size or description of any package on board, at any time during the prosecution of the voyage towards Great Britain or Ireland or any port or place for which it had cleared out from such islands, if it had on board any spirits, tobacco, snuff, tea, wine, or salt. No limit was named.

[31] By sec. 21 of 57 Geo. III, c. LXXXVII (1817), this section was repealed and re-enacted by inserting the word "or" before the words "whereof one-half of the persons on board," etc., so that the vessels now embraced were those belonging in whole or in part to His Majesty's subjects, *or* those having one-half the persons on board such subjects. This amendment is noteworthy as showing that it was the intention of the legislator continually to keep distinct, vessels that belonged in whole or in part to British subjects and those whereof one-half the persons on board were such subjects. That is, the latter vessels were not to be associated with ownership in the vessel. They were a distinct class of vessels, chosen solely by reference to the nationality of those on board.

Any open boat or vessel, so belonging, which had been in foreign parts, or which had been found with or had taken in goods at sea from a vessel coming from such parts, unless a license for such purpose had been obtained, was forfeited by sec. 21 of the Act of 1816.

were such subjects, were subjected to forfeiture if found within the British or Irish Channels or elsewhere within one hundred leagues of the coast, or if discovered to have been within such Channels or distance:

1. Any boat, wherry, pennace, barge, or galley rowing or made to row with more than four oars.

The persons using such vessels, or the owners, were subject to a fine of one hundred pounds.[32]

2. Any ship, vessel, or boat, not being a square-rigged ship or vessel of the burden of two hundred tons or upwards, (and of other specified build), for which a license had not been procured.[33]

In 1819, the same distance was designated in the Act of 59 Geo. III, c. CXXI. According to section 8, a practice had grown up of building boats with double bottoms or double side or sides, wherein customable or prohibited goods could be concealed and run into the country. It was, therefore, enacted by that section that such boats and all their materials should be forfeited when belonging in whole or in part to British subjects, or whereof one-half the persons on board were such subjects, when found or discovered to have been in the British or Irish Channels, or elsewhere within one hundred leagues of the coasts of Great Britain or Ireland.[34]

These three Acts introduced no new principle of legislation, but they show the uninterrupted exercise of jurisdiction for one hundred leagues between 1802 and 1825. In fact this jurisdiction was exercised from 1805 until 1876.[35]

---

[32] This Act did not repeal sec. 3 of the Act of 1807.

[33] Sec. 21. This section was passed in lieu of sec. 20 of 56 Geo. III, c. 104, which was repealed.

[34] The French sloop *L'Industrie* of Cherbourg was seized at the "legal quay at the port of Southampton for having a secret disguise place in the construction" of the vessel. Exchequer K. R., *Memoranda Roll,* 2 Wm. IV, Trinity Term, No. 70.

[35] See pp. 104 and 113, *infra.*

Jurisdiction for four and eight leagues was taken in several acts between 1802 and 1825.[36]   Section 10 of the Act of 59 Geo. III, c. CXXI, provided for the forfeiture of any ship or vessel, not being square-rigged, or any boat found at anchor or hovering or discovered to have been within four or eight leagues of the coast as defined above,[37] having on board any goods liable to the payment of duty, concealed between false bulkheads, or in any other place.   The goods also were declared forfeitable.

This jurisdiction was taken in an Act of 1817, passed to end the practice of smuggling liquors and tobacco carried on board under the pretension that they were for the use of the seamen.[38]   Provision was made for the seizure and forfeiture of any ship or vessel, not being square-rigged, coming from specified parts of the coast of Europe found at anchor or hovering within four leagues of the coast between the North Foreland and Beachy Head or within eight leagues of any other part of the coast, or discovered to have been within such limits, having on board for the use of seamen more than a certain quantity of brandy or other liquors, or more than a certain quantity of tobacco for the use of each seaman.[39]

These two Acts were similar to the previous ones taking jurisdiction for four and eight leagues, in that they applied to all vessels, irrespective of their ownership or nationality, or the nationality of any person on board.

The year 1819 witnessed a new type of law in the Act of 59 Geo. III, c. CXXI.   It was observed that the provisions of the laws rendering liable to forfeiture vessels or boats belonging in whole or in part to His Majesty's

[36] This jurisdiction was taken in several acts after 1825, until their final repeal in 1876. See pp. 104 and 113, *infra*.

[37] See p. 74, *supra*.

[38] 57 Geo. III, c. XXXIII, (June 16, 1817).

[39] See also sec. 2. Vessels coming from other parts of the coast of Europe were included in a similar Act in 1819, 59 Geo. III, c. CXXI, sec. 6.

subjects, or whereof one-half the persons on board were such subjects, if found or discovered to have been within certain distances of the coasts of Great Britain or Ireland with foreign spirits, tea, tobacco, or snuff on board, were being defeated by foreign vessels and boats having on board British subjects, though such subjects did not amount in number to one-half those on board, and also by such subjects pretending to be passengers. It was then enacted that the following vessels should be seized and forfeited: any foreign smuggling vessel or boat in which there was one or more British subjects, whether mariners or persons pretending to be passengers, if such vessel or boat had on board any foreign brandy or other spirits in any cask of less content than sixty gallons, or more than six pounds of tea, or any tobacco or snuff in any cask containing less than four hundred and fifty pounds, if found or discovered to have been within four leagues of the coast between the North Foreland and Beachy Head, or within eight leagues of any other part of the coasts of Great Britain or Ireland.[40]

It will be recalled that the previous Acts calling for these distances applied to all vessels, irrespective of their nationality or the nationality of any person or persons on board. But under the present Act, the vessel found within these distances was forfeited only when one or more British subject was on board when the forbidden goods were present.[41] No new principle of law was introduced by this Act so far as jurisdiction over foreign vessels was concerned. Smuggling craft, of whatever

[40] Under sec. 2, this distance of eight leagues was to be measured as defined in the Act of 42 Geo. III, c. 82, p. 74, note (6), *supra*. By sec. 4, British subjects found masked on vessels hovering within those distances in which such vessels were forfeitable, were declared to be guilty of felony.

[41] For examples of cases enforcing this Act, see *The Providence*, p. 124, *infra; Le Georges*, p. 125, *infra; The Petit Jules*, p. 125, *infra; The Marie*, p. 133, *infra; L'Abandance*, p. 134, *infra*.

nationality, usually had at least one British subject on board, who served as a pilot or assisted in the running or landing of the cargo, or who was the owner of the cargo,[42] and his presence was, by this Act, made conclusive evidence that such foreign vessel was a smuggler. In 1875, the Board of Customs explained in a letter to the Treasury that the mention of one or two British subjects on board pointed to the fact that small craft generally employed in smuggling seldom carried a crew of more than three or four men, and frequently only one man and a boy. But the fact remains that large foreign vessels with one or more Englishmen on board were frequently seized within four or eight leagues of the coast and condemned under these Acts.[43] It was also said that if boats generally were not made liable by reason of being manned by British subjects, smugglers would always evade forfeiture of the boats they used by manning foreign vessels for their ventures.

In 1816, in order to insure the more effectual enforcement of the various acts passed to prevent smuggling, it was again provided by the Act of 56 Geo. III, c. CIV, section VIII, that when any vessel, liable to seizure or examination under any act of Parliament, should not bring to when required to do so, she should be shot into. This would authorize the shooting into vessels at the various distances named in the various acts in force in 1816, namely, two miles off the coast of Alderney and two, three, four, eight and one hundred leagues off other parts of the coasts and the Channel Islands, when such vessels came within the terms of such acts. The repetition of this provision at this time shows the determination on the part of Parliament to enforce the various acts

[42] See the report to the House of Commons in 1733, p. 21, *supra*. In nearly all cases of seizures of foreign smuggling vessels, at least one Englishman was found on board, and usually more than one.

[43] See p. 124, et seq., *infra*.

against vessels within the distance prescribed by such acts.

In 1809, provision was made by the Act of 49 Geo. III, c. LXII, for the seizure of certain goods concealed at sea within one hundred leagues of the coast. The preamble declared that seizures were frequently prevented by the smugglers throwing their cargoes overboard during chase; and section 2 declared that smuggling had been carried on by means of sinking small casks of spirits at sea, and "getting them up as opportunity offers." That section then provided for the taking up by customs officers of any spirits concealed within the British or Irish Channels, or elsewhere within one hundred leagues of the coasts of Great Britain or Ireland. The purpose of this Act was to prevent the smugglers, when found with illicit wares on board, from saying that such wares were picked up at sea,[44] and to break up the practice of sinking spirits on the coast and taking them up later when a favorable opportunity presented itself.[45]

§ 19. Efficacy of the New Laws

Turning to a consideration of the results accomplished by the several laws passed before 1825, it was observed in a letter of February 5, 1816, from the chairman of the Revenue Boards to the Board of Treasury that the Acts of 24 Geo. III, c. 47, 42 Geo. III, c. 82, and those of 45

[44] Opinion of Solicitor to the Board of Customs, 1864.

[45] For example, the port of Plymouth reported to the Board of Customs on February 22, 1815, that the "smuggling of spirits has of late increased . . . in small vessels and in small kegs that are sunk on different parts of the coast . . . when no opportunity offers for landing, but when suitable opportunity offers they are taken up and brought to land."

Certain provisions of the Act of 5 Geo. I, c. XI, were made perpetual in the year 1810, by the Act of 50 Geo. III, c. X; namely, those that penalized the taking of the goods "at sea" by certain vessels, in order to land them or to put them into any vessel within the limits of any port, and the boarding of certain vessels under fifty tons hovering on the coasts within the limits of any port. See p. 6, *supra*.

and 47 Geo. III,[46] all extending the distance "within which vessels are in certain cases forfeited, no less than one hundred leagues" have resulted in great advantage and "evince the propriety of strong measures." [47] It will be recalled that the first of the Acts referred to [48] extended jurisdiction over all hovering craft for four leagues; the second, for eight leagues for certain parts of the coast and four leagues for other parts;[49] the third, for one hundred leagues and to the British and Irish Channels, and two leagues for the Channel Islands;[50] while the fourth broadened the jurisdiction within these distances.[51]

It was observed in this letter that beneficial results would follow from a consolidation of the various acts into one general statute; but this consolidation did not take place until nine years later,[52] in spite of the fact that by 1816 the numerous laws in force had become very involved, intricate, and difficult to apply.

§ 20. General Instructions to Coast Guard Officers

The *General Instructions for Cruisers employed in the Revenue Coast Guard*, for 1822, show that the statutes were literally enforced. The pertinent sections of the Instructions read:

"You will use your utmost endeavors to come up with and seize all vessels or boats employed in smuggling, or attempting to smuggle, and all goods forfeited by law, particularly directing your attention to vessels of suspicious appearance, and from their size, build, and construction, adapted for smuggling; and also to Boats

[46] Presumably, 45 Geo. III, c. CXXI, and 47 Geo. III, c. 66 (2d sess.), were meant.

[47] *Parliamentary Papers*, 1816, vol. XVIII, No. 180, p. 9.

[48] See p. 59, *supra*.

[49] See p. 73, *supra*.

[50] See p. 77, *supra*.

[51] See p. 81, *supra*.

[52] See p. 101, *infra*.

calculated for carrying on an illicit traffic (especially French Boats, at present frequently used therein); and likewise to arrest and convey before a magistrate agreeably to the Act, 57 Geo. III, Cap. 87, sections 5 and 6, all persons employed on such vessels and boats, or in any way aiding or assisting in the clandestine unshipping, landing, or carrying off, such goods." [53]

The commanders were instructed also to go on board any foreign ship laden with wine or tobacco from parts beyond the sea and demand the manifest, and attention was called to the fact that the law required two copies to be delivered to the officer who first went on board within the limits of a port or within four leagues of the coast. If there was no manifest on board, or if delivery of it was refused, a report was to be made to the Comptroller General. [54]

If vessels were met with which were suspected of having on board commodities intended for smuggling, the officers were instructed to watch their movements, "taking care that they do not unlade any goods by the way into Boats within the limits prescribed by Act of Parliament. . . ." [55]

If upon any vessel bound for a port concealed goods were found, an officer was instructed to board the same and go into port with her and deliver her and her cargo to the port officers. [56]

Instructions were given to guard especially carefully East India ships to their moorings [57] and to guard against

[53] P. 18.

[54] P. 23.

There seems to have been no statute in force in 1822, requiring the production of a manifest within four leagues of the coast. Such a statute was passed in 1825. (See p. 103, *infra.*) This instruction of 1822 may have been based upon an Order in Council.

[55] P. 24.

[56] P. 27.

[57] P. 28.

the practice "amongst ships that have been over to Holland, France, etc. with coals, of putting their goods, on their return, into lightships from London or on the coast, but chiefly into Cobles or small fishing-boats, at sea. You are carefully to search such vessels when you meet them at sea (if within the limits of your Port)."[58]

Officers were instructed to acquaint themselves with the Acts of Parliament,[59] and "to act in strict conformity to the said Acts,"[60] and carefully to note the distance from the shore of each seizure.[61]

§ 21. Court Decisions

The French galley *La Victoire* of Rochester, of 5 16/94 tons burden, was seized six leagues southeast from the North Foreland and forfeited under one of the statutes giving jurisdiction for four and eight leagues, though it does not appear which one. No further details are given. This proceeding was also against the *P. O.* of Dover, seized ten miles from the North Foreland.[62]

§ 22. Seizures on the High Seas Reported by the "Preventive Service"

There are records of seizures of foreign vessels during this period in the accounts of the "Preventive Service," relating to seizures made by cruisers and the Land and Water Guard. The place of the seizures is seldom given

[58] P. 29.

[59] P. 17.

[60] P. 38.

[61] P. 39.

[62] Exchequer K. R. *Memoranda Roll*, 58 Geo. III, Michaelmas Term, No. 535 (1818).

This proceeding was against the following vessels, in addition to *La Victoire*:

The yawl *William and Elizabeth* of Rochester, 15 32/94 tons, seized one quarter mile off Gun Fleet Beacon, west, northwest; and

The sloop *Lotto* of Middlebury, seized one mile from Long Sand, John Stock of Dunkirk, Master.

See, also, p. 64, *supra*, for the case of *The Four Brothers* (1823).

except in most general terms; but it is sufficient to observe that the statutes were being enforced literally against all craft embraced within their terms. The following accounts of seizures are reported in 1821, 1823, and 1824:

The Dutch lugger, *Bykorf*, in ballast, seized by cruisers on the Irish Station in 1820;[63] The Dutch lugger, *De Zee Meeuno*, with a cargo of tobacco, some spirits and tea; The Dutch lugger, the *Blue-Eyed Maid*, with like cargo; *L'Eole*, French cutter, with a cargo of tobacco, and eighty gallons of geneva; *L'Isis*, French cutter, with tobacco and some spirits; all from January 5, 1822, to January 5, 1823;[64] and the lugger *L'Alouette*, 1821.[65]

Records of seizures of many foreign and domestic vessels are scattered through these reports.

The Times, (London) gives brief accounts of other seizures at this period, which show that smuggling continued on a large scale from 1802 to 1825. In some instances, these accounts give the nationality of the vessel and of the crew, the character of the cargo smuggled, and occasionally the distance from the shore where the seizure took place. One vessel was chased when sighted six leagues off the coast, but its nationality is not given. An American smuggling schooner was captured "between Irishtown and Glenegadhead (coast Ireland)," but the exact location is not given. A French vessel was boarded at Katlindean; it refused to surrender, put to sea, and twenty miles out the smugglers compelled the revenue officers to get into a tub-boat and return to shore. Another vessel was taken "in the Channel" and another "off the Needles." A Dutch vessel was taken "coming from France."[66]

[63] *Parliamentary Papers*, 1821, vol. XXI, No. 577, p. 8.

[64] Ibid., 1823, vol. XIV, No. 100, p. 1.

[65] Ibid., 1824, vol. XI, p. 335 of the 10th Report of the Commissioners of Inquiry into the Revenue of Ireland.

[66] These cases are reported in the following issues of *The Times*: Sept. 22, 1819; Nov. 30. 1820; Feb. 26, 1821; Nov. 16, 1824; Nov. 3, 1829; June 15, 1811.

CHAPTER VII

JURISDICTION OVER FOREIGN SUBJECTS DURING
THE EIGHTEENTH AND THE FIRST QUARTER
OF THE NINETEENTH CENTURIES

§ 23. Legislation Summarized

Before entering upon a discussion of the legislation of the second quarter of the nineteenth century, it seems desirable to summarize the legislation before that period extending jurisdiction over *persons* in the marginal seas The general principles of this legislation only are traced.

1. The early Act of 5 Geo. I, c. XI, section 3 (1718), provided for the forfeiture, by the masters of certain in-taking and all unlading vessels, of treble the value of any goods taken in "at sea." This applied to all masters of whatever nationality. By section 8, the master of every vessel of fifty tons or under, found hovering within the limits of any port, could be compelled to come into port.[1]

2. By the Act of 6 Geo. I, c. XXI (1719), section 31, masters of all ships of fifty tons or under were declared to be subject to the same penalty, rules, and procedure prescribed by section 8 of 5 Geo. I, c. XI, if found at anchor or hovering within two leagues of the coast.

3. By the Act of 9 Geo. II, c. XXXV, section 23 (1736), the masters of all in-taking vessels and unlading vessels were subjected to the penalty provided in the Act of 6 Geo. I, c. XXI, when goods were unladen within four leagues of the coast. This law applied to all persons assisting in the unshipping.

[1] See, also, 8 Anne, c. 7 (1709), p. 6, *supra*.

4. The masters of all vessels of seventy tons burden or under were subjected to fines or penalties, when their vessels were found hovering within two leagues with certain goods on board, by 24 Geo. II, c. XLI, section 26 (1751).

5. By 24 Geo. III (2d sess.), c. XLVII, section 11 (1784), it was made a felony for anyone to shoot at any vessel in the service of the customs, or at a customs officer on board or going to or returning from on board any vessel within four leagues.[2] By section 3 all persons in charge of forbidden goods on vessels hovering within that distance were subjected to a fine of treble their value, if such goods were on board without the knowledge or privity of the owner or master.

6. By 42 Geo. III, c. LXXXII, the provisions of the last Act were extended to eight leagues; and the master was subjected to the fine prescribed in that Act within the extended distance. This applied to all masters of whatever nationality.

7. By 45 Geo. III, c. CXXI, section 7, any subject of His Majesty, not being a passenger, found on any ship or vessel liable to forfeiture for having been found at anchor or hovering within the distance named within that Act or any other act, with goods on board which subjected the vessel to forfeiture, and *every person* found aiding in unshipping goods to be laid on land or found carrying or concealing any liquor subject to forfeiture under any law, were subjected to a forfeiture of treble the value of the goods that should be found or taken from such person, or of one hundred pounds. And any such person, being a subject of His Majesty, could be stopped and arrested and carried before a Justice of the Peace, where the vessel was carried or where the person was taken or arrested and placed under bail of one hundred pounds to answer

[2] See, also, 34 Geo. III, c. L, sec. 5, (1794).

any indictment and to pay such penalty, in default of which he was to be committed; or at the option of the officer arresting him, or of the Justice of the Peace before whom he was carried, he could be impressed as a seaman or marine on board His Majesty's ships of war for five years.

It will be recalled that the distances named in this Act ranged from two miles to one hundred leagues,[3] so that a British subject found on a vessel subject to forfeiture within such distances came within the provisions of section 7. This provision did not apply to foreign persons unless they were found aiding in unshipping goods to be laid on land; and even in such cases its application is uncertain; for it possibly referred to unshipping at the shore. At any rate, this section was aimed primarily at British subjects. After 1805, one finds legislation applicable to such subjects found on certain vessels at many miles from the coast. This distinction was, perhaps, due to the fact that most of the smuggling was carried on in British vessels by British subjects, and to the further fact that a large navy was being built up at that time, and Parliament was sweeping the high seas in order to secure as many recruits as possible under any pretext that it could seize upon. The smugglers were trained seamen and were, therefore, thought to be good material for the navy. This law called forth considerable complaint on the part of the regularly enlisted men as well as from members of Parliament.[4]

8. The Act of 49 Geo. III, c. LXII (1809), provided for the detention of every British subject, not a passenger, *found on board* any vessel belonging in whole or in part to British subjects, for which the owners were required to

---

[3] See p. 77, *supra.*

[4] See *Parliamentary Debates* (Hansard), 1834, Third Series, vol. 22, col. 931.

have a license for navigating the same, when found within four or eight leagues of the coast as specified by any act of Parliament, or within the British or Irish Channels or elsewhere within one hundred leagues of the coast, if cargoes were thrown overboard by anyone during chase.

9. By the Act of 50 Geo. III, c. LXII (1810), provision was made for the forfeiture of £100 by every British subject not being a passenger, found on any vessel at anchor or hovering within three leagues of the coast of the Isle of Man, having on board certain forbidden goods, and by every person assisting in unshipping certain goods within the limits of any port, without payment of duties.

These last two Acts providing for the arrest of British subjects on vessels within the distances named therein, would seem to authorize the boarding of any vessel of whatever nationality for the purpose of making the arrest. While the jurisdiction is a personal one, nevertheless control over the foreign vessel was exercised while the arrest was being made.[5]

10. By the Act of 57 Geo. III, c. LXXXVII, section 15 (1817), the owners of, or all persons using, any boat, wherry, pennace, barge, or galley rowing or made to row with more than four oars, if belonging in whole or in part to British subjects or if one-half the persons on board were such subjects, were subject to a forfeiture of one hundred pounds when found within the British or Irish Channels or elsewhere within one hundred leagues of the coast.

11. By the Act of 58 Geo. III, c. LXXVI (1818), it was provided that every person, not being a subject of His Majesty or a passenger, found or discovered to have

---

[5] See p. 112, *infra,* for reports of the arrest of British subjects on foreign vessels eight leagues from the shore, and *The Providence,* p. 124, *infra.*

been on board any vessel, ship, or boat within one league of the British "Dominions," when such vessel was liable to forfeiture under the Act of 45 Geo. III, c. CXXI, or any other act, for having been found at anchor or hovering within such distance and with such goods on board as subjected the vessel or the goods to forfeiture, should forfeit treble the value of such goods, or one hundred pounds. It should be noted that while the foreigner was subject to the fine only if found on the vessel within one league of the coast, yet the offense of the vessel upon which his presence made him subject to the fine might have been committed anywhere from two miles to one hundred leagues from the shore.[6]

This is the first time that jurisdiction for one league was associated with the foreigner, as distinct from the British subject. It is probable that the reason for this distinction made between the foreigner and the British subject, which had its beginning in legislation at this time, is found in the facts that most of the smuggling was carried on by British subjects and that recruits were being sought for the navy. The offense defined by this legislation was simply *being present* on certain vessels. Other laws provided for the arrest and punishment of foreigners for other offenses at much greater distances from the shore than one league.

12. By the Act of 59 Geo. III, c. CXXI, section 4, any British subject found or discovered to have been on board any ship, vessel, or boat liable to forfeiture under this or any other act for being found at anchor or hovering within any such distances of the Dominions of His Majesty with such goods on board as subject such vessel to forfeiture, wearing any mask, was declared guilty of felony and upon conviction was to be transported for

---

[6] See p. 121, *infra,* for the case of *Attorney-General* v. *Schiers* (1835), for the application of a similar statute to a French vessel.

seven years.[7] This provision did not apply to foreign subjects. By this same Act, foreign vessels were forfeitable when found within four or eight leagues of the coast with forbidden goods on board.[8] This difference in the treatment of the foreign vessel and the foreign subject supports the view that the wider jurisdiction was extended over British subjects for the reasons already given.

[7] For the conviction of an Englishman for having been on board a vessel liable to forfeiture under 6 Geo. IV, c. 108, for having been within one hundred leagues of the coast, contrary to sec. 3 thereof, see *In the Matter of Nunn* (1828), 108 Eng. Reps., 1182. It was held that he must be tried by the magistrate at the place where he is first carried, following *Kite and Lane's Case* (1822), 107 Eng. Reps. 38.

[8] See p. 87, *supra*, and *The Providence*, p. 124, *infra*.

CHAPTER VIII

FROM 1825 TO 1876

§ 24. Repeal of all "Hovering Laws"

By the end of the second quarter of the nineteenth century the hovering laws had become very numerous and complicated. As already noted, the Chairman of the Revenue Boards had recommended a consolidation of these laws in 1816.[1] As new methods and devices for smuggling arose, as larger and different types of craft were employed in its practice, and as the distance from which it was carried on at sea was increased, legislation underwent many sweeping changes. New acts were passed without repealing the old ones. Parliament legislated rapidly to meet new conditions as they arose, without regard to laws that were already on the statute books. This resulted in much duplication. A repealing act and simplified legislation were inevitable. This act was passed in the early years of the reign of George IV.[2] It repealed practically all the laws from the Act of 5 Geo. I, c. XI, passed in 1718, to that of 59 Geo. III, c. 121, passed in 1819, inclusive.[3]

[1] See p. 91, *supra.*

[2] 6 Geo. IV, c. CV (July 5, 1825).

[3] The following Acts were repealed by the following sections of the repealing statute:

Acts repealed:	By section:
5 Geo. I, c. XI	65
Made perpetual by 50 Geo. III, c. X, 6 Geo. I, c. 21, secs. 31 and 62	68
8 Geo. I, c. 18	71
2 Geo. II, c. 28, sec. VIII	76
9 Geo. II, c. 35	85

§ 25. The New Legislation

(1) *Introduction of Four Leagues for Breaking Bulk and Production of the Manifest and Visitation after Clearance Outwards*

The repealing statute was followed by a series of new acts, whose provisions formed the basis of the English law down to the passage, in 1876, of the Act now in force.

The first of these acts, "An Act for the general regulation of the Customs," was that of 6 Geo. IV, c. CVII, which came into force on January 5, 1826. It brought legislation of an entirely new type.[4]

According to section 2, it was found "expedient that the Officers of Customs shall have full cognizance of all ships coming into any port in the United Kingdom or in the Isle of Man, or approaching the coasts thereof, and of all goods on board, or which may have been on board such ships, and also of all goods unladen from any ship in any port or place in the United Kingdom or in the

---

3 Geo. III, c. 22............................... 109
5 Geo. III, c. 39................................ 115
5 Geo. III, c. 43, secs. 27 and 38, 19 Geo. III, c. 69 154
24 Geo. III, c. 47 (2d sess.)...................... 169
34 Geo. III, c. 50............................... 202
35 Geo. III, c. 31, sec. VI...................... 205
42 Geo. III, c. 82.............................. 226
45 Geo. III, c. 121............................. 237
47 Geo. III, c. 68 (2d sess.)..................... 258
49 Geo. III, c. 62.............................. 270
50 Geo. III, c. 62.............................. 279
56 Geo. III, c. 104............................. 323
57 Geo. III, c. 33.............................. 326
57 Geo. III, c. 87.............................. 328
58 Geo. III, c. 76.............................. 333
59 Geo. III, c. 121............................. 339

A general repealing Act, repealing all laws relating to customs and smuggling in force on January 5, 1826, besides those repealed by 6 Geo. IV, c. CV, was passed on May 26, 1826. 7 Geo. IV, c. XLVIII, sec. LII.

[4] It is possible that the provisions of this Act were modelled after a law passed by the Congress of the United States in 1790. See p. 184, *infra*.

Isle of Mann." This section subjected the master of
every ship to a fine of £100 when bulk was broken after
arrival of the ship within four leagues of the coasts of the
United Kingdom or the Isle of Man, before due report of
the ship and entry of the goods had been made, and a
warrant granted. Any alteration in the stowage, so as to
facilitate unlading, or any staving, destroying, or throwing overboard of the cargo or the opening of any package
after the ship's arrival within four leagues of such coasts
were declared to be a breaking of bulk.

Section 7 provided that the master of every ship
required to have a manifest on board [5] should produce
the same and a copy thereof to any officer of the customs
who should go on board such ship after her arrival within
four leagues of the aforesaid coasts, and demand the same
for inspection. If he refused to produce either, he was
subject to a forfeiture of one hundred pounds. He was
required to produce another copy to any officer who
should go on board within the limits of the port to which
the ship was bound. Both copies were to be transmitted
to the collector of the port.

Under section 79, a customs' officer was permitted to go
aboard any ship, after clearance outwards, within four
leagues of the coast, and demand the file of cockets and
the victualling bill. Any goods found on board not named
in these documents were forfeitable; and the master was
subject to a fine of twenty pounds for every package
named in such documents, but not found on board.
Every person falsifying a cocket forfeited £100.[6]

[5] By sec. 3, British vessels from parts beyond the sea, coming to the
United Kingdom or the Isle of Man, and every ship with tobacco on
board, were required to have a manifest on board.

[6] Sec. 2 was retained by sec. 2 of the Act of 3 and 4 Wm. IV, c. LII,
while secs. 3, 7, and 84 of that Act retained the provisions of secs. 3, 7,
and 79 of the old Act, respectively. These provisions were again carried forward in 8 and 9 Vict., c. LXXXVI, secs, 2, 3, 4, 6, and 93,
respectively. Sec. 3 of that Act declared that no goods should be

(2) *Jurisdiction for Three, Four, Eight and One Hundred Leagues Retained; One League Introduced*

The second new Act, namely 6 Geo. IV, c. CVIII,[7] also brought some sweeping and far-reaching changes into the law. The distances of two and three leagues were dropped altogether, and there was no re-enactment of the provisions of the Act of 34 Geo. III, c. 50, giving jurisdiction over the so-called "King's Chambers."

The new Act extended jurisdiction over foreign smuggling vessels when found at various distances from the shore ranging from one league to one hundred leagues. They were subjected to forfeiture when found within four and eight leagues, depending upon the part of the coast, in some cases when one-half the persons on board were British subjects, and in other cases when only one such subject was on board, or when the vessel was owned in whole or in part by such subjects. Forfeiture was incurred when the vessel was found within one hundred leagues, only when one-half the persons on board were such sub-

---

imported into the United Kingdom or the Isle of Man from parts beyond the sea in any British ship, unless the master had on board a manifest. Sec. 4 provided that "before any ship shall be cleared out or depart from any place in any of the British possessions abroad, . . . with any goods for the United Kingdom or for the Isle of Man, the master of such ship shall produce the manifest to the collector . . . of the customs."

The Act of 16 and 17 Vict., c. CVII, sec. 53, re-enacted sec. 2 of 6 Geo. IV, and sec. 146 re-enacted sec. 79 of that Act.

The Board of Customs explained to the Treasury on March 31, 1875, that sec. 146 of 16 and 17 Vict., c. 107, came into operation after a vessel had cleared out of a port and there was reason to suspect that she had clandestinely carried out any goods without the requisite official documents, or that dutiable goods included in such documents had been secretly relanded, in either of which cases she could have been boarded within port or within four leagues of the coast. It was added, however, that a vessel was practically never boarded beyond the limits of British ports, for, as a ship clearing one port sometimes proceeded to another port before her final departure from the country on her outward voyage, the officers of the latter port, being satisfied that everything was in order, interfered no further.

[7] January 5, 1826.

jects, or when the vessel was owned wholly or in part by such subjects. When the vessel was owned wholly by foreigners, and if no English subject was on board, the foreign vessel was not forfeitable unless it was found within one league of the coast. Jurisdiction over all vessels, British and foreign, was taken for one league off the coasts of the Channel Islands, the Isle of Man, and the British possessions in America.[8] This Act repeats many of the provisions of the laws repealed but a complete summary of it is given, as it forms the basis of the English law until 1876. The minor changes introduced are not, as a rule, commented upon, unless they represent a new principle of law.

The pertinent provisions of the Act are as follows:

The following vessels, belonging in whole or in part to British subjects, or whereof one-half the persons on board or discovered to have been on board were such subjects, were declared forfeited:

1. Any vessel or boat found or discovered to have been within four leagues of the coast between the North Foreland and Beachy Head or within eight leagues of any other part of the coast, not proceeding on her voyage, having or having had on board any goods liable to forfeiture, by any act, upon being imported into the United Kingdom.

[8] The Act fixing one league for the American possessions is 6 Geo. IV, c. CXIV, sec. 50. All vessels hovering within that distance could be visited, and if the vessel did not depart in twenty-four hours, it was carried into port and searched. The ship and cargo were then forfeited if prohibited goods were found on board.

By sec. 84 of this Act, all persons, British or foreign, found on any vessel liable to forfeiture within one league of the Channel Islands, were subject to a fine of £100.

The provisions of this Act were re-enacted by sec. 58 of 3 and 4 Wm. IV, c. LIX, and by sec. 65 of 8 and 9 Vict., c. XCIII; but by sec. 15 of 20 and 21 Vict., c. LXII, it was provided that the Acts of 16 and 17 Vict., c. CVII, and 18 and 19 Vict., c. XCVI, both of which are considered later, should extend to "the several British possessions abroad," unless otherwise provided in the said Acts, or unless limited by express reference to the United Kingdom or Channel Islands, except as to any such possessions as had by law or ordinance provided or might thereafter provide for the regulation of the customs.

The goods and containers were forfeited, also.[9] These distances and the requirements as to ownership and the persons on board are not new.[10]

2. Any boat or vessel, not being square-rigged, found or discovered to have been in the British or Irish Channels or elsewhere within one hundred leagues of the coast, having or having had on board any brandy or other spirits in casks of less content than forty gallons, more than six pounds of tea, any tobacco or snuff in any cask containing less than four hundred and fifty pounds, any cordage adapted for slinging small casks, and other enumerated contrivances to be used for smuggling.

The goods and containers were also forfeited.[11]

3. Any vessel or boat found within the British or Irish Channels or within one hundred leagues, or within four or eight leagues of the coasts as aforesaid, from which any part of the cargo was thrown overboard or staved or destroyed to prevent seizure when chase was given or signal made to bring such vessel or boat to.[12]

4. Any vessel sailing from the Islands of Guernsey, Alderney, Jersey, Sark, or the Isle of Man, which was navigated by a greater number of men than this Act allowed (as specified in sec. 21), or which sailed from such Islands with,

[9] Sec. 2. The distance of eight leagues is to be measured as in sec. 3 of 42 Geo. III, c. LXXXII. See p. 74, *supra,* note (6). Sec. 2 of 3 and 4 Wm. IV, c. LIII, sec. 2 of 8 and 9 Vict., c. LXXXVII, sec. 212 of 16 and 17 Vict., c. CVII, and sec. 25 of 18 and 19 Vict., c. XCVI, re-enacted this section. A few minor changes, such as changes in the minimum size of the containers for tobacco and snuff, and in the cargoes were made; but these changes are of no legal significance. See p. 139, *infra,* for an explanation of this section by the Board of Customs.

[10] See p. 87, *supra,* for similar provisions.

[11] Sec. 3. This section was re-enacted by sec. 2 of 3 and 4 Wm. IV, c. LIII, and by sec. 2 of 8 and 9 Vict., c. LXXXVII. Sec. p. 85, *supra,* for similar acts.

[12] Sec. 6. Sec. 5 of 3 and 4 Wm. IV, c. LIII, re-enacted this section. It was provided, in addition, that all persons escaping during the chase should be deemed to be British subjects unless it was proved to the contrary. This provision was carried forward in sec. 5 of 8 and 9 Vict., c. LXXXVII, and in secs. 216 and 217 of 16 and 17 Vict., c. CVII. See p. 142, *infra,* for an explanation of the use of the term "one hundred leagues" in this section.

or which "shall take or have taken" on board during the voyage, certain equipment adapted for slinging small casks, or otherwise used for smuggling.[13]

No distance was named in which seizures were to be made.

5. Any vessel or boat, after its departure from the islands named in sec. 10, with any spirit, tobacco, snuff, tea, or wine on board, upon which bulk was broken or from which any cargo was unladen, or its size or description altered, at any time during the voyage towards the United Kingdom or any other place for which such vessel or boat cleared out.[14]

6. Any vessel or boat, not being a lugger and at the time fitted and rigged as such, navigated by a greater number of men than in certain specified proportions to the tonnage (for example, if of thirty tons and under and above five tons, four men; if of one hundred tons or under and above eighty tons, seven men), found within any of the aforesaid distances, that is, within four, eight, or one hundred leagues as specified in this Act, unless it had a license for that purpose.[15]

Section 4 provided for the forfeiture of the following vessels: Any foreign vessel or boat, not being square-rigged, in which there was one or more subjects of His Majesty, found or discovered to have been within four or eight leagues of those parts of the coast as specified in sec. 2, not proceeding on her voyage, having or having had on board any brandy or other spirits in any cask of less content than forty gallons, more than six pounds of tea, or any tobacco or snuff in any cask containing less than four hundred and fifty pounds.[16]

[13] Sec. 10.

[14] Sec. 12.

[15] Sec. 21. If the vessel was a lugger, the proportions were different. See p. 82, *supra*, for a similar provision.

This section was re-enacted by sec. 17 of 3 and 4 Wm. IV, c. LIII, and sec. 17 of 8 and 9 Vict., c. LXXXVII.

[16] See p. 88, *supra*, for a similar provision.

Sec. 2 of 3 and 4 Wm. IV, c. LIII, re-enacted this section; and 5 and 6 Vict., c. XLVII, sec. 36, re-enacted it except that the offense defined was the throwing overboard or destroying the cargo to prevent its seizure, instead of the possession of certain goods. This provision was declared necessary by the later Act because vessels from which goods

Section 5 provided for the forfeiture of any foreign vessel whatsoever, found within one league of the coast, not proceeding on her voyage, having or having had on board any goods liable to forfeiture by any act for being imported into the United Kingdom.[17]

Jurisdiction over foreign craft was confined to one league only when the vessel was not owned in whole or in part by British subjects, or when no such subject was on board; for, as provided in other sections of the Act, when the foreign vessel was so owned, or when one or more British subjects was on board, the vessel was subject to forfeiture when found much farther from the coast than one league. There was, thus, no intention on the part of the legislator to confine jurisdiction over foreign craft to one league. There are many cases of forfeiture of foreign vessels seized within four or eight leagues of the shore when one or more British subjects were found on board.[18] Foreign vessels with no British subject on board whatever, seldom, if ever, engaged in smuggling.

Section 9 provided for the forfeiture of any vessel or boat, "whether British or foreign," found within one league of the Channel Islands or the Isle of Man, not proceeding on its voyage, having or having had on board any goods which were liable, by any act of Parliament,

---

were thrown overboard were not liable to seizure, although British subjects found on such vessels were liable to prosecution. Sec. 4 was again re-enacted by secs. 2 and 6 of 8 and 9 Vict., c. LXXXVII, and by sec. 216 of 16 and 17 Vict., c. CVII.

[17] This section was extended to all foreign boats, also, by 7 Geo. IV, c. XLVIII, sec. 15 (1826).

Sec. 2 of 3 and 4 Wm. IV, c. LIII, sec. 2 of 8 and 9 Vict., c. LXXXVII, sec. 212 of 16 and 17 Vict., c. CVII, and sec. 25 of 18 and 19 Vict., c. XCVI, re-enacted this section. See p. 139, *infra,* for an explanation of this provision by the Board of Customs.

[18] See p. 124, et seq., *infra,* and pp. 133 and 134, *infra.*

to forfeiture for being imported into or exported from such islands. The goods also were forfeited.[19]

This section reduced the distance from two leagues for the Channel Islands and three leagues for the Isle of Man to one league. Two leagues for the Channel Islands had been adopted in 1805, by the Act of 45 Geo. III, c. CXXI, and had remained in force until the passage of the present Act; while the Act of 5 Geo. III, c. XXXIX, had adopted three leagues for the Isle of Man.

By section 16 all vessels made use of in the removal or carriage of any goods liable to forfeiture under this or any other act relating to the revenue of the customs were forfeited.

This section was applicable to all vessels used in the removal of goods anywhere within those distances within which such goods were declared forfeitable by this Act. It would apply to foreign vessels, though vessels used for this purpose were largely British.[20]

Section 14 provided for the firing at or into any vessel (after the proper signal had been given), which did not bring to upon being required to do so, or upon being chased, when liable to seizure or examination under any act for the prevention of smuggling.[21]

Section 57 prescribed the death penalty for anyone who shot at or upon any vessel in the service of the revenue,

[19] This section was re-enacted by sec. 2 of 3 and 4 Wm. IV, c. LIII, sec. 2 of 8 and 9 Vict., c. LXXXVII, by sec. 212 of 16 and 17 Vict., c. CVII, and sec. 25 of 18 and 19 Vict., c. XCVI (1855). Under sec. 2 of the Act of 3 and 4 Wm. IV, in all cases of forfeiture of the vessel, the forbidden goods on board were also subjected to the same penalty.

[20] This section was re-enacted by sec. 10 of 3 and 4 Wm. IV, c. LIII, by sec. 11 of 8 and 9 Vict., c. LXXXVII, and by sec. 222 of 16 and 17 Vict., c. CVII.

[21] See p. 89, *supra,* for a similar provision.

Sec. 8 of 3 and 4 Wm. IV, c. LIII, sec. 7 of 8 and 9 Vict., c. LXXXVII, and sec. 218 of 16 and 17 Vict., c. CVII, re-enacted this section.

or at any officer in the execution of his duty in the British or Irish Channels or elsewhere within one hundred leagues of the coasts of the United Kingdom.[22]

Section 74 provided that in case any offense should be committed or any penalty of forfeiture incurred upon the high seas under this or any other act, the former should be deemed to have been committed and the latter incurred at the place on land where the persons committing such offense or incurring such penalty or forfeiture were taken.[23]

The Act of 16 and 17 Vict., c. CVII, brought one important change. Section 212 provided for the forfeiture of any foreign ship or boat, together with its cargo, having one or more British subjects on board, found within three leagues of the coasts of the United Kingdom with any spirits in casks of less content than twenty gallons or more than six pounds of tea, or any tobacco or snuff in any cask not containing two hundred pounds or any cordage or other articles to be used in smuggling.[24]

Jurisdiction for three leagues had been taken in 1765 by the Act of 5 Geo. III, c. XXXIX (sections 7 and 8).[25] This Act was repealed by the Act of 6 Geo. IV, c. CV, and was omitted in the new Acts passed during the reign of George IV.

The Act of 1876,[26] now in force, retains jurisdiction for three leagues, over the foreign vessel, carrying certain cargoes, when one-half the persons on board are British

[22] This section was re-enacted by sec. 64 of 8 and 9 Vict., c. LXXXVII, and sec. 249 of 16 and 17 Vict., c. CVII.

[23] By an Act of May 26, 1826, 7 Geo. IV, c. XLVIII, sec. 14, it was provided that when any vessel became liable to forfeiture under the Act of 6 Geo. IV, c. CVIII, on account of any goods being on board, "the goods creating such forfeiture should also be forfeited."

[24] This section was re-enacted by sec. 25 of 18 and 19 Vict., c. 96. See pp. 139 and 146, *infra,* for an explanation of this section by the Board of Customs.

[25] See p. 41, *supra.*

[25] See p. 150, *infra.*

subjects; or when it is owned in whole or in part by such subjects; or when goods are thrown overboard, during chase, regardless of the nationality of the owners or of the persons on board.[27]

§ 26. Jurisdiction over Persons

(1) *Legislation*

The Act of 6 Geo. IV, c. CVIII, retained the distinction made by 58 Geo. III, c. 76;[28] the foreigner was not subject to arrest and fine for being on certain vessels unless found within one league of the coast, while the British national could be taken from any vessel at any distance from the coast named in the Act within which the vessel was liable to forfeiture.[29] It should be noted, however, that the British subject could be arrested on any vessel, British or foreign, within any of the distances mentioned in the Act. Such an arrest on a foreign vessel was, of course, the exercise of control over it. This jurisdiction was only a personal one and had no relation to jurisdiction over vessels, except in so far as the arrest of the person meant the temporary control over the vessel.[30]

[27] See p. 154, *infra.*

[28] See p. 98, *supra.*

[29] Sec. 49. See p. 97, *supra,* for the probable reasons why this distinction was drawn between the foreigner and the British national, but not between foreign and domestic vessels.

This section was re-enacted by sec. 48 of 3 and 4 Wm. IV, c. LIII, sec. 2 of 4 and 5 Wm. IV, c. XIII, sec. 50 of 8 and 9 Vict., c. LXXXVII and sec. 235 of 16 and 17 Vict., c. CVII. The penalty was changed from fine to imprisonment by the last two Acts.

See *In re Van Boren* (1846), 115 Eng. Reps., p. 1430, for a conviction under this section of a foreigner taken from a foreign vessel within one league of the coast.

Sec. 90 of 3 and 4 Wm. IV, c. LIX, imposed a fine of one hundred pounds upon every person found or discovered to have been on board any vessel or boat liable to forfeiture under any act relating to the revenue of customs, for being found within one league of the Islands of Guernsey, Jersey, or Sark, having on board goods which subjected the vessel to forfeiture, or any vessel or boat from which any cargo was thrown overboard during chase. This section was re-enacted by 8 and 9 Vict., c. 93, sec. 97. It applied to foreigners and British subjects alike.

[30] See *The Providence,* p. 124, *infra.*

(2) *Cases of Arrest on Foreign Vessels on the High Seas.*
Reports to the House of Commons

Reports to the House of Commons show that the Act last considered was literally enforced by the customs authorities. It was reported on May 31, 1833,[31] for example, that a number of foreigners residing abroad, under confinement of smugglers, were taken aboard vessels laden with prohibited goods, and that many persons found on board vessels within eight or one hundred leagues of the shore laden with such goods were in prison for having thrown cargoes overboard during chase and for breaking bulk. Pierre Monster, Francois Quemener, Joseph M. Guilhac, and Samuel Griffin, were imprisoned for having been "taken on board a foreign boat within eight leagues of the coast of the United Kingdom with 150 gallons of foreign brandy in forty-three small casks. . . ." The nationality of these persons is not given.[32]

Some of the old acts or sections of acts, were, thus, omitted in the acts passed during the reigns of George IV, William IV, and Victoria. There was no longer a penalty attached to taking in goods "at sea," nor was any provision made for the seizure of goods concealed at sea within one hundred leagues. Jurisdiction for three, four, eight, and one hundred leagues was retained, in certain cases, over both foreign and domestic vessels; but there was no specific legislation calling for jurisdiction for two leagues or over the so-called King's Chambers, but these Chambers were embraced within the one-hundred, and in some cases, the eight-league statutes.

The law as contained in the acts passed during the reign of George IV remained the law of England, with

---

[31] *Parliamentary Papers*, 1831-1832, vol. XXXVIII, No. C. 50.
See, also, ibid., 1833, vol. XXXIII, p. 8 of No. 248 and, 1839, vol. XXX, p. 2 of No. 234.
[32] Ibid., 1839, vol. XXX, No. 234. See, also, p. 115, note (42), *infra*.

the changes noted, until the passage of the Act now in force in 1876. While smuggling reached its climax by 1825, yet it continued on a broad scale until the middle of the nineteenth century. Reports of committees to the House of Commons, showing the large amount of smuggling and the methods employed in its practice during the second quarter of the nineteenth century, and the consequent necessity for the continuation of these laws during this period, are considered later.[33]

To summarize the situation between 1826 and 1876:

1. The acts passed during the reign of George IV were repealed eight years later on August 28, 1833, by the Act of 3 and 4 Wm. IV, c. L, sections II and III.[34] New acts were passed on the same date,[35] and these remained in force until their repeal in 1845.

2. The acts passed during the reign of William IV, were, in turn, repealed on August 4, 1845, by 8 and 9 Vict., c. LXXXIV. On the same date, new acts were passed,[36] which remained in force until their repeal on August 20, 1853.

3. The acts passed in 1845 were, in turn, repealed on August 20, 1853, by 16 and 17 Vict., c. CVII.[37] A new act was passed on the same day and two others later, one

[33] See p. 114, *infra.*

[34] These Acts repealed were:
    6 Geo. IV, c. CVII,
    6 Geo. IV, c. CVIII,
    6 Geo. IV, c. CXIV,
    7 Geo. IV, c. XLVIII.

[35] These new Acts were:
    3 and 4 Wm. IV, c. LII,
    3 and 4 Wm. IV, c. LIII,
    3 and 4 Wm. IV, c. LIX,
    4 and 5 Wm. IV, c. XIII,
    5 and 6 Wm. IV, c. XLVII.

[36] The new Acts were:
    8 and 9 Vict., c. LXXXVI,
    8 and 9 Vict., c. LXXXVII,
    8 and 9 Vict., c. XCIII.

[37] P. 827.

in 1855 and another in 1857, which remained in force until their repeal in 1876.[38]

The new acts in each case, for the most part, copied the ones that they repealed; so that the law of 1825 remained in force, with the few changes noted, for the fifty years that followed.

§ 27. The Necessity of the Foregoing Legislation

Smuggling Gradually Declines after 1825; and is Practically Wiped Out after 1851. Reports to House of Commons, 1843-1876

That the continuation of the legislation passed during the reign of George IV was necessary for some twenty-five years after its passage in 1826, is shown by reports to the House of Commons and by Parliamentary discussions. These reports state that smuggling was carried on from sea during these years on a very large scale. While the golden days of smuggling ended with the first quarter of the nineteenth century,[39] it continued on a large scale until the end of the first half of the century. Especially had the smuggling trade been carried on to an advantage off the coasts of Kent, Sussex, and Surrey, because of the presence of the marshes and fens, into which the small craft could not be pursued. The activities of the large gangs, such as the well-known Hawkhurst and Ruxley gangs, had ceased during the early years of the century, as a result of the execution of some of the leaders for the murder of those who stood between them and the success of their trade. The increase in the trade between 1800 and 1825 was due to the activities of the seafarers and fishermen, who looked upon smuggling as a charitable

[38] The new Acts passed were:
    16 and 17 Vict., c. CVII (1853),
    18 and 19 Vict., c. XCVI (1855),
    20 and 21 Vict., c. LXII (1857).
See p. 90, *supra*.

enterprise, since it carried goods to the poor people at a much cheaper price than they would have had to pay for the goods legitimately introduced into the country. The populace were their friends, and in many cases, abetters. Homes and churches and church yards were made convenient hiding places for contraband. Convictions were all but impossible.

The amount of smuggling from sea by all classes began rapidly to decline after 1850. The report of the Commissioners of Customs of 1843 records some seizures of forbidden goods from vessels at sea.[40] The report of 1851 [41] notes that smuggling was on the decline in most districts, and entirely suppressed in others by the vigilance of the Coast Guard and cruisers.[42] It was observed by the authorities at Falmouth that the decline was due largely to the Act of Parliament making foreigners liable to the same penalties as Englishmen for smuggling; while in another district it was said to be due to reduction of the price of spirits in France.[43]

[40] *Parliamentary Papers,* 1844, vol. XII, p. 624.

[41] Ibid., 1851, vol. LIII, No. 454.

[42] This report notes that smuggling vessels had been compelled to destroy their cargoes during chase by revenue cruisers, among which vessels there appears *La Creole, "Le Vif* of Cherbourg," on May 13, 1842.
Tobacco was being smuggled directly from America at this time. In 1846, tobacco was run from the American vessel *Sumatra.* The Belgian vessel, the *Jeanette,* was seized with tobacco on board in 1842, by the Coast Guard at Malden. Likewise the French vessel, *La Commerce,* at St. Ives, was seized in 1841, after having run forty-six tubs of spirits. There was noted "petty smuggling by French vessels" at Scarborough. And in 1842 there had been "petty smuggling by the crews of French and Dutch vessels" at Scarborough. Smuggling was "extensively carried on by the coasting and foreign vessels bound for Limerick" in 1841, and by vessels from North America in 1842, and Dutch and French fishing vessels in 1841.

[43] On April 18, 1834, when a smuggling bill was before the House of Lords, it appeared from the discussions on that day that Boulogne, Cherbourg, Dieppe, Fecamp, Barfleur, St. Valeri, Etaples, and two or three other ports between Brest and St. Maloes were "privileged ports," whose "municipal regulations and ordonnances . . . were framed

A report of the Commissioners of Customs Inquiry to the Lords of the Treasury in 1851 observed that "in proportion as the Coast Guard force, by which the coast more exposed to the smuggler is lined, has become more efficient, in the same proportion smuggling has changed its character. Runs by swift-sailing cutters are now seldom attempted," and the trade "is generally effected by means of coasting vessels, and vessels entering the ports from foreign countries with contraband goods, either secreted under their cargoes or in carefully contrived places of concealment." [44]

The reports to the House of Commons from 1857 on show that the smuggler was being successfully coped with. In the report of the Commissioners of 1857 it is stated that "with the reduction of duties, and the removal of all vexatious restrictions, smuggling has greatly diminished, and the public sentiment with regard to it has undergone a very considerable change. The smuggler is no longer an object of general sympathy or a hero of romance. . . . Smuggling proper is now almost entirely confined to tobacco, spirits, and watches." In the last ten years, it was said to have decreased about one-third. [45] The report of 1860 observed that "since the failure of the wine crop in France the attempts to smuggle brandy into this country appeared to have almost entirely ceased until 1858," but since the recovery of the vines, impetus had been given to the trade, though it was not "extensive or

---

solely . . . with a view to facilitate and encourage the illicit importation of French goods and produce into this country." The regulations consisted in reducing tonnage dues on small English smuggling vessels, and allowing brandy to be shipped from Bordeaux, Rockfort, and Rachelle in kegs containing three or four gallons. Remonstrances were made to the French Government, and assurances were given that these conditions would be amended. *Parliamentary Debates* (Hansard), 1834, Third Series, vol. XXII, col. 933.

[44] *Parliamentary Papers*, 1851, vol. XI, Part III, p. 1369.

[45] Ibid., 1857, vol. III, No. 2186, pp. 38-9.

important." "The Coast Guard have made a few seizures from time to time, principally in the neighborhood of Portsmouth and the Isle of Wight, but in no case has the number of tubs seized exceeded fifty." Eight hundred and ninety pounds of tobacco attempted to be run by a vessel called the *Telegraph* was seized.[46] There was "no great increase or decrease to report" during the past year. Attempts had been continually made in 1861 to run small quantities of tobacco from vessels arriving from America. Some cases of seizures in ports are noted.[47]

In 1864, the Coast Guard had not reported any attempts to run spirits or tobacco on any part of the coast.[48] In 1865 and in 1866, the attempts were of a petty description and unusually rare.[49] From 1866 to 1876, these reports show nothing of importance. Petty smuggling continued, and some seizures of foreign vessels and goods on vessels in port are noted. In 1874, smuggling was detected from a port one mile from the shore, but this is the only instance of the kind mentioned.[50]

§ 28. Instructions to the Coast Guard, 1829, 1841, 1866, and 1875

The instructions to the Coast Guard during this period show that the hovering laws were strictly enforced.

The *General Instructions for the Coast Guard* of 1829

---

[46] Ibid., 1860, vol. XXIII, No. 2679, p. 21.

[47] Ibid., 1861, vol. XXXI, No. 2843, p. 27.

[48] Ibid., 1865, vol. XXVII, No. 3543, p. 44.

[49] Ibid., 1866, vol. XXVI, No. 3710, p. 51, and 1867, vol. XXI, No. 3887, p. 56. The attempts at smuggling were made by seamen and passengers; all organized efforts had ceased to exist at this time.

[50] The accounts of seizures at sea reported in the London *Times* are very rare at this period. The issue of that paper of May 30, 1870, reports that the Ventnor Coastguard station had received word that a smuggler was landing goods in Steel Bay. Twenty-five minutes later when the place was reached, the smuggler had gone. He was finally captured a "good distance" out in the Channel. The vessel was a sail boat with only one person on board,—an Englishman.

admonished the officers to study the "laws for the prevention of smuggling" and "to be able on all occasions to act in strict conformity thereto. . . ."[51]   Some of the special instructions of 1822 are repeated.[52]

"When vessels are met with within 4 leagues of the coast, which are not liable to quarantine, the commander . . . is to go on board and inform himself from whence she came and where she is bound to; and if she is a vessel required by the Act of 6· Geo. IV, Cap. 107 to have a manifest on board, he is to demand the production thereof," according to section 7 of that Act.[53]   A failure to find a manifest or a refusal to deliver it must be reported to the inspecting commander.

The *General Instructions for the Coast Guard* of 1841 enjoined the officers to acquaint themselves with the acts of Parliament,[54] and they were directed to "search and strictly examine all suspicious ships, vessels, and boats, and in all cases where authorized by law, to seize the same."[55]   There were instructions to place one officer on board a vessel bound for a port when there was reason to believe, after search, that goods were concealed on board.

When a vessel was met with within four leagues of the coast, the commander was instructed to go on board and demand a manifest as required by section 3 of 3 and 4 Wm. IV, c. 52, which includes "all vessels importing tobacco."[56]   A refusal to deliver the manifest or the absence of it was to be reported to the inspecting commander.[57]

The *Special Instructions for the Coast Guard* of 1866

[51] P. 5.

[52] See p. 91, *supra*.

[53] See p. 103, *supra*, for this section.

[54] P. 2.

[55] P. 4.

[56] See notes (5) and (6), p. 103, *supra*, for this section.

[57] For the instructions of 1857, see p. 137, *infra*.

and 1875, issued by the Admiralty, likewise show that the laws passed in 1845, 1853, 1855 and 1857 were being strictly enforced. The pertinent sections of the instructions of 1866 are as follows:

"It will be their [the officers] duty to search and strictly examine all suspicious vessels or boats, and in all cases, where authorized by law, to seize the same, . . ." [58] The officers were enjoined "to make themselves thoroughly acquainted" with "the Acts of Parliament for the prevention of smuggling" so as "to be enabled to act, . . . for the benefit of the Revenue, without infringing the laws." [59] When a vessel was met with "bound to a port in Great Britain or Ireland," and after search, there was reason to believe that goods were concealed for the purpose of being clandestinely landed before the vessel arrived at her port of discharge, an officer was to be placed on board, to prevent such landing and to deliver the vessel and cargo at the port to which she was bound. [60] If a vessel was met with, and there was reason to believe that goods were on board which were intended to be smuggled, she was to be watched and accompanied till she was seen "clear of the coast." [61] "When vessels are met with within 4 leagues of the coast, which are not liable to quarantine, the Officers of the Coast Guard will be guided by the directions contained in the 25th Section of 'The Supplimental Customs' Consolidation Act, 1855. . . .' " [62] It was then added that the "officers of the Coast Guard are to be very careful how they carry out the above instructions, with

[58] Chapter X, sec. 11, p. 49,—"Duties of Officers and Men in the Protection of the Revenue."

[59] Ibid., sec. 12.

[60] Ibid., sec. 15.

[61] Ibid., sec. 20.

[62] Sec. 25 referred to is then set out in full. See note (9), p. 106, *supra;* note (17), p. 108, *supra;* note (24), p. 110, *supra,* for the provisions of that section.

respect to Foreign Vessels." [63]   "When a vessel is seized, or detained . . . at sea," the officers were instructed to take particular care "that the distance from the shore . . . be clearly ascertained." [64]

Sections 471, 495, 475 and 476 of the *Special Instructions for the Coast Guard Service,* which took effect January 1, 1875, repeated sections 15, 12, 24, and 25, respectively, of the *Instructions* of 1866. Section 474 prohibited the approach by Coast Guard vessels within one league of the coast of France, Holland, Belgium, "etc.," and the boarding and examining foreign vessels or the exercise of "any belligerent rights of search beyond the limits of British jurisdiction." "Should any suspicious vessels under foreign colours be fallen in with, the cruizers are to keep company with them, to see that, if they have contraband goods on board, they do not land them on any part of the British coast, nor transfer them into British vessels."

§ 29. Court Decisions: Interdepartmental Correspondence Discussing the International Status, the Necessity for and the Proper Interpretation of the "Hovering Laws," 1850-1875

(1) *Cases from Memoranda Rolls*

The *Memoranda Rolls* record many cases of seizures and forfeitures of vessels under the acts passed between the years 1825 and 1876. The cutter *Eliza* of Cherbourg was forfeited for being within one league with liquor on board in casks containing forty gallons.[65] The French sloop *Le Pierre* was seized on the high seas within one

---

[63] Chapter X, sec. 24 of the instructions.
[64] Ibid., sec. 25.
[65] Exchequer K. R. *Memoranda Roll,* 6 Wm. IV, Easter Term, No. 51. This forfeiture was under sec. 2 of 3 and 4 Wm. IV, c. LIII.

league of the shore.[66] And the smack *Unternehming,* "a foreign vessel found within one league of the coast," was seized.[67] The French smack *John* of Cherbourg was seized within one league for having divers articles on board for sinking small casks.[68]

Under section V of 6 Geo. IV, c. CVIII,[69] and the corresponding sections of the later acts, a foreign vessel was not subject to arrest or forfeiture beyond one league, unless at least one Englishman was on board or unless the vessel was owned in whole or in part by British subjects.

(2) *The Attorney General* v. *Schiers* (*The Bien Aimé*)

A case arose in 1835, *Attorney General* v. *Schiers,*[70] which interprets a somewhat vague provision in section V of 6 Geo. IV, c. CVIII, which declared forfeited any foreign vessel found within one league of the coast, *having had on board* any goods liable to forfeiture by any act for being imported into the United Kingdom.[71] It was an information filed by the Attorney General, upon 3 and 4 Wm. IV, c. LIII, section 2, which is a re-enactment of section V of 6 Geo. IV, c. CVIII, praying for the forfeiture of a French vessel, the *Bien Aimé,* for being found within one league of the shore,[72] having had on board certain parcels of foreign spirits in casks of prohibited size. The *Bien Aimé* had never had spirits

[66] Ibid., 7 Vict., Hilary Term, No. 24. This forfeiture was under the same law.

[67] Ibid., 10 Vict., Michaelmas Term, No. 32. This forfeiture was under sec. 2 of 8 and 9 Vict., c. 87.

[68] Ibid., 1 Vict., Easter Term, No. 47. This forfeiture was under sec. 2 of 3 and 4 Wm. IV, c. LIII.

[69] See p. 108, *supra.*

[70] 150 Eng. Reps. 124; 2 C. M. and R. 286; 1 Gale 223; 5 Tyr. 1029; 4 L. J. Ex. 324.

[71] See, also, p. 154, *infra,* for a similar provision in the Act now in force.

[72] The vessel was apparently seized about one-half mile from shore.

on board while within one league of the coast but had had them on board and delivered them to another vessel, *La Marie*, beyond one league, and had later come within one league herself. *La Marie* was taken about one-half mile from the shore, and three French and two English sailors were on board with "casks of foreign spirits, in half ankers, slung." The Lord Chief Baron told the jury that in his opinion the *Bien Aimê* was liable to forfeiture under the statute if she unshipped the prohibited goods more than a league from the coast, and afterwards came within that distance. A verdict was given for the Crown. Counsel for defendant moved for a new trial on the ground that the words in the Act "having had on board," must be taken in connection with the words "so found or discovered," that is, found or discovered "to have been within one league of the coast"; and he contended that "it is not sufficient to subject the vessel to forfeiture, that she has unshipped the goods at a greater distance, and afterwards come, as an innocent vessel, within the prohibited limits."

The rule was refused. Lord Abinger, C. B., said: "The statute seems indeed to be directed against the very case of a vessel, having had goods on board in prohibited packages, discharging them before she enters the specified limit and then following, to assist in the landing or receive back the crew." [73] But the provision, he added, "is applicable only to the particular voyage in which she both discharges the goods and enters the prohibited limits."

The English law in force today contains a provision similar to that under which this case was decided.[74] It, thus, subjects to forfeiture a foreign vessel for an act committed on the high seas beyond one league from

[73] See *The Coquitlam*, p. 203, *infra*, and *The Grace and Ruby*, p. 217, *infra*.

[74] See p. 154, *infra*.

the shore, when that vessel later comes within that distance.[75]

The will of Parliament, as expressed in the laws from 1699 to 1876, is quite clear. Legislation has been consistent. The laws, during this period, as has been repeatedly pointed out, were framed to meet the smuggler on his own ground. With the safety of the revenue only in mind, Parliament experimented in legislation until laws were found that fell so heavily upon the smuggling trade that it was, for all practical purposes, eventually wiped out. Many seizures were made and foreign vessels condemned under these laws. They had, thus, served a high purpose: they had brought order out of chaos in the coast countries and in the neighboring seas, and they had saved the revenue many millions sterling. No foreign government ever lifted its voice in complaint or protest.[76] There had never been any intimation by any such government or by any department of the British Government that these laws were in contravention of International Law. These laws had held and hold today a rather unique position; they have persisted in the municipal codes of nearly all maritime countries, while some of these countries maintain a narrower jurisdiction for other purposes.

In December, 1850, their legality came under discussion for the first time by several departments of the British Government, in the famous, unpublished case of *The Petit-Jules.*[77] These discussions, which continued until

---

[75] The British Government was, therefore, inconsistent when it protested in 1892 against a proceeding by the United States against a Canadian vessel, the *Coquitlam,* which was seized about one-fourth of a mile from the shore for an act committed between three and seven miles of the coast, in violation of the hovering laws. See pp. 203 and 271, *infra.*

[76] See pp. 140 and 148, *infra.*

[77] This case, together with all other cases for which no citations are given, was taken from the original records in the library of His Majesty's Customs in London.

1875, disclose the views of several departments of the place in International Law of the so-called "hovering laws," and in some cases, they clarify some of their obscure provisions. Two cases arose only a few months before that of *The Petit-Jules,* which should be discussed first.[78]

(3) *The Providence* (1850)

The first was *The Providence.* A large French tub boat "not square-rigged, lugger rigged," of Cherbourg, was observed on March 22, 1850, lying about six and one-half miles off the Coast of Dorset, not within the limits of a port, ostensibly waiting for an opportunity to run ashore. After chase, she was captured eight or nine miles from land. She threw her cargo overboard when the revenue cruisers began firing to bring her to. The casks thrown over were fitted with sinkers and, therefore, could not be found, but they were seen to have the appearance of small casks of the size and description ordinarily used in smuggling; there was found on board an empty cask, some large stones adapted for slinging, and one gallon of brandy. The vessel carried a crew of six Frenchmen and the usual one Englishman. She was cleared out for England, according to her manifest.

The Englishman was convicted and given six months' imprisonment under section 50 of 8 and 9 Vict., c. 87,[79] "for having been found on board a vessel within 8 leagues of the coast from which goods were thrown overboard to prevent seizure." The Frenchmen were released under the same section of the same Act, for they had not been found at any time within one league of the coast. The vessel was proceeded against, condemned, and sold under sections 2[80] and 88 of that Act, for having been within

---

[78] The unpublished case of *The Four Brothers,* decided in 1823, has already been discussed. See p. 64, *infra.*

[79] See p. 111, note (29), *supra,* for this section.

[80] See p. 107, note (16), *supra,* for this section.

eight leagues of the coast with one or more English subjects on board and with spirits in casks of forbidden size.[81]

(4) *Le Georges* (1850)

In the second of the two cases, *Le Georges,* a French smuggling vessel, of thirty-one tons, was boarded on April 21, 1850, about eight or nine miles from the shore. One Englishman was found on board, but no forbidden goods were found. But as she was suspected of having "a concealment about her," officers were placed on board to accompany her to Portsmouth, where she was bound. No cause for an action against her was found at Portsmouth, where she was examined. This proceeding, however, was a clear exercise of authority over the vessel at the point where she was boarded.

In *The Providence* and *Le Georges,* the French Government made no protests, and no department of the British Government questioned the legality of the seizure and the legal proceeding in the one case and the boarding of the vessel in the other.

Le Georges was seized on August fourth of the same year about two miles from the shore and forfeited under section 2 of 8 and 9 Vict., c. 87, for having on board, within one league of the shore, articles prepared for slinging small casks. The French crew were imprisoned under section 50, for being on board within the same distance, with the articles named on board.

(5) *The Petit-Jules* (1850)

The next case of seizure of a foreign vessel under the eight-league statute, the one which gave rise to discussions by several departments of the English Government, was that of *The Petit-Jules.* This vessel was a French smug-

---

[81] Sec. 88 provided for the imprisonment of the offenders upon conviction before two or more Justices of the Peace, until a fine of one hundred pounds was paid.

gler, entirely French owned, "filled with tubs," manned by eight Frenchmen and three Englishmen. She was seized on December 9, 1850, about twenty-five miles from the shore, bound to England with spirits on board with the intention of smuggling them ashore or of sinking them off the coast.[82] While being carried to port, the crew rose against the boarding officers, and the vessel made her escape. It was thought at the time that one of the boarding officers was killed in the fight that took place. One of the French crew, Fanin, was later taken at Alderney; and the *Petit-Jules* was taken again on January 6, 1851, about sixteen miles from the shore with spirits on board. There was no evidence that she had violated the statute on this occasion, but the Solicitor to the Board of Customs advised that if on the occasion of her first capture (i.e., on December 9, 1850), she was within eight leagues of the shore with one Englishman on board, she was liable to forfeiture under section 2 of 8 and 9 Vict., c. 87, and that any member of the crew on board on that occasion was liable under sections 2, 50,[83] and 88 of that Act. The crew on board at the time of the second capture were released, as they could not be identified as those on board at the time of the first capture, but the vessel was retained

[82] She was seized by the *William and Mary,* which was cruising under the following orders:

"You are hereby directed to cruize in the Prize William and Mary tomorrow off Barfleur, [France] and use your best endeavors to capture contreband vessels, returning back to the Nab Lights tomorrow at sunset and waiting there for me.

Given under my hand this 8th day of December, 1850.

(Signed), Robert Willcock
Lieut't R. N.
in Command."

[83] See p. 111, note (29), *supra,* for sec. 50. Under that section only the Englishmen were liable for being on board within eight leagues; the Frenchmen were not liable unless they were within one league. Sec. 2 had no application to the crew. See note (81), p. 125, *supra,* for sec. 88, which provided for imprisonment, after conviction, until the fine was paid.

as she had on board, at the time of her first capture, casks of illegal size.

While the authorities were still under the impression that one of the boarding officers had been killed, the Board of Customs presented the case to the Lords of the Treasury with the view to obtaining, through the Secretary of State for Foreign Affairs, the delivery of the French crew for trial.[84] The Lords of the Treasury, in turn, called upon the Queen's Advocate General, an officer of the Admiralty, for an opinion as to what steps might be taken that would lead to the apprehension of the crew of the *Petit-Jules,* who were then safely lodged in France. An opinion was asked on the further questions of whether the capture of the vessel was a lawful act or whether the resistance of her crew and her recapture by the crew were lawful acts. The Advocate General advised that "it is now generally understood and admitted that the territory of a country within which the rights of sovereignty may be exercised extends to a distance of 3 miles from the shore and that it would be an unwarranted assumption of power against which other nations would have a right to remonstrate, if a government were to attempt to enforce its municipal regulations beyond those limits." He, therefore, concluded that the seizure of the French vessel "was not warranted by the Law of Nations," and that His Majesty's Government had no right to insist upon the surrender of the French crew for the purpose of trial in an English court, but that any English subject that was on board the vessel could be tried if found within British territory. He rendered another opinion in which he held that proceedings against Fanin, the Frenchman, who had been taken at Alderney, and was then confined in England,

[84] It should be noted that the French Government made no protest against this or any other seizure of French vessels under the English eight-league statutes.

would involve a serious violation of the principles of International Law and recommended that he be released.

The Advocate General cited no authority for these opinions. They are the first utterances by any department of the British Government to the effect that the Law of Nations prohibited the enforcement of this legislation against foreign vessels beyond three miles from the shore. His position fails to differentiate between the general jurisdiction of a nation over a narrow strip along the shore which he called "territory," [85] and a special jurisdiction, which England and most other maritime powers had exercised, for the sole purpose of defense, or of preventing infractions of their revenue laws. It is true that England and the United States had agreed, by treaty, that for some purposes, such as fisheries and neutrality, three miles, or one league, would be the extent of jurisdiction, but they had never agreed upon that distance for the purpose under consideration. It is possible that the Advocate General was influenced in his opinions by the existence of these treaties; but they were not in point. Where three miles, or one league had appeared, it was only in certain treaties, for certain purposes, and there was no excuse for holding that a wider distance for defensive and revenue purposes was inhibited by the Law of Nations. The practice of nations had been contrary to such a view. This point will be developed more fully later.[86]

Furthermore, this opinion was rendered under rather singular circumstances: there was no protest by the French Government;[87] it is only the opinion of the Advocate General rendered to another department of the Gov-

---

[85] There is even to-day a dispute on the question of whether this strip is "territory."

[86] See p. 375, et seq., *infra*.

[87] The owners petitioned for the vessel's release on the ground that they had purchased it after the capture in ignorance of the fact that this liability had attached.

ernment, and, perhaps, therefore, without the caution that usually characterizes an opinion when it is a question between governments. Other departments of the Government did not share this opinion, and after much discussion between them, it was decided not to change the existing laws. It would seem, therefore, that this opinion is of little value to the international lawyer, as subsequent developments show.

It should not be overlooked that the Advocate General was called upon for an opinion as to whether the British Government might insist upon the surrender by a foreign government of the latter's citizens found in the latter's territory for an offense committed on the high seas many miles from shore. This was an embarrassing question, and the opinion rendered was one answer to it. If the crew of the *Petit-Jules* had been before an English court, whether proceedings could properly have been had against them for the offense charged would, doubtless, have presented different considerations and might have elicited a different opinion from the Advocate General.[88]

One other probable reason for the opinion expressed was a political one,—the British Government was especially desirous at this time of avoiding all friction with France, and her courtship terminated favorably: the two countries, three years later, were allies in the Crimean War.[89]

Furthermore, as has been noted, the golden age of

[88] Furthermore, the criminal and forfeiture proceedings would have taken place without the opinion of the Advocate General or without any question, from any source, as to their legality.

[89] See p. 133, *infra*, where it is shown that a treaty with France was spoken of, whereby France was to allow the seizure of her vessels for eight leagues, but no such proposal was to be presented to the other powers. This is significant as showing that the English Government was endeavoring to avoid all friction with France especially; and the Advocate General's opinion might have reflected this desire of his Government.

smuggling had passed, and that trade by 1850 was no longer a menace. The severe laws had served their purpose. Their observance was, therefore, no longer necessary.

The chief reason for this opinion lies, perhaps, in the fact that the Advocate General was an officer of the Admiralty, which was pressing for this narrow limit for purposes of neutrality in time of war.[90]

The opinion of the Advocate General was communicated by the Lords of the Treasury on January 15, 1851, to the Board of Customs with instructions to issue orders to the commanders of the revenue cruisers to obstain from making seizures "beyond the limit of the British Jurisdiction." These proposed instructions immediately developed a controversy, with the result that they were never issued, and the Coast Guard continued to operate under the existing laws. The Solicitor to the Board and the Board itself pointed out to the Treasury that a large part of the Act then in force designed to prevent smuggling would be rendered nugatory by the instructions and would, moreover, tend to increase smuggling to the great injury of Her Majesty's revenue.[91] The Board pointed out that this was the first time that any objection had been made to "the liability to seizure under the smuggling laws, of a foreign vessel with one or more British subjects on board, when found within eight leagues"

[90] For further possible reasons for the opinion of the Advocate General, see p. 149 and note (129), ibid., *infra.*

[91] He reiterated his opinion that the vessel was liable to forfeiture under sec. 2 of the Act then in force, and the crew to prosecution under secs. 66 and 95.

As to the *Petit-Jules,* upon the recommendation of the Solicitor, the Board consented to its release upon the condition that no compensation be paid for its detention. This consent was based, apparently, upon the letter from the Treasury of January 15, though it was pointed out again that the vessel was liable to forfeiture under sec. 2 of the Act. No claim was ever presented for compensation. Fanin was also released.

of the coast, with liquors on board in casks of illegal size.

As a result of the opinion of the Advocate General, the Lords of the Treasury expressed the opinion that it would be advisable to repeal the existing law which asserted a power of seizure beyond "the limits of territorial jurisdiction," and they requested the Board of Customs to prepare a clause for insertion in a bill that would accomplish that purpose. They asked the opinion of the Board upon the probable results that would flow from such a repeal. The Board, in its reply, referred to the previous observations on this point, and submitted letters from the Comptroller General, the Deputy Comptroller General, and from some of the most experienced Inspecting Commanders on the coast, all of which confirmed the Board's views that the repeal of section 2 of 8 and 9 Vict., c. 87, would result in an enormous increase in smuggling and a great loss to the revenue. The Board pointed out that during the past year (from January 5, 1850, to April 5, 1851), as well as in previous years, the records of the department showed that the revenue cruisers had caused many illicit cargoes to be cut away and destroyed some leagues from the coast, on their passage from France to England in foreign vessels, each of which vessels had one or more British subjects on board; that the smuggler had always destroyed the cargo in order to prevent the capture of his vessel under section 2 of the Act. It was pointed out that with the repeal of that section, foreign vessels, having on board a British subject well acquainted with the creeks and landing places on the coast, would be able to come within three miles of the coast in open day, and hover there with impunity until night-fall and, by means of signal or by sending in a boat, communicate with the agent on the shore and arrange for the landing of his goods. Also, by being permitted to hover so near the coast, the smuggler would be able to send his cargo ashore by means of small boats in small quantities at a time, which could not be done very successfully if the boat were liable to seizure within eight leagues of the coast. Furthermore, it was pointed out that the smugglers would be able to meet vessels engaged in the coasting trade and deliver to them their cargoes, which could easily be concealed beneath their coasting cargoes. The repeal of the law, it was said, would mean the employment in the trade of many inferior and poorly constructed vessels, whereas the smuggler was then forced to use the more expensive and swifter vessels, which were rarer and more difficult to secure and maintain. In view of these considerations, the Board observed that with the repeal of the law, "no amount of force afloat would be of material use" in preventing smuggling from sea.

The Board took occasion to observe that a foreign vessel engaged in legitimate trade could not suffer from the law, inasmuch as such a vessel would probably not have a British subject on board, and it would, therefore, not be liable to forfeiture unless found or discovered to have been within one league of the coast, with contraband goods on board. It was reiterated that no complaint had ever been made by any "foreign power as to the operation of the law which has been for so long a period in force with great benefit to the Revenue."[92]

[92] The commander of the revenue cutter, the *Vigilant*, observed that the repeal would lead British subjects to employ foreign vessels, for they would be immune from seizure just beyond three miles, where they could stand and say to the cruisers, "Thanks to the alteration of the law, you are here powerless." He also noted that a large fleet of French, Dutch, and Flemish vessels and boats which fished between the one and eight-league lines would be employed in smuggling during the fishing season.

It was reported from Folkstone that most of the illicit cargoes were brought over in large French fishing vessels; and when these were forced to stand off eight leagues, the shore boats that went out for their cargoes would have to depart before sunset, and would, therefore, be observed and followed.

The Secretary of State for Foreign Affairs considered that the reasons advanced by the Board against the repeal of the law were conclusive, and the matter was dropped. It was suggested, however, that some reciprocal arrangement might be entered into with the French Government for the purpose of protecting the revenue and checking, as far as possible, the illicit trade between the two countries. A draft treaty was drawn, but the whole matter was dropped without approaching the French Government on the subject, in view of the fact that no protest had ever been made against the law, and because the promulgation of such a treaty would proclaim to foreign vessels other than French that they might hover off the coast just beyond three miles without liability to seizure except under a special treaty.

(6) *The Marie* (1852)

The *Marie,* a French vessel with a crew of four Frenchmen and two Englishmen, was taken on August 19, 1852, while anchored about seven miles from shore, with tobacco on board.[93] The tobacco was sold and the Englishmen convicted and imprisoned under sections 2 and 50 of the Act of 8 and 9 Vict., c. 87.[94] The French members of the crew were released, because they were not within one league of the coast. The vessel was held liable to forfeiture in order to enforce against the Englishmen

---

The report from Southampton stated that cargoes were brought over in foreign vessels, for they were not liable to seizure beyond eight leagues; and that the repeal of the law would witness swarms of foreign vessels on the coast, "a fine nursery."

Many other objections were pointed out by other commanders of the cruisers.

[93] This was a collusive seizure. The officers and crew of the vessel, by prearrangement, stationed themselves at a point where they might be seized. This was done as a scheme to secure the reward granted in cases of captures of smuggling vessels and their cargoes.

[94] See note (16), p. 107, and note (29), p. 111, *supra.*

the penalties of the Act, but the forfeiture was "waived" as between the two countries and the vessel released after the Englishmen were prosecuted, in accordance with the opinion of the Advocate General rendered in *The Petit-Jules* case.

The French Government made no protest in this case.[95]

An interesting case arose three years after *The Petit-Jules.*

(7) *L'Abandance* (1853)

L'Abandance, a French fishing lugger of twenty-seven tons, laden with tobacco, was seized on September 16, 1853, ten or twelve miles from the shore. One Englishman, the owner of the cargo, was on board.[96] It does not appear how far out the vessel lay, except that "she was standing out to sea," when the revenue officers were informed of her presence, or when they put out to sea to make the seizure. But she was seized ten or twelve miles out, because, according to the watchman, "she had been within three miles of the coast," between two and three miles out, within the limits of a port. The Solicitor to the Board of Customs advised that the officers should be prepared to show that the vessel, when first seen, was within

---

[95] During the year 1851, the following French vessels were seized within three miles of the coast:

The *Anna-Joseph* seized one mile out, which was released because of insufficient evidence against her. The French Consul applied for indemnity, which was refused because the vessel's conduct created suspicion.

The *Henri,* seized one-quarter of a league from shore, with tobacco on board. The vessel, cargo, and crew were proceeded against under secs. 2, 50, and 88 of 8 and 9 Vict., c. 87. The French Ambassador applied for the release of the seamen, and asked for favorable consideration of their case, but the reasons for the request and application, which were refused, do no appear.

An open boat, whose nationality was not known, was taken four miles from the shore in the same year. She was "supposed to be French built." Two Englishmen only were on board.

[96] He had gone ashore the previous day to arrange for getting the cargo ashore.

the limits of a port. It would seem that the justification for the seizure ten or twelve miles out was that the vessel had previously been within three miles of the coast. This is the only fact to distinguish the case from *The Petit-Jules*, except that *L'Abandance* was seized about twelve or fifteen miles nearer the shore than the *Petit-Jules*. Proceedings were had under sections 213, 236, and 281 of 16 and 17 Vict., c. 107.[97] The French crew were convicted and fined £100 each for having been on board the vessel laden with tobacco within the limits of a port. The vessel and cargo were forfeited.

This case presents the reverse of *Attorney General* v. *Schiers*,[98] in which a foreigner was arrested within three miles of the coast, and prosecuted for an act he had committed beyond that distance, while in the instant case, a vessel and the crew were taken beyond that distance, and proceeded against for an act previously committed within it.

The French Government made no protest in this case.[99]

[97] Sec. 213 provided for the forfeiture of any ship or boat found or discovered to have been within any port, bay, harbor, creek, or river of the United Kingdom or Channel Islands, having on board any liquor in casks not capable of containing twenty gallons, or any tobacco or snuff in casks not containing two hundred pounds, unless such goods were on board without the knowledge or "neglect" of the owner or master, in which case the vessel was to be delivered to the owner or master. By sec. 236, persons found or discovered to have been on board such vessels were subject to a fine of £100, in default of which they were, under sec. 281, to be imprisoned.

[98] See p. 121, *supra*.

[99] Upon representations by the French Consul, two boys of twelve and fifteen years of age were released as being irresponsible parties. Many of the foreign smuggling vessels carried young boys as part of the crew, so that in the event of capture they would be released because of their tender years.

The French Consul also requested the release of the vessel and the adult members of the crew on the ground that the master did not know of the character of the voyage, but had been "the dupe of some designing Englishmen"; but the request was refused, as the evidence showed that the master knew he was violating the law.

(8) *Discussions in 1859*

The case of *The Petit-Jules* and the question of the seizure of foreign vessels subsequent to that case came under discussion again in August, 1859. In reply to an inquiry from the Foreign Office, it was stated by the Solicitor to the Board of Customs that the proposed instructions of 1851 to commanders of the revenue cruisers not to make seizures beyond three miles from the coast, which arose in connection with *The Petit-Jules*,[100] were never, in fact, issued, for the reason, it was decided, that it would tend to the injury of the revenue by inducing foreign vessels to transship illicit cargoes to small craft just beyond three miles. The Coast Guard Office, then under the Admiralty, in response to an inquiry from the Board on the question of how far from the coast it was competent for the revenue vessels to pursue and detain vessels sailing under foreign flags, referred to section 212 of the Act of 16 and 17 Vict., c. 107, as the law and authority governing the question. It will be recalled that that section subjected foreign vessels to forfeiture when found, under varying circumstances, within one, three, four, or eight leagues from the coast. The Coast Guard announced that it had never received any instructions relating to seizures at the time of or subsequent to the case of *The Petit-Jules*.[101] It was added that the cruisers were not likely to look "too minutely into proceedings of foreign vessels beyond 2 leagues off the coast of the United Kingdom."

This communication also referred to certain sections of

---

[100] See p. 125, *supra*.

[101] It was observed that had such instructions been issued, they would have become known to the foreigners, who would have taken advantage of the change, whereas, on the contrary, no such vessels had lately attempted to smuggle, and none had been seized for that offense.

the Coast Guard Instructions for 1857, which were in force in 1859. Section 26, c. VIII, of these Instructions reads:

"When vessels are met with within 4 leagues of the coast, which are not liable to quarantine, the officers will be guided by the directions contained in the 212th section of the Customs Consolidation Act, viz.: . . . ." Section 212 is then set out in full.[102] Section 14 required the officers to acquaint themselves with acts passed to prevent smuggling in order "to be enable to act and instruct those under their command to act, . . . for the benefit of the revenue. . . ." Section 17 provided for the placing of an officer on board any vessel which is "met bound to a British port," if, after search, it was suspected that prohibited or dutiable goods were on board, such officer to keep a constant watch to prevent any such goods from being landed and to deliver the vessel and its cargo to the officers of the port to which it was bound. Section 12 was a general direction to search suspicious vessels, without designating a distance in which they were to be searched, but presumably the distances named in the statute were implied.

Section 5 of c. V of these instructions reads:

"They [the officers in command of cruisers] are on no pretense whatever to approach within the distance of one league of the coast of France, Belgium, Holland, etc., or commit a violation of territory, nor to board or examine foreign vessels, nor exercise any belligerent rights of search beyond the limits of British jurisdiction, nor to enter any foreign port; but should any suspicious vessels under foreign colors be fallen in with, the cruisers are to keep company with them, so as to see that if they have

---

[102] For this section, see notes under secs. II, V, and IX of 6 Geo. IV, c. 108, pp. 106 and 108, *supra*.

contraband goods on board, they do not land them on any part of the British coast, nor transship them into British vessels." [103]

Since the Coast Guard was still governed by section 212 of the smuggling Act, and since no instructions were ever issued to that office or to the commanders of the revenue cruisers in conformity with the opinion of the Advocate General in 1851, that opinion had no effect upon the application of the smuggling laws to foreign vessels. As has been noted, *L'Abandance,* a French vessel, seized in 1853 ten or twelve miles out, though it had previously been within three miles of the coast, was forfeited; while in the case of *The Marie,* which was a collusive seizure, a French vessel, taken seven miles out in 1852, was held liable to forfeiture in order to prosecute the Englishmen on board, but the forfeiture was "waived" and the vessel released in conformity with that opinion. The revenue cruisers had never ceased to make seizures under the laws in force. The reason why more foreign vessels were not taken between 1851 and 1859 under those laws is found in the statement from the Coast Guard Office that no such vessels had made any attempt at smuggling because of their liability to seizure within eight leagues of the shore. [104]

[103] The "limits of jurisdiction" referred to in this section are defined in sec. 26 of c. VIII of the Instructions, which incorporated sec. 212 of the Act of 16 and 17 Vict., c. 107, as already noted.

It is significant to note that while the cruisers were given instructions to follow sec. 212 of the smuggling law, which authorized the seizure of foreign vessels as far out as eight leagues, yet it forbade them to approach within the distance of one league of foreign coasts. It would seem that the Commissioners for executing the office of Lord High Admiral, who issued the Coast Guard Instructions, recognized the distinction between the "territory" of a nation or "territorial waters," which they conceived in 1857 to be one league seaward, and a limited jurisdiction beyond that distance for the purpose of enforcing custom laws.

[104] P. 136, note (101), *supra.* See p. 114 et seq., *supra,* for reports to the House of Commons, showing the decline of smuggling after 1850.

During the same year (1859), the Foreign Office made inquiry as to the regulations and usage in regard to seizing foreign vessels, and as to the statutory enactments in force. The Board, in reply, discussed sections 215,[105] 216, 217, 218, 219,[106] and 223 [107] of 16 and 17 Vict., c. CVII, and sections 25, 26,[108] and 27 [109] of 18 and 19 Vict., c. 96; it explained that a "foreign vessel wholly navigated by foreigners is not liable to detention unless she be found or discovered to have been within one league of the coast . . . with contraband goods on board," [110] but that if there were on board "one or more British subjects," she was "liable to detention if found within 3 leagues of the coast," [111] or "if half the persons on board be British subjects, she is then liable to detention if found within 4 leagues of the coast between the North Foreland and Beachy Head or 8 leagues of any other part of the coast." [112]

The Solicitor, in his statement to the Board which grew

[105] Sec. 215 provided that any ship or boat, found within the limits of a port of the United Kingdom with cargo on board, and afterwards found light or in ballast, was forfeitable if the master was unable to give a due account of the port where he had discharged.

[106] An officer, under sec. 219, could go on board any vessel within the limits of any port and rummage for uncustomed and prohibited goods and remain on board as long as such vessel remained in such limits.

[107] Under sec. 223, all vessels, goods, and persons liable to be detained for any offense under this act were to be detained "in any place, either upon land or water" and delivered into the care of an officer authorized to receive them.

[108] This section refers to boats found in a bay or harbor.

[109] This section makes certain exceptions to the application of the law, of no importance here.

[110] P. 108, *supra*.

[111] P. 110, *supra*. The Board overlooked the provisions of sec. 216 of 16 and 17 Vict., c. CVII, which forfeited foreign vessels with one or more British subjects on board, within four or eight leagues of the coast. See p. 107, note (16), *supra*.

[112] P. 105, *supra*.

Nothing was said of the jurisdiction for one hundred leagues over foreign vessels, when one-half the persons on board were British subjects. See p. 106, note (12), *supra*.

out of the inquiry from the Foreign Office, observed that
the laws then in force had in view "smuggling vessels
throughout" and that it did not touch foreign vessels
beyond "the national league" unless there was something
to "identify them with English sail, such as being wholly
or partly British-owned or manned." He observed in
answer to the possible contention that these laws were not
reconcilable with the principles of International Law
that they had, from a very early period, formed part of
the "Customs Code," and that no complaint had ever
been made by any foreign power "either of their existence
or of the exercise of them—possibly for the obvious reason
that they have never been brought to bear upon any but
smuggling craft in *flagrante delicto*." He explained that
they had operated wholesomely *in terrorem* and that
their repeal would be attended with disastrous conse-
quences to the revenue and with increased cost to the
Coast Guard. He also pointed out that in most cases
the suspected vessels were marked out and pursued
upon definite and certain information that they were
actually engaged in illicit trade, or were in connivance
with persons on British soil, adding that it would be
"straining the high principles and policy of International Law to hold that in such cases the prevention
of a known premeditated infraction of municipal
law" would meet with opposition by any civilized country.

The Foreign Office made no reply, and the matter was
dropped with these explanations from the Board of Customs and its Solicitor.

(9) *Discussions in 1861-1865*

In 1861, the Legislature of Victoria had passed an Act,
section 174 of which was practically a transcript of section 25 of 18 and 19 Vict., c. 96; and sections 177, 178, and

388 were transcripts of sections 216, 217, 242,[113] respectively, of the Act of 16 and 17 Vict., c. CVII. This Act was submitted to the Secretary of State for the Colonies, who had submitted it to the Treasury in 1861 and again in 1864, before confirming it. The Treasury referred it to the Board of Customs. The discussions that followed brought the case of *The Petit-Jules* and the so-called hovering laws to the fore once more.

It was noted in these discussions that the Law Officers of the Crown in 1854 had given an opinion on a British Guiana Ordinance of that year, and had held that the jurisdiction of a British colony was confined to the distance of three miles from the shore.[114] The Solicitor to the Board now rendered an opinion on the Victoria law, confirming that of the Law Officers in 1854, on the ground that the grant of the crown extended no farther than three miles seaward. "It may be held," he said, "that the Colonial jurisdiction seaward is bounded by the league whether the crown has any inherent jurisdiction beyond or not." He added that if the powers granted by the Colonial Act were curtailed, some difficulty would be encountered if the question were raised against similar provisions of the Imperial Acts. "In strictness," he said, "it is an assumption in either case and the acts following upon it can only be justified by their merits." He concluded, therefore, that it would be "inexpedient" to modify the provisions of the Victoria Act.

The Board reported to the Treasury that the colonies did not have the power to impose penalties on persons

[113] Sec. 242 provided that no subject of Her Majesty should take up spirits in casks of less content than twenty gallons, which were found floating upon or sunk in the sea within one hundred leagues of the United Kingdom, upon penalty of forfeiture of such goods and the vessel upon which they were found.

[114] The ordinance and the opinion are not available. Guiana, it was said, repealed the law assuming jurisdiction beyond three miles.

other than inhabitants thereof, or to confiscate vessels not owned by them, for acts committed beyond the distance of three miles from the shore, and that, therefore, the Victoria law should be modified in so far as it affected ships and inhabitants of the mother country or of other colonies beyond that limit.[115]

On January 2, 1865, the Committee of Privy Council for Trade wrote to the Board of Customs, declaring that section 25 of the Imperial Act of 18 and 19 Vict., and sections 216, 217, 235, 242, of the one of 16 and 17 Vict., to which the Victoria Act corresponded, appeared to be of so questionable a character that before recommending to the Secretary of State for the Colonies the allowance of the provisions of the Colonial Act, they would like to be informed if such Acts had ever been enforced or could be enforced, and if it would serve any useful purpose to retain them. This statement, it should be noted, was made at a time when smuggling from sea was all but a thing of the past. The Board, in reply, called attention to the seizure of several English vessels in 1855 from nine to thirteen miles out, and of one French vessel eight leagues from the Isle of Wight,[116] all of which, it was said, were condemned and their crews imprisoned;[117] and it recommended that the statutes be continued in force. It was observed that with respect to sections 217 and 242,[118] the term one hundred leagues was merely "a definite used for an indefinite or uncertain limit, and is intended to apply to persons who may become amenable to the Revenue Laws wherever they may be met with."

---

[115] See p. 163, et seq., *infra,* for a discussion of colonial legislation.

[116] This is probably a reference to the French *Petit-Jules,* taken, in 1850, off the Isle of Wight. As already noted, the Coast Guard Office reported in 1859 that there had been no attempts at smuggling after 1851.

[117] In the case of *The Petit-Jules,* however, the vessel and the crew were finally released. P. 125, *supra.*

[118] See p. 106, note (12), and p. 141, note (113), *supra,* for these sections.

The Solicitor, upon whose report the Board's reply was based, stated in a letter to the Board that but for the wholesome power of interception beyond the league smuggling would be rendered comparatively easy. He added: "The facts always justify the law and the courts never question it." If the vessel came to and no goods were found to justify the seizure, no harm was done; and if a seizure was wrongful, that is, one in which the proved facts were insufficient to sustain it, the owners were entitled to compensation. His conclusion was that so long as the protection to the revenue rendered such laws essential, on the one hand, whilst the "common law" afforded ample indemnity against injustice on the other, "it is better to let well alone."

The Committee of Privy Council for Trade addressed another letter to the Treasury shortly after the one of January 2, and asked the Treasury to consider the expediency of retaining the laws, which, it was said, "are at variance with the Law of Nations, and which experience has shown . . . are liable to be adopted as models by Colonial legislatures"; reference was made to the Victoria Act. The Treasury referred this letter to the Board of Customs whose Solicitor replied that he was not so satisfied as the Board of Trade that the laws were at variance with the "alleged principles of International Law," or that they ought to be sacrificed to some "supposed incongruity with the non-written doctrines of the Law of Nations, the creatures of expediency and common consent undefined by statute and varying with circumstances." It was not so clear, he added, that a known wrongdoer apprehended in the act is not a "rightful prize," though taken on the common highway of nations; but if the vessel were taken within a league of a foreign country, it would be a stronger ground of complaint. However, on December 5, in a letter to the Board in connection with the Victoria Act, he had expressed some doubt as to whether a case could be made out for the retention of the laws, if the question were raised. He said that in case of a seizure of a foreign vessel beyond one league, satisfaction could be demanded, unless, perhaps, the offense were committed in British waters and the vessel captured after pursuit on the common highway. He stated that the laws were of great value as a justification to the service and officers when seizures were made, and advocated their retention.

The Solicitor noted that this question had been "vigorously fought before and that what is now contended for by the Customs was acceded to by the Government." He suggested that it might satisfy the Board of Trade if the Colonial law were varied to meet their views, even though this action might admit a principle which might prove inconvenient. He reiterated that well enough should be let alone, and added that it would be time enough "to mutilate wholesome and necessary municipal laws when some foreign power challenges the Act of the British Crown," and that if such a challenge were presented in the event of a seizure not justifiable in itself, it would only involve the payment of damages, but not an alteration of the law, with which a foreign country could not interfere.

The Board of Customs reported to the Treasury (after first referring to the case of *The Petit-Jules* and the discussions at the time that case arose, of the question of retaining the customs acts) that it was still of the opinion that it would not be advisable to disturb the laws, for any alteration would be attended with considerable risk to the revenue. The Treasury advised the Board of Trade to the same effect.

(10) *Discussions in 1875*

The Petit-Jules and the principle involved in that case were discussed at great length again in 1875. On February 25, of that year, the Foreign Office pointed out, in a letter to the Treasury, that a long-standing difference had arisen, from time to time, between the British and Spanish Governments, based upon Spain's claim to exercise maritime jurisdiction at a distance of two leagues, or six nautical miles, from her coasts, whereas Great Britain contended that according to the "rule recognized by all nations," Spain was not entitled to exercise jurisdiction at a greater distance than one league, or three nautical miles.[119] It was said by the Foreign Office that up to a very recent date, the Spanish Government, in arguing the question, had claimed maritime jurisdiction to the extent of two leagues generally without any exception or reservation, but that in the last communication to the British Government, a distinction was drawn between the limit of "Military jurisdiction," as to which the Spanish Government did not seriously dispute the rule contended for by the British Government,[120] and "fiscal jurisdiction," as to which it maintained that every independent state had "the right to fix the limit at such a distance from its coasts as may be necessary to defend itself from the attacks which may be made against it, and to prevent intended fraud upon its revenues by boats engaged in smuggling," and that the Spanish Minister justified this claim by the example of other countries, especially that of Great Britain, whose law (8 and 9 Vict., c. 87)[121] fixed the limit at various distances, for different classes of

[119] See p. 257, *infra,* for the correspondence in 1875 between the United States and British Governments on the subject of Spain's claims. For other discussions of Spain's claim, see pp. 265 and 394, *infra.* The Foreign Office had no objection to the enforcement of hovering laws beyond three miles from the shore, but its opinion was influenced by its desire to establish this narrow limit for purposes of neutrality, in time of war.

[120] This is not the position of the Spanish Government to-day, which claims six miles for both defensive and revenue matters. It has made this claim consistently. The communication of that Government referred to is not available.

[121] 16 and 17 Vict., c. CVII, had supplanted 8 and 9 Vict., c. 87, though it had not changed the law essentially.

vessels, far in excess of three miles. The Foreign Office requested certain information upon the existing British law and the method of applying it. The questions propounded, among others, were whether revenue vessels under the laws in force stopped or searched foreign vessels beyond one league from the· shore and whether foreign vessels, having on board one or more British subjects, were held to be liable to seizure if found within the distances specified in the laws (four and eight leagues), or whether such laws were applied only to vessels having entered British ports and then found or discovered to have been within those distances. This information was, in turn, requested of the Board of Customs by the Treasury. The Board, in reply, interpreted the pertinent provisions of the Acts then in force, as follows:

In order to make section 25 of 18 and 19 Vict., c. 96, applicable, the ship or boat had to fall under one of the three following "separate conditions":

1. She had to possess the "elements of British ownership," or at least one-half of her crew had to be British subjects, and she had to have on board the goods or apparatus specified, in which case she could be visited within the distances of four and eight leagues as specified in that section.[122]

2. The ship, if foreign, with one or more British subjects on board and certain prohibited goods or apparatus, could be visited within three leagues of the coast of the United Kingdom.[123]

3. The ship or boat, if foreign, whatever her crew was, with the forbidden goods or apparatus on board, could be visited within one league of the coast of the United Kingdom or the Channel Islands.[124]

The Board in commenting upon section 216 of the Act

[122] See p. 105, *supra.*
[123] See p. 110, *supra.*
[124] P. 108, *supra.*

of 16 and 17 Vict., which forfeited foreign vessels with one or more British subjects on board within four and eight leagues of the coast,[125] said that this provision was necessary to prevent British subjects from employing foreign vessels.

It was added that it was always upon "reliable information" that the parties intended to smuggle their cargo into British ports that such visitations were made; and that if by mistake an innocent foreign ship were overhauled, she was entitled to compensation "unless perhaps sailing under false colours."

It was said that the reason for giving the right of visitation beyond the league of foreign vessels with British crews was that British smugglers sometimes hired foreign boats in which to carry on their trade. It was explained that the presence of foreign craft with one or more British subjects on board, within the distances specified in the Act, was not of itself sufficient to render the vessel liable to seizure; but there had to be, in addition, the deliberate intention to smuggle, and the presence of prohibited goods or smuggling apparatus, or the destruction or throwing overboard of such goods or apparatus to prevent seizure. No foreign vessel would be seized beyond one league, although it had prohibited goods on board, without evidence of an intention to land them clandestinely. Without this evidence, she would not be seized even in British waters, or the limits of a port, even though she carried forbidden goods, provided she were pursuing a legitimate voyage. The mention of one or two British subjects on board, it was explained, pointed to the fact that small craft, generally employed in smuggling, seldom carried a crew of more than three or four men, and frequently only one man and one boy.

The Board's reply stated further that it was not the

---

[125] See note (16), p. 107, *supra*.

practice to stop and search foreign vessels beyond the distance of one league from the shore, even when they were carrying goods not legally admissible into the country, unless "the British character of crew" were found, as already explained, which rendered them liable to seizure beyond that distance, and not even then except upon reliable information or demonstrative evidence of the fact that the vessel was actually approaching the British coast with and for the express purpose of clandestinely landing prohibited goods. When it was proved that the vessel was innocent, she was liberated at once and the right of the owner to compensation admitted in respect of damages or inconvenience from the delay.

The Foreign Office inquired further whether any foreign vessel had in recent years been stopped or seized on the high seas under the provisions of the laws in force, and if so, whether such seizure had led to a claim on the part of the flag state or the owner of the vessel. The Board of Customs reported that *The Petit-Jules* was the last case of seizure beyond the one league; but this statement was erroneous, for, as already noted, the *Marie* [126] was seized seven miles out in 1852, and *L'Abandance* [127] was seized in 1853 ten or twelve miles out. The *Marie,* however, was released. Attention was called again to the fact that no protest was ever received from the French Government. It was noted at this time that the *Petit-Jules* was not "the subject of information," but was discovered with the prohibited goods on board while the revenue vessel was cruising for another vessel. The Board enclosed its report of October 7, 1859, on this subject [128] and explained that it contained strong reasons for not materially weakening the existing provisions of the law. It further

[126] See p. 133, *supra.*
[127] See p. 134, *supra.*
[128] See p. 139, *supra.*

expressed the opinion that no serious harm could be apprehended if Spain were permitted to adopt provisions similar to those in the English laws, with the understanding that any interference, by Spanish authorities, with British vesels beyond one league, unless justified by proof of illegal or contraband traffic with Spain, would be the subject of compensation to the owners, the master, and crew, and the owners of the cargo, for any damage, loss, or inconvenience arising from such interference. It was said that it was possibly this liability to which Great Britain had always considered herself subject that Spain wished to avoid.[129]

The Foreign Office made no reply, and the matter once more rested where the discussions began.

[129] In this statement there is reflected a possible further reason why the Foreign Office of the British Government was pressing for one league for revenue laws; the British merchant fleet was very large, and if British vessels were subject to search beyond a greater distance, say two leagues, many of them would be arbitrarily subjected to annoyance without any more claim for redress than if the power of search were confined to one league.

The Board also called attention to the fact that when smugglers were taken, they were not treated as criminals, but were debtors to the crown, and were committed to "clean, wholesome, and well ventilated gaols," and were tried without delay.

Sec. 205 of 16 and 17 Vict., c. 107, was said by the Solicitor to refer to vessels departing from the Channel Islands, which were guilty of a breach of the bond that had been given as to their cargoes; that it had no reference to a distance and, therefore, had no application to the present question. That section provided that no ship, belonging wholly or in part to British subjects, should sail from the Channel Islands without a clearance, whether in ballast or having a cargo; and if a ship sailed with cargo, the master should give bond for the due landing of the cargo at the port for which the vessel cleared; and any ship or boat which did not have a clearance, or which, having a clearance for her cargo, should be found light or to have discharged any part of its cargo before arrival at the port specified in her clearance, should be forfeited.

He said that sec. XXVIII of 18 and 19 Vict., c. 96, referring to vessels within any port, bay, harbor, river, or creek, referred to smugglers within the league. It related to a penalty against any person found or discovered to have been on board certain vessels in any port, bay, harbor, river, or creek of the United Kingdom or the Channel Islands.

CHAPTER IX

FROM 1876 TO 1927

§ 30. Repeal of All Laws: New Legislation, Retaining Jurisdiction for One, Three, and Four Leagues

As already noted, there was very little smuggling after 1851, and certainly after 1865, by vessels devoted exclusively to the trade. When attempted at all, it was by means of a concealment of the illicit goods under legitimate cargoes on vessels that came into port; and, as the report of 1865 stated, the attempts were of a "petty description and unusually rare." It was brought out in the interdepartmental discussions that there was no longer any need for the laws extending jurisdiction as far as eight and one hundred leagues. In 1876, a new act was passed,[1] repealing all the acts in force at that time,[2] and considerably simplifying the law. This new Act has remained in force since the date of its passage.[3] No debate took place on the bill when it was before Parliament; Mr. W. H. Smith, in moving that it be read the second time, said that "its main object was to consolidate the existing Customs laws, the sole alteration in those laws being in the direction of reducing the penalties now in force in respect of infractions of the Customs

---

[1] 39 and 40 Vict., c. 36 (July 24, 1876),—"An Act to Consolidate the Customs Laws."

[2] The Acts repealed were:

 16 and 17 Vict., c. CVII,
 18 and 19 Vict., c. XCVI,
 20 and 21 Vict., c. LXII.

[3] As will be noted later, certain minor changes were made in 1890 in the size of the craft to be forfeited. P. 154, *infra*.

laws." [4] It contains some of the provisions of the earlier statutes, but the great distances of eight and one hundred leagues are abolished; while the old distances of one, three, and four leagues are retained.

The provisions of this new Act must be read in the light of the many acts of Parliament that have preceded it, the reports to the House of Commons that have been analysed from time to time, and the methods usually employed by the smuggler. It would be difficult to arrive at a satisfactory interpretation of this Act, without a knowledge of the previous acts and of the conditions that produced them. It must be remembered that it is an outgrowth of one hundred and seventy-five years of legislative development and experiment; and, like much other legislation, it cannot be understood without a knowledge of this development, especially since some of its provisions are defined with less particularity of detail than the acts that went before it. The detailed analyses of the previous acts and the reasons set forth for their numerous provisions, will, it is hoped, render clear the provisions of the present Act without very much discussion at this point.

Section 53 of the new Act re-enacts the provisions of section 53 of 16 and 17 Vict., c. CVII, and the corresponding sections of 6 Geo. IV, c. CVII, and of the other acts passed between 1825 and 1853, in regard to breaking bulk within four leagues of the coast. It provides that if bulk is broken, or if any part of the cargo is staved, destroyed, or thrown overboard, or if any package is opened, after the vessel's arrival within four leagues of the coast, the master shall be fined £100.

This section is applicable to all vessels of what-

[4] *Parliamentary Debates* (Hansard), 1876, vol. 229, col. 1962. The Act was prepared and brought in by Mr. Raikes, Mr. Smith, and the Chancellor of the Exchequer.
Parliamentary Papers, 1876, vol. II, no. 154.

ever nationality, irrespective of the nationality of any person or persons on board. It has been in force since 1825.

By section 134, the distance for visitation after clearance outwards for the purpose of demanding the ship's clearance is reduced from four leagues as provided in the old acts, to one league, or to the limits of any port. If the master refuses to produce the clearance within that distance or those limits, or to answer questions concerning the ship, the cargo, or the intended voyage, he is subject to a forfeiture of £5.

Section 179 provides for the forfeiture of the following vessels, which have false bulkheads, false bows, double sides or bottoms, or any secret or disguised place for concealing the goods, or any device for running goods, or which have or have had on board any spirits, tobacco, or snuff in packages in which their importation into the United Kingdom or the Channel Islands is prohibited:

1. Any ship or boat, belonging wholly or in part to British subjects, or whereof one-half the persons on board are such subjects,[5] found or discovered to have been within any port, harbour, river, or creek of the United Kingdom or the Channel Islands, or within three leagues of the coasts.

It has been pointed out that a vessel belonging only in part to British subjects may not be a British ship,[6] whereas, by the law of several European countries, foreigners may be part owners of vessels under their registry and carrying their flag;[7] and that vessels whereof one-half the persons on board are British subjects may be of any nationality, for the nationality of the persons on

---

[5] When the Act was first drawn, these requirements as to ownership and persons on board were omitted, and *all* vessels within three leagues were brought within the terms of this section.

[6] See p. 61, *supra.*

[7] See pp. 62-63, note, *supra.*

board has nothing to do with the nationality of the ship.[8] This section thus takes jurisdiction over foreign vessels for three leagues, when such vessels are owned in whole or in part by British subjects, or if one-half of the persons on board such vessels are British subjects, and this is frequently the case with small foreign smuggling craft.[9]

This is the third time that the three-league limit has been adopted in the law of England. It was first adopted in 1765 by the Act of 5 Geo. III, c. XXXIX, section VII, for all vessels arriving from the Isle of Man at Great Britain, or vice versa, with certain goods on board. In 1853, it was adopted by 16 and 17 Vict., c. CVII, for any foreign vessel upon which there was one or more British subjects, with certain goods on board.

The only change made in the present law is the requirement as to the number of British subjects that must be on board; that is, under the present law, one-half of the persons on board must be such subjects, whereas under the Act of 1853, only one person on board was required to be a British subject. The present Act also introduces the element of part ownership by a British subject.

2. Any ship or vessel, if not British, found or discovered to have been within one league of the coast.[10]

That is, if the foreign vessel is not owned in whole or in part by British subjects or if one-half of the persons on board are not British subjects, it is not subject to forfeiture unless it is found within one league of the coast, or is discovered to have been therein.[11] This provision is a re-enactment of the principle of section V of 6 Geo. IV, c. CVIII, and of the corresponding sections of the subsequent acts.

[8] See p. 78, *supra.*

[9] See p. 147, *supra.*

[10] The forbidden goods or articles are also subject to forfeiture.

[11] See the case of *L'Abandance,* p. 134, *supra,* for a case of the seizure of a vessel beyond three miles from the shore for having been discovered in that distance under forbidden circumstances.

Section 179 provides for the forfeiture of any ship or boat, belonging in whole or in part to British subjects, or whereof one-half the persons on board are such subjects, or any foreign ship or boat, "which shall be found or discovered to have been within three leagues of any part of the coast of the United Kingdom from which any part of the lading shall have been thrown overboard, or on board which any goods shall have been staved or destroyed to prevent seizure."

This part of section 179 seems to apply to all vessels, irrespective of their nationality or of the nationality of any person or persons on board.[12]

By the Act of 53 and 54 Vict., c. 56, passed on August 18, 1890, it was declared that it is expedient "that the law as to the forfeiture of ships or boats for offenses against the customs acts as provided in section 179" of the Act under consideration "shall be modified." Section I provides that "no ship or boat shall be liable to forfeiture under the said section [i.e., section 179] for having or having had on board . . . any goods as therein specified, or for any unlading, throwing overboard, or destruction of goods, unless such ship or boat shall be under 250 tons burden." Section II provides that any ship or boat of or exceeding two hundred and fifty tons burden may be fined in any sum not exceeding £50, in case a responsible officer of the ship or boat is "implicated either actually or by neglect," which fine shall be enforced by requiring a deposit of a sum not exceeding £500; and in default of the payment of such deposit the ship or boat may be detained. But if the Commissioners of Customs consider the fine of £50 an inadequate penalty for the offense com-

---

[12] When this Act was presented to Parliament, it was accompanied by a "Synopsis" prepared to aid in the discussion of the bill. This "Synopsis" notes that section 179 is "Existing Law. Consolidation of Four Sections of different Acts, with limitation of right of search beyond the league." *Parliamentary Papers,* 1876, vol. II, No. 154a.

mitted, they may take proceedings for condemnation of such ship or boat in a sum not exceeding £500. And a deposit of such sum may be required to abide the decision of the court, in default of which such ship or boat may be detained. By section IV, the goods remain liable to forfeiture, regardless of the size of the vessel upon which they are found.

Section 180 of the Act of 1876 provides for the forfeiture of any ship or boat, belonging in whole or in part to British subjects, or whereof one-half the persons on board are such subjects, which shall not bring to when signal is given, and upon chase being given, from which goods are thrown overboard or upon which they are staved or destroyed to prevent seizure.[13]

This section corresponds with section 179 with respect to the two classes of ships named. It does not apply in express terms either to British or to non-British ships, though, as already pointed out, the vessels enumerated must in some cases be foreign, and in others, they may be either foreign or domestic. There is no defined area of the high sea within which the signal to bring to may be made or must be complied with; but it may be implied that it must be within the distance from the coast in which some offense may be committed under the provisions of the Act. If chase is begun anywhere within those limits, presumably, it may be continued on the high seas, until the waters of a foreign country are reached.[14]

Section 181 re-enacts section XIV of 6 Geo. IV, c. CVIII, and the corresponding section of the acts passed subsequent to that Act, providing for the firing into any ship or boat liable to seizure and examination, which shall

[13] Persons escaping during chase shall be deemed to be British subjects unless the contrary is proved.

[14] The Synopsis accompanying the bill referred to in note (12), p. 154, *supra*, noted that this section was the "Existing Law (leaving out the surplusage about 100 leagues)."

not bring to when required to do so. The master is subject to a fine of £20, in addition.[15]

Section 200 provides that if any person, not being an officer of the navy, customs, or excise, "shall intermeddle with or take up any spirits being in casks of less content than 20 gallons found floating upon or sunk in the sea, such spirits shall be forfeited, together with any vessel or boat in which they may be found." Interpreted literally, this section applies to all vessels of whatever nationality on the high seas.[16]

Section 202 provides that "all ships, boats, . . . made use of in the importation, landing, removal, or conveyance of any uncustomed, prohibited, restricted, or other goods liable to forfeiture under the customs acts shall be forfeited, and all ships, boats, . . . and things liable to forfeiture, and all persons liable to be detained for any offense under the customs acts, . . . shall or may be seized or detained in any place either upon land or water. . . ." [17]

Section 193 makes it a felony for anyone to shoot maliciously at any vessel or boat in the service of the revenue or at any officer of the customs in the execution of his duty.[18]

[15] See comments under section 180, p. 155, *supra*.

[16] See p. 90, *supra*, for the old law, forfeiting spirits taken up within one hundred leagues of the coast.

[17] The "Air Force (Application of Enactment) (No. 2) Order, 1918" ordered that this section shall "apply in relation to the Air Council, the President of the Air Council, and the Air Force and the officers and men thereof and the air force property and institution." *Statutory Rules and Orders*, 1918, No. 548, vol. 1, p. 50, at p. 54.

[18] Section 177 provides that if any goods subject to payment of any duty or restriction in respect of importation shall be found or discovered to have been concealed in any manner on board any ship or boat within the limits of any port of the United Kingdom either before or after landing, all such goods together with the goods concealed with them shall be forfeited.

Section 229 provides that "where any offense shall be committed in any place upon the water not being within any county of the United Kingdom, or where the officers have any doubt whether such

Section 179 provides for the detention and punishment of British subjects within three leagues and foreigners within one league of the coast, when found or discovered to have been on board any ship or boat liable to forfeiture under section 179 or on board any vessel in Her Majesty's service or any foreign post office packet carrying mails between the United Kingdom and any foreign country, having the forbidden goods on board.[19] The British subject, it would seem, may be taken from any vessel made liable to forfeiture under that section within three leagues.[20]

This section relates to jurisdiction over the person, but not the vessel. This distinction between jurisdiction to arrest foreigners and British subjects is a very old one. It is found as early as 1805 in the Act of 45 Geo. III, c.

---

place is within the boundaries or limits of any such county, such offence shall for the purposes of the customs acts be deemed and taken to be an offence committed on the high seas; and for the purpose of giving jurisdiction under such acts every offence shall be deemed to have been committed," either in the place in which it was actually committed, or at any place on land where the offender may be brought. That is, if an offence is committed "upon the water not being within any county," it is to be deemed to be an offense committed upon the high seas. Offenses in the Dominion waters are, therefore, treated as having been committed within the county: and where there is any doubt on the question, the offense is to be treated as having been committed on the high seas.

Section 151 provides that "The customs acts shall extend to and be of full force and effect in the several British possessions abroad," unless otherwise provided by such acts or "limited by express reference to the United Kingdom or the Channel Islands," and unless any such possession shall have provided or may hereafter provide for the management and regulations of the customs. Section 284 defines British possessions as used in this Act as any colony, plantation, island, territory, or settlement belonging to His Majesty. Section 277 declares that the Isle of Man shall be deemed to be part of the United Kingdom for all the purposes of the Customs Acts.

[19] The Act of 50 Vict. (sess. 2), c. 7 (May 23, 1887), sec. I, provides that a person shall not be liable to conviction under this section unless he "was concerned in, or privy to, the illegal act or thing proved to have been committed."

[20] See pp. 111 and 112, *supra*.

CXXI,[21] and is carried forward in several acts after that date. Hence, the retention, in the present Act, of this distinction does not represent any change in legislation since 1805. This section, under the decision of *Attorney General* v. *Schiers,* applies to foreigners arrested within three miles of the coast, when found on vessels that have committed offenses for which they are subject to forfeiture, beyond that distance.[22]

The offense for which this jurisdiction is given is that of being on board a vessel liable to forfeiture under section 179. Section 181, however, subjects every master to a fine of £20 when a vessel does not bring to when required to do so; and foreign vessels, in some cases, may be required to bring to within three leagues. Under section 53, any foreign master is subject to a fine of £100 if bulk is broken, or if the cargo is destroyed or thrown overboard, or if any package is opened after the arrival of his vessel within four leagues of the coast.

§ 31. Air Navigation (Consolidation) Order, 1923

The "Air Navigation (Consolidation) Order, 1923,"[23] provides that the following sections, among others, of the Act of 1876, "shall, so far as they are applicable, . . . apply to air craft and to goods, mails and persons carried in or landed from them as they apply to ships and to goods, mails, and persons carried in or landed from ships":

Sections 53, 151, 180, 190, 193, 202, 229, 277, and 284.

[21] See p. 96 for this Act, and pp. 95 to 100 and p. 111, *supra,* for a summary of the laws relating to jurisdiction to arrest foreigners and British subjects.

[22] See p. 121, *supra,* for this case, and p. 203, *infra,* for the case of *The Coquitlam,* in which the United States proceeded against a British vessel arrested within three miles of the coast for an act committed three and seven miles from the coast.

[23] *Statutory Rules and Orders,* 1923, No. 1508, p. 13, sec. 23.

§ 32. Smuggling from Sea Practically Wiped Out

Annual Reports of the Commissioners of Customs

After the year 1876 only an occasional seizure of a smuggling vessel was made at sea. What little smuggling there was, was carried on largely from vessels in port. According to the report of the Commissioners of Customs for the year 1882, a cutter carrying a foreign crew was seized about one mile out with tobacco on board; her papers showed that she was ostensibly on a voyage from Ostend to Dieppe.[24] By 1886, attempts at illicit importation were confined largely to tobacco.[25] The report of 1887 notes the following captures:

The Dutch coopers *Merchant* and *De Kenan* and the German cooper *Martha,* at the Shetland Islands and at Hartlepool.

Smuggling was said to be growing less on account of the vigilance of the customs officers.[26] The report of 1890 states that with the "increased use of steam launches," operations of the "craft plying in the more frequented rivers and roadsteads of the Kingdom" were held in check.[27] The reports after 1890 comment upon the fact that the character of smuggling was very petty.

The report of 1904 [28] notes the seizure of "209 lbs. of tobacco and 6 gallons of spirits . . . from the small boats of two Dutch coopers, which had ventured inside the three-mile limit." In 1906, five thousand pounds of tobacco were seized from two Dutch coopers, *Nordster* and *Active,* which were captured "inside the three-mile limit off the Humber." These vessels, it is said, formed part of a fleet of seven coopers ("floating spirit and

[24] *Parliamentary Papers,* 1882, vol. XXI, No. 3269, pp. 50-4.

[25] Ibid., 1886, vol. XX, No. 4891, p. 8.

[26] Ibid., 1887, vol. XXVII, C. 5183. See *The Times* (London) of August 16, 1886.

[27] Ibid., 1890, vol. XXVI, C. 6185, p. 18.

[28] Ibid., 1904, vol. XVIII, Cd. 2227, p. 29.

tobacco shops"), all of Dutch nationality, whose cargoes were usually shipped in Holland and were sold chiefly to the crews of the Fishing Fleet, which collected at various places around the coast during the herring fishing season. Vessels patroled the coast "to intercept contraband goods being conveyed from the coopers to the shore." "Coopering," it is added, "is a constant source of anxiety, and its control is dependent upon the co-operation of the Admiralty cruisers." [29] The report of 1907 [30] mentions a seizure of "1108 lbs. of tobacco and cigars forming part of a cargo of contraband goods on the Dutch cooper 'Maria,' which was captured by H.M.S. 'Argus' inside the three-mile limit off the Humber and confiscated together with her cargo." In the report of 1908,[31] it is stated that on May 30, 1907, "a Dutch cooper named the 'Cosmopoliet,' with a cargo of contraband goods, chiefly tobacco, was captured by H.M.S. 'Skipjack' within the three-mile limit, off Cape Clear, on the south-west coast of Ireland." Judgment was given by the Lord Chief Baron of the High Court of Justice of Ireland that the vessel remain forfeited. The master and the crew were not convicted.

No further details are given in connection with the seizures of these Dutch coopers inside "the three-mile limit." It does not appear from the reports whether these vessels or any other smuggling craft after 1853 were observed beyond that distance.[32] If these vessels were not owned in part by British subjects, or if half the persons on board were not British subjects, they would not be liable to seizure and forfeiture after 1876, except when found within one league of the coast. If these requirements as to ownership or as to persons on board were

[29] Ibid., 1906, vol. XXVI, Cd. 3079, p. 29.

[30] Ibid., 1907, vol. XX, Cd. 3701, p. 27.

[31] Ibid., 1908, vol. XXIV, Cd. 4232, p. 28.

[32] *L'Abandance,* seized about twelve miles from the shore in 1853, is the last case of seizure beyond three miles that was found. P. 134, *supra.*

present, these vessels would have been liable to seizure anywhere within three leagues of the coast.[33]

After the report of 1908, there is no mention of any seizures of foreign vessels under the circumstances of interest in this connection.

§ 33. Coast Guard Instructions for 1887, 1898, 1905, and 1911

Sections 802, 809, and 833 of the *Special Instructions for the Coast Guard Service, 1887*,[34] repeated sections 20, 15, and 12, respectively, of the Special Instructions for the Coast Guard, 1866,[35] and section 812 repeated section 474 of the Special Instructions for 1875.[36]

Section 813 provided that "when vessels are met with within 3 leagues of the coast, which are not liable to quarantine," the officers should be guided by section 179 of the Act of 1876.

The *Coast Guard Instructions, 1898*, repeated sections 20 and 15 of the Special Instructions of 1866, by sections 855 and 862 respectively. Under section 862, "The action enjoined above must not be taken outside the territorial waters. If taken outside the territorial waters, except as

[33] According to *The Times* (London), of August 31, 1886, foreign vessels engaged in coopering cruise about without coming to a standstill at any particular point. At the trial of the crews of the *Martha* and the *Merchant* it was said that the sheriff, in giving his decision in the *Merchant* case, said that "It seemed very clear in his mind that this vessel at the time she was seized was liable to forfeiture and that a contravention of the act [i.e., the Act of 1876] had been committed. There was no doubt that the vessel was inside the three-mile-limit. There was no proof that she was there for any illegal purpose, but the fact that illegal sized packages of spirits were found on board was sufficient for a conviction under the statute." The captains and crews of both vessels were fined, and the vessels and their cargoes were forfeited.

The same paper on September 21, 1886, reported the release of the Dutch cooper *May of Dord*, captured "off Dover." "It was proved that she was taken outside *English waters*." Nothing is given as to the nationality of those on board or as to the ownership of the vessel.

[34] September 16.

[35] See p. 118, *supra*.

[36] See p. 120, *supra*.

regards a British ship, it would be illegal." "Territorial waters" are not defined. Section 865 repeated section 474 of the instructions of 1875. Section 866 repeated section 813 of the Special Instructions of 1887; it summarizes section 179 of the Act of 1876, as follows:

"That any British ship within 3 leagues of the coasts of the United Kingdom or the Channel Islands, or any ship not British, within one league of the said coasts," under the circumstances named in section 179 of the Act of 1876, shall be forfeited.

Section 871 enjoined the search and examination of "all suspicious vessels or boats only in British Territorial Waters," and their seizure when authorized by law. "Territorial Waters" are not defined.

The Coast Guard Instructions of 1905 repeated sections 862, 865, 866, and 871, of those of 1898 by sections 1202, 1205, 1206, and 1211, respectively; while section 20 of the Special Instructions of 1866 was repeated by section 1194. Section 1199 enjoined the cruisers to fire at a vessel when necessary, as provided in section 181 of the Act of 1876.

The Coast Guard Instructions, 1911, section 547, enjoin the officers to search all suspicious vessels in British territorial waters and to make seizures when authorized by law. Article 549 provides that "If vessels are met with within 3 leagues of the coast," the officers will be guided by the directions of section 179 of the Act of 1876, which is said to apply to any ship or boat which "shall be found or discovered to have been . . . within 3 leagues of the coast if belonging wholly or in part to British subjects, or having half the persons on board subjects of Her Majesty, or within one league if not British. . . ." Article 563 repeats section 862 of the Instructions of 1898. Article 565 provides that "If any cooper is discovered in British Territorial Waters," she shall be seized.

PART II

THE LAW OF THE BRITISH EMPIRE

INTRODUCTION

It has been noted in another connection that in 1854 the Law Officers of the Crown rendered an opinion to the effect that the jurisdiction of a British colony is confined to the distance of three miles from the shore. The Solicitor to the Board of Customs rendered an opinion in 1864, confirming that of the Law Officers in 1854, on the ground that the grant of the Crown extended no farther than three miles seaward. "It may be held," he said, "that the Colonial jurisdiction seaward is bounded by the league whether the Crown has any inherent jurisdiction beyond or not." [1]

As a result of this last opinion, the Board reported to the Treasury that the colonies did not have the power to impose penalties on persons other than inhabitants thereof, or to confiscate vessels not owned by them, for acts committed beyond the distance of three miles from the shore, and that, therefore, the Victoria law, which was submitted to the Secretary of State for the colonies, and, in turn, to the Treasury for an opinion of certain of its sections taking jurisdiction for the same distance adopted by the Imperial acts then in force,[2] should be modified in so far as it affected ships and inhabitants of the mother country or of other colonies beyond that distance.

[1] See p. 141, *supra*.

[2] Sec. 25 of 18 & 19 Vict., c. 96, and secs. 216, 217, and 242 of 16 & 17 Vict., c. CVII.

CHAPTER I

LEGISLATION

§ 34. Scotland

Article eighteen of the Treaty of Union between England and Scotland provided that the laws of the customs and excise should be the same in both countries, so that the legislation for England after the union in 1707 applied to Scotland.[3]

§ 35. Ireland

Legislation for Ireland by the English Parliament was passed as early as 1719. By the Act of 6 Geo. I, c. XXI, jurisdiction was taken over the hovering vessel for two leagues from the coast.[4] Generally speaking, the various acts of Parliament passed during the eighteenth and the nineteenth centuries applied to Ireland, unless they provided otherwise.

§ 36. The British Possessions in America

By the Act of 4 Geo. III, c. XV, section XXXIII (1764),[5] any vessel, British or foreign, hovering within two leagues of the coasts of any British colony or terri-

---

[3] Green, *Encyclopedia of Scots Law* (2d ed., 1910), vol. 4, p. 176. Article 19 of the treaty provided that a new Court of Exchequer should be established in Scotland with the same authority in revenue cases as the Court of Exchequer in England. This new court was established by the Act of 6 Anne, c. 26. The Exchequer was abolished in 1856 as a separate court by the Court of Exchequer Act 19 and 20 Vict., c. 56, and its jurisdiction and functions were transferred to the Court of Session.—Ibid., vol. 5, p. 239.

[4] See p. 14, *supra.*

[5] See p. 38, *supra.*

tory in America, which did not depart when requested to do so, was forfeitable; and by section XXIX, any vessel bound for such coasts could be stopped and seized within the same distance, in order to remove from such vessel any goods for which there was no cocket. This Act was in force for all British possessions in America until the United States became independent, after which it remained in force for the coasts of the remaining possessions until 1825. By the Act of 6 Geo. IV, c. CXIV, section 50 (1825), jurisdiction was taken over any vessel, British or foreign, hovering within one league of the coasts of such possessions, for the purpose of visiting such vessel and of placing an officer on board as long as it remained within such distance. This section was re-enacted by 3 and 4 Wm. IV, c. LIX, section 58 (1833), and by 8 and 9 Vict., c. XCIII, section LXV (1845). This last Act remained in force until 1857, when by the Act of 20 and 21 Vict., c. LXII, section XV, the provisions of 16 and 17 Vict., c. CVII (1853), and 18 and 19 Vict., c. XCVI, were extended to "the several British possessions abroad," except as provided otherwise in that Act or limited by express provision to the United Kingdom or the Channel Islands, and except as to such possessions as had already provided or might thereafter provide for the regulation of its customs, so that the provisions of 16 and 17 Vict., c. CVII, and 18 and 19 Vict., c. XCVI, which took jurisdiction for one, three, four, eight, and one hundred leagues, were now applicable to the possessions abroad which had not legislated on the subject.[6]

Section 151 of the Act of 39 and 40 Vict., c. 36, provided that that Act should extend to the British possessions abroad that had not legislated, so that after 1876 jurisdiction was taken for one, three, and four leagues.[7]

[6] See p. 105, note (8), *supra*.
[7] See p. 156, note (18), *supra*.

§ 37. The Dominion of Canada

In 1867, by the British North American Act, 30 Vict., c. III, Canada, Nova Scotia, and New Brunswick were united into one Dominion under the name of Canada. By section 122 of this Act, the customs and excise laws of each province were to remain in force until altered by the Parliament of Canada. The first Act passed by the Canadian Parliament was in 1877. The provisions of that Act were, for the most part, re-enacted in 1883, 1886, and in 1906. These four Acts extend jurisdiction for one league for some purposes, and for three leagues for other purposes. The last Act passed by the Canadian Parliament is "The Customs Act" of 1906.[8] Section 13 provides that bulk shall not be broken within three leagues of the coast until entry of the goods has been made and warrant granted; any alteration in stowage or the throwing overboard of any goods after the vessel's arrival within three leagues, is deemed a breaking of bulk. Appropriate penalties are provided.[9] Section 191 prescribes a penalty of two hundred dollars against the master if bulk is broken contrary to section 13.[10]

Under section 15, any vessel bound for a port may be boarded within three marine miles of the "anchorage ground," and demand made for a copy of the "report inwards." [11]

Section 147 provides that an officer may, upon information, or grounds of suspicion, "go on board of and enter into any vessel, . . . and may stop and detain the same,

---

[8] *Rev. Stat. of Canada*, 1906, c. 48; *Brit. and Forn. State Papers*, vol. 105, p. 10.

[9] This section is a re-enactment of the *Rev. Stat.* (1886), vol. 1, c. 32, sec. XXI, of sec. 16 of "The Customs Act, 1883," 46 Vict., c. 12, and of sec. VIII of 40 Vict., c. X (1877).

[10] This section is a re-enactment of sec. 16 of the Act of 1883 and of sec. 24 of the Act of 1886.

[11] This section is a re-enactment of sec. 26 of the Act of 1883 and of sec. 24 of the Act of 1886.

whether arriving from places beyond or within the limits of Canada, and may rummage and search all parts thereof" for any "goods respecting which there has been any violation of any of the requirement of this act," and any such goods may be seized, together with the vessel.[12]

Section 154 provides for bringing into port any vessel found hovering within one league of the coast, if she is bound elsewhere, and if she continues hovering for twenty-four hours after being required to depart.[13] By section 210, if any goods, whose importation into Canada is forbidden, are found on such hovering vessel, both the vessel and the cargo are forfeitable. The master is subject to a penalty of four hundred dollars if he refuses to comply with the directions of the officer boarding the vessel.[14]

Section 211 provides that if any prohibited or smuggled goods or "goods respecting which there has been any violation of any of the requirements of this act" are found in any vessel of any description, "whether arriving from places beyond or within the limits of Canada," such goods and the vessel shall be seized and forfeited.

Section 216 provides that any person, having been on board any vessel liable to forfeiture for having been found within one league of the coasts, having on board anything subjecting such vessel to forfeiture, or any vessel from which any part of the cargo has been destroyed or thrown overboard, shall incur a penalty of one hundred dollars.[15]

---

[12] This section is a re-enactment of sec. 91 of the Act of 1877, sec. 172 of the Act of 1883, and sec. 134 of the Act of 1886.

[13] This section is a re-enactment of sec. 84 of the Act of 1877, of sec. 163 of the Act of 1883, and of sec. 113 of the Act of 1886.

[14] This section is a re-enactment of sec. 163 of the Act of 1883 and of sec. 113 of the Act of 1886.

[15] This section is a re-enactment of sec. 85 of the Act of 1877, of sec. 164 of the Act of 1883, and sec. 199 of the Act of 1886.

By sec. 259, every master refusing to stop a vessel when required

The Canadian law has never made any discrimination between foreigners and Canadian subjects or between foreign and domestic vessels in so far as the extent of jurisdiction in the marginal sea is concerned. The provisions of the foregoing acts have applied to all persons and to all vessels, regardless of their nationality.

§ 38. The Commonwealth of New Zealand

An act of 1913 [16] forbids breaking bulk within one league of the coast. Under section 28, the master must bring his ship to within that distance for boarding, when hailed. By section 168, a vessel may be fired into which is not brought to when required to do so.

By section 165, an officer may board any ship, "within or without the territorial waters," and by section 166 he may search any ship whether within or without such waters. In 1922, these sections were amended so as to confine the boarding and searching to "territorial waters." [17]

Section 206 provides that when any statute imposes a penalty on the master in respect of any act or event in waters not within the territorial limits, such person shall be guilty of an offense, punishable if he comes into New Zealand within one year after the commission of the

---

to do so, is liable to a penalty of two hundred dollars. This section is a re-enactment of sec. 214 of the Act of 1886 and sec. 174 of the Act of 1883.

By sec. 196, "all vessels, . . . made use of in the importation or unshipping or landing or removal of any goods liable to forfeiture under this act, shall be seized and forfeited." Any person who assists or is concerned in unshipping such goods shall incur a penalty of two hundred dollars, or treble the value of such goods. This section is a re-enactment of sec. 196 of the Act of 1883, and of sec. 162 of the Act of 1883.

[16] "An act to make provisions for the collection of Duties of Customs," *Statutes,* 4 Geo. V, December 15, 1913, No. 63, sec. 27.

[17] "An Act to Amend the Customs Act, 1913," *Statutes,* 13 Geo. V, No. 14, p. 48, sec. 6.

offense. This section was repealed by section 6 of the amendment of 1922.

By section 253, any "goods may be seized and forfeited wherever found, whether on land or in New Zealand or in the territorial waters of New Zealand, or at sea." This section was amended by section 6 of the amendment of 1922, by omitting the words "or at sea," so that after 1922 seizure of goods was confined to "territorial waters."

Section 268 provides that, "Except in case of a ship which has unlawfully departed from a port of entry, no ship shall be seized elsewhere than in a port of entry or the territorial waters of New Zealand, but the right of seizure shall not be affected by the fact that the ship was not within any such port or waters at the time of the act or event which rendered it liable to detention." By section 6 of the amendment of 1922, this section was amended by omitting the words, "except in the case of a ship which has unlawfully departed from a port of entry," and all of the section following the last comma, so that that section now reads, "no ship shall be seized elsewhere than in a port of entry or the territorial waters of New Zealand."

By section 270, it is provided that every ship seized may be detained by the customs until security is given for the payment of any penalties or costs which may be imposed upon the owner or master, in respect of the offense which rendered the ship liable, "or in respect of the offence of coming into New Zealand after such offence committed in waters out of New Zealand." By section 6 of the amendment of 1922, the clause in quotation marks is omitted.

It is provided by section 177 that when this Act authorises the exercise of any power or authority or the doing of any act on or in respect of any ship or boat "being in waters not comprised within the territorial limits of New Zealand," the exercise of such power or the doing of such act shall in all courts be deemed and taken as "lawful and valid, notwithstanding that such power or authority was exercised or such act was done beyond the territorial limits aforesaid." The amendment of 1922 does not expressly alter this section, but other sections of the amendment have, in effect, rendered this section inoperative by withdrawing authority for the exercise of jurisdiction beyond "territorial limits," wherever it had been taken by the Act of 1913.[18]

By section 169, provision is made for fastening down the hatchways or other openings into the hold "while any ship remains in port or in the territorial waters of New Zealand."

Section 216 penalises the master and owner of any ship found "within one league of the coast of New Zealand or within the territorial waters of New Zealand," having false bulkheads, bows, sides, or bottoms, or any device adapted for the purpose of smuggling.

§ 39. The Commonwealth of Australia

Before 1901, each of the colonies now comprising the Commonwealth of Australia had its own customs laws and administration. By the Commonwealth of Australia Constitution Act of July 9, 1900,[19] the six Provinces of Tasmania, New South Wales, Victoria, Queensland, South Australia, and Western Australia were united under the name of the Commonwealth of Australia. Section 88 of that Act provides that "Uniform duties of customs shall be imposed within two years after the establishment of the Commonwealth"; and section 90 provides that "on

---

[18] The Act does not define "territorial limits" or "territorial waters."
[19] 63 & 64 Vict., c. 12.

the imposition of uniform duties of customs all laws of the several states imposing duties of customs or exercise, . . . shall cease to have effect."

"The Customs Act 1901" of the Commonwealth of Australia [20] and several amendments since that year form the law of to-day. Section 228 of the Act of 1901, as amended by The Customs Act of 1910, No. 36, section 10, and substituted by The Customs Act 1923, No. 12, section 32, provides for the forfeiture of the following ships or boats not exceeding 250 tons registered tonnage and the following aircraft:

"2. Any ship, boat or aircraft found within one league of the coast or of land failing to bring to, or failing to land at an aerodrome, for boarding upon being lawfully required to do so.[21]

"3. Any ship, boat or aircraft hovering within one league of the coast or of land and not departing within twelve hours after being required to depart by an officer.[22]

"4. Any ship, boat or aircraft from which goods are thrown overboard, staved or destroyed to prevent seizure by the Customs. . . .[23]

"6. Any ship, boat or aircraft within one league of the coast or land having false bulk heads, false bows, sides or bottoms or any secret or disguised place adapted for the purpose of concealing goods or having any hole pipe or other device adapted for the purpose of running goods."

[20] No. 6 of 1901.

[21] See, also, sec. 59. In commenting on this provision the Permanent Head of the Department of Trade and Customs and Comptroller General of Customs for Australia says: "In regard to Australia and this act, the Customs, till otherwise advised, maintained the right of search for a clear three nautical miles from a line drawn in the case of gulfs, inlets, bays, etc., from point to point of the coast. It would, however, be probably difficult to obtain a conviction under this section unless the ship were actually within a league of the land." *Commonwealth of Australia, Customs Law and Regulations*, by H. N. P. Wollaston, 1904.

[22] See, also, sec. 185.

[23] No distance is named.

If the ship exceeds 250 tons, it is not forfeited, but the owner is liable to a penalty not exceeding £1,000, for which the ship may be detained.

By section 226 (f) and (k) of the Act of 1901, the goods in respect of which bulk is unlawfully broken and the cargo of any ship, boat, or aircraft hovering "about the coast or land" that does not depart within twelve hours after being required to do so, are forfeited. By section 73, the breaking of bulk is prohibited after the arrival of the ship or aircraft within one league of the coast.

By section 184 of the Act of 1901, as amended by No. 12 of 1923, any ship or aircraft may be chased and fired into which does not bring to when required to do so.

§ 40. The Union of South Africa

The "South African Act" of September 20, 1909 [24] united the colonies of the Cape of Good Hope, Natal, the Transvaal, and the Orange River Colony under the name of the Union of South Africa.

The Union of South Africa passed an Act in 1913 dealing with the subject of customs.[25] Section 4 provides that an officer may board "any ship arriving at any port in the Union, or being within one marine league of the coast thereof." Section 35 provides that "no goods shall be unladen, or water-borne to be laden, on board any ship, or unladen from any ship," until due entry has been made and warrant granted for the lading or unlading.

In 1923, an act was passed giving effect to the International Convention for Regulating Air Navigation. Section 12 provides that the Customs Act of 1913 shall, with

[24] 9 Edw. VII, c. 9.

[25] "Act to provide for the Management of Customs of the Union of South Africa," Act No. 9 of 1913, *Statutes of the Union of South Africa*, 1913, p. 24.

the necessary modifications, apply to the importation and exportation by aircraft.[26]

§ 41. India

Section 53 of c. VII of the Sea Customs Act, 1878,[27] provides that the local government may "fix a place in any river or port, beyond which no vessel arriving shall pass until a manifest has been delivered to the pilot, officer of the customs. . . ." "If, in any river or port wherein a place has been fixed by the local government under this section, the master of any vessel arriving remains outside or below the place so fixed, such master, shall . . . within twenty-four hours after the vessel anchors, deliver" such manifest. Under section 57, no vessel, arriving in any customs port, shall break bulk until a manifest has been delivered.

[26] Ibid., 1923, p. 68 at p. 80.
[27] *The Unrepealed General Acts of the Governor General in Council from 1868 to 1878,* vol. II, p. 605.

PART III

DEVELOPMENT OF THE LAW
OF THE UNITED STATES

CHAPTER I

FROM 1775 TO 1920

§ 42. Extent of Smuggling

(1) *In the American Colonies*

In 1660, Parliament passed laws forbidding the shipment of certain goods of the growth or manufacture of any English plantation in America, Asia, or Africa to any place except another plantation of His Majesty or to England, under penalty of forfeiture of the goods shipped and the ship importing them.[1] In 1663, it was provided that no goods of the growth or manufacture of Europe should be imported into the colonies of America except from English ports.[2] These laws, among others, resulted in an extensive smuggling trade by some of the colonists.

During the eighteenth century, much smuggling was carried on along the Connecticut coast. Incoming vessels from foreign ports would anchor off Fisher's Island, send their illicit cargoes ashore, and then sail to New London or other ports with their manifested cargoes; while later, the contraband would be run in in small craft, as opportunity afforded. As in England, the smugglers frequently had the support of the community.

[1] 12 Chas. II, c. 18.
[2] 15 Chas. II, c. 7. See p. 164, *supra*, for legislation by Parliament for the British possessions in America.

In discussing Lord Abbington's motion for support of the army, Mr. William Innes said in the House of Commons on November 8, 1775:

"It is notorious to every merchant in the *American* trade, that the most northern of the Colonies have long been in the practice of smuggling every article of goods they could from *Holland* and *Germany;* and all the Colonies, without exception, have discovered great partiality to the *French* Islands, in preference to the *British*." [3]

The North Carolina Council of Safety passed the following resolution on July 26, 1776:

"Whereas it is necessary that the directions of the Congress, respecting Exportation, be fully and strictly observed:

"Resolved, That the Commissioners of the different Ports do receive from the Captains of all Vessels, on oath, a Manifest of their Cargo, before they grant any clearance or permit to leave this Colony; and that the Commanders of the Armed Vessels, the Companies of Militia on the sea-coast, and of the different Forts in this Colony, are hereby empowered and required to stop and to detain all Vessels, and prevent their leaving this Colony until they produce proper clearances from the Commissioners of the Ports of *Edenton, Bath, Newbern,* or *Wilmington*." [4]

(2) *In the United States*

The practice of smuggling by no means ended when the American colonies became independent. During the first quarter of the nineteenth century, it was especially prevalent. During this period, there are many reported cases of seizures of vessels in ports for bringing in dutiable

[3] *American Archives,* Fourth Series, vol. VI, col. 151.

[4] Ibid., Fifth Series, vol. I, col. 1367. This resolution was aimed primarily at contraband of war.

goods clandestinely, though there is no reported case of a seizure on the high seas, for reasons that will be considered later. There was much illicit trading until the outbreak of the Civil War, after which it did not appear again with its old vigor.

The need of the Treasury of cutters to be used in combating smuggling during the early years of the nineteenth century is discussed in a communication from Albert Gallatin to the House of Representatives on November 29, 1808.[5] It was observed that three additional cutters would be sufficient for the execution of the ordinary revenue laws, viz., "one for the District of Maine, one for Rhode Island and the southern coast of Massachusetts, and one for Ocracock, in North Carolina."

"But, for the purpose of carrying into effect laws which prohibit exportation and restrain importations, more efficient means must be used than are now authorized. And amongst these an increase of revenue cutters is necessary, in addition to the assistance of gun boats, which are better calculated as a stationary force, and for the purpose of stopping, in certain places, than of pursuing, vessels. We want small fast sailing vessels, ten of which will require a less number of men than the smallest frigate, and will cover much more ground. For you will be pleased to observe, that there are but six vessels belonging to the navy, under the size of frigates; and that number is inadequate to the extent of coast, and number of harbors to be watched. An easy draught of water is also a material consideration. But it seems to me that it cannot be doubted, that, if all the navy was employed in that service, they are not sufficient, in point of number, for the object, and that ten or twelve small vessels, in addition, will form a very useful appendage. I propose that they should be revenue cutters, because, in time of peace,

[5] *American State Papers,* Class III (Finance, vol. II), vol. VI, p. 306.

and when employed solely in carrying the laws into effect, they will be under the control of the collectors; which, in relation to that object, is preferable; and because, in case of war, they might, according to the existing laws, be placed under the direction of the Navy Department. Their size would vary from 70 to 130 tons; they would carry from six to ten four-pounders, or, if they can be procured, twelve-pounder carronades; and be manned with from fifteen to thirty men each, which is amply sufficient for the object in view."

The practice of smuggling was carried on in England from the seventeenth century on, in comparatively small craft, from the continent across very narrow bodies of water. Except through Canada, Mexico, or the West Indies, however, the smuggler had great difficulty in carrying his wares to America from overseas. The journey across the Atlantic required large vessels; it consumed much time and entailed great hazard. The larger craft, moreover, could not enter the small coves or escape notice or outsail the swift revenue cutters. The smuggling vessels were, therefore, usually American vessels under one hundred tons burden, which received their illicit wares off the coast from ocean-going merchantmen; and, for the most part, they cruised along near the coast for these cargoes. To meet this practice, Congress provided on July 31, 1789, that no dutiable goods, wares, or merchandise of foreign growth or manufacture should be brought into the United States in any other manner than by sea, or in any ship or vessel of less than thirty tons burden, except within the district of Louisiana, under penalty of forfeiture of the vessel and the goods.[6] The

---

[6] 1 *Stat. at Large,* 1st sess., c. 5, sec. 40, p. 48.

This section was re-enacted in 1790 (ibid., p. 177, sec. 70), and in 1799 (ibid., p. 697, sec. 92), when other districts than Louisiana were excepted, and when it was also provided that no drawbacks on such goods should be allowed on exportation from the United States otherwise than by sea, and in vessels of not less than thirty tons burden;

object of this provision was "to prevent the landing of foreign goods in the United States except at regular ports of entry, where the custom-house officers could secure the duties due the government without difficulty, and to prevent smuggling by small sloops that could run into rivers and small streams where no custom-houses are established, and to avoid patrolling the entire coast, against smugglers." [7] Other acts passed during the early years of the century prohibited the importation of many commodities into the United States from any foreign port or place, except in casks or containers of specified content, or in vessels of specified tonnage, on pain of forfeiture of the commodities and the vessel in which they were imported.[8]

The provisions of the foregoing Acts show that the United States, as well as England, had to contend with the small smuggling craft plying near the coast and running into creeks and coves and other obscure places, and with the old practice of transporting liquors and other goods in small containers, in order to facilitate their transshipment and the running of them inland. Doubtless, in these early Acts, Congress profited from the old laws passed by Parliament in the early years of the eighteenth century.[9]

The instructions to the officers of the revenue cutters for the years 1834 [10] and 1843 [11] reported that there was reason to believe that "many vessels, ostensibly employed

---

and, again in 1878 (*Rev. Stat.* sec. 3095). These exceptions as to other districts made in 1799 were made as a result of a recommendation by Alexander Hamilton, Secretary of the Treasury, on April 22, 1790. *American State Papers,* Class III (Finance vol. I), vol. V, p. 49.

[7] *U. S.* v. *The Sloop Theophile* (1882) 11 Fed. 696, (D. C. W. D. Texas, Turner, Dist. Judge.)

[8] See, for example, 1 *Stat. at Large,* 3d sess. (1791), c. 15, sec. 83, p. 207, and ibid., vol. 4, 2d sess. (1827), c. 55, p. 235.

[9] See p. 8, note (4), *supra.*

[10] P. 193, *infra.*

[11] P. 195, *infra.*

in the fisheries and coasting trade" were engaged in smuggling foreign merchandise. With the advent of the Civil War in 1861, the smugglers, for the most part, joined the armies or navies, or devoted themselves to blockade running, for which their experience had admirably equipped them. After the war, the trade did not rise again with its old vigor.

The reports of the Revenue-Cutter Service show that many vessels were boarded and examined as a matter of routine, or were seized or reported for violations of revenue laws, but the place of boarding and examination and the nature of the violations are not given.[12] The annual reports of this Service for the years 1912, 1913, 1914, 1915, and 1916 state that it was "the general impression that there is little or no smuggling in bulk at the present time, and it is true that this form of lawlessness is not very common, but this fact is evidence of the high state of efficiency in which the Revenue-Cutter Service has been and is being maintained, and is a result of the accumulated deterrent effect of years of vigilant patrolling. Along our borders there is still more or less smuggling of Chinese persons, opium, and spirits in violation of the law, and it keeps the Revenue-Cutter Service in those localities busy to prevent operations of this kind. Lawlessness in any guise and in any locality is kept in check only by physical force, and it is clear that without an armed coast patrol smuggling would soon spring into existence along our many miles of seacoast."[13]

[12] *Annual Report of the Chief of the Revenue Marine Bureau* for June 30, 1872, p. 14; for 1873, p. 6; and for 1881, pp. 12-13; *Report of the Chief Division of the Revenue-Cutter Service*, 1887, p. 17; *Annual Reports of the United States Revenue-Cutter Service* for the following years: 1913, p. 5; 1914, p. 83; 1915, p. 20; 1916, p. 16; 1917, p. 25.

[13] *Annual Report of the United States Revenue-Cutter Service* for 1912, p. 60. These observations were made again in the reports of 1913, 1914, 1915, p. 19, and 1916, p. 15.

§ 43. Legislation

(1) *Requirement of Manifest*

Before Congress legislated upon this subject in 1790, some of the States had passed revenue laws, and their courts had forfeited vessels for violations of these laws. For example, the case of *Phile quitam* v. *The Ship Anna* [14] was a proceeding against a vessel for landing goods not manifested, in violation of a law of Pennsylvania of March 15, 1787, which provided, among other things:

"That every vessel, or boat from which goods, wares, or merchandise, shall be unladed before due entry thereof, at the office of the Collector of the port of Philadelphia, ... shall be forfeited."

The Act of Congress of 1789 [15] provided that the master of every ship or vessel bound to any port of the United States from any foreign port or place, should deliver, upon demand, to any officer who should first go on board, two manifests, specifying, among other things, a true account of the loading on board at the port from which she last sailed, and to what port in the United States she was bound.[16] The officer was required to transmit one of the manifests to the collector of the district to which the vessel was bound. Section 11 prescribed a penalty of $500 against any master refusing to "deliver his manifests and documents, pursuant to the directions of this act."

Another Act was passed on August 4, 1790,[17] which

[14] (1787) 1 Dallas (Pa.) 197. See also: *Douglas* v. *Roan* (1790), 4 Call. (8 Va.) 353; *Bentley* v. *Roan* (1790), ibid., 153.

[15] P. 178, *supra*.

[16] Sec. 10, p. 38. This Act was repealed in 1790. (1 *Stat. at Large*, 2d sess., c. 35, sec. 74, p. 178).

[17] "An act to provide more effectually for the collection of duties imposed by law on goods, wares, and merchandise, imported into the United States. . . ." 1 *Stat. at Large*, 2d sess., c. 35, p. 145. This Act was repealed March 2, 1799. Ibid., 3d sess., c. 22, sec. 112, p. 704. For a general discussion of this Act by Alexander Hamilton in 1790, see *American State Papers*, Class III (Finance, Vol. I), vol. V, p. 45, et seq. See, also, *The Antilles* (1875), Fed. Case No. 489, 8 Benedict 9; and *U. S.* v. *26 Diamond Rings* (1855), Fed. Case No. 16,572.

has remained the basis of the American law. Section 9 required the presence of a manifest on board, specifying, among other things, the name of the port or ports in the United States to which the goods named in such manifest were consigned, the name of the port or the place to which the vessel belonged, and a true account of all goods laden on board, the build of the vessel, its name, and tonnage, before any goods, wares, or merchandise could be brought into the United States from any foreign port or place, in "any ship or vessel belonging in the whole or in part to a citizen or citizens, inhabitant or inhabitants of the United States." [18]

A vessel owned only in part by a citizen of the United States could not have been an American vessel. The American law on this point has corresponded with the English law.[19] Therefore, such a vessel was foreign or

[18] Sec. 10 provided that if any goods, wares, or merchandise were imported or brought into the United States in any vessel so belonging, from any foreign port or place, without such manifest or manifests in writing, or if they were not included in such manifest, the master should forfeit the value of the goods not included in the manifest. The forfeiture was not incurred if no part of the cargo had been unshipped, and the manifest lost, or mislaid without fraud or collusion.

Alexander Hamilton, Secretary of the Treasury, in a communication to the House of Representatives on April 22, 1790, declared that this section "renders more difficult those collusions between masters and owners, which often take place after the arrival of vessels upon the coast, or within port." *American State Papers*, Class III (Finance, vol. I), vol. V.

[19] For the English law, see p. 61, *supra*.

The law of the United States is as follows:

1. By an Act of September 1, 1789, the following vessels only could be registered and were deemed to be and denominated vessels of the United States, and entitled to the benefits granted by any law of the United States:

> Any ship or vessel built within the United States, and owned wholly by a citizen or citizens thereof, or not built within the United States, which on May 16, 1789, belonged, and thereafter continued to belong, wholly to a citizen or citizens thereof, and whose master was a citizen of the United States.

1 *Stat. at Large*, 1st sess., c. XI, sec. I, p. 55, "An Act for Registering and Clearing Vessels. . . ."

By section 5 of that Act, no ship or vessel, owned in whole or in part by any citizen of the United States, "usually residing in any

nondescript as to its flag. A vessel owned in part or wholly by an *inhabitant* of the United States could have

---

foreign country, shall, during the time he shall continue so to reside, be deemed a vessel of the United States, entitled to be registered by virtue of this act, unless he be an agent for, and partner in, some house or co-partnership, consisting of citizens of the United States, actually carrying on trade in the said States." This section was carried forward in section 4133 of the *Revised Statutes*. By section 6, before registry of a vessel could be made, an oath by the owner or owners had to be made that they were citizens of the United States "and that no foreigner, directly or indirectly, hath any part or interest in the said ship or vessel." By section 9, when the certificate of registry was given, a bond had to be given, conditioned, among other things, that such certificate would be surrendered "if any foreigner, or any person or persons for his use and benefit, shall purchase and become otherwise entitled to the whole or any part or share of, or interest in such ship or vessel."

The foregoing provisions were substantially re-enacted in 1792. 1 *Stat. at Large,* 2d sess., 1792, secs. 1, 2, and 4, p. 287, et seq. They correspond with the provisions of 26 Geo. III, c. 60. See p. 61, note, *supra,* and Abbott, *Shipping* (1812), p. 28.

By an Act of June 27, 1797, it was provided that no ship or vessel registered pursuant to any law of the United States, which should be seized or condemned under the authority of any foreign prince, or which should by sale become the property of a foreigner, should be entitled to or capable of receiving a new register, even if such ship or vessel should afterwards become American property; but all such ships and vessels were to be taken as foreign vessels, unless the person regaining the property therein was the owner at the time of the seizure or capture. 1 *Stat at Large,* 1st sess., c. V, p. 523.

By an Act of March 4, 1804, it was provided that no ship or vessel should be entitled to be registered as a ship or vessel of the United States, or, if registered, to the benefits of such a vessel, if owned wholly or in part by any person naturalized in the United States and residing for more than one year in the country of his origin, or for more than two years in any foreign country, unless such person was a consul or other public agent of the United States. 2 *Stat. at Large,* 1st sess., c. LII, p. 296. This section was re-enacted in sec. 4134 of the *Revised Statutes*.

By sec. 4132 of the *Revised Statutes,* only the following vessels may be registered:
1. Vessels built within the United States and belonging wholly to citizens thereof;
2. Vessels which may be captured in war by citizens of the United States and lawfully condemned as prizes, or
3. Vessels which may be adjudged to be forfeited for a breach of the laws of the United States, being wholly owned by citizens.

By sec. 4131, the foregoing vessels are the only ones which may be deemed vessels of the United States.

been a foreign vessel, for such a person could have been a foreigner, and his ownership would not have controlled the nationality of the vessel. According to Judge Story, the vessels named in this section embraced American ships, or "foreign ships having on board goods on American account."[20] This section was nothing more than a provision made especially for vessels owned wholly or in part by American citizens or inhabitants. Other vessels, that is, vessels of which such persons were not owners, in whole or in part, were also required to carry manifests.

This Act of 1790 was repealed in 1799, but its provisions were re-enacted in the same year with greater particularity of detail.[21] Section 23 of the Act of 1799 re-enacted section 9 of the Act of 1790, except that by section 23, when goods were imported by "citizens or inhabitants of the United States in vessels other than the United States," special provisions were made for the description of the vessel in the manifest. This section provided that all wines, spirits, and teas, constituting the whole or any part of the cargo of "any vessel," should be inserted in the manifest in the order in which they were to be delivered, when delivery was to be made at different ports. Section 2806 of the *Revised Statutes* prohibits the importation into the United States in any vessel, of any goods, unless the master has a manifest on board, so that the restrictions as to ownership of vessels and cargo were omitted altogether after 1878.

(2) *Production of Manifest and Examination of Vessels within Four Leagues*

Section 11 of the Act of 1790 provided that the master of "any ship or vessel, belonging in the whole or in part to a citizen or citizens, inhabitant or inhabitants of the

---

[20] *The Betsy* (1818), Fed. Case No. 1365.

[21] "An Act to regulate the collection of duties on imports and tonnage," March 2, 1799. 1 *Stat. at Large*, 3d sess., 1799, c. 22, p. 627.

United States," laden with such goods, and bound to any port or place in the United States, should, upon his arrival "within 4 leagues of the coast thereof," or within any bays, rivers, harbors, or inlets, upon demand, produce, for inspection, such manifest and a copy thereof, which such master is "herein before required to have on board," to such officers as should first go on board the vessel.[22] The officer was required to certify the fact of the delivery of the original on the back thereof and to transmit the copy to the collector of the district to which the goods should appear, by the manifest, to be consigned. A like procedure was required after the vessel arrived "within the limits of any district of the United States." This section was re-enacted by section 25 of the Act of 1799.[23]

Section 2811 of the *Revised Statutes* provided that "Every master of any vessel laden with merchandise, and bound to any port in the United States, shall, on his arrival within four leagues of the coast thereof," or within any bays, harbors, ports, creeks, or inlets, "upon demand, produce the manifests in writing, which such master is required to have on board his vessel, to such officer of the customs as first comes on board his vessel, for inspection." Section 2812 provided a like procedure after any such vessel arrived within the limits of any collection district in which the cargo was intended to be discharged. These two sections of the *Revised Statutes,* together with section 2813, correspond to section 11 of the old Act of 1790, and section 25 of the Act of 1799, except that all qualifications as to ownership are removed, so that after 1878 the law requiring the production of a mani-

[22] In English and American law, the league, as employed in the revenue laws, has been used synonymously with three miles.

[23] The Act of 1799 added that when any master produced any manifest to a collector of the district upon which no certificate of delivery had been endorsed, he should make oath that no officer had applied for such a manifest and that no endorsement had taken place on any manifest.

fest within four leagues of the coast applied to all vessels.[24]

Section 12 of the Act of 1790 provided for the forfeiture
of a sum not exceeding $500 by the master of "any ship or
vessel laden as aforesaid," and bound as aforesaid, who
should not, upon his arrival within four leagues of the
coast or the limits of any district where the cargo was
intended to be discharged, produce such manifest and such
copy upon demand, or should not give an account of the
"destination of such ship or vessel," or should give "a
false account of the said destination, in order to evade the
production of the said manifest. . . ." This section was
re-enacted by section 26 of the Act of 1799 [25] and by sections 2814 and 2815 of the *Revised Statutes*. The application of sections 12 and 26 was not limited to vessels
belonging in whole or in part to citizens or inhabitants
of the United States. The foregoing sections of the Acts
of 1790 and 1799 whose application was not specifically
restricted as to ownership, applied to all vessels, domestic
and foreign, so that in many cases those statutes applied
to foreign vessels which were not owned in part or wholly
by United States citizens or inhabitants of the United
States.[26] All restrictions as to ownership found in all

[24] Sec. 2809 provides: "If any merchandise is brought into the
United States in any vessel whatever from any foreign port without
having such a manifest on board [as described in section 2807], or
which shall not be included or described in the manifest, or shall not
agree therewith, the master shall be liable to a penalty equal to the
value of such merchandise not included in such manifest; and all such
merchandise not included in the manifest belonging or consigned to
the master, mate, officer, or crew of such vessel, shall be forfeited."

[25] Sec. 26 added that if the customs officer should not receive full
satisfaction from the master "respecting any of the provisions in this
and the foregoing sections," he should make a written return of the
name of the vessel and master so offending to the collector of the
district to which the vessel was considered to have been bound.

[26] Judge Story held in *The Betsey* (1818), Fed. Case No. 1365 (C. C.
D. Mass.), that sec. 13, in which the foregoing qualifications as to ownership were omitted, as in sec. 12, applied to foreign ships; the same
reasoning employed in that case applies to sec. 12. See p. 188, *infra*, for
sec. 13. See Instructions to Revenue Cutters, p. 193, et seq., *supra*.

sections of these Acts were omitted in the provisions of the *Revised Statutes* in 1878.[27]

By section 31 of the Act of 1790, it was made lawful for all collectors, and other named officers to go on board of "ships or vessels in any part of the United States, or within four leagues of the coast thereof," if bound to the United States, for the purposes of "demanding the manifests aforesaid," and of "examining and searching the said ships or vessels." The officers were allowed free access to every part of the ship; and if any package was found anywhere on the ship in a "place separate from the residue of the cargo," a description thereof was to be taken or a seal placed thereon and a report made thereof to the collector of the district to which the ship was bound. If any such package was missing, or the seal broken upon the vessel's arrival at port, the master was subject to a forfeiture of $500. These sections were re-enacted by sections 3067, 3069, and 3070 of the *Revised Statutes*.[28] By section 64 of the Act of 1790, officers of the Revenue boats and cutters were empowered to go on board "every ship or vessel," which should arrive "within the United States, or within four leagues of the coast thereof," if bound for the United States, and to search and examine every part thereof, and to demand, and certify "the manifests, hereinbefore required to be on board of certain ships or vessels," and to affix fastenings on the hatches, and to remain on board until such vessels had arrived at their

[27] By an Act of July 18, 1866, "An Act further to prevent Smuggling and for other Purposes," (1 *Stat. at Large,* c. CCI, sec. 25, p. 184), it was provided that the several provisions of the Act of March 2, 1790, "relating to manifests, shall apply as well to vessels owned in whole or in part by foreigners, as to vessels of the United States." The Secretary of State was instructed to send copies of this section to all consular officers of the United States in foreign countries. In other words, this Act of 1866 had the effect of making the provisions of the Act of 1799 applicable to all vessels within four leagues of the shore, regardless of their ownership.

[28] See note (24), p. 186, *supra,* for sec. 2809 of the *Revised Statutes,* requiring a manifest for all merchandise brought into the United States.

places of destination. This section was re-enacted by section 99 of the Act of 1799; but section 99 provided, in addition, that the commander of every revenue cutter should make a weekly return in writing, specifying "the vessels that have been boarded, their names and descriptions, the names of the masters, and from what port or place they last sailed, whether laden or in ballast, whether ships or vessels of the United States, or to what other nation belonging, and whether they have the necessary manifest or manifests of their cargoes on board. . . ."[29] This section was re-enacted by sections 2760 and 2761 of the *Revised Statutes*.

(3) *Unloading within Four Leagues*

By section 13 of the Act of 1790, the master and mate were subjected to a fine of $1,000 if any part of the cargo was unladen for any purpose (necessity excepted), from "any ship or vessel so laden with goods as aforesaid,"

[29] On December 7, 1814, the Treasury Department, in a communication made to the Congressional Committee of Ways and Means, in answer to a request for information "as to the defects of the present revenue laws," stated that "smuggling is extensively prosecuted, on the Northern frontier, by citizens of the United States, sometimes with, and sometimes without, the cover of a neutral character; in the course of which the enemy obtains important intelligence; he is furnished with cattle, and other essential supplies; and he is enabled to introduce his merchandise surreptitiously into our markets." The Department noted that on the arrival or the approach of vessels, officers were empowered to go on board for the purpose of demanding manifests and of searching vessels. This was to be done by way of precaution without any special deputation from a collector, naval officer, or a surveyor. If, however, there was reason to suspect that any goods subject to duty were concealed in any vessel, an officer could not enter such vessel to search for, seize, and secure such goods without being specially appointed for that purpose by the officers just named. The act to be performed was not an act of precaution, but one of detection. Any vessel and its goods which were liable to seizure by virtue of any act of the revenue could be seized and secured. The act to be performed was founded on the fact that the property was liable to seizure, but that it was not necessary to enter the ship to ascertain whether such goods were so liable and were there concealed. *American State Papers*, Class III (Finance, vol. II), vol. VI, p. 881.

that is, with goods from a foreign place, and bound to the United States, after her arrival within the limits of any district or within four leagues of the coast, before she should come to a proper place for the discharge of her cargo, and should be duly authorized to unlade the same. The goods so unladen were forfeitable.[30]   This section was re-enacted by section 27 of the Act of 1799, and by section 2867 of the *Revised Statutes*. It is applicable to all vesels of whatever nationality, and irrespective of their ownership.[31]

Under section 14 of the Act of 1790, any ship, vessel, or boat was forfeitable into which any goods, wares, or merchandise so unladen should be placed; that is, the in-taking vessel was forfeitable if the goods were taken in within four leagues of the shore. The master of the in-taking vessel was subject to a forfeiture of treble the value of the goods. This section was re-enacted by section 28 of the Act of 1799, and by section 2868 of the *Revised Statutes*.

[30] If the unlading was from necessity, the master was required to give notice to the collector of the customs of the district within which the unlading took place, or within which the ship afterwards arrived when the unlading was within four leagues of the coast but not within the limits of any district.

The Cargo ex Lady Essex (1889), 39 Fed. 765 (D. C. E. D. Mich., Brown J.), was an information against a cargo of lumber of the schooner *Lady Essex*, forfeiture of which was claimed under sec. 2867 of the *Revised Statutes*, which was a re-enactment of sec. 13, on the ground that the cargo had been unladen without a permit. The cargo had been taken from a Canadian vessel which was bound for an American port and which had been stranded after its arrival within the limits of a collection district. The *Lady Essex* began to unload its cargo on shore without reporting that it had the cargo. On exception to the information, it was held that sec. 2867 does not work a forfeiture of the cargo for being unladen when no notice is given in case of necessity or accident, and the goods may not be forfeited for being smuggled into the United States if the master of the Canadian vessel had no authority to sell them to the master of the *Lady Essex*, for no act with reference to them can be done to the prejudice of the owner in the absence of such authority.

[31] In *The Betsey* (1818), Fed. Case No. 1365, 1 Mason, 354 (C. C. D. Mass.), Judge Story says, ". . . the policy of the act applies equally , to all vessels; and indeed more strongly to foreign vessels."

In 1791, provision was made for the forfeiture of both the in-taking and unlading vessels, and the spirits unshipped, when any spirits, after being shipped for exportation, were unladen for any purpose, necessity excepted, "either within the limits of any port of the United States, or within four leagues of the coast thereof." [32]

(4) *Penalties for Resisting Customs Officers*

By section 51 of the Act of 1790, every person was subjected to a fine in a sum not exceeding $400 who should resist or impede any customs officer in the execution of his duty. Since the duty of the officer had to be performed within four leagues of the coast under several sections of the Act, this section applied to any act of interference within that distance. [33]

Section 67 provided for the seizure, libel, and prosecution of all vessels and goods which should become forfeited by virtue of the Act. The corresponding section of the *Revised Statutes* is section 3072.

Section 102 of the Act of 1799 provided that the master of a cutter or boat in the service of the revenue should fire at or into any ship or vessel liable to seizure or examination which should not bring to when required to do so, or upon being chased. This section was re-enacted by section 2765 of the *Revised Statutes*.

Section 3088 of the *Revised Statutes* provided that whenever a vessel or the owner or master had become subject to a penalty for the violation of the revenue laws, the vessel should be held for payment and seized and proceeded against to recover such penalty.

(5) *Slave Vessels Hovering on the Coast*

The reports of several departments of the Government

---

[32] 1 *Stat. at Large,* p. 212, sec. 55.
[33] See also, sec. 12, p. 186, *supra.*

in the early years of the nineteenth century show that there was a great deal of smuggling of slaves from Africa, which, however, was wiped out by 1827. This trade called for a special law, which was passed in 1807.[34] It was provided that any ship or vessel should be forfeited if found "in any river, . . . or on the high seas, within the jurisdictional limits of the United States, *or hovering on the coast thereof,*" having on board any negroes for the purpose of selling them as slaves, or "with intent to land the same." The President was authorized to cause any of the armed vessels of the United States "to cruise on any part of the coast of the United States, . . . where he may judge attempts will be made to violate the provisions of this act" and to direct the seizure of the offending vessels, and to seize "all ships or vessels of the United States, wheresoever found on the high seas." This provision was re-enacted in sections 5555 and 5557 of the *Revised Statutes* and *the Federal Penal Code of 1909.*[35]

[34] "An Act to prohibit the importation of slaves into . . . the United States," March 2, 1807. 2 *Stat. at Large,* p. 428, sec. 7.

[35] 35 *Stat. at Large,* Part I, p. 1140, secs. 258 and 260. A large number of New England whalers were employed in the slave trade. The following interesting report shows something of the necessity for this law:

The Navy Department, on July 16, 1817, in its instructions to the Commanding Officer of the United States brig *Saranac* stated that "The recent occupation of Amelia Island by an officer in the service of the Spanish revolutionists occasions just apprehensions that, from the vicinity to the coast of Georgia, attempts will be made to introduce slaves into the United States contrary to the existing laws, and further attempts at illicit trade in smuggling goods in violation of our revenue laws.

"You are hereby directed to detain and search every vessel, under whatever flag, which may enter the river St. Mary's or be found hovering upon the coast under suspicious circumstances, and seize every vessel freighted with slaves, or whose doubtful character and situation shall indicate an intention of smuggling.

"In the execution of these orders, you will take special care not to interrupt or detain any vessel sailing with regular papers, and of a national character, upon lawful voyages to or from a port or ports of the United States.

"The traffic in slaves is intended to be restrained, and in the performance of this duty you will exercise your sound judgment in regard

§ 44. Summary of Laws Passed between 1789 and 1920

To summarize, the laws passed by Congress between 1789 and 1920 were as follows:

1. By the Act of 1789, which was repealed in 1790, the master of every vessel, bound to the United States, was required to produce a manifest, when his vessel was boarded for that purpose.

2. The Acts of 1790, 1799, 1866, and certain sections of the *Revised Statutes* of 1878 required the masters of all vessels, foreign or domestic, when bound for the United States, to produce manifests of the cargoes when they had arrived within four leagues of the coast; the first two of these Acts and certain sections of the *Revised Statutes* forbade unlading by such vessels within the same distance.

3. The Act of 1791 forbade the unlading of spirits after their exportation, within four leagues of the coast.

4. By the Act of 1807, any "slaver" could be seized if found hovering on the coasts of the United States; and cruising was authorized on any part of the coast where violations of the Act were likely to be attempted.

Severe penalties were attached to the violation of these Acts.[36]

---

to all vessels you may visit." *American State Papers*, Class III (Finance, vol. II), vol. VI.

After the first quarter of the nineteenth century, smuggling in slaves was successfully coped with, and, in large measure, suppressed. In 1827, the United States schooner *Shark* gave chase to a French "slaver" off the coast of Little Bassa (St. Thomas), for a long time. It was said that "the slave trade is nearly extinct" on that part of the coast. *American State Papers*, Class VI (Naval Affairs, vol. III), p. 58.

For other references to this illicit trade in slaves and the smuggling of merchandise, see:

American State Papers, Class III (Finance, vol. III), p. 238; Ibid., Class I (Foreign Relations, vol. IV), pp. 133-4, and 134-44.

[36] By an Act of Congress of February 8, 1881, it was provided that ". . . no vessel used by any person or corporation, as common carriers, in the transaction of their business as such common carriers, shall be

§ 45. Instructions to Commanders of Revenue Cutters and Coast Guard Vessels, 1834-1916

The instructions to officers of the revenue service from year to year have been based upon the laws just discussed. Those of 1834 called attention to the fact that the general outline of the duties of the officers and men employed in the Revenue Cutter Service was contained in the Act of March 2, 1799, particularly in sections 98, 99, 100, and 101.[37]

The commander was ordered to "take care that a constant and regular watch be kept on board the Cutter, whether cruising or in port. . . ."[38]

No cutter was permitted to leave the ground assigned to it "except forced by stress of weather . . . or in the pursuit of vessels suspected of being engaged in violating the revenue laws; and which have either escaped from the limits of the Cutter's station, or have been discovered hovering about in the vicinity of her cruising ground. . . ."[39]

"It may be observed, generally, that it is the special duty of the officers of the cutters to guard the revenue laws from violation. It is for this purpose that they are made officers of the customs, and invested with extensive power. It is the indisputable duty of officers commanding Cutters, to board every vessel arriving from a foreign country, and being within four leagues of the coast, and bound to a port in the United States, carefully to search

---

subject to seizure or forfeiture by force of the provisions of title thirty-four of the *Revised Statutes* of the United States, unless it shall appear that the master or owner of such vessel, at the time of the alleged illegal act, was a consenting party or privy thereto."

21 *Stat. at Large*, c. 34, p. 322. See *U. S.* v. *The Walla Walla* (1891), 44 Fed. 796 (1891), and *The Saratoga* (1881), 9 Fed. 322.

[37] *Instructions to Officers in the United States Revenue Cutter Service*, Oct. 3, 1834, p. 1.

[38] Ibid., p. 5.

[39] Ibid., p. 9.

and examine her, to demand and certify the manifests (where she is required to have them), cause the hold to be fastened, and under circumstances of well-grounded suspicion, to place an officer on board, who will continue in charge until relieved on her arrival in port, unless previously relieved by an Inspector. It is their duty to seize all vessels and merchandise liable to seizure, under the revenue laws; and for this purpose they are authorized to enter any vessel in which they have good reason to suspect goods subject to duty are concealed, and to search for, and secure such goods. It being strictly forbidden, after the arrival of any vessel laden with goods, and bound to the United States, within the limits of any district thereof, to break bulk or put out any part of her cargo previously to entry, and permit obtained for that purpose, except in case of accident. . . . There being good reason to believe that many vessels, ostensibly employed in the fisheries and coasting trade, are engaged in the illicit introduction of foreign merchandise, the officers of the cutters are enjoined to keep a watchful eye on such vessels; and when they are discovered under suspicious circumstances, to examine them with the view to such further measures as may be found proper; and if probable cause appear to suspect them of being engaged in violating the revenue laws of the United States, to cause the hatches to be fastened down, and an officer to be put on board, who will continue in charge until relieved by an Inspector, or his arrival or report to the Collector." The officers were enjoined to examine the papers of coasting vessels and watch vigilantly "outward bound vessels to foreign ports, with the view to prevent the relanding of goods subject to drawback." [40]

Officers were enjoined to act with "vigilance and firm-

---

[40] The Act of 1791 forbade the unlading of exports within four leagues of the coast. P. 190, *supra*.

ness," since the performance of these duties was "so important in their operation to the revenue, on the one hand, and to the interest of commerce and navigation, on the other. . . ." They were further enjoined to make themselves acquainted with the laws, so that they would be able to use all legal and proper means to protect the revenue.[41]

The same instructions were issued almost verbatim in 1843.[42] It was noted that smuggling was being carried on by the same vessels mentioned in the instructions of 1834.

While the *Revised Regulations for the Government of the Revenue Marine* of 1871 do not mention specific distances in which vessels were to be examined or seized, the officers were enjoined to become acquainted with all the laws relating to the revenue.[43] They were "authorized to board any vessel which they may have good and sufficient reasons for believing has concealed goods which are subject to duty, and to search for and secure all such goods." It was stated that "it is strictly forbidden all vessels to break bulk or land any part of their cargoes previous to entry and a custom-house permit to land their goods obtained, except in cases of distress; . . . it therefore becomes the special duty of the commanding officers of revenue vessels to arrest all persons who attempt to violate the revenue laws in this respect." [44]

Officers were required to be "vigilant and firm in the performance of their duties, and to act at all times with a proper discretion, in protecting the revenue, by employing proper and legal means. . . ." [45]

The regulations for 1894, 1907, and 1916 pointed out

[41] *Instructions to Officers in the United States Revenue Cutter Service,* Oct. 3, 1834, pp. 9-10.

[42] *Rules and Regulations for the Government of the United States Revenue Marine,* Nov. 1, 1843, pp. XV and XVI.

[43] Ibid., p. 6.

[44] Ibid., p. 25.

[45] Ibid., p. 26.

the pertinent sections of the *Revised Statutes* which it was the duty of the officers to enforce as a protection to the revenue. Among these sections was section 2760, authorizing them to go on board all vessels bound for the United States upon their arrival within four leagues of the coast, in order to search them and to certify the manifests.[46]

§ 46. Court Decisions

The condemnation proceedings before 1922 were, for the most part, under section 50 of the Act of 1799, which subjected to forfeiture any goods, brought from any foreign place, which were unladen within the United States except "in open day," or at any time without a permit from the collector, as well as the vessel, if the goods unladen were of the value of $400.[47] The four-league statutes were frequently discussed by way of dicta in many early cases. In these discussions, no distinction was drawn between jurisdiction over domestic and foreign vessels. Three cases were before the Supreme Court of

[46] Art. VII, sec. 98 (1) of the regulations of 1894 mentioned secs. 2747, 2760, 2762, and 3059 of the *Revised Statutes*. Sec. 415 admonished the officers to acquaint themselves with the laws relating to their service. (Art. VII names 18 different services to be performed by the revenue vessels.)

The regulations of 1907 [Chap. II, sec. 10 (1)] add secs. 2758 and 5318 of the *Revised Statutes* to those named in the instructions of 1894. The regulations for the Coast Guard of 1916 (Chap. II, sec. 102) mention secs. 2747, 2758, 2761, 2762, 2773, 2764, 2765, 3059, 3061, 3067, and 3068 of the *Revised Statutes*. Sec. 2760 is omitted. The author is advised, however, that it was omitted through error, and that it was followed by the Coast Guard until 1922, when a new law came into force.

The regulations for 1907 (p. 12), and 1916 (Chap. II, sec. 101) declared that the President may direct any vessel of the Coast Guard "to perform any duty or make any cruise which, in his judgment, may be necessary for the public service."

[47] For cases of seizures of vessels in port for unlading without a permit, or for having on board goods not manifested, see: *134901 ft. of lbr., Fed. Case* No. 10,523 (1858); Fed. Cases Nos. 13,355, 11,229 (1859), 4,633 (1858), 15,785 (1872).

the United States in the early years of the nineteenth century, in which the revenue laws were discussed by Chief Justice Marshall with great clarity and forcibleness of language. While his remarks are *obiter dicta,* they reflect rather decided views of the Chief Justice and the universal view of his time; and since they have doubtless influenced the opinions of writers and the decisions of many courts, if not legislation, they should not be overlooked in a discussion of this question. If there has been a tendency to place too much stress upon them, it is for the reasons, perhaps, that they are from such a great jurist, and that there is a dearth of judicial authority squarely in point until many years later.

(1) *Church v. Hubbart*

Church v. *Hubbart* is the first of these cases.[48] It was an action on an insurance policy written on a vessel, the *Aurora,* which excepted from its terms losses arising from "illicit trade with the Portuguese." The vessel was seized by Portuguese authorities four or five leagues off the Brazilian coast for alleged illicit trade with Portuguese possessions. It was contended by the insured that the underwriter should be held to respond under the policy for a seizure of the ship so far from shore while merely attempting to violate the Portuguese trade laws, for such a seizure was unlawful and that the conduct of the vessel at the point of seizure could not be in violation of Portuguese law. It was held, however, that the underwriter was relieved from all liability under the policy. The language of the Chief Justice is very strong. "The authority of a nation within its own territory," he says, "is absolute and exclusive. The seizure of a vessel within the range of its cannon by a foreign force is an invasion of that territory, and is a hostile act which it is its duty

[48] (1804) 2 Cranch 187.

to repel. But its power to secure itself from injury may certainly be exercised beyond the limits of its territory. Upon this principle the right of a belligerent to search a neutral vessel on the high seas for contraband of war is universally admitted, because the belligerent has a right to prevent the injury done to himself by the assistance intended for his enemy: so too a nation has a right to prohibit any commerce with its colonies. Any attempt to violate the laws made to protect this right, is an injury to itself which it may prevent, and it has a right to use the means necessary for its prevention. These means do not appear to be limited within any certain marked boundaries, which remain the same at all times and in all situations. If they are such as unnecessarily to vex or harass foreign lawful commerce, foreign nations will resist their exercise. If they are such as are reasonable and necessary to secure their laws from violation, they will be submitted to.

"In different seas, and on different coasts, a wider or more contracted range, in which to exercise the vigilance of the government, will be assented to. Thus in the Channel, where a very great part of the commerce to and from all the north of Europe, passes through a very narrow sea, the seizure of vessels on suspicion of attempting an illicit trade, must necessarily be restricted to very narrow limits; but on the coast of South America, seldom frequented by vessels but for the purpose of illicit trade, the vigilance of the government may be extended somewhat further; and foreign nations submit to such regulations as are reasonable in themselves, and are really necessary to secure that monopoly of colonial commerce, which is claimed by all nations holding distant possessions.

"If this right be extended too far, the exercise of it will be resisted. It has occasioned long and frequent contests, which have sometimes ended in open war. The English, it will be recollected, complained of the right claimed by Spain to search their vessels on the high seas, which was carried so far that the *guarda costas* of that nation seized vessels not. in the neighborhood of their coasts. This practice was the subject of long and fruitless negotiations, and at length of open war. The right of the Spaniards was supposed to be exercised unreasonably and vexatiously, but it never was contended that it could only be exercised within the range of the cannon from their batteries. *Indeed, the right given to our own revenue cutters, to visit vessels four leagues from our coast, is a declaration that in the opinion of the American government, no such principle as that contended for has a real existence.*" [49]   (Italics the author's.)

(2) *Rose* v. *Himely*

The second of these cases is *Rose* v. *Himely*.[50] In this case, an American vessel was seized ten leagues out for a breach of a French municipal law (*arrete*) promulgated for Santo Domingo. It was later condemned by a French Court in Santo Domingo *while lying in South Carolinian waters*, after it had been sold. Some of the cargo was sold to Himely, shipped to Charleston, South Carolina, and there libelled by the original owner in this suit. The court, speaking again through Chief Justice Marshall, held that the French decree of sale was void, because: (1) the vessel was not within the jurisdiction of the French court; (2) the *arrete*, under which the seizure was made, provided for seizure for only two leagues from the shore, while the seizure was made over ten leagues from the shore; and (3) the seizure of a vessel not belonging

---

[49] See, also, *Cuculla* v. *La. Ins. Co.* (1827), 5 Martin, N. S. (La.), 464; and *The Alexander* (1894), 60 Fed. 914.

[50] (1808) 4 Cranch 241.

to a subject, made on the high seas, for the breach of a municipal regulation, is an act which the sovereign cannot authorize. "A power to seize for the infraction of a law . . . must be exercised . . . within those limits which circumscribe the sovereign power." The Court does not define the "limits which circumscribe the sovereign power." The language quoted is dictum, for the decision rests upon the well recognized principle of law that an admiralty or prize court may not proceed against a vessel which is not within its jurisdiction, because it has no power over the *res*. Justices Livingstone, Cushington, and Chase concurred in the "result," because of that very principle; and one Justice dissented on the ground that a state may seize a vessel on the high seas for breach of its municipal law in its territory, because on the high seas, "rights of sovereignty are concurrent." Justices Livingstone, Cushington, and Chase expressed no opinion on this point.[51]

(3) *Hudson* v. *Guestier*

In the third case, *Hudson* v. *Guestier*,[52] a vessel had been seized six leagues from the shore for violating a municipal law of France prohibiting trading with colonies in revolt. Her cargo, which was at Baracoa, a Spanish port, had been condemned by a French tribunal at Gaudaloupe and sold to the defendant, against whom this action of trover was brought. It was held that this sale was valid. The court refused to hold that the condem-

---

[51] Judge John Bassett Moore considers that this case represents a change of view by Chief Justice Marshall from that expressed in *Church* v. *Hubbart,* and that it announced "the wise and salutary exemption of ships from visitation and search on the high seas in time of peace." Moore, *Digest of International Law,* vol. VII, p. 312. But the case went off on a point of procedure. Even if this decision had the effect that Judge Moore says that it had, the next case that went to the Supreme Court of the United States, *Hudson* v. *Guestier,* contains equally strong dictum in accord with *Church* v. *Hubbart.*

[52] (1810) 6 Cranch 281.

nation of the vessel and cargo by a French tribunal while they were in the port of another nation, had failed to pass the title, but it rested its decision upon the question of whether it made any difference if "the vessel were taken on the high seas, or more than two leagues from the coast." Mr. Justice Livingstone, in delivering the opinion of the court, said that if the *res* can be proceeded against when not in the possession or under the control of the court, it was not material whether the vessel was captured beyond or within the jurisdictional limits of France. He added, "By a seizure on the high seas, she [France] interfered with the jurisdiction of no other nation, the authority of each being there concurrent." Chief Justice Marshall said, ". . . the principle of that case (*Rose* v. *Himely*) is now overruled."

These three cases have been variously interpreted.[53] It is sufficient to observe here that in view of the language in *Church* v. *Hubbart* and in *Hudson* v. *Guestier*, the four-league statutes would, doubtless, have been enforced against any foreign vessel seized anywhere within that distance from the shore.

(4) *The Betsey*

In 1818, in the case of *The Betsey*,[54] Judge Story, in discussing section 27 of the Act of 1799, forbidding an unlading within four leagues of the coast, said:

"And the policy of the act applies equally to all vessels; and indeed more strongly to foreign vessels; since

[53] For a discussion of these cases, see 15 *Fur Seal Arbitration Proceedings* (1893), pp. 128-131, *William* v. *Armroyd* (1813), 7 Cranch 423; and Dickinson, Edwin D., "Jurisdiction at the Maritime Frontier," 40 *Harvard Law Rev.*, p. 4, et seq.

See *The Antelope* (1825), 10 Wheaton (U. S. Sup. Ct.) 66, in which a Spanish slaving vessel was seized and proceeded against under the Act of 1807 (p. 190, *supra*) while "hovering near the coast of the United States," attempting to smuggle slaves ashore.

[54] Fed. Case No. 1365; 1 Mason, 354 (C. C. D. Mass.).

frauds committed by them in evasion of the revenue laws are less easily detected, than like frauds are under the regulations applicable to American vessels."

In this case, the vessel, whose nationality is not given, was condemned and forfeited for taking in cargo from a Spanish steamer within four leagues of the coast, in order to introduce the same into the United States without payment of duties. It was forfeitable under section 28 of the Act, only if the foreign vessel had violated section 27. The decision is a necessary holding, therefore, that section 27 was applicable to the act of unlading by a foreign vessel within four leagues of the coast.[55]

[55] In *The Hunter* (1806), Fed. Case No. 15,428, Pet. C. C. 10 (C. C. D. N. J., Washington Cir. Judge), the libel alleged that the *Hunter,* a foreign vessel bound for the United States, "after her arrival within the limits of the United States and before she had gone to the proper place for the discharge of her cargo" unloaded spirits without a permit. It was held that sec. 27 applied, while sec. 50 applied to an unlading after the vessel's arrival in port. See, also, *United States* v. *Brant* (1806), Fed. Case No. 14,637 (C. C. D. N. J.).

In *The Active* (1866), Fed. Case No. 33, Deady, 165 (D. C. D. Oregon, Deady, Dist. Judge), the vessel unladed "within the limits of the collection district of Oregon, on the Columbia river, below the port of Astoria" . . . "within the limits of the United States." The court followed *The Hunter,* and held that sec. 27 applied.

In *U. S.* v. *The Virgin* (1806), Fed. Case No. 16,625 (1 Pet. C. C. 7), which was a proceeding under sec. 28 to condemn the *Virgin,* the vessel into which the *Hunter* unladed, it was held that the libel must allege that the unlading took place within four leagues of the coast, for the court said that, "If the rum was taken out before the arrival of the *Hunter,* [a foreign vessel] within four leagues of the coast, the act is not prohibited by law."

In *The Industry* (1812), Fed. Case No. 7028, 1 Gallison, 114 (C. C. D. Mass., Story, Cir. Judge), an information was filed against a foreign vessel for unlading at the port of Edgartown during the night without a permit. It was held that she was forfeitable under sec. 50 of the Act of 1799. The court said that sec. 27 did not reach a case where the illegal unlading took place after the vessel's arrival at her intended port of discharge, but that it clearly applied to a vessel which had not reached such port, but had arrived within the limits of the districts of the United States or within four leagues of the coast. Sec. 50, the court said, applied to any unlading at any port in the United States, whether or not it was the port of the vessel's ultimate discharge and destination. See, also, *Clark* v. *Protection Ins. Co.* (1840), Fed. Case No. 2832, 1 Story, 109 (C. C. D. Mass., Story, Cir. Judge), and *The Harmony* (1812), Fed. Case No. 6081, 1 Gallison, 123.

(5) *The Coquitlam*

Not every unlading within four leagues of the coast constitutes an offense against sections 27 and 28, or the corresponding sections 2867 and 2868 of the *Revised Statutes*. The cargo unladed within that distance must be destined to the United States, and there must be an intention to defraud the United States of customs duties. In *The Coquitlam*,[56] a Canadian vessel met some Canadian fishing vessels at Tonki Bay, to which they had gone from their fishing grounds, to arrange to unload their catch of seal skins and take on supplies from the *Coquitlam*. They went out to a point between three and seven miles from the shore, where the exchange was made and where the masters thought an unlading would not be a violation of the laws of the United States. After the exchange at this point, the fishing vessels returned to their fishing grounds. The *Coquitlam*, the supply vessel, had no intention of introducing the skins received from the fishing vessels into the United States. That vessel was arrested "at or near Port Etches," less than one-half a mile from land.[57]

The Circuit Court of Appeals, in reversing the District Court, held that this unlading was not in violation of sections 2867 and 2868, and that, therefore, the cargo received from the fishing vessels and the receiving vessel, the *Coquitlam*, were not forfeitable, since the fishing vessels were not bound to the United States and had not arrived in a collection district as contemplated by section 2867; for under that section, the unlading vessel must be bound to the United States for the purpose of her voyage, and her cargo must be a cargo which is destined to the United States and to be there discharged, since

[56] (1893) 57 Fed. 706 (D. C. D. Alaska); (1896) 77 Fed. 744 (C. C. A.).

[57] This fact appears from the *British Memorial*, vol. II, p. 36, filed with the arbitral tribunal to which this case was later submitted. See p. 270, *infra*.

the penalty is confined to an unlading before the vessel has come to the proper place for the discharge of her cargo. The court said that "it is not every casual arrival of a vessel within the waters of the United States, and the unlading of a portion of her cargo within such waters, therefore, that comes within the prohibition of the statute." The District Court had held that when a vessel comes within four leagues of the shore and makes an unlading, it has "arrived," and should be treated as bound to the United States within the meaning of sections 2867 and 2868.

The question of the jurisdiction of the United States to make arrests of foreign vessels for violations of revenue laws anywhere within four leagues of the coast was not raised by counsel in the trial or appellate court; but the trial judge in his opinion commented upon the Act of 9 Geo. II, c. 35, and the American Act of 1799, and added that judicial authority in England and the United States had declared that such laws were consistent with the laws and usage of nations, citing *Church* v. *Hubbart*.[58]

[58] It was held also that secs. 2806, 2807, and 2809 of the *Revised Statutes,* requiring a manifest for all goods brought into the United States and forfeiting all goods belonging to the officers and crew for which there was no manifest were not violated, for it was not alleged that such goods belonged to the officers and crew. The District Court had held that the cargo was forfeitable under these sections. Sec. 2806 reads:

"Section 2806. No merchandise shall be brought into the United States, from any foreign port, in any vessel unless the Master has on board manifests in writing of the cargo, signed by such Master."

There was no attempt to enforce the fine against the Master provided in sec. 2809. See p. 186, note (24), for this section.

It was also held that the *Coquitlam* was not forfeitable under sec. 3109, which contemplates an arrival for the purpose of receiving or discharging and of proceeding further inland. That section reads:

"The Master of any foreign vessel, laden or in ballast, arriving in the waters of the United States from any foreign territory, adjacent to the northern, northeastern, or northwestern frontiers of the United States, shall report at the office of any collector or deputy collector of the customs, which shall be nearest to the point at which such vessel may enter such waters; and such vessel shall not proceed farther inland,

The case of *The Coquitlam* was, no doubt, properly decided. The laws under which her forfeiture was sought are designed to intercept smuggling attempted by means of unlading or running goods or by bringing into port concealed or unmanifested cargoes. The *Coquitlam* was not engaged in an attempt to smuggle. There was no intention to introduce her cargo into the United States, much less to smuggle it. The waters near the coast of the United States were simply used as a convenient rendezvous for an innocent exchange of cargoes. The United States Government admitted its liability after the case was dismissed by the Circuit Court of Appeals, and the matter was submitted to the British-American Claims Commission for an assessment of damages.[59]

It was held in *The Javirena*[60] that a Spanish vessel, which had come within the limits of a collection district to repair her sails, but which was not bound for a port and which had on board no goods destined for a port, had not violated section 2773 of the *Revised Statutes*, which provide that any vessel having arrived within such limits must make report and entry before her departure.

Before 1920, the United States had been troubled very little with the foreign hovering vessel or the foreign vessel engaged solely in smuggling by running its goods ashore under cover of night upon an unguarded coast. The illicit trade, for the most part, had been carried on from foreign and domestic merchant vessels in port, a

---

either to unlade or take in cargo, without a special permit from such collector or deputy collector, issued under and in accordance with such general or special regulations as the Secretary of the Treasury may in his discretion, from time to time, prescribe. For any violation of this section such vessel shall be seized and forfeited."

In *The C. G. White* (1894), 64 Fed. 579 (C. C. A. 9th Cir.), a vessel was condemned under secs. 3088 and 2867 for unlading skins into another vessel at Caton Harbor, Alaska.

[59] This arbitration will be considered later. See p. 270, *infra*.

[60] (1895) 67 Fed. 152 (C. C. A. 5th Cir., Pardee, Cir. Judge).

part of whose cargoes was legitimate and manifested, or from small American vessels that cruised near the coast, seeking an opportunity to run their cargoes ashore.[61] For this reason, there are few cases against foreign vessels for violations of the four-league statutes before that year.[62]

[61] P. 178, *infra.*
[62] See pp. 217 and 234, *infra,* for further decisions.

CHAPTER II

FROM 1920 TO 1928

§ 47. Increase in Smuggling from Sea after 1920

The "Rum Fleet"

After the enactment of the American prohibition law in 1919, prohibiting the importation into the United States and the sale therein of intoxicating liquors, a new condition of affairs arose. Liquors were hard to obtain. Fabulous prices were offered, so that large profits loomed in sight for the smuggler. As a result, foreign vessels from many countries set sail for the waters off the coasts of the United States. In order to get their liquors ashore, the "rum-runners" had to hover off the coast and run their cargoes as opportunity afforded, or send them ashore by means of their own small boats or by boats sent out from the shore. This practice resulted in the seizure of many foreign vessels within four leagues of the coast, and their forfeiture by the Federal Courts for violations of the four-league statutes considered in the previous chapter.

The conditions that existed off the American coast reminds one of those described in the reports to the House of Commons in 1783,[1] when the vessels laden with tea from India anchored in the English Channel, where the scenes of their activities, it was said, resembled public fairs. These rum vessels carried liquors from all parts of the world—the West Indies, Holland, England, Scot-

---

[1] See p. 53, *supra*.

land, Spain, Portugal, Panama, Chile, Germany, and other countries. Other wares, such as drugs, rugs, silks, laces, furs, gloves, shoes, and aliens were eventually added to their cargoes. They constituted another menace: according to *The Times* (London), of January 17, 1923, the masters of vessels entering New York harbor complained that this fleet, anchored off the shore without lights, was an obstruction to navigation and that collisions had been narrowly averted and time lost. The crews of some of these vessels turned pirate, and accounts were received of the most reckless plundering and robbery near the American coast.[2] According to the *Annual Report of The Attorney General* of the United States of December 7, 1922,[3] since the 18th Amendment of the Constitution, and Title II of the National Prohibition Act became effective January 16, 1920, rum-running vessels of American and foreign registry, carrying liquor from foreign ports to our shores, have "swarmed along our seaboards, smuggling liquors into the United States in violation of our laws." It was said that eighteen vessels of foreign registry and eleven of American registry with their liquor cargoes had been seized; that ten of the foreign vessels were found transporting and smuggling liquors within "the 3-mile limit of our shores," while the other eight were seized while hovering off the shores "beyond the 3-mile limit, but within the 4-league zone of our shore line and unlading their cargoes to other boats to be brought ashore in violation of the hovering acts." His report of December 4, 1923,[4] shows that the conditions were not improved. It states that "The liquor smuggling business is the most gigantic criminal problem the United States has ever faced on the high seas." The

[2] *Parliamentary Debates* (Hansard), 1926, vol. 194, col. 1184; *The Times* (London), February 10, April 17, and March 4, 1923.

[3] P. 84, et seq.

[4] P. 88, et seq.

amount of liquor smuggled into the United States, the report continues, cannot be approximated. From Nassau, liquors valued at $7,059,294 were shipped to the United States during the calendar year ending December 31, 1922, and a part of the year 1923. The American Consul General at London reported shipments of 143,660 gallons of liquors, 428 barrels of beer, and 27 gallons of wines, from Glasgow from March 3, 1923, to April 24, 1927.

The Attorney General gave an opinion at the request of the Treasury on November 1, 1920,[5] to the effect that under the decision of *St. Clair v. U. S.*[6] and other cases, American ships were "American territory" and that they could not transport liquors on the high seas, and that American citizens could not possess them on such vessels except in violation of the law. This ruling caused some of the American owners to obtain from the United States Shipping Board permits to transfer their vessels to foreign registry,[7] and thereafter to employ their vessels in this trade.[8] This scheme was circumvented by the Shipping Board's inserting in the permits and bills of sale "a warrant clause running with the title to the vessel that the purchaser, his successors and assigns, shall not use said vessel to import into or export from the United States beverage liquors or contraband merchandise, and in case of breach of said warranty clause," the vessel was to be forfeited to the United States. The Attorney General reported that upon the sale of some American vessels for foreign registry, a diplomatic controversy arose over this "warrant clause," but the American Government insisted upon its right to insert the clause, and that its insertion

[5] 32 *Opins. Atty. Gen.,* p. 332.

[6] (1894) 154 U. S. 134.

[7] 41 *Stat. at Large,* pp. 997, 1005, et seq.

[8] This was done in order to invoke the protection of the foreign governments whose flags they flew, when taken on the high seas.

was believed to have become an "established American policy." [9]

The *Annual Report of the Attorney General* of December 5, 1924,[10] notes that seizures of vessels were being made in increasing number. Mr. Hudson stated in the House of Representatives on December 30, 1924, that the work of the Coast Guard had become enormous, as the "smuggling and piracy" then existing on the coast made the stories of the nineteenth century in the Carribean Sea and the Gulf of Mexico "fade into insignificance." Great fleets of vessels carrying reckless and lawless crews, he said, stood off the shore at various points in the Atlantic and Pacific—"a grave menace to the peace, health, and prosperity of our country." [11]

The questions of appropriations and the construction of additional vessels to be employed in combatting this evil case constantly before Congress.[12] *The Annual Report of the Coast Guard* for 1924 [13] states that the Secretary of the Treasury, in his report for the fiscal year ended June 30, 1923, recommended a substantial increase in the

[9] According to *The Times* (London) of May 4, 1923, the Canadian authorities refused to register American vessels sold subject to this condition. This was said to be a "projection of sovereignty" and was without parallel.

[10] P. 82.

[11] *Congressional Record*, 68th Congress, 2d sess., Part I, p. 1040.

[12] Ibid., 69th Congress, 1st sess., Part III, p. 3305.
On January 3, 1924, a joint resolution was introduced into the House directing the President to employ the Army and Navy, the militia of several states, and the "resources of the government in suppressing all smuggling into the United States of intoxicating liquors, narcotics, and aliens, and to suppress the insubordinate rebellion now being waged by those in authority in several states and large cities of the United States against the fundamental laws of the Republic, . . ." and to prohibit the possession of or transportation into the United States by any foreign ambassador and other representatives, any intoxicating liquors for beverage purposes, in violation of the 18th Amendment of the Constitution. H. J. Res. 119, *Congressional Record,* 68th Congress, 1st sess., Part I, p. 570. See, also, ibid., Part II, p. 1181, for the introduction of a bill into the Senate for the same purpose.

[13] Pp. 27-28.

appropriation for the Coast Guard for the purpose of combatting the smuggling of liquor into the United States, and that on February 1, 1924, the President transmitted to Congress estimates of appropriations for the Treasury Department for the fiscal year, amounting to $13,853,989, for increasing the equipment and personnel of the Coast Guard. This sum, it was said, would be used in the equipment of twenty torpedo boat destroyers, and two mine sweepers, and other suitable types of vessels, and the construction of two hundred and twenty-three "Cabin Cruiser" type motorboats and one hundred smaller motorboats.[14]

This report states that "very satisfactory results" in regard to the law enforcement program had been attained. Comment is made upon the inadequacy of the equipment then in use for "overtaking the fast craft employed in smuggling operations," and upon the enormous task that had been set the Coast Guard to prevent the smuggling of liquor along the coasts.

The *Annual Report of the Attorney General* of December 9, 1925,[15] reports the seizures of foreign vessels during the fiscal year 1924-25 as follows:

British	28
French	4
Honduran	2
Norwegian	2
Italian	1
Cuban	1
Costa Rican	1

[14] As a further means of combatting this evil, Congress passed an Act approved March 3, 1925, providing that upon application by the Treasury, any vessel or vehicle summarily forfeited to the United States for violation of the customs laws was to be taken and used for the enforcement of the customs laws or the National Prohibition Act. Procedure for reporting forfeitures was outlined. *Treasury Decisions,* 1925, vol. 47, p. 331, No. 40,760, and ibid., p. 516, No. 40,855.

[15] Pp. 49-50. See, also, *Parliamentary Debates* (Hansard), 1923, vol. 164, col. 2212.

a total of 39. Ten of these vessels had been forfeited by the courts, six released, four cases were on appeal, and sixteen were pending in the trial courts. Seven hundred and fifty-three American vessels had been seized during the same period.[16] The smuggling operations, it was said, had been conducted for the most part from Halifax, Nova Scotia; Nassau, Bahama Islands; Havana, Cuba; and Vancouver, British Columbia. The liquor was brought from these places by vessels flying foreign flags, which proceeded to a place in close proximity to the shore of the United States, but outside territorial waters, where the cargoes were transferred into smaller boats for illegal introduction into the United States. The foreign vessel seldom came within the territorial jurisdiction, and the actual smuggling over the United States line was done by American vessels and American citizens. During the year and for a reasonable time prior thereto, over three hundred foreign vessels, the large majority of which were British, had been engaged, from time to time, in the liquor-smuggling trade.[17]

[16] Ibid., p. 48.

[17] For greater details as to the methods of the smugglers and the extent of the trade on various parts of the coast from time to time, see *The Times* (London), of:

November 26, 1923, reporting rumors of the presence of one hundred rum vessels anchored off the coast of New Jersey;

January 13, 1923, reporting that twenty-three vessels were off the coast of New York;

March 5, 1923; December 14, 1923; June 11, 1923, reporting the presence of fifteen ships off the coast of New Jersey between Atlantic City and Atlantic Islands, and ten off Montauk Point, Long Island, and the employment of five hundred motor boats and other small craft in carrying their cargoes to the shore;

October 6, 1924, reporting the capture of the British trawler *Fred B,* which revealed a conspiracy of American, British, and Canadian bootleggers to smuggle $1,000,000 worth of liquar into the United States.

December 17, 1924, stating that $120,000,000 worth of liquor had been sent into California, Washington, and Oregon from British Columbia during the year, and that a fleet of vessels, ranging from 30-foot motor launches to schooners from two to three hundred tons, were plying regularly out of Vancouver, ostensibly headed for South American

Some of these vessels operated from the British West Indies, Cuba, and Canada, while others received their cargoes directly from European countries, while anchored at "rum row." They were often armed; and some of them resisted arrest. Some were manned, in part, by foreign crews. The owner of the cargo or his representative was usually on board directing the vessel's movements,[18] so that there was nearly always at least one American on board. The old practice of the smugglers of carrying two clearances was again adopted, so that the master could produce the one calling for a foreign port if boarded and examined on the high seas by customs officers, while if he succeeded in unlading his illicit cargo without detection, he could go into the American port named in the other clearance for a return cargo.[19] The liquors were in "triangular-shaped packages," so that they could be easily unloaded and a large quantity carried by small craft.[20]

---

ports; these vessels were lying off twelve miles from shore, waiting to deliver their cargoes to vessels from the shore; some of them carried cargoes valued at $3,000,000;

February 9, 1925, estimating that five million gallons had been smuggled into the United States in 1924, to the loss of the revenue of $87,150,000;

August 14, 1924, reporting that the new "dry fleet" consisted of over three hundred craft, manned by about two thousand prohibition enforcement officers;

July 1, 1925, reporting the organization in the Bahamas of a $100,000 corporation for smuggling liquors into the United States.

[18] These facts appear from the court decisions, diplomatic correspondence, and departmental reports. See also, *The Times* (London), April 3, 1922, Jan. 30, March 5, and November 27, 1923.

[19] According to *The Times* (London), of December 20, 1923, the Canadian Department of Marine and Fisheries had received a protest from the Venezuelan Consul in Montreal against these vessels being given clearance papers at Niagara for Venezuela.

[20] Some of these practices are graphically depicted in a note by the American Secretary of State, Mr. Charles Evans Hughes, to the British Ambassador on June 26, 1922, as follows:

"I have the honor to lay before you certain important considerations with respect to a possible coöperation on the part of British and Ameri-

The United States had, thus, a reproduction, on an even larger scale, of the conditions against which Eng-

---

can authorities with regard to the smuggling of liquor. The authorities of the United States charged with the duty of enforcing the law of this country with respect to this matter are confronted by serious difficulties which they feel might be effectively met with the assistance of British authorities in British territories, which it appears are made bases of operations in flagrant violation of constitutional and statutory provisions of the United States. It is understood that the importation of intoxicating liquors into the Canadian provinces of Nova Scotia, Manitoba, Saskatchewan and Alberta, is also prohibited by law. . . ."

"It has been found that many of the ships engaged in the illegal smuggling of liquor into the United States are registered under the British flag and that large quantities of liquor are carried by such vessels from the Bahama Islands and from Bermuda. It appears that, in order to evade the customs officers and prohibition agents of the United States, the persons engaged in this illicit traffic of smuggling liquor into the United States from the Bahama Islands have adopted the practice of packing the liquor so that it can be easily taken ashore in the United States. Liquor is placed in triangular-shaped packages consisting of six bottles carefully sewed in burlap, so that it can very easily be unloaded, and even a small ship can carry a very large consignment in a comparatively small hold space. Liquor is carried on both large and small ships; schooners carry cargoes out to sea from Nassau and unload them off the coast of the United States, and smaller boats carry their cargoes to Bimini and Gun Key, and from these places it is transported to West Palm Beach, Daytona, and Fort Lauterdale. A list of vessels said to be plying between the United States and the Bahamas is herewith enclosed.

"This Department's attention has been drawn to the ease with which it seems vessels of American registry are transferred to British registry for the purpose of preventing the authorities of the United States from taking the necessary steps to thwart these smuggling operations. It is understood that British laws require that vessels to be entitled to British registry must be owned by British subjects. Apparently reliable information indicates that American citizens of questionable reputation who are known to be engaged in the smuggling business have succeeded in obtaining British registry at the Bahama Islands for a large number of American vessels by means of the execution of paper transfers purporting to convey title to vessels to British subjects in the Bahamas, although the actual interest in the vessels continues to vest in American citizens.

"Reference may be made in this connection to the fact that, under the laws of the United States relating to the transfer of registry, it is necessary for the owner of an American vessel to obtain a certificate from the United States Shipping Board showing that the vessel has first been tendered to the Board before the privilege of transferring it to a foreign register can be obtained. It would be of great assistance to this Government in combating the illicit traffic in liquors if authori-

land battled for many years, aided by legislation extending jurisdiction over foreign vessels from two to one

---

ties at Bermuda and in the Bahama Islands should refuse the privilege of registry to American vessels unless a certificate from the United States Shipping Board is produced showing that the vessel has first been tendered to it. It is understood that for some time British laws have imposed restrictions necessitating some form of acquiescence of British authorities to the transfer of registry. It would seem that laws of this character cannot well be effectively administered unless the authorities of one nation are disposed to take cognizance of the legislation of another nation.

"There is information before the Department indicating that the authorities at the Bahama Islands have in many cases issued two sets of clearance papers to ships which have taken on board cargoes of liquor. It is said that persons engaged in this traffic have openly made the statement that they have no trouble in obtaining from the Bahamas' customs officials one set of clearance papers for a cargo of liquor declared to be destined for Halifax, Tampico or St. Pierre, and other clearance papers issued 'in ballast' for an American port. This procedure is adopted by the liquor smugglers so that the ship may come within unloading distance of American shores, and if caught with a cargo of liquor on board the master can exhibit the clearance to Mexico or Canada; if the ship has succeeded in unloading the cargo on the shore without being captured, it proceeds into an American port with the second clearance papers.

"In this connection I beg to quote for your information three paragraphs from an affidavit executed by a federal prohibition agent of this Government with respect to the proposal declared to have been made to him by Mr. M. Cole, who signs clearance papers for the Comptroller of Customs for the British Government at Nassau, Bahamas, concerning the issuance of two sets of clearance papers for liquor ships:

"That deponent asked Mr. Cole how the liquor runners arranged their clearance papers and if it was possible to get an extra set of clearance papers. Mr. Cole said, 'Just a minute' and then went to the other side of the room and motioned deponent to come over which deponent did. Mr. Cole then stated substantially as follows:

"That 'there are a number of ways to handle it but the best and simplest way we find is, First to give you clearance papers with your liquor, then in an hour or so come back and state that you had discharged your cargo of liquor on the high seas and then we will give you another set of papers for "in ballast" for any American port.' Mr. Cole explained that the first set of papers referred to would be for a Foreign port and that if you were searched they could not touch you and that after you had discharged your cargo of liquor you could enter the American Port with your papers showing 'in ballast.'

"Deponent states further that Mr. Cole did not say that there would be any money required outside the regular fees but intimated that he and the boys expected to be taken care of. . . ."
Press release, Feb. 16, 1927.

hundred leagues seaward. It is doubtful if the situation finds a parallel in the history of smuggling. Smuggling vessels of all types, sizes, and nationalities anchored almost within sight of the shore, waiting for favorable opportunities to sell their wares to all who should visit them, or to run them ashore at night or at any time that it seemed safe to do so. This fleet shifted from one part of the coast to another. Public sentiment in America ran high. The Government began a vigorous campaign to clear the front door of the nation of this traffic, even as England has always done when she has been confronted with similar conditions, though the jurisdiction in the marginal seas exercised by the United States for that purpose has never been anything like as extended as that exercised by the English Government.

§ 48. Seizure and Forfeiture of the Rum Vessels under the Four-League Statutes and the National Prohibition Act

When the "rum fleet" appeared off the coast, and seizures began under the four-league statutes, four principal types of cases came before the Federal Courts:

1. The unlading vessel stands within four leagues of the coast, but beyond one league, and by means of her own small boats and crew, assists in getting her cargo into port or within one league of the shore.

2. The unlading vessel comes within four leagues of the coast, but remains beyond one league, and by pre-arrangement, sends her wares ashore by small boats not her own, that come out from the shore.[21]

3. The vessel stands within four leagues of the coast without a manifest calling for an American port.[22]

4. The unlading vessel comes within four leagues of

[21] P. 222, *infra.*
[22] Pp. 222 and 226, *infra.*

the coast, but remains beyond one league, and sells her wares to vessels that visit her.

(1) *The Grace and Ruby*

The first few cases arose under those sections of the *Revised Statutes* already considered and the National Prohibition Act. The first type is represented by the case of *The Grace and Ruby*.[23] A British schooner, the *Grace and Ruby*, carrying one Sullivan, the American owner of a part of the cargo, sailed from the British West Indies with a St. John, New Brunswick, clearance. She moved to a point about six miles off Gloucester, where Sullivan was set ashore. She remained always more than three miles from the shore. While ten miles out, Sullivan returned in a motorboat to carry supplies to the *Grace and Ruby* and to take some of her liquors ashore. Three members of the crew of the *Grace and Ruby* returned with Sullivan in the motorboat, and one of her dories was towed along to be used in landing the liquor or to enable the three members of the crew to get back to their ship. By this means, some of the cargo was carried ashore at night.

The *Grace and Ruby* was seized four miles from land with the rest of the liquor cargo on board, where she was hovering for the purpose of delivering it.[24] She was carried to Boston, the present libels filed, and a warrant for her arrest issued. Her forfeiture was asked under sections 2872 and 2874 of the *Revised Statutes* and the National Prohibition Act.[25] The above facts were stipu-

[23] (1922) 283 Fed. 475 (D. C. D. Mass., Morton, Dist. Judge).

[24] According to *The Times* (London), of March 16, 1922, this vessel was taken after several hours' chase, but this does not appear from the official report of the case.

[25] Secs. 2872, 2873, and 2874 read:

Sec. 2872. Except as authorized by the preceding section, no merchandise brought in any vessel from any foreign port shall be unladen or delivered from such vessel within the United States but in open

lated, and the libels were heard upon exceptions reserving solely the question of jurisdiction. It was held that the facts constituted an unlawful unlading at night within the territorial limits of the United States in violation of sections 2872 and 2874. Judge Morton said: "The act of

day—that is to say, between the rising and the setting of the sun—except by special license from the collector of the port, and naval officer of the same, where there is one, for that purpose, nor at any time without a permit from the collector, and naval officer, if any, for such unlading or delivery.

Sec. 2873. If any merchandise shall be unladen or delivered from any vessel, contrary to the preceding section, the master of such vessel, and every other person who shall knowingly be concerned, or aiding therein, or in removing, storing, or otherwise securing such merchandise, shall each be liable to a penalty of four hundred dollars for each offense, and shall be disabled from holding any office of trust or profit under the United States, for a term not exceeding seven years; and the collector of the district shall advertise the name of such person in a newspaper printed in the State in which he resides, within twenty days after each respective conviction.

Sec. 2874. All merchandise, so unladen or delivered contrary to the provisions of section twenty-eight-hundred-and-seventy-two, shall become forfeited, and may be seized by any of the officers of the customs; and where the value thereof, according to the highest market price of the same, at the port or district where landed, shall amount to four hundred dollars, the vessel, tackle, apparel, and furniture shall be subject to like forfeiture and seizure.

The pertinent provisions of the National Prohibition Act (41 *Stat. at Large,* Part I, p. 308) read:

Title II, sec. 3: No person shall on or after the date when the Eighteenth Amendment to the Constitution of the United States goes into effect, manufacture, sell, barter, transport, import, export, deliver, furnish or possess any intoxicating liquor except as authorized in this Act, and all the provisions of this Act shall be liberally construed to the end that the use of intoxicating liquor as a beverage may be prevented.

Liquor for nonbeverage purposes and wine for sacramental purposes may be manufactured, purchased, sold, bartered, transported, imported, exported, delivered, furnished and possessed, but only as herein provided, and the commissioner may, upon application, issue permits therefor: *Provided,* That nothing in this Act shall prohibit the purchase and sale of warehouse receipts covering distilled spirits on deposit in Government bonded warehouses, and no special tax liability shall attach to the business of purchasing and selling such warehouse receipts.

Title II, sec. 26: When the commissioner, his assistants, inspectors, or any officers of the law shall discover any person in the act of transporting in violation of the law, intoxicating liquors in any wagon, buggy, automobile, water or air craft, or other vehicle, it shall be his duty to

unlading, although beginning beyond the three-mile limit, continued until the liquor was landed, and the schooner was actively assisting in it by means of her small boats and three of her crew, who were on the motorboat for that purpose."

---

seize any and all intoxicating liquors found therein being transported contrary to law. Whenever intoxicating liquors transported or possessed illegally shall be seized by an officer he shall take possession of the vehicle and team or automobile, boat, air or water craft, or any other conveyance, and shall arrest any person in charge thereof. Such officer shall at once proceed against the person arrested under the provisions of this title in any court having competent jurisdiction; but the said vehicle or conveyance shall be returned to the owner upon execution by him of a good and valid bond, with sufficient sureties, in a sum double the value of the property, which said bond shall be approved by said officer and shall be conditioned to return said property to the custody of said officer on the day of trial to abide the judgment of the court. The court upon conviction of the person so arrested shall order the liquor destroyed, and unless good cause to the contrary is shown by the owner, shall order a sale by public auction of the property seized, and the officer making the sale, after deducting the expenses of keeping the property, the fee for the seizure, and the cost of the sale, shall pay all liens, according to their priorities, which are established, by intervention or otherwise at said hearing or in other proceeding brought for said purpose, as being bona fide and as having been created without the lienor having any notice that the carrying vehicle was being used or was to be used for illegal transportation of liquor, and shall pay the balance of the proceeds into the Treasury of the United States as miscellaneous receipts. All liens against property sold under the provisions of this section shall be transferred from the property to the proceeds of the sale of the property. If, however, no one shall be found claiming the team, vehicle, water or air craft, or automobile, the taking of the same, with a description thereof, shall be advertised in some newspaper published in the city or county where taken, or if there be no newspaper published in such city or county, in a newspaper having circulation in the county, once a week for two weeks and by handbills posted in three public places near the place of seizure, and if no claimant shall appear within ten days after the last publication of the advertisement, the property shall be sold and the proceeds after deducting the expenses and the costs shall be paid into the Treasury of the United States as miscellaneous receipts.

Forfeiture of a vessel under this section may not be had until there has been an arrest and conviction of the person in charge. *The Sagatind* (1926), 11 Fed. (2d) 673, (C. C. A., 2d Cir.., Hough, Cir. Judge); *The J. Duffy* (1926), 14 Fed. (2d) 426, (D. C. D. Conn., Thomas, Dist. Judge); *The Squanto* (1926), 13 Fed. (2d) 548, (C. C. A. 2d Cir., Manton, Cir. Judge); *The Homestead* (1925), 7 Fed. (2d) 413, (D. C. S. D. N. Y., Augustus N. Hand, Dist. Judge).

On the question of jurisdiction, the court said that the schooner was held in the proceedings on the arrest made by the marshal after she was brought into port, and not under the seizure made by the revenue cutter four miles out.[26]   After noting that it was not the question whether the schooner could have been seized beyond three miles from the shore for an offense committed wholly beyond that distance, Judge Morton said:

"The high seas are the territory of no nation; no nation can extend its laws over them; they are free to the vessels of all countries. But this has been thought not to mean that a nation is powerless against vessels offending against its laws which remain just outside the three-mile limit. . . .

"The mere fact, therefore, that the *Grace and Ruby* was beyond the three-mile limit, does not of itself make the seizure unlawful and establish a lack of jurisdiction.

"As to the Seizure:

"The line between territorial waters and the high seas is not like the boundary between us and a foreign power. There must be, it seems to me, a certain width of debatable waters adjacent to our coasts. How far our authority shall be extended into them for the seizure of foreign vesels which have broken our laws is a matter for the political departments of the government rather than for the courts to determine.

"It is a question between governments; reciprocal rights and other matters may be involved. . . .

"In directing that she be seized . . . and brought into the country to answer for her offense, I am not prepared to say that the Treasury Department exceeded its power." [27]

[26] See Beale, "The Jurisdiction of a Sovereign State" (1923), 36 *Harvard Law Rev.,* p. 241 and ibid., pp. 609-613; *The Tenyu Maru* (1910), 4 Alaska 129; and *The Ray of Block Island,* 11 Fed. (2d) 522.
[27] Judge Morton quoted with approval the language of Chief Jus-

The court said, by way of dictum, that the unlading within four leagues of the coast was a violation of sections 2867 and 2868 of the *Revised Statutes* (which sections are considered in the next case), which rendered the motor boat and the liquors liable to seizure and forfeiture and the masters of the boat and the schooner liable to the penalties prescribed by those sections.

In *The Tenyu Maru*,[28] the principle of this case was applied; a Japanese vessel was forfeited for fishing within three miles of the coast, though she herself stood 11½ miles out to sea, at which point she was seized, while the actual fishing was carried on within 2.6 miles from the shore by her small boats.[29]   She was forfeited because to "all intents and purposes," she was engaged in sealing within three miles of the shore.[30]

---

tice Marshall in *Church* v. *Hubbart*, p. 197, *supra*, and said that the principle there stated is "a sensible and practical rule," and that it ought to be followed until it is authoritatively repudiated.   He also noted that certain communications of the Department of State to the Spanish Government in which the marine league was said to be the limit of jurisdiction (see p. 265, *infra*), do not relate to "vessels committing unfriendly or hostile acts against the country on whose coast they were hovering."

[28] (1910) 4 Alaska 129.

[29] See, also, *United States* v. *The Jane Gray* (1896), 77 Fed. 908, at 918 (*obiter dictum*).   This principle was followed by the British Government in 1890 in *The Araunah*, p. 311, *infra*.

[30] The Court said:

"The schooner was therefore just as much 'engaged in' killing the seals, under the statutes, when the small boat was captured within the three-mile limit on July 9th as though she had been standing within the zone at the time, in the absence of any evidence showing extenuating circumstances. . . .

"The principle that a man who, outside of a country, wilfully puts in motion a force to take effect in it is answerable at the place where the evil is done is recognized in the criminal jurisprudence of all countries. . . .

"While the authority above mentioned holds that the inherent right rests in a sovereign to punish violations of its laws when such violations are occasioned within the sovereign's domain, even though the force causing a wrongful act came from without, yet it finds the difficulty, as we find in this case, to obtain jurisdiction of the person or object; but in my opinion, in this case, so far as this court is concerned, the

(2) *The Henry L. Marshall*

The case of *The Henry L. Marshall* [31] represents the second and third types of cases. [32] It was a case of libels for the forfeiture of 1250 cases of liquors, the British sailing vessel, the *Henry L. Marshall*, [33] upon which the liquor was laden, and for penalties. The liquor was taken on board the *Marshall* at the British West Indies, from which she departed with two clearances, one calling for Canada with fifteen hundred cases of liquor, the other for the United States in ballast. She had no manifest on board. Her real object was to peddle liquor along the coast of the United States. On various occasions she accomplished her purpose, while lying off the coast nine or ten miles, by sending her wares to the shore by means of motor boats not belonging to her or to her owner. Her previous registered owner, an American, was ashore directing her movements, and representing the new owner. She was seized beyond three miles from the shore, brought into port, where, with her cargo, she was seized, and libelled.

Tenyu Maru is before this court under its civil process, the respective proctors having filed a stipulation herein now in evidence, admitting that the Tenyu Maru was libeled by the service of process from this court at Dutch Harbor, Unalaska, within the Third judicial division, territory of Alaska, and I apprehend it is not a judicial question for this court to determine by what means or under what circumstances she became so situate, in the event she was not brought there contrary to the provisions of any treaty existing between the United States and Japan."

The Twee Gebroeders (1800), 3 C. Rob. 162 and 336, presents the converse of this case. The English High Court of Admiralty held that a capture of a prize made by small boats outside neutral waters is illegal if the mother ship is lying within such waters.

[31] (1922) 286 Fed. 260, (D. C. D. N. Y. Hazel, Dist. Judge); (1923) 292 Fed. 486, (C. C. A. Hough, Cir. Judge). Certiorari denied, 263 U. S. 712.

[32] See p. 216, *supra*.

[33] The vessel was proceeded against and condemned as British, but it appears that after the condemnation had taken place, the British Government declared that it was not entitled to British registry though it was sailing under such registry. P. 314, *infra*.

The following forfeitures and penalties were decreed under the following sections of the *Revised Statutes:*

1. The vessel was declared forfeited under sections 2872 and 2874 [34] for introducing liquors into the United States "by the participation of small boats which came to the vessel for transference. . . . The transfer and deliveries of the liquor at night without the permission of the officials specified in section 2872 was an unlawful unloading. Even though the act of unloading began beyond the three-mile limit, it continued until the liquor was landed. . . . The vessel here, as in *The Grace and Ruby,* actively assisted in the unloading, and by the use of motor boats, or other craft caused the fraudulent introduction of the merchandise into the commerce of the United States." Judge Hough of the Circuit Court said: "We are entirely in accord with the decision in the *Grace and Ruby.* . . . The difference between the facts there presented and those at bar is that, instead of arranging to unload and deliver the cargo of the schooner by, through, or with some assistance from the schooner's crew or equipment (as in the case cited), the whole matter was performed by previous arrangement with those controlling the Marshall, but with small boats that did not belong to the schooner, and were not even partially manned by men from her crew.

"But it is just as true in this case, as it was in that of *The Grace and Ruby,* that 'the act of unlading, although beginning beyond the 3-mile limit, continued until the liquor was landed.' "

2. The master was held liable to a fine of $1,000 under section 2867 [35] for unlading within four leagues of the coast, and to a fine of $500 under section 2814 [36] for not

---

[34] P. 217, *supra.*

[35] P. 189, *supra,* for this section.

[36] P. 186, *supra,* for this section.

producing a manifest within that distance. Under section 3088, both of these fines become liens against the vessel.[37] It should be noted that the first two sections are applicable when the vessel is bound to the United States. The Court held that a vessel engaged as the *Marshall* was, would not be heard to deny that it was so bound. This decision is clearly in accord with the intention of the legislator; for this vessel was engaged in the very conduct at which all legislation since 1790 in the United States and since 1699 in England has been aimed. These laws have been passed to end *smuggling* and, therefore, they apply to vessels attempting to get their cargoes ashore unlawfully by means of unlading or otherwise, whether or not they are technically bound for some port, that is, are expecting to enter some port, so long as the goods are destined to the United States.[38] The case is distinguishable from *The Coquitlam*,[39] in which it was held that the statute was not violated by an unlading within four leagues of the coast, for there was no attempt or intention to introduce the cargo into the United States.

The court held that the liquor remaining on board at the time of seizure was forfeitable under paragraph H, of Section III, of the Tariff Act of 1913,[40] which declares that when any consignor, seller, etc., introduces or

---

[37] P. 190, *supra*, for this section.

[38] If any doubt existed on this point, it was removed in favor of the decision in the *Marshall* case by secs. 581 and 586 of the "Tariff Act of 1922." See pp. 228 and 231, *infra*.

[39] P. 203, *supra*.

[40] 38 *Stat. at Large*, c. 16, pp. 114, 183. "An Act to reduce tariff duties and to provide revenue for the Government, and for other purposes."

"That if any consignor, seller, owner, importer, consignee, agent, or other person or persons, shall enter or introduce, or attempt to enter or introduce, into the commerce of the United States any imported merchandise by means of any fraudulent or false invoice, declaration, affidavit, letter, paper, or by means of any false statement, written or verbal, or by means of any false or fraudulent practice or appliance whatsoever, or shall make any false statement in the declarations provided for in paragraph F without reasonable cause to believe the truth of such statement, or shall aid or procure the making of any such false

attempts to introduce any merchandise into the United States by any fraudulent means, or is guilty of any willful act by means whereof the United States shall or may be deprived of duties accruing upon such merchandise, the merchandise shall be forfeited; since the master of the *Marshall* was attempting to introduce the cargo into the United States. It was held that this section is violated by an attempt to introduce merchandise whose importation is forbidden, such as liquors, even though section 2766 of the *Revised Statutes* defines the word *merchandise* as goods capable of being imported.[41] It was held that it is not necessary to show a deprivation of revenue

---

statement as to any matter material thereto without reasonable cause to believe the truth of such statement, or shall be guilty of any willful act or omission by means whereof the United States shall or may be deprived of the lawful duties or any portion thereof, accruing upon the merchandise or any portion thereof, embraced or referred to in such invoice, declaration, affidavit, letter, paper, or statement, or affected by such act or omission, such merchandise, or the value thereof, to be recovered from such person or persons, shall be forfeited, which forfeiture shall only apply to the whole of the merchandise or the value thereof in the case or package containing the particular article or articles of merchandise to which such fraud or false paper or statement relates. That the arrival within the territorial limits of the United States of any merchandise consigned for sale and remaining the property of the shipper or consignor, and the acceptance of a false or fraudulent invoice thereof by the consignee or the agent of the consignor, or the existence of any other facts constituting an attempted fraud, shall be deemed, for the purpose of this paragraph, to be an attempt to enter such merchandise notwithstanding no actual entry has been made or offered."

[41] Between the rendering of the opinion of the lower court and that of the Circuit Court of Appeals, the Supreme Court, in the case of *U. S.* v. *Cischo* (1923) (262 U. S. 165), held that goods whose importation is forbidden (in that case opium) must suffer the penalty prescribed by sec. 2809 for being brought into port without a manifest. That is, forbidden goods are "merchandise," as the word is used in sec. 2809, and the failure to manifest them is a violation of that section. The lower Federal Court and the Circuit Court of Appeals in the Cischo case had held to the contrary, while the case of *U. S.* v. *Santini* (1922) 279 Fed. 534 (C. C. A. 5th Cir.), had taken the view of the Supreme Court in the Cischo case.

The Circuit Court of Appeals in the instant case, in following the Cischo case held that intoxicating liquor, though "incapable of lawful importation, [under the prohibition laws] must, nevertheless, be manifested as if it were lawful. . . ."

before this section is violated. The Circuit Court of Appeals said that "rum-running" deprives the United States of duties, for "The government may, and in instances like this does, tax unlawful liquor as it did lawful product for importation." It was held that section 2809 was not violated, for the merchandise in question did not belong to the officers and crew.[42]

(3) *U. S.* v. *Bengochea*

The third type of case is again represented in the case of *U. S.* v. *Bengochea.*[43] A Cuban schooner, the *Reemplago,* had cleared from Havana, carrying a clearance certificate for a fishing trip. After her clearance, she took some liquors and Chinamen on board, sailed and anchored within seven or eight miles of the coast of the United States, where she was seized while waiting for boats to go out to her to receive the liquors and Chinamen for transportation to the shore. She carried no manifest. In forfeiture proceedings, the Circuit Court of Appeals held that the vessel was forfeitable under sections 2811, 2814, and 3088 of the *Revised Statutes,*[44] for not producing a manifest within four leagues of the coast. It was contended by the claimants of the vessel that the libel should be dismissed on the ground that the manifest was demanded beyond a marine league from the shore; but it was held that the United States did not exceed its "power or jurisdiction" in authorizing such action within four leagues of the coast as the statutes provide for. Circuit Judge Walker said:

"In view of the great length of time the above-quoted provision of section 2811 has been in existence and acted on, without complaint, so far as appears, by foreign

---

[42] P. 186, note (24), *supra,* for this section.

[43] (1922) 279 Fed. 537 (C. C. A. 5th Cir., Walker, Cir. Judge).

[44] See pp. 186, 190, and 185, *supra,* for secs. 2814, 3088, 2811, respectively.

nations whose vessels are affected by the exercise of the right which the provisions assert, and of the long-continued recognition by the courts of the validity of the provision, for reasons disclosed, though not in cases calling for a decision on the question, we are of opinion that there is an absence of justification for the contention that the United States went beyond any power or jurisdiction with which it is vested in authorizing, for the protection of its revenue and the enforcement of its commercial regulations, such action as the statute in question provides for within four leagues of our coast. To sustain that contention would mean that a foreign vessel hovering near our coast, for the purpose of violating, or aiding in the violation of, our laws, would be, so long as it keeps more than three miles from shore, beyond the reach of reasonable and appropriate action by the government for the protection of its rights, not involving any needless or harassing interference with legitimate commerce. The conclusion is that the seizure in question is not subject to be declared invalid on the ground that it was made more than three miles from the Florida coast." [45]

As in the case of *The Henry L. Marshall*, it was held that the sections of the *Revised Statutes* just referred to were applicable, although the vessel did not itself enter or intend to enter a port, but was merely intending to

[45] As the libel did not specifically allege a failure to have the required manifest on board, or claim the penalty for such failure provided in sec. 2809, the libellant was given leave to amend.

The District Court had dismissed the libel on the ground that sec. 2811 was not applicable, since the vessel was laden with goods whose importation was forbidden. The Circuit Court of Appeals reversed the lower court on this point. (See p. 225, note [41], *supra*.) But on the claimant's contention that the libel should be dismissed on the ground that the demand for the manifest was made beyond a marine league, the District Court said: "The validity of the four-league limit has not, to my knowledge, been directly passed on by the courts, but in many cases it seems to be recognized as valid and binding upon all ships laden with merchandise bound to a port in the United States." 279 Fed. 538.

introduce its cargo into the United States by delivering it at sea more than three miles from the shore.[46]

§ 49. The Tariff Act of 1922, Broadening the Jurisdiction for Four Leagues

The remaining cases involving seizures under the four-league statutes arose under the provisions of the "Tariff Act of 1922," [47] which had not come into force when the cases just discussed were decided. It will be necessary to consider the provisions of the Act before proceeding to the new cases, for these provisions made some important changes in the law. This Act took effect on September 21, 1922.

(1) *Demand of manifest*

Section 581 [48] corresponds to section 31 of the Act of 1790, section 54 of the Act of 1799, and sections 3067 and

[46] Cf. an article by Edwin D. Dickinson, "Jurisdiction at the Maritime Frontier" (1927) 40 *Harvard Law Rev.*, p. 1.

[47] 42 *Stat. at Large,* Part I, p. 858.

[48] Sec. 581 reads:

"Boarding vessels. Officers of the customs or of the Coast Guard, and agents or other persons authorized by the Secretary of the Treasury, or appointed for that purpose in writing by a collector may at any time go on board of any vessel or vehicle at any place in the United States or within four leagues of the coast of the United States, without as well as within their respective districts, to examine the manifest and to inspect, search, and examine the vessel or vehicle, and every part thereof, and any person, trunk, or package on board, and to this end to hail and stop such vessel or vehicle, if under way, and use all necessary force to compel compliance, and if it shall appear that any breach or violation of the laws of the United States has been committed, whereby or in consequence of which such vessel or vehicle, or the merchandise, or any part thereof, on board of or imported by such vessel or vehicle is liable to forfeiture, it shall be the duty of such officer to make seizure of the same, and to arrest, or, in case of escape or attempted escape, to pursue and arrest any person engaged in such breach or violation."

A distinction must be drawn between this section and section 431, which requires the master of every vessel "arriving in the United States and required to make an entry," to have a manifest on board. *The Vinces* (1927) 20 Fed. (2d) 164, 177.

3069 of the *Revised Statutes*. It provides that officers of the customs or of the Coast Guard "may at any time go on board of any vessel or vehicle at any place in the United States or within 4 leagues of the coast of the United States . . . to examine the manifest, and to inspect, search, and examine the vessel or vehicle, or any part thereof, or any person, trunk, or package on board, and to this end to hail and stop such vessel or vehicle, if under way, and to use all necessary force to compel compliance, and if it shall appear that any breach or violation of the laws of the United States has been committed," whereby the vessel or any part of the merchandise on board of or imported by such vessel is liable to forfeiture, the vessel shall be seized, and any person engaged in such violation shall be arrested, and if he attempts to escape, pursued and arrested. This section does not require that the vessel boarded and examined be bound for the United States, as previous legislation did. By the omission of this requirement at this time, Congress, no doubt, wished to bring unmistakably within the terms of the law the "rum fleet" that were now hovering off the coast in large numbers with no intention of entering a port, but were waiting for small vessels to visit them from the shore to receive their liquors.[49]

This section does not take jurisdiction generally over all vessels (i.e., vessels passing on legitimate voyages) that come within four leagues of the coast. If it did, it would certainly merit the protest of foreign nations. It does nothing more than to subject to search and surveillance craft whose movements or other conduct create suspicion of an illicit voyage. No vessel is subject to search

[49] As just noted, under the decisions in the *Marshall* and *Bengochea* cases, the previous legislation was interpreted to embrace vessels which were not actually "bound" to a port, but were standing off shore and sending their liquors ashore by means of their own small boats or by boats sent out from the shore.

or seizure unless its conduct or some previous information gives rise to the belief that it is bent upon smuggling.[50]

Section 583 provides that the master of every vessel bound to a port or place in the United States shall deliver to the officer of the customs or Coast Guard who first demands it, the original and a copy of the manifest. The officer must certify such delivery on the original.[51]

By section 584, any master of a vessel bound for the United States who does not produce the manifest as required in section 583, is liable to a fine of $500. If any merchandise is found "on board of or after unlading from such vessel" which is not included in the manifest, or which does not agree therewith, the master is liable to a penalty equal to the value of such merchandise. The master is also liable to a $500 fine if any merchandise described in the manifest is not found on board. If any of the merchandise so found is opium prepared for smoking, the master is liable to a penalty of $25 for each ounce thereof, which is a lien against the vessel that may be enforced by a libel *in rem*. No distance from the coast where the demand for the manifest may be made is specified in these two sections, but they are limited by section 581.[52]

[50] P. 147, *supra*, for a similar view of the English laws. Sec. 581 also provides that the officers of the Department of Commerce may go on board any vessel in the United States or within four leagues of the coast thereof and hail, stop, and board such vessel in the enforcement of the navigation laws, and arrest any person engaged in their breach.

[51] This section reads: *"Certification of Manifest.* The master of every vessel and the person in charge of every vehicle bound to a port or place in the United States shall deliver to the officer of the customs or Coast Guard who shall first demand of him, the original and one copy of the manifest of such vessel or vehicle, and such officer shall certify on the back of the original manifest to the inspection thereof and return the same to the master or other person in charge."

[52] *The Mistinguette,* p. 238, *infra*. See, also, *The Pictonian,* (1927) 20 Fed. (2d) 353. Under sec. 584, the penalty is imposed if no manifest is on board. *The Vinces* (1927) 20 Fed. (2d) 164.

(2) *Unlading within Four Leagues*

Section 586 corresponds to section 13 of the Act of 1790, section 27 of the Act of 1799, and section 2867 of the *Revised Statutes* in regard to unlading within four leagues of the coast. The master of any vessel from a foreign port or place who allows any merchandise (including sea stores) to be unladen at any time after the vessel's "arrival within 4 leagues of the coast of the United States" and before it has come to a proper place of discharge and received a permit to unlade, is liable to a fine of twice the value of the merchandise, but not less than $1,000; and the vessel and the merchandise are subject to seizure and forfeiture. If the unlading is from necessity, the master must notify the collector within the district in which the transshipment occurred or at which the vessel first arrives.[53]

By section 587, the master of the vessel receiving such merchandise unladen in violation of section 586 is subject to the same fine, and the receiving vessel and the merchandise are liable to seizure and forfeiture.[54]

[53] Sec. 586 reads:

"*Unlawful Unlading. Exception.* The master of any vessel from a foreign port or place who allows any merchandise (including sea stores) to be unladen from such vessel at any time after its arrival within four leagues of the coast of the United States and before such vessel has come to the proper place for the discharge of such merchandise, and before he has received a permit to unlade, shall be liable to a penalty equal to twice the value of the merchandise, but not less than $1,000, and such vessel and the merchandise shall be subject to seizure and forfeiture: *Provided,* That whenever any part of the cargo or stores of a vessel has been unladen or transshipped because of accident, stress of weather, or other necessity, the master of such vessel shall, as soon as possible thereafter, notify the collector of the district within which such unlading or transshipment has occurred, or the collector within the district at which such vessel shall first arrive thereafter, and shall furnish proof that such unlading or transshipment was made necessary by accident, stress of weather, or other unavoidable cause, and if the collector is satisfied that the unlading or transshipment was in fact due to accident, stress of weather, or other necessity the penalties above described shall not be incurred."

[54] Sec. 587 reads: "*Unlawful Transshipment.* If any merchandise

Under sections 586 and 587, the unlading vessel is not required to be bound to the United States, and in this regard is different from the corresponding sections of the older laws.

(3) *Introduction of Merchandise by Fraudulent Practice*

Sections 591 and 592 correspond to section III, paragraph H of the Act of 1913,[55] subjecting to forfeiture all goods introduced or attempted to be introduced into the United States by means of any fraudulent or false invoice or any fraudulent practice. The offense is punishable by a fine not exceeding $5,000 or imprisonment for two years.[56]

(including sea stores) unladen in violation of the provisions of section 586 of this Act is transshipped to or placed in or received on any other vessel, the master of the vessel on which such merchandise is placed, and any person aiding or assisting therein, shall be liable to a penalty equal to twice the value of the merchandise, but not less than $1,000, and such vessel and such merchandise shall be liable to seizure and forfeiture."

This section corresponds to sec. 14 of the Act of 1790, sec. 28 of the Act of 1799, and sec. 2868 of the *Revised Statutes.*

[55] P. 224, note (40), *supra.*

[56] Sec. 591 reads: *"Fraud—Penalty—Personal.* If any consignor, seller, owner, importer, consignee, agent, or other person or persons enters or introduces, or attempts to enter or introduce, into the commerce of the United States any imported merchandise by means of any fraudulent or false invoice, declaration, affidavit, letter, paper, or by means of any false statement, written or verbal, or by means of any false or fraudulent practice or appliance whatsoever, or makes any false statement in any declaration under the provisions of section 485 of this Act without reasonable cause to believe the truth of such statement, or aids or procures the making of any such false statement as to any matter material thereto without reasonable cause to believe the truth of such statement, or is guilty of any willful act or omission by means whereof the United States shall or may be deprived of the lawful duties, or any portion thereof, accruing upon the merchandise, or any portion thereof, embraced or referred to in such invoice, declaration, affidavit, letter, paper, or statement, or affected by such act or omission, such person or persons shall upon conviction be fined for each offense a sum not exceeding $5,000, or be imprisoned for a time not exceeding two years, or both, in the discretion of the court: *Provided,* That nothing in this section shall be construed to relieve imported merchandise from forfeiture by reason of such false statement or for any cause elsewhere provided by law."

Section 594 re-enacts section 3088 of the *Revised Statutes*, providing that whenever any vessel or its owner or master has become subject to a penalty for a violation of the customs laws, the vessel may be held for payment and may be seized and libelled to recover such penalty.

Section 642 repealed, by specific reference, all sections of the *Revised Statutes* of interest in this connection except sections 2760 and 2765; but section 644 repealed "all laws and parts of laws inconsistent with the provisions of this Act." [57]   Section 2765, providing for the firing into a vessel liable to seizure or examination which

---

Sec. 592 reads: *"Same—Penalty against Goods.* If any consignor, seller, owner, importer, consignee, agent, or other person or persons enters or introduces, or attempts to enter or introduce, into the commerce of the United States any imported merchandise by means of any fraudulent or false invoice, declaration, affidavit, letter, paper, or by means of any false statement, written or verbal, or by means of any false or fraudulent practice or appliance whatsoever, or makes any false statement in any declaration under the provisions of section 485 of this Act without reasonable cause to believe the truth of such statement, or aids or procures the making of any such false statement as to any matter material thereto without reasonable cause to believe the truth of such statement, or is guilty of any willful act or omission by means whereof the United States is or may be deprived of the lawful duties or any portion thereof accruing upon the merchandise or any portion thereof, embraced or referred to in such invoice, declaration, affidavit, letter, paper, or statement, or affected by such act or omission, such merchandise, or the value thereof, to be recovered from such person or persons shall be subject to forfeiture, which forfeiture shall only apply to the whole of the merchandise or the value thereof in the case or package containing the particular article or articles of merchandise to which such fraud or false paper or statement relates. The arrival within the territorial limits of the United States of any merchandise consigned for sale and remaining the property of the shipper or consignor, and the acceptance of a false or fraudulent invoice thereof by the consignee or the agent of the consignor, or the existence of any other facts constituting an attempted fraud, shall be deemed, for the purposes of this paragraph, to be an attempt to enter such merchandise notwithstanding no actual entry has been made or offered."

This section does not apply unless the merchandise actually arrives within the territorial jurisdiction of the United States. *The Vinces,* (1927) 20 Fed. (2d) 164.

[57] The following sections were repealed by reference: 2811, 2812, 2814, 2815, 2806, 2867, 2868, 3067, 3049, 3070, 3088.

does not bring to when required to do so, or upon being chased, remains in force, since it was not specifically repealed by section 642, and since no provision of the Act of 1922 is inconsistent with it; but section 2760 is repealed, for its provisions are covered by section 581.

§ 50. Court Decisions under the Tariff Act of 1922

The Federal Courts have enforced the provisions of the Act of 1922 in some very clear decisions.

(1) *The Muriel E. Winters*

The fourth type of case in the classification made above,[58] is represented by the case of *The Muriel E. Winters.*[59] This was a libel of information against a British vessel which had been regularly engaged in bringing liquors from the Bahama Islands to the vicinity of the United States and selling them as completed transactions, beyond twelve miles from the shore, to operators of small boats over which the *Winters* had no control, but which were known by those in charge of the *Winters* to be engaged in smuggling the liquors sold by it to the United States. Some of the cargo had been unladen within twelve miles of the shore; but the vessel had never come within three miles. She had come within twelve miles of the coast for protection against high winds when she was seized. The claimants attacked the libel on the ground that the seizure was unlawful, because it was made beyond three miles from the shore, and because no offense was committed within twelve miles.

It was held that the act of unlading within twelve miles, even though the vessel was never bound to a port, subjected the vessel and the cargo unladen to forfeiture under sections 586 and 594, but that that part of the

[58] See p. 216, *supra*.
[59] (1925) 6 Fed. (2d) 466 (S. D. Texas, Hutchinson, Dist. Judge).

cargo remaining on board was not subject to forfeiture, for there had been no attempt to unlade it.[60] The court held, however, that no law was violated by the completed sales more than twelve miles out. The Government had sought forfeiture of the vessel for such transactions under sections 591 and 592, on the theory that the *Winters* was introducing foreign merchandise into the United States contrary to law by means of false practices and by connivance with certain persons and small boats.

(2) *The Cherie*

In *The Cherie,*[61] a French vessel, seized seven or eight miles out, where she had been selling liquor to various persons and where, at the time of her seizure, she was anchored for the purpose of disposing of the balance of her cargo, was forfeited under section 586 for unlading within twelve miles of the coast. The Court said, by way of dictum, that there was no law making sales beyond three miles from the shore an offense, but that the unlading within twelve miles was, apart from the sales, a distinct offense under section 586. The entire cargo found on the *Cherie* was held forfeitable under the same section.[62] In the previous case, *The Muriel E. Winters,* the District Court held that only that part of the cargo which had been unladen was forfeitable. It is submitted that the holding on this point in *The Cherie* is the proper construction of the section. Section 2867 of the *Revised Statutes,* to which section 586 of the *Tariff Act* of 1922 corresponds, distinctly limited the forfeiture to the goods "so unladen" within four leagues, while that

[60] The next case considered, *The Cherie,* is contra on this point.

[61] (1926) 13 Fed. (2d) 992 (C. C. A. 1st Cir.). For the report of the case in the District Court, see 9 Fed. (2d) 640 (D. C. D. Maine, S. D., Peters, District Judge). There was no appeal from the decree penalizing the master in the sum of $1,000 under sec. 586. For diplomatic discussion of this case, see p. 322, *infra.*

[62] Bingham, Cir. Judge, dissenting.

limitation is omitted in section 586. That omission was, doubtless, purposely made by Congress in order to bring within the forfeiture clause the entire cargo of the rum-laden vessels that appeared off the coast at this time. This construction makes for the suppression of the evil against which the Act was passed.

(3) *The Island Home*

In *The Island Home*,[63] a British schooner unladed liquor to small boats that went out from the shore; she remained always beyond three miles, but made deliveries within twelve miles from the shore. One American was on board. When boarded, no manifest was found, and a part of her cargo was missing.[64] She was seized and carried to Galveston.[65] The libels against the vessel set out a number of violations of the customs laws and the National Prohibition Act, relied upon for the forfeiture of the vessel and its cargo; namely, the unlawful unlading without a permit by means of small boats, after her arrival within four leagues of the coast, a failure to report her arrival and to enter the vessel, and a failure to have a manifest on board in violation of sections 433, 436, 439, 584, 586, 591, 596 of the Act of 1922, and section 26, Title II of the National Prohibition Act. It was contended by claimants of the vessel that the seizure was illegal, because made beyond three miles from the shore, and that, therefore, the evidence secured by such seizure was inadmissible; and that the vessel could not be considered as having come to the United States, and that no mani-

[63] (1926) 13 Fed. (2d) 382 (C. C. A. 5th Cir., Foster, Cir. Judge); reported as *Arch* v. *U. S.*

[64] According to *The Times* (London) of November 26, 1923, she was seized five miles from land.

[65] Her crew and master and certain persons residing in the United States were thereafter convicted of a conspiracy to violate the customs laws and the National Prohibition Act. *Canada* v. *U. S.*, 5 Fed. (2d) 488.

fest was, therefore, required. In decreeing forfeiture of the vessel and her cargo, and in holding that the evidence was admissible, Circuit Judge Foster said:

"Conceding that the criminal laws of the United States such as the National Prohibition Act are not effective more than three miles from the shore, nevertheless, from the earliest times, the United States has claimed and exercised jurisdiction over the marginal sea to at least four leagues for the purpose of enforcing her revenue and customs laws. Jurisdiction was so assumed by the Act of March 2, 1799 . . . and continued to the present day by the various tariff and customs administrative acts. Great Britain also claimed the same extent of territory by the Hovering Act of 1736, 9 Geo. II, C. A. P. 35, and doubtless, every maritime nation claims the same right. The Supreme Court has recognized the right of a nation to enforce her customs and navigation laws on the high seas beyond the three-mile limit. *Church* v. *Hubbart*, 2 Cranch, 187, 2 L. Ed. 249. And we have so held in *U. S.* v. *Bengochea*, 279 F. 537, a case in all its essential features similar to this one. . . . When she [the *Island Home*] reached a point within four leagues of the shore, she was as much within the jurisdiction of the United States as if actually in port, and was required to observe all the customs laws and regulations. When the Coast Guard observed her at anchor they had the authority to board her for the purpose of making inquiry as to her cargo and destination, and, finding no manifest, had the right to search without the necessity of procuring a search warrant. . . .

"If the *Island Home* had merely sailed through the customs zone without it being shown she had the intention of anchoring within it, and clandestinely introducing her cargo into the country, or if her intention had been only to anchor without the jurisdictional limits, and there sell to chance customers, the case presented would have been different."

If a foreign vessel unlades within twelve miles of the coast and is later seized within three miles, she is forfeit-able[66] under section 586.

(4) *The Mistinguette*[67]

A vessel of French registry was boarded and seized within four leagues, but beyond three miles of the coast, taken to port, and charged with violation of sections 581-584 and 594 of the Act of 1922, under which her condemnation was sought. Liquor was found on board for which there was no manifest, and upon demand, no manifest was produced. It was held that the vessel was liable to forfeiture for the penalty prescribed under section 584. Since no distance within which the demand of the manifest may be made is named in section 584, it was contended that the application of that section should be confined to three miles from the shore, but it was held that section 584 refers to vessels within four leagues of the coast, as designated in section 581.[68]

(5) *The Vinces*[68a]

A vessel of British registry, the *Vinces*, took on board on the high seas liquors from another vessel; she was later observed by a Coast Guard vessel within twelve miles

[66] *The Gemma*, (1926) 13 Fed. (2d) 149 (D. C. D. R. I., Brown Dist. Judge). Cf. *Attorney General* v. *Schiers*, p. 121, *supra*, and *The Squanto*, (1926) 13 Fed. (2d) 548 (C. C. A. 2d Cir., Manton, Cir. Judge).

[67] (1926) 14 Fed. (2d) 753 (D. C. S. D. N. Y., Augustus N. Hand, Judge).

[68] See *The Pesaquid*, (1926) 11 Fed. (2d) 308 (D. C. D. R. I.), for the enforcement of a penalty under secs. 584 and 594 against a British vessel seized a mile from the shore.

[68a] (1927) 20 Fed. (2d) 164 (D. C., E. D. S. C., Cochran, Dist. Judge). See, also, p. 360, *supra*, for a discussion of this case in connection with a treaty with Great Britain.

of the coast, bound to the United States, attempting to land the liquors within the United States. While bound for the United States, she came within 7.5 miles of the coast, but upon being pursued she turned and fled and was seized 12¾ or 13 miles from the coast. A manifest was demanded at the point where she was seized, but there was none on board. The master falsely stated that the clearance paper, which he produced, was a manifest, and that it covered the liquors on board, and that he was not bound for the United States, but for Nassau. The vessel was carried to port, and she and her cargo libelled. For causes of action it was alleged: 1. The master failed to produce a manifest, and no manifest was on board, and that liquors were on board, which were claimed by the master; 2. The *Vinces* was endeavoring fraudulently to import liquors into the United States, within twelve miles of the coast, and that the master and crew were endeavoring to introduce it into the commerce of the United States by making false statements; 3. The master was endeavoring fraudulently to import liquors within the territorial jurisdiction of the United States, and within twelve miles of the coast of the United States. It was held: 1. Under section 581, a foreign vessel may be pursued beyond the twelve-mile zone and searched and seized beyond it, when pursuit is begun within it. The Act itself provides for pursuit and arrest "in case of escape or attempted escape," and this pursuit and arrest are not confined to twelve miles from the shore. The court said: "It is the duty of every foreign vessel bound to the United States, coming within the 12-mile limit, to submit to search and seizure. . . . If this right may be defeated simply by escaping beyond the limit, then the object to be obtained would in many cases be absolutely frustrated." It is added that it was "a continuous hot pursuit and a capture on the high seas." 2. The penalty prescribed by section 584 for not producing the manifest within four leagues of the coast may be enforced when the seizure is made beyond four leagues under the circumstances of this case. The court said: "When hailed within the 12-mile limit, it is the duty of such vessel to halt and submit to the visitation and the demand for the manifest. This is a right which the United States has asserted, and which is not in conflict with international law, and which has been recognized and acquiesced in by Great Britain and other nations. When this right once attaches, it cannot be defeated by any act of such foreign vessel in attempting to escape, provided the United States officials pursue and arrest upon the high seas. The right having once attached within the 12-mile limit, when the vessel is seized beyond that limit and the demand there made for the manifest, such demand is to be deemed as constructively made within the 12-mile limit, and, if there is a failure to produce at that time, the penalties of law may be imposed. Such a construction of the revenue statutes in question is a fair and reasonable one, and one that necessarily follows from the original basis of such statutes, namely, the law of necessity for the protection of the nation and the enforcement of its laws."

(6) *The Sagatind*

An unlading twenty miles from the coast, however, by a Norwegian vessel, where she was seized, is not a violation of sections 585 and 586; for under those sections the vessel must be physically present within four leagues of the shore when the unlading takes place.[69] It was argued by the Government that the unlading

[69] *The Sagatind,* (1926) 11 Fed. (2d) 673 (C. C. A. 2d Cir., Hough, Cir. Judge). For reports of the case in the District Court, see (1925) 4 Fed. (2d) 928 (Augustus N. Hand, Dist. Judge) and (1925) 8 Fed. (2d) 788. The Canadian vessel, the *Diamantina,* was taken alongside the *Sagatind* and was libelled in this case.

twenty miles out brought the vessel constructively within twelve miles of the coast. This case held also that the cargo unladen twenty miles out is not forfeitable under section 592,[70] for by the terms of that section, seizure is not lawful "outside the territorial jurisdiction of the United States."

An indictment against the master and crew of a British schooner seized twenty-four miles out, charging that they aided in the possession of liquors, engaged in the transportation and importation of them, and a conspiracy to possess and sell and deliver and transport them at the point of seizure and in the Bahama Islands, was held demurrable in *United States* v. *Archer,*[71] because there was no charge that the unlading was within twelve miles of the coast, or that the defendants had agreed to commit any act in the territorial waters of the United States or within twelve miles of the coast.[72]

(7) *The Panama*

In *The Panama,*[73] a British vessel was seized 12.1 miles off Galveston for having delivered "into the port of New Orleans," five days previously, liquors "through" small shore boats sent out from the shore by prearrangement; but the distance from which she made the deliveries to the small boats off New Orleans is not given. The claimant contended that the seizure was unlawful, because made beyond twelve miles from the shore. The

[70] P. 233, note (56), *supra.*

[71] (1926) 12 Fed. (2d) 137 (D. C. S. D. Alabama, Ervin, Dist. Judge). This seizure was made under the treaty with Great Britain to be considered later. P. 369, *infra.*

[72] In *Cunard* v. *Mellon,* (1923) (262 U. S. 100) it was said, by way of dictum, that the application of the National Prohibition Act was limited to a marine league.

[73] (1925) 6 Fed. (2d) 326 (D. C. S. D. Texas, Hutchinson, Dist. Judge). For a further discussion of this case, see p. 365, *infra.* This seizure was made under a treaty with Great Britain, but it proved to be at a point farther out than the terms of the treaty called for.

court found that the vessel had violated the laws by making "actual contact" and by an unlading, off New Orleans, and that Galveston being the first port into which she was brought after seizure, she was forfeitable there. As to the jurisdiction to seize beyond the distance of twelve miles named in the statute and the distance named in the treaty with Great Britain,[74] the court said that "the right of the executive to seize and search for violations of our laws is not limited by any particular distance from the shore." This language goes quite far, unless the facts showed that the shore boats were under the control and direction of the officers on the *Panama*, as in *The Marshall* case, or that they belonged to the *Panama*, as in the case of *The Grace and Ruby*. Whether a seizure may be made when the vessel stands beyond twelve miles and sends her small boats within that distance from the shore or controls vessels from the shore within that distance, has not been decided. Under the decisions in *The Grace and Ruby, The Araunah,*[75] and *The Marshall*, the answer would seem to be in the affirmative.

(8) *The Zeehond*

A "gift" fifteen miles from the shore, of two cases of liquors from a hovering Dutch vessel to a prospective purchaser who went out in his own boat from the shore, was held not to be a violation of section 592 of the Tariff Act of 1922, which prohibits the introduction of merchandise into the commerce of the United States by means of any fraudulent practice.[76] The court distinguishes this case from *The Marshall* case, in that there was no attempt

[74] P. 346, *infra*.
[75] P. 311, *infra*.
[76] *U. S.* v. *2180 Cases of Intoxicating Liquors,* (The Zeehond) (1926) 9 Fed. (2d) 710 (C. C. A., Hough, Cir. Judge) ; 4 Fed. (2d) 735; 8 Fed. (2d) 765. The vessel was taken within three miles from the shore.

in this case to introduce the cargo into the United States, while in *The Marshall* case arrangements were made to put the liquors ashore, in small boats sent out from the shore. It should be noted, also, that in *The Marshall* case, the unlading was within twelve miles, while in this case, it was fifteen miles out, and therefore, not within the terms of the statute.[77]

(9) *The J. Duffy*

In the case of *The J. Duffy,*[78] which was a libel against a vessel and her liquor cargo seized in Long Island Sound, it was held that the waters of the Sound are "territorial waters," that "the municipal law reaches over them," and that, therefore, the distance of the seizure of a foreign vessel from the shore within those waters is immaterial. It was held by the District Court that the mere act of concealing goods in the waters of the Sound is not a punishable offense, that section 593(b) of the Act, prohibiting the concealing of goods after importation in the United States, is not violated until the goods have passed the customs barriers;[79] but the Circuit Court of

[77] The court said that sec. 2806 of the *Revised Statutes,* requiring a manifest for goods brought into the United States, was not violated. P. 184, *supra.* That section had been repealed and substituted by sec. 583 of the Act of 1922.

[78] (1926) 14 Fed. (2d) 426 (D. C. D. Conn., Thomas, Dist. Judge); (1927) 18 Fed. (2d) 754 (C. C. A. 2d Cir., Manton, Cir. Judge.

[79] Sec. 593(b) reads: "If any person fraudulently or knowingly imports or brings into the United States, or assists in so doing, any merchandise, contrary to law, or receives, conceals, buys, sells, or in any manner facilitates the transportation, concealment, or sale of such merchandise after importation, knowing the same to have been imported or brought into the United States contrary to law, such merchandise shall be forfeited and the offender shall be fined in any sum not exceeding $5,000 nor less than $50, or be imprisoned for any time not exceeding two years, or both. Whenever, on trial for a violation of this section, the defendant is shown to have or to have had possession of such goods, such possession shall be deemed evidence sufficient to authorize conviction, unless the defendant shall explain the possession to the satisfaction of the jury."

Appeals reversed the case on this point, and held that the mere transportation and concealment of the liquors without an unlading, was a violation of section 593(b).[80]

(10) *The Louise F and Latham* v. *U. S.*

Sections 583, 585, and 586 of the Tariff Act and the National Prohibition Act are not violated when the crew mutinies and the vessel is run into the "waters of the United States" and liquor unladen on the beach against

[80] Other cases of seizure more than three miles from the shore are reported by the newspapers as follows:

The *T. M. Gardner,* a British vessel, seized twenty-two miles out; but according to the officials seizing her, she was only seven miles out. A long chase followed before her capture. *The Times* (London), September 15, (9c) and 16 (7f), 1922.

The British *Kaduskak,* seized eight miles out, was taken to Boston, and her captain charged with a rum-running conspiracy near Bar Harbour. Nothing is said of any proceedings against the vessel. Reports from Boston stated that she was seized more than twenty-five miles out. Ibid., July 20, (12e) and 21 (9f), 1923.

The British schooner *Madeline Adams* was captured and brought into New York after a chase for many miles at sea. Ibid., April 15, 1925 (10f).

The British schooner *Tomaka* was seized seven miles off the coast of New York. The members of her crew were placed under bail, and the British Charge d'Affaires secured their release. All the crew were United States citizens. Two shots were fired across her bow. She carried two machine guns, and resisted arrest, but gave in when re-enforcements arrived and when four more shots were fired across her bow. She seems to have been owned by Americans, but had circumvented the Merchant Shipping Act, and had been registered in a "British Office." Ibid., January 5, 1924 (10f); November 27, 1923 (14f); November 26, 1923 (13g).

The British trawler *Fred B* was captured sixteen miles out, within an hour's steaming. This capture uncovered a large conspiracy of American, Canadian, and British bootleggers, some of whom were socially prominent. Ibid., October 6, 1924 (11c).

The *Marion Mosher* was taken eight miles out. Ibid., October 5, 1922, and October 16, 1923.

The *Emerald* was seized beyond three miles from the shore. Ibid., October 19, 1922.

See, also, *The Gemma,* (1926) 13 Fed. (2d) 149 (D. C. D. R. I., Brown, Dist. Judge); and *Parliamentary Debates* (Hansard) 1924, vol. 169, p. 484, where it is said that the *Kwasind* was seized seventeen miles out with liquor on board. There was some question as to her being in distress.

the will of the officers.[81]   According to a long and generally accepted principle, a vessel entering the adjacent waters in distress or by accident, or if forcibly taken therein, is not, generally speaking, subject to the laws of such country so long as her extremity exists. While in such waters, she is in a position similar to that of the passing vessel in the exercise of the so-called "right of innocent passage." Such a vessel must obey the local laws of navigation and sanitation, though she is not subject to the customs and revenue laws, and is not an offender if she has on board goods whose introduction into the territory of the littoral state is forbidden. In this connection, a very nice question is presented where a vessel is forced into the customs zone by stress of weather, accident, or by a mutinous crew, while she is hovering or sailing along the coast beyond such zone for the purpose of smuggling its illicit cargo into the country by running it in as opportunity affords or by some other means, but with no intention of entering the zone herself. In such case, the principle stated in *The Louise F* does not protect her. Such a case is presented in *Latham* v. *U. S.*[82] Defendants, in that case, were charged with possession and transportation of liquors on board a British schooner, the *Pesaquid,* within two miles of the coast, where she was seized with the defendants on board. She had been sailing along the coast selling liquors to shore boats. The defendants testified that the vessel reached the waters where she was seized by accident. Circuit Judge Woods, in rejecting that defense, aptly said:

"One who ranges along the land or water line of any

[81] *The Louise F,* (1923) 293 Fed. 933 (D. C. S. D., Fla., Call, Dist. Judge). The vessel was seized four or five miles out. It does not appear from the report of this case that the vessel was upon a smuggling voyage.

[82] (1924) 2 Fed. (2d) 209 (C. C. A., 4th Cir., Woods, Cir. Judge). But see *The Hazel E. Herman,* (1927) 19 Fed. (2d) 397 (D. C. S. D. Ga.).

country with the design of aiding in the subversion of its laws challenges that country to enforce its laws and assumes the risk of his own mistakes and the action of wind and tide and all the forces of nature."

It is submitted that the *Louise F*, seized four or five miles out, should have been forfeited under the appropriate sections, on the principle announced by Circuit Judge Woods, if it was or had been engaged in smuggling or was assisting in smuggling or was attempting to smuggle, when it lay beyond twelve miles from the shore. In such a case, a vessel would not be entitled to exemption when taken within the customs zone, even though it were forced into it. There would seem to be no difference between the position of a smuggling vessel forced into that zone by accident or weather and the one forced in by a mutinous crew.

If the officers and crew of a vessel have been tried and acquitted on a charge of conspiracy to transport and possess liquors within the United States contrary to section 37 of the *Penal Code*[83] in violation of the National Prohibition Act, that proceeding is *res adjudicata* as to the libel against the liquors taken within four miles of the shore, brought under section 592 of the *Tariff Act* of 1922 and section 2806 of the *Revised Statutes;*[84] for the acquittal on the criminal charge is a necessary finding that there was no criminal intent to run liquors when the ship (the Dutch *Zeehond*) was within three miles of the shore, where she was seized with liquors on board.[85]

[83] Sec. 37, 35 *Stat. at Large*, p. 1096; *Comp. Stat.* § 10201 (1909), reads: "If two or more persons conspire either to commit any offense against the United States, or to defraud the United States in any manner or for any purpose, and one or more of such parties do any act to effect the object of the conspiracy, each of the parties to such conspiracy shall be fined not more than ten thousand dollars, or imprisoned not more than two years, or both."

[84] This section had been repealed.

[85] *U. S.* v. *2180 Cases of Intoxicating Liquors* (1926) 9 Fed. (2d) 710 (C. C. A., Hough, Cir. Judge).

It was maintained by claimants of the liquor in the libel proceeding against it that the vessel had taken refuge at the point where she was seized and that she had not gone there voluntarily; but the District Court had found that she was not there in distress but was "seeking to perpetuate the attempted fraud described in section 592." [86] The Circuit Court of Appeals reversed this decision for the reason stated.[87]

§ 51. The Seizure of American Vessels on the High Seas

With the enactment of the prohibition law, many American vessels appeared on the high seas with liquor cargoes, and there was presented again the question of whether the Coast Guard had authority to seize such vessels more than twelve miles from the shore.[88]

(1) *The Richmond*

In the case of *The Richmond*,[89] Chief Justice Marshall

[86] (1925) 4 Fed. (2d) 735 (E. D. N. Y., Garvin, Dist. Judge); ibid., vol. 8, pp. 763, 764.

[87] As to the sufficiency of evidence on the questions of possessing and of transporting liquors into the United States or the "territorial waters" thereof, in violation of sec. 593 of the Act of 1922 and the National Prohibition Act, and of conspiring so to possess or transport them, see:

Romano v. *United States,* (1925) 9 Fed. (2d) 522 (C. C. A., 2nd Cir., Manton, Cir. Judge).

Latham v. *United States,* (1924) 2 Fed. (2d) 209 (C. C. A., 4th Cir., Woods, Cir. Judge).

Hill v. *United States,* (1926) 12 Fed. (2d) 504 (C. C. A., 5th Cir., Bryan, Cir. Judge).

Burns v. *United States,* (1924) 298 Fed. 468 (C. C. A., 5th Cir., Bryan, Cir. Judge).

The vessels in these cases were all seized in port or within three miles of the shore, except in the Burns case, in which an American vessel was seized eighteen miles out, after pursuit was begun at a point within three miles of the shore.

[88] The files of the Coast Guard for September 1, 1922, to February 10, 1927, show that seventy-five American vessels had been seized more than four leagues from the shore, and that twenty-one of this number were seized about thirty miles from the coast.

[89] 9 Cranch 102. See, also, (1839) 3 *Opins. Atty. Gen.,* p. 405.

had held in 1818, that the owner of an American vessel before a Federal Court in a condemnation proceeding could not complain of the court's jurisdiction on the ground that the vessel was taken in Spanish waters. The vessel was seized in St. Mary's River, then Spanish territory, and libelled under forfeiture proceedings in the United States District Court of Georgia for a violation of the law requiring vessels to give a bond upon their departure for a foreign port or place, that they would not proceed to a prohibited port. It was found that the law was violated, but claimant contended that since the vessel was seized in Spanish territory, all the proceedings were void. In reply to this contention, the Chief Justice said that "the majority of the court is of opinion that the law does not connect that trespass, if it be one, with the subsequent seizure by the civil authority under the process of the district court, so as to annull the proceedings of that court against the vessel." [90]

(2) *U. S.* v. *Lee*

This reasoning seems applicable to an American vessel before a court, seized anywhere on the high seas. This question, upon which there had been a split of authority in the Circuit Courts of Appeals, was recently decided by the Supreme Court in the case of *U. S.* v. *Lee*.[91] That case was an indictment for conspiracy to import liquors into the United States contrary to sections 591 and 593 of the Act of 1922, and section 3, title II of the Act of October 28, 1919.[92] Lee was taken from an American vessel while alongside another vessel twenty-four miles out, from which the American vessel had just taken on

[90] The court said that the seizure in Spanish waters might have been a cause of complaint by the Spanish Government.

[91] 47 Sup. Ct. Rep. 746; (1926) 14 Fed. (2d) 400 (C. C. A., 1st Cir-, Bingham, Cir. Judge).

[92] 41 *Stat. at Large,* Part I, c. 85, p. 308.

liquors. He had intended to go ashore with the liquors on board. All the evidence against the defendant was obtained by this seizure, and it was admitted by the trial court over his objection. On motion before the Circuit Court of Appeals to suppress the evidence on the ground that it was obtained by an unlawful search at a point twenty-four miles from the shore, it was held that the evidence was not admissible, and a new trial was ordered. The court said that there is no authority to seize any vessel, American or foreign, beyond twelve miles from the shore, as provided in section 581 of the Tariff Act of 1922. The court added that the seizure would have been lawful if the government had "adopted" the act by instituting legal proceedings to enforce the forfeiture against the vessel and its liquor cargo. It was said also that no law was violated by the act charged on the high seas.

On certiorari to the United States Circuit Court of Appeals, the judgment was reversed by the Supreme Court on May 31, 1927; it was held that the "officers of the Coast Guard are authorized, by virtue of *Revised Statutes* #3072 (*Comp. St.* § 5775), to seize on the high seas beyond the 12-mile limit an American vessel subject to forfeiture for violation of any law respecting revenue," citing *Maul v. United States* (*The Underwriter*) (47 Sup. Ct. Rep. 735), decided on the same day. "From that power," the court continues, "it is fairly to be inferred that they are likewise authorized to board and search such vessels when there is probable cause to believe them subject to seizure for violation of revenue laws, and to arrest persons thereon engaged in such violation." The court said that this authority is not as broad as "the belligerent right to visit and search even without probable cause," but that in the instant case there was probable cause that the laws of the United States were being violated by an American vessel and the persons thereon, "in such manner as to render the vessel subject to forfeiture." Under these circumstances, it was said, the search and seizure of the vessel and the arrest of the persons thereon were lawful and were like the search and seizure of an automobile and the arrest of persons therein by officers on land, and the failure of the government to institute proceedings against the vessel and the liquors aboard it did not render the search and arrest illegal.[93]

(3) *The Underwriter*

In the case of *The Underwriter*,[24] an American vessel was seized thirty-four miles from the shore with liquor on board, and charged with the violation of various sections of the Tariff Act of 1922, the National Prohibition Act, section 26, Title 2, and several sections of the *Revised Statutes*. She was licensed for the coasting trade, and was proceeded against for having "gone foreign." The trial court considered only the question of jurisdiction, and held that the court had no jurisdiction based on a seizure beyond twelve miles from the shore, as Congress had established that distance for seizures. On appeal to the Circuit Court of Appeals,[95] the decision was reversed, and it was held that an American vessel may be seized anywhere on the high seas, and that section 581, among others, of the Act of 1922 was a grant of authority to seize *foreign* vessels within four leagues of the coast. It was held, further, that the possession of the *res* in the collector of the port is sufficient to give the court jurisdiction, and the particular method of bringing the vessel

---

[93] This decision has the effect of overruling *U. S.* v. *Bentley* (1926) 12 Fed. (2d) 468 (D. C. D. Mass., Brewster, Dist. Judge).

[94] (1925) 6 Fed. (2d) 937 (D. C. D. Conn.). See, also *The Chiquita*, (1926) 18 Fed. (2d) 673 (1927), ibid., vol. 19, p. 417 (C. C. A., 5th Cir.).

[95] (1926) 13 Fed. (2d) 433 (C. C. A., 2d Cir., Manton, Cir. Judge).

into port is of no importance.[96]   This case went to the Supreme Court on a writ of certiorari as *Maul* v. *U. S.,* and was affirmed on May 31, 1927.[97]

(4) *The Homestead*

In *The Homestead,*[98] it was held that the seizure of an American vessel twenty-five miles from the shore was so far valid that it could be libelled for violation of the law when brought within the jurisdiction of the court.[99]   In *The Rosalie M,*[100] an American vessel, seized 19.5 miles out with liquor on board headed to the shore, was condemned and forfeited under section 4377 of the *Revised Statutes* for engaging in a trade other than that for which she was licensed.   In answer to claimant's contention that the seizure was unlawful, because the seizing officers had no authority beyond twelve miles from the shore, the court said that an American vessel operated "in violation of the laws of the United States can be apprehended on the high seas as well as within the territorial waters," and that, at any rate, after she was brought into the

[96] The vessel was forfeited under sec. 4377 of the *Revised Statutes* for engaging in a trade for which she was not licensed and under sec. 4377 for proceeding to a point on the high seas without giving up her enrollment or license or procuring a certificate of registry.

It was held that she had not violated secs. 593 and 594 of the Act of 1922 or sec. 3450 of the *Revised Statutes,* for no merchandise was brought within the boundary of the United States; nor secs. 2867, 2868, 3088 of the *Revised Statutes,* or secs. 586 and 587 of the Act of 1922, for there was no unlading within four leagues of the coast; nor sec. 26, Title 2 of the National Prohibition Act, for no liquor was transported into the United States.

[97] 47 Sup. Ct. Rep. 735.   See, also, *The Amriald,* (1925) 6 Fed. (2d) 413.

[98] (1925) 7 Fed. (2d) 413 (D. C. S. D. N. Y., Augustus N. Hand, Dist. Judge).

[99] This case follows *The Underwriter* on the application of sec. 4377 of the *Revised Statutes* and secs. 593, 594, 585, 586 of the Act of 1922 to an American vessel.

[100] 1926) 12 Fed. (2d) 970 (C. C. A., 5th Cir., Foster, Cir. Judge).

custody of the marshal, any irregularity in the original seizure is immaterial.

(5) *U. S. v. Tello*

In *U. S. v. Tello*,[101] it was held that it is a crime under section 37 of the *Criminal Code*[102] for two or more persons to conspire together, on an American vessel twenty-five miles from the shore, to smuggle dutiable or prohibited merchandise into the country, and that, therefore, a count setting up these facts is not demurrable. It was said that it is not an offense against the laws of the United States for such a vessel to possess liquors on the high seas, so that an indictment merely charging that an American boat threw liquor overboard twenty-five miles from shore to prevent seizure is demurrable.[103]

[101] (1925) 6 Fed. (2d) 579 (D. C. D. Mass., Morton, Judge). See, also, *Burns* v. *United States* (1924) 296 Fed. 468 (C. C. A., 5th Cir., Bryan, Cir. Judge), and *The Evelyn D.* (1926) 14 Fed. (2d) 321 (D. C. S. D. Ga., Barrett, Dist. Judge).

[102] P. 246, note (83), *supra*.

[103] According to an opinion of the Attorney General of the United States of October 6, 1922, the practice of selling liquors on American ships outside the territorial waters of the United States is not permissible under the law. 33 Opins. Atty. Gen., p. 336. See, also, ibid., vol. 32, p. 332.

PART IV

DIPLOMATIC CORRESPONDENCE; TREATIES; INTERNATIONAL ARBITRATIONS

INTRODUCTORY REMARKS

THE hovering laws have very seldom been under discussion through diplomatic channels. It is only within recent years that the validity of these laws of one country has been questioned by another government. As a matter of fact, it was not until the last half of the last century that these laws came directly under discussion diplomatically, when Great Britain began to object to Spain's claim to a general jurisdiction for all purposes in the marginal seas for two leagues. In some cases, the discussions are incomplete, because some of the communications are not available; but whenever the question has arisen, all available materials have been included. In most cases, however, there has been sufficient material to present, in a general way, the position of the Governments involved. Some early materials are included, in order to show the continuity of the position of the Government in question.

CHAPTER I

DIPLOMATIC DISCUSSIONS, 1806-1892

§ 52. Mr. Madison, Secretary of State, to Messrs. Monroe and Pinkney, Ministers Extraordinary and Plenipotentiary to London, 1806 [1]

The American Ministers had been sent to London in 1806 to treat with Great Britain with reference to some "maritime wrongs which have been committed, and the regulation of commerce and navigation" between the two countries. In referring to the "insults and injuries committed by British cruisers in the vicinity of our shores and harbors," the Secretary of State wrote to the Ministers on May 17, 1806, as follows:

". . . it is proper that all armed belligerent ships should be expressly and effectually restrained from making seizures or searches within a certain distance from our coasts, or taking stations near our harbors commodious for those purposes.

"In defining the distance protected against belligerent proceedings, it would not, perhaps, be unreasonable, considering the extent of the United States, the shoalness of their coast, and the natural indication furnished by the well defined path of the Gulf stream, to expect an immunity for the space between that limit and the American shore. *But at least it may be insisted that the extent of the neutral immunity should correspond with the claims maintained by Great Britain, around her*

---

[1] *American State Papers,* Class I, Forn. Rel., vol. III, p. 119 at 121.

own territory. Without any particular inquiry into the extent of these, it may be observed: 1st. That the British act of Parliament in the year 1736, 9 G. II, c. 35, supposed to be that called the Hovering Act, assumes, for certain purposes of trade, the distance of four leagues from the shore. [Italics the author's.] 2d. That it appears that, both in the reign of James I, and Charles II, the security of the commerce with British ports was provided for by express prohibitions, against the roving or hovering of belligerent ships so near the neutral harbors and coasts of Great Britain, as to disturb or threaten vessels homeward or outward bound, as well as against belligerent proceedings generally, within an inconvenient approach toward British territory.

"With this example, and with a view to what is suggested by our own experience, it may be expected that the British Government will not refuse to concur in an article to the following effect:

" 'It is agreed that all armed vessels belonging to either of the parties engaged in war, shall be effectually restrained by positive orders, and penal provisions, from seizing, searching, or otherwise interrupting or disturbing vessels to whomsoever belonging, whether outward or inward bound, within the harbors or the chambers formed by headlands, or anywhere at sea, within the distance of four leagues from the shore, or from a right line from one headland to another; it is further agreed, that, by like orders and provisions, all armed vessels shall be effectually restrained by the party to which they respectively belong, from stationing themselves, or from roving or hovering so near the entry of any of the harbors or coasts of the other, as that merchantmen shall apprehend their passage to be unsafe, or in danger of being set upon and surprised; and that in all cases where death shall be occasioned by any proceeding contrary to these stipulations, and the offender cannot conveniently be brought to trial and punishment under the laws of the party offended, he shall, on demand made within —— months, be delivered up for that purpose.'

"If the distance of four leagues cannot be obtained, any distance not less than one sea league may be substituted in the article. It will occur to you that the stipulation against the roving and hovering of armed ships on our coasts so as to endanger or alarm trading vessels, will acquire importance as the space entitled to immunity shall be narrowed."

This reference to the British hovering laws by Secretary Madison was made at a time when England was exercising jurisdiction for revenue purposes for two, three, four, eight, and one hundred leagues.[2] This jurisdiction was maintained down to 1876, when the distances of three and four leagues were retained, and one league, which was introduced in 1825 for certain vessels, was again adopted.[3] The United States has exercised jurisdiction for four leagues since 1790.[4] This note is not only tacit acquiescence in the jurisdiction exercised for four leagues by Great Britain, but it shows a disposition and determination on the part of the United States Government to protect trade with its ports not only through the enforcement of hovering laws then in force against smuggling vessels, but, also, by inhibiting the interference, by foreign belligerent vessels, with vessels engaged in legitimate trade.

[2] See pp. 72 and 79, et seq., *supra*.
[3] See p. 151, et seq., *supra*.
[4] See pp. 184 and 228, et seq., *supra*.

§ 53. Discussion in 1874-1875 Between the United States and Great Britain of Spain's Claim to a Zone of Six Nautical Miles for General Maritime Jurisdiction: Distinction Between General Maritime Jurisdiction and Jurisdiction to Protect the Revenue

It has been noted under the discussion of the British law [5] that on February 25, 1875, the British Foreign Office addressed a communication to the Lords of the Treasury, stating that a long-standing difference had arisen, from time to time, between the British and Spanish Governments, growing out of Spain's claim to exercise a general maritime jurisdiction for two leagues, or six nautical miles, from her coasts, whereas Great Britain had contended that according to "the rule recognized by all nations," Spain was not entitled to exercise jurisdiction at a greater distance than one league, or three nautical miles, from the Spanish shore. [6] It was said by the Foreign Office that up to a very recent date the Spanish Government, in arguing the question, had claimed jurisdiction for two leagues generally without any exception or reservation, but that in the last communication to the British Government, a distinction had been drawn between the limit of "military jurisdiction," as to which the Spanish Government did not seriously dispute that three miles was the rule, and "fiscal jurisdiction," as to which it maintained that every independent state had "the right to fix the limit at such a distance from its coasts as may be necessary to defend itself from the attacks which may be made against it, and to prevent intended fraud upon its revenues by boats engaged in

[5] P. 144, *supra.*

[6] In *Regina* v. *Keyn,* II Exchequer Div. 63, decided a year later, the majority of the judges found that no such rule existed. Very few nations had recognized such a rule. See p. 145, note (119), *supra,* for the reason why the Foreign Office was pressing for three miles.

smuggling," and that the Spanish Minister justified this right by the example of other countries, especially by that of Great Britain, whose law (which was referred to as 8 and 9 Vict., c. 87)[7] fixed the limit at various distances for different classes of vessels, far in excess of three miles. Information was asked as to the provisions of the English law then in force and the practice under such laws. In the interdepartmental correspondence that followed this communication, the provisions of the law then in force (16 and 17 Vict., c. 107), taking jurisdiction far beyond three miles in many cases, were discussed, and it was brought out that no complaint had ever been received by any foreign government against their existence or enforcement. The Commissioners of Customs pointed out the dangers to the revenue that would arise from a weakening of the law, and expressed the opinion that no serious harm would be apprehended if Spain should adopt provisions similar to those in force in Great Britain, with the understanding that any interference with British vessels beyond one league, unless justified by proof of illegal or contraband traffic with Spain, would be the subject of compensation to the owners of ship and cargo. With this, the discussions were dropped.

There was no agreement among the different departments of the Government on the question of whether this special jurisdiction was exercised in violation of International Law.

This brief reference to the correspondence in 1875 is made here as a necessary background for the diplomatic correspondence that took place at this time between the British and the United States Governments on the subject of Spain's claims referred to in the letter of the Foreign Office of February 25.[8]

---

[7] P. 105, et seq., *supra*.

[8] Pp. 127-149, *supra*, should be read for the interdepartmental discussions of this question from 1850 to 1875, inclusive.

On October 17, 1874, the British representative at Washington addressed a note to the Department of State, asking for the views of the United States Government as to "the extent of maritime jurisdiction that . . . can properly be claimed by any power," and whether the United States Government "ever recognized the claim of Spain to a 6-mile limit," or "ever protested against such a claim." [9]   This request was accompanied by a copy of a note which the British Chargé d'Affaires at Washington had received from the British Foreign Office, dated September 25, of the same year,[10] and which reads, in part, as follows:

"For many years past questions have, from time to time, arisen between the Governments of Great Britain and Spain with regard to the limit of the maritime jurisdiction of the last-named Power.

"The Spanish Government claim the right to exercise such jurisdiction at a distance of *2 leagues, or 6 nautical miles,* from the Spanish coast, and they found this claim upon a Royal 'Cedula' issued on the 17th December, 1760, confirmed by a Royal Decision of the 1st May, 1775, and by Article 15 of the Royal Decree of the 3rd May, 1830; the present Spanish Minister for Foreign Affairs asserting, in a note addressed to Her Majesty's Chargé d'Affaires at Madrid, on the 4th ultimo, that no protest or reclamation whatever has been presented against those orders, all maritime Powers having acquiesced therein.

"As regards the Government of Great Britain, this assertion of Señor Ulloa is entirely contrary to fact, and Her Majesty's Government can only suppose that it was made through inadvertence. The British Government have always uniformly and strenuously resisted the pretensions of the Spanish Government to exercise jurisdic-

---

[9] *Brit. and Forn. State Papers,* vol. 70, p. 185.
[10] Ibid., p. 186.

tion at a greater distance than *1 league, or 3 nautical miles,* from the Spanish coast seawards, or within bays of the Spanish shore.

"This distance the British Government have always held to be the proper limit of maritime jurisdiction, and Her Majesty's present Government, after consulting the Law Officers of the Crown, entirely concur in that view, which they are advised is supported by the authority of all writers upon international law, and by the decisions of the Tribunals of various countries."

It must be borne in mind that the objection raised in this note was principally to Spain's claim to general jurisdiction over a zone of six miles; the hovering laws, which did nothing more than assert a special jurisdiction over vessels engaged in violating revenue laws, were not referred to in this note. This note probably avoided the mention of these laws because of their long existence in English jurisprudence. The British Government could not very well have protested against the exercise by the Spanish Government of jurisdiction for fiscal purposes beyond one league, as being in contravention of International Law; for, as the Spanish Government had pointed out, England's own laws took jurisdiction for this purpose for a much greater distance than those of Spain. It would be no answer for the British Government to say that it had ceased to enforce its own laws beyond one league from the shore, for, since the large majority of the maritime Powers had enforced similar laws for many years beyond that distance, a sudden change of position by one Government could not have the result of upsetting this long-established practice and of ushering in a new principle of International Law.

The reply of the United States Government draws the distinction which it has always made between a claim of general jurisdiction beyond one league from the shore, and the boarding of foreign vessels beyond that distance for a special purpose, under the revenue, or hovering laws. Mr. Fish, the Secretary of State, replied to the British note on January 22, 1875, in part, as follows:

"In reply I have the honor to inform you that this Government has uniformly, under every administration which has had occasion to consider the subject, objected to the pretension of Spain adverted to, upon the same ground and in similar terms to those contained in the instruction of the Earl of Derby.

"We have always understood and asserted that, pursuant to public law, no nation can rightfully claim jurisdiction at sea beyond a marine league from its coast.

"This opinion on our part has sometimes been said to be inconsistent with the facts that, by the laws of the United States, revenue-cutters are authorized to board vessels anywhere within four leagues of their coasts, ...

"*It is believed, however, that in carrying into effect the authority conferred by the act of Congress referred to, no vessel is boarded, if boarded at all, except such a one as, upon being hailed, may have answered that she was bound to a port of the United States. At all events, although the act of Congress was passed in the infancy of this Government, there is no known instance of any complaint on the part of a foreign government of the trespass by a commander of a revenue-cutter upon the rights of its flag under the law of nations.*" [11] (Italics the author's.)

As already noted, the Federal Courts have interpreted the law of the United States in force in 1875 as applying to a vessel engaged in sending goods ashore or unlading

---

[11] *U. S. Forn. Rel.* (1875), Part I, p. 649; *Brit. and Forn. State Papers,* vol. 70, p. 187.

within four leagues of the coast, even though the vessel itself is not technically bound to a port.[12]

The British Government made no reply to the American note. This correspondence shows that no government had ever protested against the hovering laws of the United States, Great Britain, and Spain, as late as 1875. It has been noted that the validity of the British hovering laws, extending jurisdiction from two to one hundred leagues, was discussed by several departments of the British Government on several occasions between 1850 and 1875, that there was no agreement on the question among the departments, and that the laws were allowed to remain unchanged, though after 1850 they were seldom enforced against foreign vessels for reasons already stated.[13] The British and United States Governments at this time questioned only the general jurisdiction claimed by Spain for all purposes. One possible reason why the United States and Great Britain took the position at this time that one league was the limit of

[12] See p. 222, et seq., *supra.*

This position of the United States Government was taken again in 1880 and 1886. See pp. 265 and 268, *infra.*

The note of January 22 discussed a treaty between the United States and Mexico, the treaty of Guadalupe-Hidalgo, of February 2, 1848, Art. V of which reads as follows:

"The boundary line between the two Republics shall commence in the Gulf of Mexico, three leagues from land, opposite the mouth of the Rio Grande, . . . from thence up the middle of that river, following the deepest channel. . . ." 9 *Stat. at Large,* p. 926.

In referring to this treaty, Mr. Fish said that it "may be remarked that it was probably suggested by the passage in the act of Congress referred to, and designed for the same purpose, that of preventing smuggling. By turning to the files of your legation, you will find that Mr. Bankhead, in a note to Mr. Buchanan of the 30th of April, 1848, objected on behalf of Her Majesty's Government, to the provision in question. Mr. Buchanan, however, replied in a note of the 19th of August, in that year, that the stipulation could only affect the rights of Mexico and the United States, and was never intended to trench upon the rights of Great Britain, or of any other power under the law of nations."

[13] See pp. 129-130, *supra.*

general jurisdiction in the marginal seas is found in the fact that both these Powers had enacted certain laws and had become parties to several treaties adopting that distance as the extent of jurisdiction to regulate the fisheries and to enforce neutrality laws.[14]   On the other hand, various other distances had been adopted in other treaties and laws.[15]   None of these laws or treaties, however, dealt with the question of smuggling from sea, which has always been treated as a subject of special legislation by the littoral state, as the laws of the United States, Great Britain, and other Powers show.[16]

§ 54. The Mina Bell (1879)

The only facts of this case obtainable are found in a single communication from the Secretary of State to the American Minister to Mexico; [17] and as they are very incomplete, the case is, therefore, not very helpful. According to this communication, the *Mina Bell*, an American vessel, was chartered for a voyage from San Francisco to a Mexican port; she carried duty-free goods. On August 9, 1879, the vessel arrived off the coast of San Blas, Mexico, and, encountering rough weather, anchored about four miles from that port. A Mexican customs boat went out to her, and without warning, began firing on her; she was then boarded, taken into port, where the goods were seized and proceedings were instituted against the vessel. After a sham trial, the

[14] For a list of some of these treaties and laws, see *The Extent of the Marginal Sea* (1919) by Henry C. Crocker, p. 532, et seq., and p. 630, et seq. See p. 300, *infra*, and p. 145, note (119), *supra*, for other reasons why the British Government was pressing for three miles.

[15] Ibid., pp. 547, 548, 552, 649.

[16] The seizure of smuggling vessels has been a subject of treaty between several Powers within quite recent years. See pp. 346, 352, 353, *infra*.

[17] *MS., Instructions to Mexico*, vol. 19, pp. 570-5. The brief reference to this case in Moore, *Digest of International Law*, vol. I, p. 731, is misleading.

master was fined $1,200, for which the ship and goods were held. The Secretary of State wrote to Mr. Foster, the American Minister to Mexico, that this case presented a claim for damages, including loss of time, for the goods were duty-free, and the acts complained of were committed by officials of the Mexican Government. The Secretary of State added that the conduct of the marines in firing on the ship, forcibly boarding and taking control of her when she was beyond a marine league from the shore and outside the maritime jurisdiction of Mexico, was in itself an outrage which, in the opinion of the Department, should not be allowed to pass unnoticed, and that the practice of the Mexican frontier customs officers in seizing and making illegal exactions of small defenseless American vessels had occurred with sufficient frequency to be a source of disquietude to the United States Government. Instructions were given to lay the facts before the Mexican Government for the purpose of obtaining reparations.

It is difficult to see how the fact that the firing into and the unwarranted interference with this innocent vessel took place beyond a marine league, could affect the merits of the case. The fact remains that the vessel was not a smuggler and that it was fired upon and forcibly taken without having been given the usual signal. These considerations would have given rise to a claim against the Mexican Government, even if the firing and seizure had taken place within one league of the shore, or even in port. The sham nature of the trial was further cause for complaint. The Secretary's casual reference to the marine league in connection with this case was not an intimation that the United States Government objected to an interference beyond that distance with an American vessel engaged in the violation of Mexican laws. This vessel was bound to a Mexican port; and since the

United States exercised jurisdiction for four leagues over vessels bound to her ports, she could not have complained if another country boarded, searched, and arrested a vessel bound to one of its ports, flying the American flag, only four miles out. The substance of the complaint was that the ruthless conduct of the officials towards this vessel was unwarranted, and not that it took place beyond a marine league.

§ 55. Diplomatic Discussions Between the United States and Spanish Governments in 1880-1881

The United States had complained repeatedly of the indiscriminate visitation and search as a belligerent measure, of all American commercial vessels passing the Cuban coast, by armed cruisers of Spain. After considerable correspondence had taken place on this question with the Spanish Government, Mr. Evarts, Secretary of State, in a note of August 11, 1880, to Mr. Fairchild, Minister to Spain, again upheld the principle of the revenue laws, explained their special purpose and function, and pointed out the distinction that must be drawn between such laws and the general jurisdiction which Spain was claiming, to stop and search all vessels passing within six miles of the coast, whether they were apparently engaged upon an illicit voyage or not. He said:

"The revenue regulations of a country framed and adopted under the motive and to the end of protecting trade with its ports against smuggling and other frauds which operate upon vessels bound to such ports have, without due consideration, been allowed to play a part in the discussions between Spain and the United States on the extent of maritime dominion accorded by the law of nations which does not belong to them. In this light are to be regarded the royal decrees which it has been claimed by the Spanish Government had for more than a hundred years established two leagues as the measure of maritime jurisdiction, asserted and exercised by the Spanish crown, both in peninsular and colonial waters. Of this character, obviously, are the regulations of our revenue system in force since 1799, which not only allow but enjoin visitation of vessels bound to our ports within four leagues from land, which, in her diplomatic correspondence with this government, Spain has much insisted on as equivalent to its own dominion as asserted off its coasts, except that our authority was exerted at twice the distance from land.

"But the distinction between dominion over the sea, carrying a right of visit and search of all vessels found within such dominion, and fiscal or revenue regulations of commerce, vessels and cargoes engaged in trade as allowed with our ports to a reasonable range of approach to such ports, needs only to be pointed out to be fully appreciated. Every nation has full jurisdiction of commerce with itself, until by treaty stipulations it has parted with some portion of this full control. In this jurisdiction is easily included a requirement that vessels seeking our ports, in trade, shall be subject to such visitation and inspection as the exigencies of our revenue may demand, in the judgment of this government, for the protection of the revenues and the adequate administration of the customs service. *This is not dominion over the sea where these vessels are visited, but dominion over this commerce with us, its vehicles and cargoes, even while at sea. It carries no assertion of dominion, territorial and in invitum, but over voluntary trade in progress and by its own election, submissive to our regulations of it, even in its approaches to our coasts and while still outside of our territorial dominion.* [Italics the author's.]

"You will observe, therefore, that the American vessels

which have been interfered with thus unwarrantably were not engaged in trade with .Cuba, and were in no degree subject to any surveillance or visitation of revenue regulation. The acts complained of, if, indeed, as our proofs seem to make clear, without the league accorded as territorial by the law of nations, have no support whatever from the principle of commercial regulation which I have explained. Spain had no jurisdiction over the waters in which our vessels were found, no jurisdiction over the trade in which they were engaged; and no warrant under the law of nations, to which alone these vessels in this commerce were subject, can be found for their arrest by the Spanish gunboats." [18]

In referring to this same practice of Spain, the Secretary of State again wrote to Mr. Fairchild in 1881 as follows:

"The wide contradiction between the several statements does not suffice to bring the position of three of the vessels at the time within the customary nautical league. This government must adhere to the three-mile rule as the jurisdictional limit, and the cases of visitation *without that line* seem not to be excused or excusable under that rule.

"This government frankly and fully accepts the disclaimer of the Government of His Majesty that any intention of discourtesy existed in these proceedings. *It insists, however, on the importance of a clear understanding of the jurisdictional limit. It insists, likewise, on the distinction between the verification (according to the usual procedure of revenue cruisers), within a reasonable range of approach, of vessels seeking Spanish ports in the due pursuit of trade therewith, and the arrest by armed force, without the jurisdictional three-mile limit,*

[18] *U. S. Forn. Rel.,* 1880, pp. 922, 926.

of vessels not bound to Spanish ports." [19]   (Italics the author's.)

A note embodying this language was sent to the Spanish Government,[20] asking for the views of that Government "in regard to the question of jurisdictional limit." The Spanish Minister of State replied on April 4, 1881:

". . . it is my duty to say to you that the jurisdictional limits within which the government of His Majesty understands itself to have exercise, necessarily refers to those established by our special legislation of customs and the reglamentary dispositions for the prevention of smuggling, which covers an extension of six miles (equivalent to 11.111 kilometers) from the coast to the high seas.

"These limits were designated in 1775, repeated in 1830, and also in the royal decree of 20th June, 1852, relative to the prevention of smuggling, and finally in article 42 of the general customs ordinances of July, 1870, and as there exists no treaty which conventionally modifies these dispositions, and as no power has protested against them in the period of so many years, the Spanish Government, apart from the right which corresponds to Spain, in the use of its sovereignty, and in conformity with the regulations admitted by international law to fix the extension of its fiscal zone, deems it its duty to maintain and to cause them to be respected." [21]

§ 56. The View of the United States in 1886

In 1886, in a discussion of the question of jurisdiction over the fisheries in the marginal seas, the Secretary of State wrote a letter to the Secretary of the Treasury, in

[19] Ibid., 1881, p. 1052. Vessels bound to the port include vessels standing off the coast endeavoring to send or engaged in sending their illicit wares ashore, that is, vessels trading with the shore. See p. 222, *supra.*

[20] Ibid., p. 1053.

[21] Ibid., 1881, p. 1054.

which he reviewed the various communications of the United States Government on this subject, and among those referred to was the note of Mr. Fish to Great Britain of January 22, 1875, which excepted the revenue laws from the so-called rule of three miles.[22]

[22] 160 *MS. Dom. Letters*, 348 (1886). See p. 261, *supra*, for Mr. Fish's note.

CHAPTER II

THE COQUITLAM (1892-1920): DIPLOMATIC CORRE-SPONDENCE AND ARBITRATION BETWEEN THE UNITED STATES AND GREAT BRITAIN

§ 57. Review of the Facts

The facts of this case and the decisions in the Federal Courts have been considered in another connection.[1] To review them briefly at this point, a Canadian vessel was seized by American revenue officers "at or near Port Etches," Alaska, less than one-half mile from shore,[2] for having taken on, several days before, the catch of a Canadian sealing fleet and delivering to such fleet some supplies, at a point between three and seven miles from the Alaskan shore, where the master thought that in making the exchange he would not be acting in violation of the laws of the United States. After the exchange, the fleet returned to its fishing grounds, and the supply vessel, the *Coquitlam,* with no intention on the part of the master or crew to unlade the catch taken from the fleet or to introduce it into the United States in any manner, touched at the point where she was seized, while en route to Canada. She was libelled, and for cause of forfeiture, among others, she was proceeded against in the Federal Court for having taken on cargo within four leagues of the shore in violation of sections 2867 and 2868 of the *Revised Statutes* then in force. The vessel was condemned as forfeited by that court, but on appeal to the Circuit Court of

[1] See p. 203, et seq., *supra.*
[2] *British Memorial,* vol. II, p. 36.

Appeals, the decision was reversed on the ground that the sealing fleet was not bound to the United States, and that its cargo was not destined for the United States. This case was in the courts for a number of years before its final disposition by the Circuit Court of Appeals, so that great loss resulted to the owners. The view has already been expressed that the seizure and proceedings were wholly unjustified and unwarranted under the laws of the United States, as the Circuit Court of Appeals pointed out, since the vessel was pursuing a peaceful voyage with no intention to smuggle any goods into the United States. The revenue laws have been applied only to vessels bent upon smuggling.[3] For this reason, the United States Government eventually acknowledged its liability in this case, and agreed to submit it to an arbitral tribunal for an assessment of damages.

The contention of the British Government in the correspondence that follows, that a government may not seize a vessel within three miles from the shore and proceed against it for an offense committed beyond that disstance is inconsistent with its own laws and court decisions. The Act of 6 Geo. IV, c. CVIII, section 5,[4] and the corresponding sections of subsequent acts,[5] subjected foreign vessels to forfeiture when found within one league of the shore, having or *having had* on board any goods liable to forfeiture for being imported into the United Kingdom; and the Act now in force subjects foreign subjects to arrest within one league, and imprisonment, for offenses committed far beyond that distance.[6]

In *Attorney General* v. *Schiers*,[7] a foreign subject was arrested within one league of the shore and imprisoned

---

[3] See p. 147, *supra.*
[4] P. 108, *supra.*
[5] P. 108, note (17), *supra.*
[6] P. 158, *supra.*
[7] P. 121, *supra.*

for having been on board a vessel *having had* on board liquors in containers of forbidden size, beyond one league from the shore. In the instant case, since the *Coquitlam* was seized within one league of the shore, the British Government could not consistently complain of the legal proceedings based upon the vessel's conduct beyond that distance. The true grounds of complaint, it is submitted, was that the vessel had violated no law of the United States, and had not engaged in the kind of conduct contemplated by the hovering laws; and these are the grounds upon which the United States Government admitted its liability.

It is important to bear in mind that this case arose at the time when the well-known dispute between the two Governments over the seal fisheries in the Behring Sea was approaching a climax. In fact, the famous Behring Sea Arbitration took place in 1893, at the very time when the controversy over this case was in progress. The United States was insisting upon exercising jurisdiction over the sealers in Behring Sea, and Great Britain was stoutly contesting this jurisdiction. The latter was naturally alert at this time to protest the interference with her vessels engaged in any pursuit or in any course of conduct beyond the acknowledged minimum distance of one league; for if it should make an exception as to vessels engaged in violating revenue laws and permit their seizure for conduct beyond the league, it would weaken her contention that her vessels should not be interfered with beyond that distance when engaged in fishing. As a matter of fact, many of the notes interchanged discussed the *Coquitlam* along with some of the sealers that had been seized. If the Behring Sea controversy had not been in full swing at this time, one is tempted to speculate upon the attitude of the British

Government with reference to the seizure of the *Coquitlam*.[8]

§ 58. Diplomatic Correspondence

The first note sent by the British Government in regard to the seizure of the *Coquitlam* was sent on July 7, 1892. This note from the British Legation to the Department of State stated that the Sealers' Association of Victoria had telegraphed to the Canadian Government, complaining of the seizure of the British steamer *Coquitlam* "at Port Etches just outside Cape Hitchin Crook, about 250 miles East of the entrance to Behring Sea," while taking in water. The purpose of her voyage was commented upon, and it was added that she was seized for transferring stores to and taking on skins from the British sealing fleet, in violation of the United States revenue laws. The Association declared that the transfer was made "outside the 3-mile limit." The Legation asked for any information that the Department might have in regard to the action of the United States authorities at Fort Etches.[9] The next day a request was made for the release of the *Coquitlam* and the skins, against security to be given; it was added that the request was made "without prejudice to any claim which may have to be advanced by Her Majesty's Government as to the illegality of the seizure of the vessel."[10]

The Department replied on July 9, 1892, that it had no information in regard to the seizure, but would furnish the same when secured. It added that the question of

[8] Sir Charles Russel in his argument before the Arbitral Tribunal in 1893, drew a distinction between the jurisdiction claimed by the United States in the Behring Sea and that contemplated by the hovering laws. See p. 375, note (1), *infra*.

[9] *Great Britain, Notes from the British Legation to the Department of State,* vol. 121 (July 1, 1892, to January 1, 1893).

[10] *Ibid.*

releasing the vessel on bond rested solely with the court.[11]
On August 1, 1892, the Department wrote that it had
been informed by the Treasury that the vessel had been
seized for violating sections 2867, 2868, 2806, and 3109 of
the *Revised Statutes* and that the District Attorney was
then preparing the necessary complaint in order to proceed against her in the District Court.[12]

A note of October 3, 1892, from the Legation to the
Department went into the facts of the case in some
detail. It first set out the purposes of the voyage of the
Coquitlam which were said to be: (1) to convey mail to
the fishing fleet, containing positive instructions to every
vessel not to enter Behring Sea; (2) to supply the fleet
with provisions and stores to aid them in continuing their
occupation in Russian and Japanese waters; (3) to bring
back all seal skins already taken by the fleet. It was
noted that no trade or communication with the shore
was contemplated and that no goods were carried for
trading purposes and that the vessel had received positive instructions not to transgress any law in any manner. She met several of the sealers in Tonki Harbour,
from which she towed them out to sea where the transfers were made "outside of the 3-mile limit." The
Coquitlam then sailed in the direction of Port Etches,
about two hundred miles northeast. She was obliged
to enter that port on June 22 in order to secure fresh
water. There were then twenty-five of the sealers in
Port Etches. After delivering mails to this fleet and
directing them to meet her the next day beyond three
miles from the shore, she began to fill her tanks. After
she dropped anchor, she was seized by a United States
revenue cutter, the *Corwin*, on a charge of transferring
stores and skins within twelve miles, or four marine

[11] *Great Britain, Notes from the Department of State to the Legation,* vol. 21 (October 1, 1888, to July 11, 1892), p. 693.
[12] Ibid., vol. 22 (July 12, 1892, to July 30, 1895), p. 29.

leagues from the Alaskan coast. She was then sent to Sitka where she was held with her cargo. The master scrupulously avoided any acts to the detriment of the United States revenue. Reference was then made to the Department's note of August 1, 1892, and the sections of the *Revised Statutes* referred to in that note were set out in verbatim. It was added that Her Majesty's Government had "carefully considered the facts set forth above, in consultation with the Legal Advisers of the Crown," and that the conclusion had been reached that "no breach of any of the sections of the United States Revised Statutes quoted above was committed by the 'Coquitlam,' and that consequently no right to seize the ship or her cargo, or to arrest her crew, or her passengers arose under those sections. It appeared to them that section 2806 [13] applied only to merchandise brought into the United States in the ordinary course of a trading adventure and for the purpose of landing there" and had no application to the facts of this case, and that section 3109 [14] applied only to vessels arriving for the purpose of unlading and taking in cargo. "These points, dealing with matters within the jurisdiction of the United States, are such as might properly have been the subject of a decision by a court of competent jurisdiction, but they do not appear to have been relied upon as justifying the arrest."

"But in so far as the case against the vessel is rested on sections 2867 and 2868, Her Majesty's Government desire to point out these sections apply only to vessels bound to the United States, and further they feel it their duty to protest against any claim on the part of the United States to bring foreign vessels within the jurisdiction of their Municipal Law by reason of anything

[13] P. 204, note, *supra*.
[14] Ibid.

done outside the limit of 3 miles from the coast." Release of the vessel was requested.[15]

On October 17, 1892, the Department, in reply to this note, wrote that the question of the applicability of the appropriate sections of the *Revised Statutes* and all the material facts and allegations offered in defense of the *Coquitlam* "are proper for consideration by the competent court having jurisdiction of the charge of the violation of the laws laid against the vessel." It was added that the case would have to take its course in the judicial branch of the Government, where it was then lodged, free from intervention on the part of the Executive, beyond "such proper steps to expedite the proceedings as may be compelled by the interests of both parties."[16]

The British Government did not reply to the Department's letter of October 17, 1892, until January 13, 1893. The reply observed that the letter of October 17 made no allusion to the last two paragraphs of the British note of October 3, 1892, in which it was maintained that the charge originally made against the vessel was "on account of an act which was undoubtedly committed outside the 3-mile limit," and that the United States officials had no right to seize her and bring her before the court on such a charge. "Her Majesty's Government in consequence feel it to be their duty to renew the protest already entered on their behalf against the assumption that the United States Government can have jurisdiction over a foreign vessel in respect of an act committed on the high seas, an assumption which practically underlies the arguments contained in your note, that the case being in the hands of the Judiciary, the Executive cannot interfere.

[15] *Great Britain, Notes from the British Legation to the Department of State,* vol. 121 (July 1, 1892, to January 31, 1893).

[16] *Great Britain, Notes from the Department of State to the British Legation,* vol. 22 (July 12, 1892, to January 30, 1893), p. 116. This note was based upon advice of the Attorney General, *Misc. Letters,* 1892, Oct., Part I.

"The objection taken by Her Majesty's Government is . . . to the action of the Executive in seizing a British ship for an act which was done outside territorial waters, and which in the opinion of Her Majesty's Government does not even come within the terms of the United States law."

It was said that the British Government was entitled to ask that the prosecution be withdrawn on the ground that the "municipal law of the United States does not extend to British vessels on the High Seas." [17]

The reply of January 17, 1893, stated that "in view of the fact that the seizure . . . is understood to have been made in waters over which the laws of the United States for the protection of the revenue extend, and of the further fact, that the seizure is still the subject of a judicial proceeding, I can only repeat the statement made in my note to your Legation of October 17th last, that the judicial proceeding must be allowed to take its course. When that is concluded, this Department will take pleasure in examining any claim which your Legation may think (?) called upon to make growing out of the facts of the case."

On January 13, 1894, the Department wrote the British Legation, referring to a conversation relative to this case, and added that "the Attorney General is unwilling to confess error upon the record and thus terminate the judicial proceeding." It was suggested that "the international question be allowed to rest until the determination of the appeal, when its consideration can be resumed . . . without prejudice to either country." [18]

This letter was acknowledged on August 22, 1894, with

[17] *Great Britain Notes,* vol. 121 (July 1, 1892, to January 31, 1893). This position of the British Government is inconsistent with her own laws and court decisions. See p. 158, *supra.*

[18] *Great Britain, Notes from the Department to the British Legation,* vol. 22, p. 461.

the request that the appeal be heard at an early date.[19] The Department replied on August 31, 1894,[20] suggesting that the claim arising from the seizure of the *Coquitlam* be embraced in the lump-sum settlement which had been suggested in a note of the Department of August 21,[21] in payment of all claims for damage growing out of the controversy between the two Governments over seizures of British sealers in the Behring Sea, so that if this suggested lump-sum settlement were agreed upon, it would embrace the claim of the *Coquitlam*, and the subsequent proceeding of the court would appear immaterial. The British Government replied on October 17, 1894, that the United States had not admitted the illegality of the seizure of the vessel, as the vessel was still "sub-judice," and that the vessel had not been seized on any ground arising out of the Behring Sea dispute, but for a violation of the revenue laws, and that, therefore, this claim would not be embraced in the proposed settlement. A request was made to press the appeal in the case of *The Coquitlam*.[22]

The Department notified the British Legation on October 25 that the Federal Court had found that the vessel had violated sections 2806 and 3109, among others, of the *Revised Statutes*, which the British note of October 3, 1892, admitted might properly have been the subject of decision by a court of competent jurisdiction and relied upon as justifying the arrest. It was said that the owners had not yet appealed from the decree forfeiting the vessel, for a reason not known.[23]

[19] *Great Britain, Notes from the British Legation to the Department,* vol. 124.

[20] *Great Britain, Notes from the Department to the British Legation,* vol. 22, pp. 606-7.

[21] Ibid., p. 600.

[22] *Great Britain, Notes from British Legation to the Department,* vol. 124. The Department admitted that it had made a mistake in proposing that the claim of the *Coquitlam* be included in the proposed settlement.

[23] *Great Britain, Notes from the Department to the British Legation,*

The decision of the lower Federal Court condemning the vessel was reversed on November 16, 1896, by the Circuit Court of Appeals,[24] for reasons already given. It was not until July 27, 1903, however, that the British Government again brought up the case, and then in connection with certain fishing vessels. It was said that the *Coquitlam* was seized more than three miles from the shore, which was not the fact, for transferring supplies to the sealers within twelve miles of the shore; as noted above, the seizure was made about one-fourth mile from the shore. The decision of the Circuit Court of Appeals was referred to.

In view of the decree of the Circuit Court of Appeals dismissing the libel against the vessel, the United States Government admitted its liability in a note to the British Legation of December 21, 1904.[25] It was said that "the Department is disposed to recognize a liability and to recommend payment of a reasonable indemnity," but that proof of damages sustained would have to be submitted. The United States Government did not accept the view of the British Government that any liability could arise from a seizure for the violation of the hovering laws beyond three miles from the shore, but it based its admission of liability on the fact that an innocent vessel had been improperly seized and proceeded against to its great loss and damage.

---

vol. 22, p. 631. Other correspondence took place in 1896 concerning the substitution of a bond proposed by the Canadian Government in lieu of the bond then on file, but it is of no particular interest in this connection. See pp. 3-6 and 11-13 of the *Supplement to the Answer of the United States* in the Arbitration of this case.

[24] See pp. 203 and 205, *supra*.

[25] *Great Britain, Notes from the Department to the British Legation,* vol. 27, p. 141.

§ 59. The Arbitration

(1) *Contentions of the Governments*

The matter was submitted to the American and British Claims Arbitration Tribunal, and an award rendered on December 18, 1920. In the *Memorial* of the British Government in support of the claim, there was an attempt to show that the *Coquitlam* was not bound to the United States and that, therefore, her conduct was not a violation of section 2867 of the Revised Statutes, and that the exchange was far beyond twelve miles from the shore—not less than five and a half leagues.[26] It was said that she put into port under stress of necessity, and that the vessel was not one that could "arrive" within the meaning of the Act, for she was not destined to any port or place for the exchange of commerce, since the ship was only a supply ship.[27] It was further contended that the hovering laws have no application in a case where "no intention exists to proceed either to the territory or territorial waters of the country which relies on such legislation." "In any event," it was argued, "the Hovering Acts do not extend to (?) the ordinary territorial limits and as against the vessels of an objecting nation cannot be legally enforced beyond one marine league from shore."[28] It was said, further, that the taking of a ship outside the ordinary territorial limits of jurisdiction is limited by law to the case of "hot pursuit" after an infraction of the law in the territorial jurisdiction.[29] Great stress was laid upon the fact that under section 3109, the

[26] Vol. I, p. 38.

[27] Ibid., p. 39.

[28] Ibid., p. 41, citing *The Louis*, 2 Dodson 245; Wheaton, *Elements of International Law* (8th ed. by Richard Henry Dana), section 180, note 108; *The Appollon*, 9 Wheaton 362; *Crapo* v. *Kelley*, 16 Wall. 633; *The Scotland*, 105 U. S. 24.

[29] This argument is not in point, for the ship was taken within one league of the shore.

vessel had not "arrived" when merely passing through or "lying in" quays or ports of refuge.

While the United States Government had admitted liability, it denied all liability before the Arbitration Tribunal. In the *Answer of the United States*,[30] it was said that the transfer to the steamers off Tonki Bay took place "within the coastal waters bounded by the so-called twelve-mile limit," somewhere "between three and seven miles."[31] After referring to the American note of December 21, 1904, admitting liability, it denied liability on the part of the United States, for the following reasons:

(1) The revenue officers in seizing the *Coquitlam* acted in the *bona fide* belief that the revenue laws of the United States had been violated and the evidence showed that there was probable cause for that belief, and that the decree of dismissal was based upon a technical construction of the language of the statute;

(2) Sections 2806, 2807, and 2809 of the *Revised Statutes* provide that no merchandise shall be brought into the United States from any foreign port in any vessel, unless a manifest is on board, and none was on board this vessel;

(3) Sections 2867 and 2868 of the *Revised Statutes* were violated by the unlading within four leagues from the shore—"within the jurisdictional limits of the United States for revenue purposes." It was also contended that since the purpose of the meeting in Tonki Bay was to make the transfer, the necessary act of transfer included the towing out to sea, which was a part of the actual unlading and the receipt of the skins, and that, therefore, it was immaterial with respect to the question of violation of these two sections whether the actual transfer was made at a greater distance from the shore than twelve miles;

[30] P. 3.   [31] Ibid., p. 38.

(4) The vessel did not put into port from necessity.[32]

The British claim, as reflected in the diplomatic correspondence and the British *Memorial,* was based upon the following contentions:

(1) The laws of the United States were not, in fact, violated, as no merchandise was brought into the United States in the ordinary course of trading, and as the vessel had not arrived there for the purpose of unlading its cargo; the sections of the *Revised Statutes* relating to unlading within four leagues of the coast were not applicable to the case, because they apply only to vessels bound to the United States.

This was the true ground upon which the libel was dismissed by the Circuit Court of Appeals and upon which the British claim for damages actually had to rest.

(2) The act for which the vessel's condemnation was sought was committed more than one league from the shore.

As already pointed out, this contention is untenable. A vessel seized within one league of the shore may be condemned for an offense committed beyond it, in both English and American law.[33]   The question of the jurisdiction to seizure beyond three miles from the shore was not presented by the case.

(3) The *Coquitlam* put into port where she was seized in distress.

(2) *The Award*

The Award of the Arbitration Tribunal, which assessed damages at $48,000, after reviewing the facts briefly, and commenting upon the dismissal of the libel by the Circuit Court of Appeals, reads in part:

"This decision of the Judicial Authorities of the United

---

[32] Ibid., pp. 4, 5, 6, and 8.

[33] See note of United States Government of January 17, 1893, and p. 277, *supra.*

States is binding upon the Government. It decides that what sections 2867, 2868, of the *Revised Statutes* had in view were vessels bound to the United States and that there was no evidence that the *Coquitlam* was so bound, —that section 3109 contemplated vessels not merely arriving in the United States waters but intending to proceed further inland, either to unload or take on cargo, and that there was on the record no proof of any such intention—that the sections 2807, 2808 and 2809, made liable to forfeiture only such merchandise as is consigned to the master, mate, officers or crew, and that it was not alleged in this case that any merchandise was so consigned.

"The same decision goes on to say that there was no contention 'that any injury has been done to the United States by the acts which are complained of in the libel, or that the United States has in any way been defrauded of revenue, or that there was any intention upon the part of the masters or owners of the vessels to evade the provisions of the revenue laws. The merchandise was not bound to the United States, nor was it consigned to any person, nor destined to be delivered at any place, in the United States.'"

The Tribunal thus bases the liability of the United States Government upon the facts that the Judicial Authorities, whose decision was binding upon the Government, had found that the vessel was not bound to the United States, nor the cargo destined for the United States, that the United States had not been injured in any way, and that the master and owner had not intended to evade the revenue laws. The fact that the act for which the vessel's condemnation was sought in the Federal Courts was committed more than three miles from the shore was not taken into account by the arbitrators; the contention of the British Government upon this point was not even referred to. The liability was rested upon the fact that the revenue authorities had made a mistake, or error in judgment in attempting to apply to the facts of this case the United States revenue laws. In the language of the Award, "since it has been decided by the United States judicial authorities that this application was wrong, liability clearly arises." The language of the Award is very significant; it emphasises the fact that the vessel's exemption rested upon its innocence; and it is, perhaps, a reasonable inference from this language that if the voyage had been an illicit one and if the decree of the Circuit Court of Appeals had been, for that reason, one of forfeiture, the Tribunal would have found that there was no liability on the part of the United States Government.

The contention of the United States Government that it should not be liable in damages because there was probable cause of seizure, as the revenue officers acted in the *bona fide* belief that the laws had been violated, was rejected, because the Tribunal held that probable cause must rest upon a doubt as to facts "which there is good reason to believe will be established though they are not yet actually proved," whereas, in the instant case, the facts were clear, but the doubt existed as to their "wrongful character," that is, as to their being a violation of the law. The language of the Award on this point is as follows:

"Before this Tribunal the United States Government denies all liability in this case.

"It contends that the construction put upon the language of the Statutes by the Circuit Court of Appeals is a very technical construction, while the construction upon which the officer acted in making the seizure had abundant support in decisions of the United States Courts prior to this case, that it is clear when this circumstance is taken in conjunction with the facts as disclosed that the officer acted in the *bona fide* belief that the revenue laws of the United States had been infringed, and that for this belief there was probable cause.

"The good faith and fair conduct of the officers of the *Corwin* are unquestionable, but though this may be taken into account as an explanation given by the same officers to their Government, it cannot operate to prevent their action being an error in judgment for which the Government of the United States is liable to a foreign Government.

"Further, even supposing that the interpretation of the United States Customs Statutes may have given rise to some doubt, such a doubt cannot constitute a probable cause of seizure. Probable cause of seizure, as defined by Chief Justice Marshall, 'imports a seizure made under circumstances which warrant suspicion' (Locke v. United States, 1813, VII Cranch, 339, at p. 348). It implies the existence of certain facts which *prima facie* create a liability to seizure, facts which there is good reason to believe will be established though they are not yet actually proved. The doubt must be as to the existence of the fact, not as to its wrongful character.

"Since in this case there was no doubt as to the circumstances of fact under which the seizure took place, but, according to the United States contention, some possible doubt as to the application of the Statutes, their application was made by the United States naval authorities at the risk of their Government, and since it has been decided by the United States judicial authorities that this application was wrong, liability clearly arises."

CHAPTER III

DISCUSSION OF THE RUSSIAN FISHERY AND CUSTOMS LAWS, TAKING JURISDICTION FOR FOUR LEAGUES, BY THE UNITED STATES, GREAT BRITAIN, RUSSIA, AND JAPAN, 1910-1912

§ 60. The Russian Customs Law

In 1910, Russia promulgated a law which reads:

"To interpret in the following manner the fourth paragraph of the supplement to paragraph 2 of the Customs regulations (*Collection of Laws, volume VI, Edition of 1904*).

"1. The Surface of the water for twelve marine miles from extreme low-water mark from the seacoasts of the Russian Empire, whether mainland or islands, is recognized as the Marine Customs area, within the limits of which every vessel, whether Russian or foreign, is subject to supervision by those Russian authorities in whose charge is the guarding of the frontiers of the Empire.

"The President of the Council of Empire,
December 10, 1909.   "M. Akimoff." [1]

It should be noted that this law goes rather far in subjecting "every vessel" to supervision within twelve miles of the shore, whereas English and American legislation has always been confined to craft known to be engaged in or attempting to engage in illicit trade with the coast, or whose conduct invites suspicion. If the Russian law is interpreted literally, it authorizes supervision of all vessels, including those passing innocently

[1] *U S. Forn. Rel.,* 1912, p. 1289.

within twelve miles of the shore, and would, therefore, call for protest by other nations.

§ 61. Correspondence Between the Japanese and Russian Governments

The Japanese Government, by a *note verbale* of December 16/29, 1910, to the Russian Government, stated that it had learned that the law of December 10, 1909, recently established the limits of the territorial sea for customs surveillance at twelve marine miles, and declared that, in its opinion, the limits of such sea, universally admitted by international usage to be three marine miles, could not be enlarged without a previous agreement of the interested powers. It was added that the Japanese Government was sure that the Imperial Government of Russia held this view, and, in order to avoid any misunderstanding concerning the application of the Russian Law, it was sure that the Russian Government had no intention of applying the law to Japanese vessels and subjects outside the limits of three marine miles.[2]

[2] The text of the Japanese note reads:

"Le Gouvernement Impérial du Japon a appris que le Gouvernement Impérial de Russie vient d'établir, par une loi du 10 decembre 1909, les limites de la mer territoriale des côtes russes à douze milles marins, en ce qui concerne la surveillance douanière.

"Dans l'opinion du Gouvernement japonais, les limites de la mer territoriale universellement admises par les usages internationaux ne sauraient être élargies sans un accord préalable des puissances intéressées pour qu'elles puissent être appliquées aux sujets et aux navires de ces puissances.

"Fermement convaincu que cette manière de voir est partagée par le Gouvernement Impérial de Russie et désirant éviter tout malentendu concernant l'application de la loi russe susmentionnée, l'Ambassadeur du Japon a l'honneur, d'après les instructions de son Gouvernement, de faire savoir au Gouvernement Impérial de Russie que le Gouvernement Impérial du Japon aime à croire que le Gouvernement russe n'a aucune intention d'appliquer la loi en question aux sujets ou aux navires japonais en dehors des limites de trois milles marins admis comme limites de la mer territoriale par les usages internationaux."

The author is indebted to the Japanese Embassy at Washington for a copy of this note.

This Japanese note does not state whether the Japanese Government would object to the application of this law to a Japanese vessel actually engaged in smuggling; but its objection goes to the general extension of the "territorial sea" for certain purposes. As just pointed out, the Japanese note is, perhaps, justified, if the Russian law is to be applied generally to all vessels that come within twelve miles of the coast, whether engaged upon an illicit voyage or not.

The Russian Minister of Foreign Affairs replied to the Japanese note as follows:

"In reply to the note verbale of —— relative to the limits of customs surveillance along the Russian coasts the Imperial Ministry of Foreign Affairs has the honor to draw the attention of the Imperial Embassy of Japan to the fact that in modern international law there exists no generally accepted rule concerning the limits of territorial waters within which sovereign state authority may be exercised.

"The question has been given widely different solutions either by international treaties or the municipal laws of a state, and very often in an unequal manner for the various protected interests (customs regulations, fisheries, criminal or civil jurisdiction, sanitary observation, etc.).

"Thus an examination of the laws dealing with the question shows that a great many States in Europe and America exercise undisputed jurisdiction within limits that exceed the so-called ordinary zone of three nautical miles.

"Sections 2760, 2867, and 3067 of the *Revised Statutes* of the United States of America, for instance, fix the limit of the jurisdiction of American customs officers at 4 marine leagues (12 nautical miles), exactly the distance set by the new Russian law of 1909.

"The jurisdiction of British officers in all customs and quarantine cases also covers (under Article XXIII of chap. 35 of the British Act 9 Geo. II; Article XII of chap. 80 of Acts 39 and 40 Geo. III; and Article I of chap. 47 of Act 24 Geo. III) a 4 marine-league zone.

"Finally, under the law of March 27, 1817, the customs marine zone of France reaches out 2 myriameters from the coast.

"Taking into consideration the above-cited provisions of laws against which no State appears to have protested, together with the fact that Russia is not bound by any international treaty fixing the 3-mile zone for the territorial waters and that therefore its area cannot be measured from the viewpoint of international law except by the range of the cannons on the coast (which now even exceed the 12-nautical-mile limit) the Imperial Government is unable to admit that the Russian law of December 10, 1909, conflicts with international law.

"Lastly, the Imperial Ministry deems it its duty to recall to the Japanese Embassy's memory that the Institute of International Law (whose authority on such questions is unquestionable) did not hesitate to declare (as far back as 17 years ago, when it met at Paris, in 1894) that the 'usually adopted' distance of three miles was absolutely insufficient. Fully concurring in that view, the Netherlands Government soon thereafter (1895) took the initiative of an international conference (unfortunately never going beyond the stage of being contemplated) which was to give special attention to the question of territorial waters and accurately define the law common to all States, the lack of which the Imperial Government is not the last to deplore.

"It might perhaps be possible, should all the States interested therein arrive at an agreement thereon, to include that question, of such importance to international life, in the program of the approaching Third Peace Conference that is to meet at The Hague about 1915." [3]

§ 62. Correspondence Between the Russian and United States Governments

The Russian Government addressed a note to the Department of State on April 12, 1910, stating that the British Government contended that the Russian law was "contrary to the principles of international law," and inquiring if the British Government had ever protested against sections 2760, 2867, and 3067 of the *Revised Statutes* of the United States, which provided for "a zone of 4 leagues (equal to 12 miles) within which the authority of the United States Customs officers is exercised." The United States replied that "there is no record of any protest having been made at any time by Great Britain." [4]

§ 63. Position of the United States Government—Correspondence Between the American Ambassador and the Department of State

On September 30, 1910, the United States Ambassador to Russia wrote to the Secretary of State as follows and asked for instructions:

"I learn from the British Embassy that shortly after the promulgation of this law, the British Government gave notice that with reference to this question it reserved the rights of its subjects as fixed by international usage. The Russian Government replied that, in the absence of treaty provisions to the contrary, the determination of the limits to which customs supervision could be extended was a question not of international usage but of domestic regulation; and it instanced similar enactments of other Powers, including the United States (presumably refer-

[3] Ibid., p. 1308.
[4] Ibid., p. 1287.

ring to section 2760 of the Revised Statutes quoted in Moore's Digest, I, 725, § 151); and it asked for a more precise statement of the rights which the British Government had declared its intention of reserving. The British Government thereupon expressed its unwillingness to acquiesce under any circumstances in a claim to jurisdiction over marginal seas beyond the generally recognized three-mile limit. To this expression of views the Russian Government has not yet replied." [5]

This note was followed by another one of January 16, 1911, in which it was stated that the customs law was complicated with Russia's proposal to exclude foreigners from fishing within the same distance from the shore— twelve miles.

To the note of September 30, 1910, the Department of State replied on January 21, 1911, in part, as follows:

"You will inform yourself thoroughly on the nature and extent of the jurisdiction assumed under the Russian law and report fully to the Department especially as to the operation of the law upon American shipping. Meanwhile you will discreetly call the matter to the attention of the Minister for Foreign Affairs, and state that with reference to the general operation of the law over the marginal seas beyond the generally recognized three mile limit and particularly as affecting American commerce, the United States is constrained to reserve all rights of whatever nature." [6]

On February 13, 1911, the American Ambassador

[5] Ibid., p. 1288. He added that the German Ambassador had informed him that the German Government had made no protest against the law, but that one of the Secretaries of the Japanese Embassy had made inquiries at the American Embassy as to the attitude of the Department of State on this question and, "While careful not to make any specific statement, he gave the impression that his (the Japanese) Government is endeavoring to learn the attitude of the other Powers with a view to remonstrating against the Russian claim if it finds that it may rely upon support in such a protest."

[6] Ibid., p. 1298.

reported that he had carried out the instructions of January 21, and that the Minister of Foreign Affairs had promised information as to the nature and extent of the jurisdiction. He stated that the Russian Minister of Foreign Affairs, discussing the application of the customs and fishery laws for a distance of twelve miles, took the position that "the territorial jurisdiction over marginal seas is based on the theory of control from the land, and that the delimitation of this area of control at twelve miles now corresponds more nearly with actual conditions than does the three-mile limit which represented the effective range of cannon at the time when this limitation of control over the seas was recognized as a principle of international law." [7]

The American Ambassador, on May 16, reported that the British Ambassador had informed him that "the question is now under discussion of bringing the whole subject (not only of the twelve-mile limit, but of the fisheries also) before an international conference." He wrote on June 21 that he was informed by the British Chargé d'Affaires "that his Government has not yet reached any definite conclusions in its discussions of the matter with the Russian Government," and that the President of the Council of Ministers, to whom he had spoken on the subject, "seemed disposed to agree, in principle, to the submission of the question, in a limited form, to a conference, but not otherwise." He added: "I cannot learn that any of the other diplomatic representatives are taking any part whatsoever in the discussion of this matter with the Russian Government." [8]

Nothing further developed until January 19, 1912, when the Acting Secretary of State wrote to the American Ambassador to make further inquiry regarding the fishery

[7] Ibid., p. 1299.
[8] Ibid., pp. 1301-2.

law referred to in the note of January 16 of the previous year. Nothing was said of the customs law at this time. The American Ambassador replied on February 3, 1912, that, "The whole matter is most complicated and confusing, but conferences with the British and Japanese Embassies and with the Secretary of Foreign Affairs have helped me to a clearer understanding on the question." It appears from the rest of this note that the Powers were levelling their objections principally at the fishery law, or to the attempt of Russia to extend its jurisdiction to twelve miles for all purposes. The question of the customs regulations soon dropped out of consideration, and the controversy was waged over the fishery legislation. The Ambassador said:

"Russia proposes ultimately to extend her control in every way to a distance of twelve miles from all her coasts bordering on the ocean. This has not yet been fully accomplished, but only in part. The question naturally groups itself into three divisions:

"1. The exercise of customs authority to a distance of twelve miles from all her coasts on the open sea.

"This law was approved by the Emperor December 10/23, 1909, promulgated January 1/14, 1910, and is now in force. As yet, so far as can be ascertained, no case calling for special international protest has occurred under it.

"2. The extension of Russian jurisdiction over all open-sea fisheries on the Pacific coasts within twelve miles of the lands of the Russian Empire.

"This law was passed May 29/June 11, 1911, and went into force December 25/January 7, last.

"3. The law extending jurisdiction over fisheries conducted in the White Sea and within twelve miles of the Archangel Government was reported favorably by the Committee to the Duma last June, but has not yet been passed. It lies on the table and it is reported that English influence is responsible for the delay in its passage.

"England has formally protested against all three of these laws in particular and against the attitude of Russia in general in regard to the extension of jurisdiction from three miles to twelve. Not being, however, specially interested in the Pacific Coast fisheries, England has confined vigorous action to the Archangel and White Sea fisheries, where her interests are large. England hopes to be able to get this proposed law postponed long enough to permit the matter to be presented before the next Hague Conference in 1915. The President of the Duma has assured the British Ambassador that the project cannot be reached by the present Duma, and M. Sazonov practically admitted the same thing to me.

"Japan also has protested in general against the whole proposition of extension of jurisdiction to twelve miles from shore in the open sea, but she has confined her vigorous action to the fisheries in the Pacific, where her direct interests are enormous. The annual Japanese catch of fish in what are now claimed to be Russian waters is valued in gross by the Japanese Embassy at 80,000,000 roubles.

"Japan contends that the section of these laws dealing with Pacific fisheries is not only in violation of international law, but is also a violation of the spirit of the existing Russo-Japanese Fishery Agreement.

"Two Japanese delegates representing the fishing fleet of Japan are now here seeking amelioration of present conditions.

"The Japanese Embassy filed a formal note of protest on October 31 last in regard to Russia's action in the Pacific Fisheries, but as yet has received no answer.

". . . M. Sazonov in a long interview last night assured me that Russia proposed to maintain the twelve-mile limit as a permanent policy, though he hinted that it might be modified in detail, and frankly stated that Russia had agreed to hold conversations with the representatives of Japan and of England, especially on the points in which the two countries were especially interested.

"Russia contends that the three-mile limit is obsolete. The distance of three miles having been set as the conventional range of a cannon, it is claimed that with the extension of the range of modern ordnance the limit of jurisdiction should be increased to correspond."

It was said that M. Sazonov had stated that under no circumstances would Russia consent to refer such a question to "The Hague tribunal." [9]

§ 64. Summary of the Positions of the Governments

The notes of the British Government and those of the Japanese Government, referred to in the communications from the American Ambassador, except the one quoted above, are not available. This fact necessarily leaves a gap in this most important controversy. The following conclusions, however, are clear:

1. The United States Government entered no protest against the Russian customs or fishing laws, but it expressed some concern over the effect of the customs law upon American shipping in general; it did nothing more than instruct the American Ambassador to determine "the nature and extent of the jurisdiction" assumed under the law, to report as to its "operation . . . upon American shipping," and discreetly to call the matter to the attention of the Russian Minister of Foreign Affairs, and to state that with reference to the "general operation of the law" over the marginal sea beyond three miles from the

[9] Ibid., pp. 1304-5.

shore and "particularly as affecting American commerce, the United States is constrained to reserve all rights of whatever nature."

The United States Government seemed to be chiefly concerned over the possibility that the Russian Government might attempt to enforce the law against all vessels found within twelve miles of the shore, whether bound for a port or merely passing, without reference to whether such vessels were actually engaged in smuggling or were suspected of being engaged upon a smuggling voyage. Such a general application of the law might easily inconvenience or interfere with legitimate commerce, and it was such a possible interference that evoked the inquiry of the United States Government. In other words, the tenor of the American note would imply that any objection that the United States Government might have had to the law was that it assumed jurisdiction *generally* over a zone of twelve miles. Beyond this, its objection could not very well go; for its own laws had always permitted and do permit the boarding, searching, and seizing of vessels whose conduct create suspicion, within the same distance from the shore.[10]

2. The Russian Government was emphatic in its opinion that the limits of customs surveillance and "territorial waters" were not fixed at three miles by International Law, but that these were questions of domestic regulation; and in view of the laws of the United States, Great Britain, and France, it was "unable to admit that the Russian law of December 10, 1909, conflicts with International Law." It was equally firm in its position that in International Law there existed "no generally

---

[10] The United States could not very well have objected to the application of this law to an American vessel actually engaged in smuggling. See *The Coquitlam*, pp. 203 and 270, et seq., *supra*, and the laws of the United States, pp. 184 and 228, et seq., *supra*, and pp. 217 and 234, et seq., *supra*.

accepted rule concerning the limits of territorial waters within which sovereign state authority may be exercised," but that the area of such waters "cannot be measured from the viewpoint of international law except by the range of the cannons on the coast (which now even exceed the 12-nautical-mile limit). . . ."

3. The Japanese Government and, according to the American notes, the British Government, protested against this general extension of "territorial waters" to twelve miles by the Russian laws; these Powers, it was said, concentrated their attacks upon those sections of the laws which directly affected their largest fishing interests, that is, those sections that would curtail the English and Japanese fishing grounds. Great Britain could not very well have protested against the customs law, in view of her own legislation extending over a period of two hundred years.

Since the discussion of the customs law was soon lost sight of in the discussion of the fishery laws, one is tempted to ask if the discussions would have arisen at all if the customs law had not been accompanied by the fishing laws, in view of the fact that no nation had ever protested against the customs laws of the United States and Great Britain asserting jurisdiction over foreign vessels, in some cases, for the same distance as that claimed by the Russian law in question.

§ 65. Discussions in Parliament

The discussions in Parliament in 1911 throw light upon this controversy. It is significant to observe that no mention was made of the Russian customs law in these discussions, but that the remarks were addressed solely to the Russian fishery legislation.

On February 9, 1911, the question was asked in the House of Commons if the government had any information as to Russia's having introduced a bill into the Duma seeking to enlarge her territorial waters for *fishing purposes* from three miles to twelve; and, if so, if this was against treaty rights. Mr. McKinnon Wood, Under Secretary of State for Foreign Affairs, replied that the proposed extension would not be contrary to any treaty between the United Kingdom and Russia, but to the "generally accepted doctrines, i.e., of international law." He stated that His Majesty's Ambassador at St. Petersburg had made representations to the Russian Minister of Foreign Affairs, and that he had "been instructed to address an official protest to the Russian Government against the proposal to extend the fishery limits . . . beyond the ordinary distance of three miles . . . as being contrary to the generally accepted doctrines of International Law." He added that the British fishery industry would be involved.[11]

On February 13, while discussing the "claim by Russia to extend the three-mile limit to twelve miles" in *fishery matters,* Mr. Wood was asked:

"Do the government recognize the right of any State to fix the limit of territorial waters beyond the range of gun fire?" He answered: "No, Sir; we do not recognize that right." [12]

On February 16, Sir Edward Grey, Secretary of State for Foreign Affairs, stated that it would be "contrary to a generally accepted principle of International Law to prohibit foreign fishing vessels from trawling beyond three miles from low-water mark," [13] and on March 11 he stated that he was inquiring as to the interests of Canadian fishermen, and that he would communicate with the Russian Government.[14]

[11] *Parliamentary Debates* (Hansard), 1911, vol. 21, col. 421.
[12] Ibid., col. 675.
[13] Ibid., col. 1422.
[14] Ibid., vol. 22, col. 2039. See, also, ibid., 1911, vol. 21, cols. 674-5, where Mr. Wood refused to express an opinion on the question of

On April 3, Mr. Wood was asked "what was the limits in distance from the mainland of territorial waters claimed for fishery purposes by Norway, Russia, Denmark, Germany, Spain, and Portugal." He replied: "Denmark, Germany, and Portugal maintain a territorial limit of three miles for fishery purposes. Russia is at the present time claiming twelve miles, while Norway and Spain have for some time past claimed four and six miles respectively. His Majesty's Government, however, have always declined to recognize these extensions of the generally accepted three-mile limit.[15] Norway claims exclusive fishery rights in the Westfjord, which lies between the Lofoden Islands and the mainland, but no definite limit to the waters thus claimed appears even to have been specified. The distance from the most southern of the Lofoden Islands to the mainland is about fifty miles." He stated that the British claim to jurisdiction over the Ceylon pearl fisheries (which extends to a distance far beyond three miles) was based on the fact that "the beds are capable of being physically occupied in a manner analogous to the occupation of the land; and, further, because from time immemorial, and, therefore, before the adoption of the present three-mile limit, they have been treated by the successive rulers of Ceylon as subjects of property and jurisdiction, and have been so regarded with the acquiescence of other nations."[16] When asked if the

---

concluding an international agreement for the control of the methods of fishing beyond three miles from the shore, until the results of certain investigations were known. See, also, ibid., col. 849.

[15] These claims are not "extensions" of a three-mile limit, for they were asserted and maintained before the idea of a three-mile limit was ever advanced. They are limitations placed upon the old claims to jurisdiction over the high seas. Denmark and Portugal claim more than three miles.

[16] May it not be asked why this reasoning may not be applied to the hovering acts of nearly all the powers, and to the claims of Norway, Spain, Russia, and other powers for a wider jurisdiction than three miles for other purposes, since such acts and claims existed "before the adoption of the present three-mile limit"?

"three-mile limit" was not accepted by the bordering states along about one-half of the coast of Europe, he replied that, "perhaps the hon. Member would give me notice of that question." [17]

On June 20, when Mr. Harcourt made the statement that three miles were not generally acknowledged, Sir Edward Grey replied that he presumed that the member referred to the two Russian Bills, extending the limits of territorial waters along the northern coasts of European Russia and the Pacific Coasts of Asiatic Russia to twelve miles *in fishery matters*, and that representations had been made to the Russian Government "to the effect that the three-mile limit cannot be altered without international agreement." [18]

The reason why the British Government, at least, has been attempting within recent years to force a "three-mile limit" for all purposes is found in the reason for her protest against the Russian laws in 1912: she feared that the repudiation or abandonment of that limit for any one purpose, even for customs surveillance, might be the basis of an argument against its existence for other purposes, namely fisheries and neutrality. Sir Thomas Barclay observed in 1907 that the adoption of a thirteen-mile limit for fishery purposes would exclude British fishermen from an area of 135,000 square miles of the fishing grounds of Western Europe, or nearly one-third of the area available for trawling, while a nine-mile limit would exclude them from an area of 80,000 square miles; he then added that as the British steam trawling fleet is

[17] *Parliamentary Debates* (Hansard), 1911, vol. 23, cols. 1778-9. See, also, ibid., vol. 26, cols. 1294, 1304, and 1327, where several members pointed out that the so-called three-mile limit had not been generally accepted.

[18] Ibid., vol. 27, col. 132.

It was brought out in these debates that the adherence to the "three-mile limit" by the British Government in the matter of coast fisheries had almost ruined "line fishing." For example, see ibid., 1911, vol. 22, col. 2241; vol. 24, col. 430; vol. 26, cols. 1295-1306; vol. 27, col. 189, and 1899, vol. 67, col. 1347.

more than 6 times greater than that of all other countries combined, "the subject cannot be disposed of as involving legal principles only."[19]   Furthermore, it is

[19] *Problems of International Practice and Diplomacy* (1907), p. 111.

Mr. L. H. Woolsey, Solicitor to the Department of State, wrote an opinion on whether seizures of American vessels beyond the "ordinary limit of territorial waters" under customs regulations such as Russia's, "would be consistent with the rules of International Law." *U. S. Forn. Rel.*, 1912, pp. 1289-1297.   The cases and other authorities relied upon in his opinion are:

Church v. *Hubbart,*

Rose v. *Himely,* and

Hudson v. *Guestier,* which have already been considered (pp. 197, 199, 200, *supra*);

Williams v. *Armroyd* (1813, 7 Cranch 423), which was a capture for trading with the enemy;

Le Louis (1817, 2 Dods. 210), a capture for engaging in slave trade;

In re Cooper (1891, 143 U. S. 473), a fisheries case;

The Sylvia Handy (1891, 143 U. S. 513), involving sealing in the Behring Sea; and the

Behring Sea Claims Commission (1892).

Relying upon these authorities, he reached the conclusion that the question whether municipal seizures beyond the "three-mile limit" are legal, has been decided affirmatively by the municipal courts, bound by municipal law, and negatively by international tribunals governed by international law.   But these authorities confuse the issue; with the exception of the first three cases, they have no bearing upon the question of customs jurisdiction.   The one decision by an international tribunal to which he refers does not sustain his view.   See statement of M. de Courcel, President of the Behring Sea Arbitral Tribunal, *Ann. de l'Inst. de Droit Int.*, for 1894, p. 282, and Hall, *A Treatise on International Law* (8th ed.) (1924) by A. Pearce Higgins, p. 193, note.   In the case of *The Costa Rica Packet* (1897), an arbitration between the Netherlands and Great Britain, M. F. de Martens, the arbitrator, said that "the right of sovereignty of the state over territorial waters is determined by the *range of cannon measured from the low-water mark.*" (Italics the author's). Moore, *Int. Arb. Digest,* vol. V, pp. 4949-54.

The Tatsu Maru (1908), 2 *American Journal of International Law,* p. 391, et seq.   In this case, the Chinese authorities seized a Japanese vessel with a cargo of arms beyond three miles from the shore (it does not appear how far), bound for Macao, a port under Portuguese jurisdiction.   The seizure was made on the ground that the delivery of the cargo to Macao was colorable, for its real destination was ultimately the interior of China, to which it was being shipped for illicit purposes, in violation of the Chinese smuggling, or revenue laws.   The seizure gave rise to diplomatic correspondence.   China accepted the five conditions presented by the Japanese Government, namely:

"1. An apology, with the saluting of the Japanese flag in the presence of the Consul;

"2. Unconditional release of the vessel;

obviously to the interest of the British Government to maintain a narrow limit for purposes of neutrality in time of war. In other words, Great Britain, in order to make sure that her fishermen will not eventually be driven from valuable fishing grounds, and that she will not lose an advantage in time of war, has been endeavoring to enforce a three-mile zone for all purposes. She would thus assimilate the question of smuggling to the questions of the fisheries and neutrality, while the United States and other Governments, as already pointed out, have drawn a sharp and logical distinction between them. If the British Government desired a "three-mile limit" for purposes of fisheries and neutrality, it might well have announced that fact, but made the express exception as to smuggling craft made by most nations and by its own Parliament for centuries.

§ 66. Summary of Diplomatic Discussions, 1806-1912

Thus, in the diplomatic discussions considered before and during the year 1912, Russia, the United States, and

---

"3. Payment of the actual cost of the arms under detention;

"4. China to engage to investigate the circumstances of the seizure and take suitable measures against the responsible persons;

"5. An indemnity for the actual losses."

An editorial in 2 *American Journal of International Law,* at page 391, says that this case supports the view that a vessel may not be seized beyond three miles from the shore to prevent a violation of customs laws. It must not be overlooked, however, that *The Tatsu Maru* presented a special case—this vessel was not bound for a Chinese port and there was no effort to introduce the cargo into China, but the alleged violation of the Chinese laws could not have been committed unless and after the arms were landed on the territory of a third power. The law under which the seizure was made and the diplomatic correspondence that took place between the two governments are not accessible; and this mere outline of the facts from a secondary source is not very helpful in arriving at the positions of two governments, in an international controversy. At least, it would seem to indicate that under Chinese laws smuggling vessels may be seized beyond three miles from the shore; and this would place China on the side of those powers that have enacted and enforce revenue laws extending jurisdiction for a special purpose beyond three miles from the shore.

Spain have taken emphatic stands for the legality of the revenue laws extending jurisdiction beyond three miles from the shore, on the theory that necessity and long usage have given them sanction in International Law, while Great Britain and Japan protested in 1912 against a general extension by Russia of her maritime frontier to twelve miles for revenue and fisheries purposes, and these protests were levelled principally at the fishery laws in their application to those ports of the Russian coasts that most vitally affected the interests of their respective nationals.   The last two Powers named had not protested against customs legislation of other countries.   It is possible that the protests against the Russian customs legislation were based upon the general character of the jurisdiction assumed, and that they would not have been made had that jurisdiction been confined to smuggling craft.[20]

[20] See *The Coquitlam,* p. 271, *supra,* for the inconsistent position of the British Government in regard to the seizure of a Canadian vessel within three miles from the shore for an act committed within the United States customs zone of twelve miles.

CHAPTER IV

THE SEIZURE OF FOREIGN SMUGGLING VESSELS IN 1922 BY THE UNITED STATES UNDER THE NATIONAL PROHIBITION ACT AND THE FOUR-LEAGUE STATUTES AND OTHER LAWS

§ 67. The Controversy with Great Britain

It has just been pointed out that the British Government has been endeavoring for several decades to establish the so-called "three-mile limit" as the maximum limit of jurisdiction seaward for some purposes. It has been unwilling to make an exception as to jurisdiction over vessels engaged in illicit trade with the shore, except in two or three cases. The reassertion of this position in 1922, when the United States began the seizure of British "rum-running" vessels under her four-league statutes, brought the matter to a sharp issue. The British Government objected to the seizure of its vessels, in some cases, more than three miles from the shore, however menacing their conduct was; while the United States Government was equally positive in its position that such seizures under the hovering laws were, under certain circumstances, not in contravention of any principle of International Law. This led to treaties between these two Governments and between the United States and many other countries, embodying the principle contended for by the United States. The provisions of these treaties and the negotiations leading up to them will be reserved for consideration after the diplomatic discussions of the seizures made before the treaty was concluded, are dealt with.

When the United States began the seizure of the rum vessels under its four-league statutes, it suggested to the British Government the desirability of a treaty which would remove any possible friction that might arise from such seizures, for it was well aware that that Government had been advancing for some years views different from its own in regard to the so-called hovering laws. The Coast Guard had made many seizures of British vessels under these statutes, which were then before the Federal Courts in forfeiture proceedings. The British Government began a series of protests against such seizures. The proposal for the treaty had been put forward on June 26, 1922, while, according to *The Times* (London), of October 5, 1922, protests were made against the seizure of the British vessels, the *Marion Mosher* and the *Gardner,* more than three miles from the shore; while that paper of October 19, 1922, reports a protest against the seizure of the *Emerald.*[1] The United States Government was, thus, placed in a peculiar position: it felt that it could not well urge its proffered treaty of June 26 in the face of action that was calling for repeated protests. The treaty was the great need in the warfare against the "rum-row," and its swift conclusion was, therefore, the Government's chief concern. It was felt that excessive zeal in the warfare against the rum trade might embarrass the negotiations then under way, or postpone or frustrate the conclusion of a treaty altogether. The United States, therefore, in order to smooth out the way for the treaty, decided to release certain foreign vessels that had been taken beyond three miles from the shore. Instructions were sent by the Secretary of the Treasury to the Collec-

---

[1] The *Marion Mosher* was taken eight miles from shore, according to *The Times* (London), of October 5 and 16, 1922, while the *Gardner* was taken twenty-two miles from shore. Ibid., September 15 and 16, 1922. No distance is given for the *Emerald.* See, also, p. 318, note (18), *infra.* See pp. 217 and 234, et seq., *supra,* for cases before the Federal Courts.

tor of Customs at New York on November 9, 1922, in regard to the *Gardner,* and certain other foreign vessels, as follows:

"The Department is in receipt of your telegram of the 8th instant, relative to the seizure of the British Auxiliary Schooner M. M. Gardner, on September 13, 1922.

"It appears from your report that the seizure was made outside the three-mile limit, and that while the master admitted unlading part of the cargo beyond the three-mile limit there is no evidence that the vessel was communicating with the shore by means of her own boats or equipment.

"Under these circumstances it is the desire of the Department of State and the Department of Justice that all foreign vessels so seized shall be released, and you will be governed accordingly. A report should be made to the Department in each instance." [2]

It should be noted that this communication was addressed to the Collector of Customs at New York, and that it contained instructions for the release of certain foreign vessels.[3] It did not purport to give instructions as to future seizures. The court decisions already considered show that foreign vessels were seized anywhere within four leagues of the coast after this communication of November 9.[4] Instructions to the Coast Guard of December 6, 1923 [5] and the Amendments of 1924,[6] issued by the Treasury Department, authorized the continued

[2] The author is indebted to the Treasury Department for a copy of this letter.

[3] According to the newspaper reports, Treasury officials estimated that approximately twenty vessels had been seized as liquor carriers beyond three miles from the shore and were, therefore, to be released under this order. New York *Times,* October 28, 1922. See also, 32 *Yale Law Journal* 259, 36 *Harvard Law Rev.* 615, note 37, and *The Times* (London), of October 28, 1922.

[4] Pp. 217 and 234, et seq., *supra.*

[5] *Instructions, Customs, Navigation, and Motor-Boat Laws, and Duties of Boarding Officers,* 1923, pp. 1-3.

[6] *Amendments to Instructions, Customs, Navigation, and Motor-Boat Laws and Duties of Boarding Officers,* 1923, No. 3, December 11, 1924.

search and seizure of foreign vessels as provided by the *Tariff Act* of 1922,[7] within that distance from the shore.

[7] See p. 228, et seq., *supra*, for this Act. Under paragraph 1 of the Instructions of 1923, a merchant vessel of the United States may be boarded and searched at any time, "either in home waters or within four leagues of the coast of the United States (*Tariff Act* of 1922, sec. 581)" and seized for a violation of the laws of the United States. The Amendments of 1924 authorize the seizure of United States vessels anywhere on the high seas. (P. 248, *supra*, for a U. S. Supreme Court decision to the same effect.) Under paragraph 2, it is said that an officer has "the right to *board* and *search* any foreign vessel if within 3 nautical miles of the coast . . . , and to *seize* such vessel for a violation of the laws of the United States warranting seizure," but such vessel "may be held liable," "even though she herself may not have entered the territorial waters of the United States," if her boats "come within 3 nautical miles of the coast . . . and there violate any law of the United States." This was repeated in the Amendments of 1924, par. 3, citing the cases of *The Grace and Ruby* (see p. 217, *supra*), and *The Henry L. Marshall* (see p. 222, *supra*). In the first case referred to, the foreign vessel's own boat and seamen had gone within three miles of the shore, while in the second case, a shore boat had gone out to the vessel by prearrangement; and in both cases, the ship hovered and was seized more than three miles, but within twelve miles of the shore. This amendment was made to paragraph 3 of the Instructions in order to include all vessels that were communicating with the shore by means of their own vessels or by boats sent out from the shore, and to enforce the law as provided by statute and as interpreted by the Courts. Paragraph 3 authorizes an officer "to approach any foreign vessel found within 12 nautical miles of the coast . . . and by speaking or signaling the vessel ascertain if she be bound to a port of the United States," and if so bound, the vessel may be "*boarded* and *searched*" and she may be seized "upon arrival in United States territorial waters." If the vessel is not bound to a port, she may not be boarded, detained, or searched, "no matter what her cargo may be, or how suspicious her actions may be." If necessary, force may be used to make the search and seizure, but "the actual seizure may not be made until the vessel is within 3 miles of the coast." Under paragraph 4, no vessel, except a vessel of the United States, may be detained, boarded, or searched or required to stop or to heave to for the purpose of showing her identity, which is "encountered more than 12 miles from the coast." The Amendments of 1924, paragraph 2, called attention to the existence of various treaties with foreign powers covering this subject; and added that, "Except where special treaty provides otherwise," an officer "has the right to go on board of any foreign vessel . . . within four leagues of the coast . . . to examine the manifest and to inspect, search, and examine the vessel . . . if under way, and use all necessary force to compel compliance, and if it shall appear that any breach or violation of the laws of the United States has been committed, whereby or in consequence of which such vessel . . . or the

(1) *The Grace and Ruby*

The British Government has swung so far in its recent efforts to establish the "3-mile limit" as a principle of International Law for all purposes that it took the position in 1922 that its vessels should not be seized beyond that distance from the shore, even though they were in actual communication with the shore by means of their own small boats and crew, and engaged in violation of the laws of the United States. The United States Government unequivocally disagreed with that position, and pointed out the inconsistency of the British Government, which had, only a few years earlier, taken exactly the opposite view.

On December 30, 1922, the British Ambassador wrote

---

merchandise, . . . on board of or imported by such vessel . . . is liable to forfeiture, it shall be the duty of such officer to make seizure of the same," and to arrest any person engaged in such breach or violation, citing section 581 of the *Tariff Act* of 1922. As treaties had been entered into only with Great Britain, Germany, Italy, Sweden, Norway, and Denmark (see pp. 346, 352, and 353, *infra,* for these treaties), paragraph 2 of the Amendments would apply to the vessels of all other powers. This paragraph is a repetition of paragraph 10 of the Instructions of 1923, except that in paragraph 10 no reference was made to the treaties, so that before the treaties were entered into in 1924 and several years following, paragraph 10 applied to all vessels.

Paragraphs 7 and 8 of the Instructions of 1923 refer to sections 583, 586, and 587 of the *Tariff Act* of 1922, which require the production of a manifest and prohibit unlading within four leagues of the coast, and they note that this prohibition applies to "foreign as well as American vessels"; and paragraph 12 calls attention to section 2760 of the *Revised Statutes,* which authorizes the boarding, searching, examining, and certifying the manifests of all vessels that arrive within four leagues of the coast. (Paragraph 11 of the Instructions of 1923, which provide that the duties of officers indicated in the paragraphs preceding it are restricted to vessels bound to the United States, is stricken out by the Amendment of 1924. Sections 5 and 6 of the Instructions and the Amendment enunciate the so-called doctrine of "hot pursuit.")

When a foreign vessel is seized within four leagues of the coast and proceeded against for a violation of some provision of the *Tariff Act* of 1922, or of some other law, a copy of the court's judgment is transmitted by the Treasury Department to "the Collectors of Customs and others concerned," for their information. (See, for examples, *Treasury Decisions,* 1926, vol. 50, Nos. 41766, 41767, 41846, 41755, 41787, and 41749.)

to the Department that statements "purporting to be officially inspired," had appeared in the daily press to the effect that "the United States Government had decided to restrain prohibition enforcement officials from seizing, outside the three-mile limit of territorial waters, foreign vessels which are suspected of being engaged in the smuggling of liquor," except in cases where vessels were shown to be in contact with the shore, "such as the running of small craft of the ship to some point on the land," and that from "semi-official correspondence" which had passed betwen the two Governments in regard to individual British vessels "arrested outside territorial waters" on the charge of liquor smuggling, it appeared that the United States Government was acting on the principle just stated, and that all such vessels had been released by the intervention of the United States Government except "in the cases of vessels, notably the 'Grace and Ruby,' in respect of which a charge has been lodged of having been in communication with the shore by means of the ship's small boats."

It will be recalled that in that case the American cargo owner went out from the shore in a motor boat to the *Grace and Ruby,* which lay ten miles from shore, to carry her supplies and to receive some of her cargo. Three members of the crew of the British vessel returned with the cargo owner in the motorboat, and a dory belonging to the former was towed along to be used in landing the liquor or to enable the three members of the crew to return to their vessel. The *Grace and Ruby* was later arrested four miles from the shore while hovering to deliver the rest of her cargo, and was libelled and forfeited for having unlawfully unladed at night within the territorial limits of the United States. The Court remarked that "The act of unlading, although beginning beyond the three-mile limit, continued until the liquor was landed, and the schooner [the *Grace and Ruby*] was actively assisting in it by means of her small boats and three of her crew, who were on the motorboat for that purpose." [8]

Returning to the British note of December 30, it was added that the British Government was "unable to acquiesce in what they understand to be the ruling of the United States Government, namely, that foreign vessels may be seized outside the three-mile limit if it can be shown that they have established contact with shore for illegal purposes by means of their own small boats," and that the British Government reserved "their right to lodge a protest in any individual case in which action may be taken by the United States Government under this ruling." [9]

[8] For a fuller summary of this case, see p. 217, *supra*.

[9] The text of the British note reads as follows:

"On September 27th last a statement, purporting to be officially inspired, appeared in the daily press to the general effect that the United States Government had decided to restrain prohibition enforcement officials from seizing, outside the three-mile limit of territorial waters, foreign vessels which are suspected of being engaged in the smuggling of liquor. According to the same statement, however, this ruling did not apply to the searching, beyond the three-mile limit, of ships which were known to be in contact with the shore, such as the running of small craft of the ship to some point on the land.

"From semi-official correspondence which has since passed between us in regard to individual British vessels arrested outside territorial waters on the charge of liquor smuggling it appears that the United States Government are in fact acting on the principle defined above. The majority of such vessels either have, through your kind intervention, already been released or else are in process of being restored to their owners. The only exceptions to this rule appear to have been made in the case of vessels, notably the 'Grace and Ruby,' in respect of which a charge has been lodged of having been in communication with the shore by means of the ship's small boats.

"In order to avoid the possibility of any misunderstanding, I am desired by my Government to make it clear that His Majesty's Government are unable to acquiesce in what they understand to be the ruling of the United States Government, namely that foreign vessels may be seized outside the three-mile limit if it can be shown that they have established contact with the shore for illegal purposes by means of their own small boats. My Government must reserve their right to lodge a protest in any individual case in which action may be taken by the United States Government under this ruling."—*U. S. Press release,* February 16, 1927.

The reply of the Department of January 18, 1923, stated that the conclusion had been reached that the Government of the United States "should adhere to the position it has previously taken that foreign vessels outside the three-mile limit may be seized when it is established that they are using their small boats in illegal operations within the three-mile limit of the United States." In support of this position, the case of *The Araunah* [10] was cited, in which a Canadian fishing vessel was seized by Russian authorities "6 or more miles" from land, while two of her small boats were fishing within the "customs-house limits," within half a mile from the shore, in violation of Russian law. Lord Salisbury, in a note of May 9, 1890, said that Her Majesty's Government were of the opinion if the *Araunah* "was herself outside the 3-mile territorial limit, the fact that she was, by means of her boats, carrying on fishing within Russian waters without the prescribed license warranted her seizure and confiscation according to the provisions of the municipal law regulating the use of those waters." [11]

[10] *British and Foreign State Papers*, vol. 82, pp. 1043, 1058.

[11] For other cases applying this principle, see p. 221, *supra*. The following is the full text of the Department's note:

"I have the honor to acknowledge the receipt of your note No. 973 of December 30, 1922, stating that your Government desires you to make it clear that it is unable to acquiesce in what it understands to be the ruling of the United States Government, namely, that foreign vessels may be seized outside the three-mile limit if it can be shown that they have established contact with the shore for illegal purposes by means of their own small boats. You state that your Government must reserve the right to lodge a protest in any individual case in which action may be taken by the United States Government in cases of this character.

"I have the honor to state that consideration has been given to the statements contained in your note and the conclusion has been reached that the Government of the United States should adhere to the position it has previously taken that foreign vessels outside the three-mile limit may be seized when it is established that they are using their small boats in illegal operations within the three-mile limit of the United States. This conclusion is supported by the position taken by the British Government in the case of the British Columbian

The British Government made no reply, and the question was not raised again.   That Government, thus, allows this exception to the principle for which it has been so earnestly contending.[12]

(2) *The Henry L. Marshall*

The next discussion between the British and the United States Governments arose over the seizure of the *Henry L. Marshall*, a vessel which flew the British flag and was believed at the time to be British, and which was pro-

---

schooner ARAUNAH, which was seized off Copper Island, by the Russian authorities in 1888, because it appeared that members of the crew of the schooner were illegally taking seals in Behring Sea by means of canoes operated between the schooner and the land, and it was affirmed that two of the canoes were within half a mile of the shore. Lord Salisbury stated that Her Majesty's Government were 'of opinion that, even if the ARAUNAH at the time of the seizure was herself outside the three-mile territorial limit, the fact that she was, by means of her boats, carrying on fishing within Russian waters without the prescribed license warranted her seizure and confiscation according to the provisions of the municipal law regulating the use of those waters.' (Volume 82, *British and Foreign State Papers*, p. 1058.)

"I may add that it is not understood on what grounds the decision of His Majesty's Government in this matter was reached, in view of the position taken by Lord Salisbury in the ARAUNAH case and the statement in your note No. 781 of October 13, 1922, that His Majesty's Government 'are desirous of assisting the United States Government to the best of their ability in the suppression of the traffic and in the prevention of the abuse of the British flag by those engaged in it."

"As you are doubtless aware, the case of the GRACE AND RUBY, to which you refer, is now pending before the Supreme Court of the United States and I shall be glad to inform you of its decision as soon as it is rendered."

U. S. Press release, February 16, 1927.

[12] On July 4, 1923, Mr. McNeill, Under Secretary of State for Foreign Affairs, stated in the House of Commons that the United States Government had, the previous autumn, given instructions for the discontinuance of seizures except in cases where the vessel's own small boats could be shown to have entered the 3-mile limit for an illegal purpose. He did not express any objection to seizures in these cases. *Parliamentary Debates* (Hansard), 1923, vol. 166, p. 410. He had said on April 30 of the same year that His Majesty's Government had questioned the right of the United States Government to make such seizures, and that diplomatic correspondence on the subject was proceeding. Ibid., vol. 163, p. 968.

ceeded against in the Federal Courts and condemned as such.[13] It will be recalled that this vessel was seized more than three miles from the shore for having unladed and sent liquors ashore by means of small motorboats sent out from the shore by previous arrangement, while she stood nine or ten miles out. The seizure was made and condemnation was decreed under the four-league statutes, which had been in force and had been enforced since 1790.

On July 10, 1923, the British Chargé d'Affaires ad interim wrote to the Secretary of State that his attention had been drawn to comments in the press regarding this decision to the effect that "the view of many American legal experts that the United States Government has the right to seize rum-runners outside the three-mile limit is shared by the State Department, and it is hinted that the absence of a protest by His Majesty's Government against the condemnation of the 'Henry L. Marshall' by the United States Circuit Court of Appeals not only makes the case a useful precedent for similar future action by the United States authorities outside the three-mile limit against British vessels suspected of rum-running, but also implies a change in the attitude of His Majesty's Government toward the principle of such seizures outside the three-mile limit." It was added that in order to avoid the possibility of any misunderstanding as to the attitude of the British Government, he was instructed by His Majesty's Principal Secretary of State for Foreign Affairs, "to inform you that any attempt on the part of the United States authorities to seize a British ship outside the three-mile limit would be regarded by His Majesty's Government as creating a very serious situation." It was said that the absence of a protest in this case "in no way implies any alteration in the views of His Majesty's

[13] See p. 222, *supra,* for a full summary of this case.

Government with regard to the principle at stake," since the *Marshall* was not recognized as being entitled to British registry, but that owing to the circumstances under which her registry was secured, she remained an American vessel, as far as the British Government was concerned.[14]

The Department was unable to accede to the position

[14] The text of the British note reads:

"I have the honor to inform you that my attention has been drawn to certain comments in the press regarding the recent decision of the United States Circuit Court of Appeals in connection wtih the condemnation and forfeiture of the alleged British schooner 'Henry L. Marshall' for smuggling liquor into the United States in contravention of the prohibition laws. You will recollect that this vessel was seized by United States Revenue officials in July, 1921, when off the coast of New Jersey and outside the limit of United States territorial waters.

"The general trend of these comments is to the effect that the view of many American legal experts that the United States Government has the right to seize rum-runners outside the three-mile limit is shared by the State Department, and it is hinted that the absence of a protest by His Majesty's Government against the condemnation of the 'Henry L. Marshall' by the United States Circuit Court of Appeals not only makes the case a useful precedent for similar future action by the United States authorities outside the three-mile limit against British vessels suspected of rum running, but also implies a change in the attitude of His Majesty's Government towards the principle of such seizures outside the three-mile limit.

"In order to avoid the possibility of any misunderstanding on the part of the United States Government as to His Majesty's Government's attitude in this matter I have the honour, under instructions from His Majesty's Principal Secretary of State for Foreign Affairs, to inform you that any attempt on the part of the United States authorities to seize a British ship outside the three-mile limit would be regarded by His Majesty's Government as creating a very serious situation. In regard to the 'Henry L. Marshall' Case, I have been instructed to explain that the absence of a protest by His Majesty's Government against the condemnation of this vessel in no way implies any alteration in the views of His Majesty's Government with regard to the principle at stake, inasmuch as that vessel, owing to the circumstances in which she secured her British registry, was not recognized by His Majesty's Government as entitled to British registry. Consequently, His Majesty's Government have not felt called upon to assert the principle at stake on her behalf, since, as far as His Majesty's Government are concerned, the 'Henry L. Marshall' remains an American vessel."

U. S. Press release, February 16, 1927.

of the British Government in this case as in that of *The Grace and Ruby;* and, in reply, it declared that the seizure of a foreign vessel beyond the three-mile zone engaged in sending its liquors ashore in a vessel not belonging to her was not a violation of any principle of International Law. A note of Secretary Hughes, dated July 16, 1923, directed the attention of the British Chargé d'Affaires to "the precise import" of the adjudications in the Federal Courts in the case and gave a brief account of the conduct pursued by the vessel which led to her seizure and forfeiture. Attention was called to the view of the Circuit Court of Appeals that the fact of unlading, although beginning more than three miles from the shore, continued until the liquor was landed,[15] to the finding by the court that the whiskey was never manifested, that it was unladed between the rising and setting of the sun, that no special permit had been obtained for unlading at night, and that there was an unlading without a permit, all in violation of certain sections of the *Revised Statutes,* and to the conclusions of the court that the *Marshall* attempted to introduce all of its cargo "into the commerce of the United States, and that there was an actual introduction of a part of that cargo into that commerce," and that, "such attempt at introduction was by means of fraudulent practices, i.e., evasion of the provisions of the National Prohibition Act," and that "there were wilful acts (i.e., rum-running) by means whereof the United States was deprived of duties upon the merchandise (i.e., whiskey) affected by the said act." ". . . the foregoing conclusions are deemed by this Government to be self explanatory. They relate to the conduct of a vessel which was far from exercising the normal

[15] The Circuit Court of Appeals held that it made no difference if boats from the shore were used for this purpose, instead of the vessel's own boats, and that, therefore, there was no difference between this case and that of *The Grace and Ruby.*

right of passage on the high seas adjacent to American waters in the course of a voyage between British ports.[16] They show that the vessel and those controlling it started upon its sinister voyage with connivance and aid of British authority in British territory; that its direct and single effort was by fraudulent means to introduce the cargo, and all of it, within the territory of the United States; and that the vessel prior to and at the time of its actual seizure, even though more than three miles from the shore, was hovering off the coasts of the United States and was engaged in an attempt to violate the laws of the United States by the introduction of the liquor within its territory." It was added that competent judicial procedure had determined these facts, that competent judicial authority had sustained the seizure, and that, "In view of this decision, and of the tenor of your communication, my Government hopes that it may be advised that His Majesty's Government does not consider, even in the case of a vessel admittedly of valid British registry, that such a vessel pursuing the course of conduct followed by the schooner *Henry L. Marshall* is making proper use of the British flag and that His Majesty's Government would not be disposed to espouse the cause of a British merchant vessel in an effort unlawfully to introduce intoxicating liquors into the territory of the United States in the manner adopted" by the *Marshall,* "or in such a case to oppose the enforcement of the laws of the United States by means of the procedure taken in the case of that vessel and judicially approved."[17]

[16] She sailed from the British Bahamas, and one of her clearances called for Halifax.

[17] The text of the Department's note reads:

"I have the honor to acknowledge the receipt of your communication No. 578 of July 10, last, in relation to the recent decision of the United States Circuit Court of Appeals in the case of the schooner HENRY L. MARSHALL, and to certain American press comments thereon. You advert to the general trend of these comments and to the inferences which are drawn from the views of many American legal experts.

"I note your statement that under instructions from your Government you inform me that any attempt on the part of the United States authorities to seize a British ship outside the three-mile limit would be regarded by your Government as creating a very serious situation. With respect to the case of the HENRY L. MARSHALL, you state that you have been instructed to explain that the absence of a protest by His Majesty's Government against the condemnation of the vessel in no way implies any alteration in the views of your Government with respect to the principle at stake, inasmuch as the vessel was not recognized as entitled by your Government to British registry; and you add, that so far as your Government is concerned, the HENRY L. MARSHALL remains an American vessel. The Department is pleased to receive this formal statement as to the status of the vessel as it is recalled that your Embassy had made protests against the seizure of the vessel in your communications No. 623, of August 11, 1921, and No. 686, of September 9, 1921, and that the Department had also been in receipt of communications from your Embassy in respect to the progress of the cause and the detention of certain members of the crew as witnesses.

"In view of the emphasis placed in your last communication upon the principle deemed to be involved, it would seem appropriate to direct your attention to the precise import of the adjudications in the United States District Court for the Southern District of New York and, on appeal, in the United States Circuit Court of Appeals for the Second Circuit, from whose decrees it is not understood that the claimant has as yet sought by writ of certiorari to obtain a review in the Supreme Court of the United States. For this purpose I may refer to the pertinent facts as these have been judicially established and set forth in the statement of the case by the United States Circuit Court of Appeals. The vessel sailing under British registry in 1921 obtained clearance from West End, Bahama Islands, when actually laden with a cargo of intoxicating liquors. She received two clearances of the same date and signed by the same Collector of Revenue, one of which stated that she had cleared for Halifax with the cargo of liquor, the other that she had cleared for Gloucester, Massachusetts, in ballast. The same Collector furnished two bills of health, likewise differing as to destination. It was abundantly proved that the real object and only business of the HENRY L. MARSHALL was to peddle liquor along the coast of the United States. 'Particularly,' states the official report of the decision, 'did she pursue her vocation while lying some nine or ten miles off Atlantic City and there sent liquor on shore, pursuant to previous arrangement made in the United States, by motor boats,' which, however, were not a part of the schooner's equipment, and, so far as appears, did not belong to her owner. When the MARSHALL was boarded more than three miles from the New Jersey coast it was found that she had no manifest and still had on board a quantity of liquor.

To this note, the British Government made no reply.[18]

"The United States Circuit Court of Appeals in affirming the decrees which were passed upon the libels for forfeiture, held that the act of unlading although beginning beyond the three mile limit continued until the liquor was landed; that the MARSHALL'S cargo of whiskey was never manifested; that it was not unladen between the rising and setting of the sun and that no special license had been obtained for unloading at night; and that there was an unloading without a permit,— all in violation of provisions of the Revised Statutes of the United States. The United States Circuit Court of Appeals concluded: (a) that there was an attempt to introduce all of the MARSHALL'S cargo into the commerce of the United States, and that there was an actual introduction of a part of that cargo into that commerce; (b) that such attempt at introduction was by means of fraudulent practices, i.e., evasion of the provisions of the National Prohibition Act; (c) that there were wilful acts (i.e., rum running) by means whereof the United States was deprived of duties upon the merchandise (i.e., whiskey) affected by the said act.

"The foregoing conclusions are deemed by this Government to be self-explanatory. They relate to the conduct of a vessel which was far from exercising the normal right of passage on the high seas adjacent to American waters in the course of a voyage between two British ports. They show that the vessel and those controlling it started upon its sinister voyage with connivance and aid of British authority in British territory; that its direct and single effort was by fraudulent means to introduce the cargo, and all of it, within the territory of the United States; and that the vessel prior to and at the time of its actual seizure, even though more than three miles from the shore, was hovering off the coasts of the United States and was engaged in an attempt to violate the laws of the United States by the introduction of the liquor within its territory. It should be added that adequate judicial procedure, as already noted, was available and used, in order to determine these facts, and in these circumstances the competent judicial authority of the United States has sustained the seizure of the vessel.

"In view of this decision, and of the tenor of your communication, my Government hopes that it may be advised that His Majesty's Government does not consider, even in the case of a vessel admittedly of valid British registry, that such a vessel pursuing the course of conduct followed by the schooner HENRY L. MARSHALL is making proper use of the British flag and that His Majesty's Government would not be disposed to espouse the cause of a British merchant vessel in an effort unlawfully to introduce intoxicating liquors into the territory of the United States in the manner adopted by the schooner HENRY L. MARSHALL, or in such a case to oppose the enforcement of the laws of the United States by means of the procedure taken in the case of that vessel and judicially approved."

U. S. Press release, February 16, 1927.

[18] On June 6, the Under Secretary of State for Foreign Affairs, Mr. McNeill, stated in the House of Commons that some twenty or twenty-

The views of the American Government on this question were expressed even more clearly in a public address by Secretary Hughes.[19]

----

five vessels, mostly Canadian, had been seized by the United States at "varying distances from the shore, some within and some without the three-mile limit. The crews have nearly always been detained for varying periods. His Majesty's Embassy at Washington have acted repeatedly, and in the strongest possible manner, to secure the release of vessels seized outside the three-mile limit, or inside it when a genuine case of distress seemed to be made out." *Parliamentary Debates* (Hansard), 1923, vol. 164, col. 2212.

On June 11, he stated that in the large majority of such cases the vessel was seized more than three miles from the shore. Ibid., vol. 165, col. 23.

On July 4, when Sir W. Davidson called the attention of Mr. McNeill to the seizure ten miles out and condemnation of the *Marshall,* and asked what action the British Government proposed to take, "seeing that the effect of the above decision is contrary to the accepted rules of international law, and applies American Municipal law to foreign ships on the high seas outside the accepted three-mile limit," Mr. McNeill referred to his statement of June 6, and added that last autumn the United States Government gave instructions to discontinue seizures "except in cases where the vessel's own small boats could be shown to have entered the three-mile limit for an illegal purpose." He stated that *The Marshall* case was an exception, since the vessel had obtained British registry by fraudulent means. Ibid., vol. 166, col. 410.

On November 13, in reply to the question if it was true that "we have refused to recognize the twelve-mile limit with the United States," he said, "I cannot answer that question 'yes' or 'no,' except to say that there will be no infringement of the general rule as to the three-mile limit." Ibid., vol. 168, col. 11.

On May 2, Sir A. Shirley Benn asked if the British Government has "at any time, with any nation, recognized any limit outside the three-miles limit." Lt. Colonel Buckley replied, "Not that I am aware of." Ibid., vol. 163, col. 1346. It was brought out in this discussion that "a number of states have at different times claimed to exercise jurisdiction for various specific purposes over a wider limit" than three miles, but Lt. Colonel Buckley said that the only rule generally recognized "as defining the *extent of territorial waters* is that prescribing a limit of 3 miles drawn from low water mark." Mr. Ormsby Gore, the Under Secretary of State for the Colonies, made the statement on this occasion that the "limit of 12 to 20 miles claimed by the British Government" in Ceylon, was claimed "under very special conditions." Mr. Trevelyan asked the very pertinent question, "Is there any country which claims more than a three-miles limit which does not do so for very special reasons?" Ibid., col. 1347.

[19] (1924) 18 *American Journal of International Law,* p. 231.

"It is quite apparent," he said, "that this Government is not in a position to maintain that its territorial waters extend beyond the three-mile limit and in order to avoid liability to other governments, it is important that in the enforcement of the laws of the United States, this limit should be appropriately recognized. It does not follow, however, that this Government is entirely without power to protect itself from the abuses committed by hovering vessels.[20] There may be such a direct connection between the operation of the vessel and the violation of the laws prescribed by the territorial sovereign as to justify seizure even outside the three-mile limit. This may be illustrated by the case of 'hot pursuit' where the vessel has committed an offense against those laws within territorial waters and is caught while trying to escape. The practice which permits the following and seizure of a foreign vessel which puts to sea in order to avoid detention for violation of the laws of the state whose waters it has entered, is based on the principle of necessity for the 'effective administration of justice.' (Westlake, Part I, p. 177.) And this extension of the right of the territorial state was voted unanimously by the Institute of International Law in 1894.

"Another case is one where the hovering vessel, although lying outside the three-mile limit, communicates with the shore by its own boats in violation of the territorial law. Thus Lord Salisbury said, with respect to the British schooner *Araunah*, that Her Majesty's Government were 'of opinion that, even if the *Araunah* at the time of the seizure were herself outside the three-mile territorial limit, the fact that she was, by means of her boats, carrying on fishing within Russian waters without the prescribed license warranted her seizure and confisca-

[20] This is a clear recognition of the distinction repeatedly pointed out between the idea of "territorial waters," and of a more extensive zone for the application of revenue laws against the smuggling vessel.

tion according to the principles of the municipal law regulating the use of those waters.' A case similar to this was that of the *Grace and Ruby* (283 Fed. 476).

"It will be noted that in the case of the *Araunah* it was the vessel herself that was deemed subject to seizure outside the three-mile limit, and not simply her small boats, and this was manifestly because of the direct connection between the conduct of the vessel and the violation of the law of the territory. It may be urged with force that this principle should not be limited to the case of the use by the vessel of her own boats, where she is none the less effectively engaged, although using other boats, in the illegal introduction of her cargo into the commerce of the territory. Such a case was that of the *Henry L. Marshall*, recently decided by the Circuit Court of Appeals of the Second Circuit (292 Fed. 487-488).

"The vessel was thus found to be engaged, not in the exercise of her admitted rights upon the high seas, but in unlawfully unloading her cargo into the territory of the United States, in 'an actual introduction of a part thereof into the commerce of the United States' contrary to its laws. It should be added that while the British Government originally made a protest in this case, it was finally withdrawn upon the ground that the vessel was not of *bona fide* British registry, and it should be said that in this withdrawal the British Government did not acquiesce in the principle of the ruling. In view, however, of the historic practice of nations in the protection of their territory from the violation of their laws by hovering vessels, the United States Government can not admit that the accepted rules of international law preclude such action as that taken in the circumstances of the Marshall case."

§ 68. Diplomatic Discussions with France

(1) *The Mousmée*

The French Ambassador, upon being informed that a French vessel, the *Mousmée,* had been seized about eight miles from the nearest land, asked the Department for the facts of the case, and expressed the hope that if it were found that the vessel had been seized outside of "territorial waters," the Department would issue instructions for its release. "Territorial waters" were not defined. The Department advised that the vessel was first sighted two and one-half miles off Nantucket Island, under way, and upon immediate and continuous pursuit, she was seized eight miles from shore, in accordance with established principles of International Law. The French Government made no reply.

It was not necessary, in this case, for the United States Government to rely upon the principle of the hovering laws, for the case was covered by the doctrine of "hot pursuit," which permits the littoral state immediately to pursue and seize upon the high seas a foreign vessel which has offended against its laws within the zone of "territorial waters."

(2) *The Cherie*

This French vessel [21] was seized seven or eight miles from the nearest land, where she had been selling liquors to various persons, and where, at the time of seizure, she was anchored for the purpose of disposing of the balance of her cargo. She was forfeited under section 586 of the *Tariff Act* of 1922, for unlading within twelve miles of the shore in violation of that section.[22] She had not sent

[21] There was some question as to this vessel's being French, as her French registry, issued by a French Consul, was only provisional, and a visit to Bordeaux, which was not made, was necessary to procure a permanent French document.

[22] For a full report of this case, see p. 235, *supra.*

any of her wares ashore by means of her own boats or any boats under her control from the shore, and was, therefore, not like the case of *The Grace and Ruby* or that of *The Henry L. Marshall*. The French Ambassador was under the impression that the vessel was seized some fifteen or twenty miles from shore, and, therefore, some distance beyond "territorial waters," and he asked for the release of the vessel, if that were the case. Here, again, he did not define "territorial waters." The matter was dropped when he was informed that the seizure was made in "territorial waters." The basis for the statement that the place of seizure was in "territorial waters" is found in the fact that it was made just inside of a line drawn three miles from and parallel to a line connecting the outermost points of the Isle au Haut and Duck Island. The distance between these two points, or headlands, is about eleven and one-half miles. The Department of Commerce has ruled that bays, whose headlands are no further apart than twenty miles, are territorial waters; and, therefore, such waters would embrace the waters three miles from a line connecting such headlands.[23] Thus, the basis for saying that the seizure in this case was made in "territorial waters" as defined by that Department must be found in the fact that it was made within three miles of a line connecting headlands eleven and a half miles apart. The French Government made no objection to this method of calculation.

It, thus, acquiesced in the seizure of two of its smuggling vessels more than three miles from the shore; the one was seized eight miles out for having been within two and one-half miles of the shore with liquor on board, and the other was seized seven or eight miles from shore for unlading within that distance, at a point defined by the

[23] See p. 288, et seq., of the *Navigation Laws of the United States,* 1923, for the lines establishing "inland waters."

Department of Commerce to be within "territorial waters."

So far as is known, no objection was raised by the French Government to the seizure of the *Mistinguette* beyond three miles from the shore.[24]

§ 69.   Diplomatic Discussions with the Netherlands

The Zeehond

It will be recalled that the Dutch vessel, the *Zeehond*, was seized within four miles from the shore and her liquor cargo libelled, but the libel was dismissed because it was found that the operators of the vessel had no criminal intent to introduce liquors into the United States, but had come near the coast for shelter. It was found also that no law had been violated by a gift of two cases of liquor fifteen miles out.[25]

The Netherlands Government brought this case to the attention of the United States Government with the request for a statement of the facts. It was under the impression that the ship was seized outside the "territorial waters" of the United States, or beyond three miles from the shore, when headed for the shore in distress; it had learned, also, of the gift of the two cases of liquor fifteen miles out. No protest was entered, nor was release of the vessel requested, but after the crew and officers were acquitted, some doubt was expressed as to whether the seizure and the long detention of the vessel were justifiable under International Law.

§ 69a.   Diplomatic Discussions with Panama

The Federalship

A vessel flying the Panaman flag, the *Federalship*, was seized 270 miles from shore, and her crew, which proved

---

[24] See p. 238, *supra*.
[25] See pp. 242 and 246, *supra*, for a full report of this case.

to be British, indicted for a conspiracy to violate the *National Prohibition Act* and the *Tariff Act* of 1922. The Panaman Government refused to enter a claim against the United States Government on behalf of the British crew.[26] Under Article I of Law 54 of 1926 of Panama, any merchant vessel which has acquired Panaman nationality loses that nationality if it is habitually devoted to smuggling, illicit commerce, or piracy.

[26] See p. 366, *infra*, for a fuller statement of this case. The vessel was, in fact, owned by a Canadian corporation.

CHAPTER V

THE RUM TREATIES

§ 70. The Treaty with England

(1) *The Negotiations Leading up to the Treaty*

The "rum-row" presented many menaces to the enforcement of law and the preservation of order. The United States Government was faced with a serious problem, which called for immediate and drastic action. It wished to be able to move against this rum fleet and to sweep it from its coasts with as little resistance, or opposition, as possible, especially from the nation whose vessels were the chief offenders. It wished to clear the way for unrestricted action under its four-league statutes. As repeatedly pointed out, it has always upheld the validity of the so-called hovering laws taking jurisdiction far beyond three miles from the shore, but at the same time, it was aware of the wavering attitude of the British Government on this question. In order, therefore, to forestall possible repetition of protests by the British Government, which might handicap its action against the rum fleet, it approached that Government on the question of a treaty under which the United States might seize these vessels on the high seas as far out as twelve miles without objection.[1] It seemed better to avoid opposition than to

---

[1] In the language of the Secretary of State, "But it is apparent that, whatever measures this Government may believe that it is free to adopt in accordance with the principles of international law, these, so far as they are practicable, are far from adequate to meet the exigency; and, further, the diplomatic history of the United States reveals the fact that maritime powers, including the United States itself, are highly sensitive to attempts by foreign authorities to seize their vessels on

oppose it, should it arise.[2] With this in view, Mr. Hughes wrote at length to the British Ambassador on June 26, 1922, with regard to the possibility of aid by the British Government by means of "co-operation on the part of the British and American authorities with regard to the smuggling of liquor," which presented "serious difficulties," and which, it was felt, "might be effectively met with the assistance of the British authorities in British territories, which it appears are made bases of operations in flagrant violation of constitutional and statutory provisions of the United States."

It has been pointed out in another connection that many American-owned vessels were proceeding to near-by British ports and obtaining British registry by means of the execution of paper transfers purporting to convey title to vessels to British subjects in order to be able to appeal to the British Government if seized, and that vessels were procuring from the British authorities at the Bahamas two clearances before starting on their illicit voyages. These practices were referred to in the note of Mr. Hughes, who added, "It is believed that effective measures for this purpose might be taken by a careful supervision of the issuance of registries to vessels suspected of being engaged in illegal traffic and of the issuance of clearance papers for such vessels. . . ." It was

---

the high seas in time of peace. In each case of seizure there are likely to be serious questions of fact and law, and at any time there may be collisions of authority which would be embarrassing to friendly relations. It is precisely in matters of this description, where the sense of grievance and resentment are so easily aroused, that the effort should be made to reach an international agreement suited to the case. We need to put the measures that are required for the adequate enforcement of our laws on an impregnable basis and to invite and secure the friendly co-operation of the maritime powers." (1924) 18 *American Journal of International Law*, pp. 231, 233.

[2] It has been noted that certain vessels seized more than three miles from the shore were ordered released, pending the negotiation of the treaty. See p. 306, *supra*.

suggested that the British authorities in the Bahamas might refuse the privilege of registry to American vessels unless a certificate from the United States Shipping Board were first produced, showing that the vessel had first been tendered to that Board before it could be transferred to foreign registry, as was required by the law of the United States.

The second point raised in the note was a possible "international arrangement between the United States and Great Britain under which the authorities of each nation would be authorized to exercise beyond the three-mile limit of territorial waters a measure of control over vessels belonging to the other." It was said that ". . . the situation with which the authorities of this Government are confronted has become so serious that this Government feels prompted to inquire whether your Government would be disposed to enter into a treaty for the purpose of checking the illegal practices in question. Such a treaty might contain reciprocal provisions authorizing the authorities of each Government to exercise a right of search of vessel of the other beyond the three-mile limit of territorial waters to the extent of twelve miles from the shore. It would appear that no inconvenience would be experienced as a result of the exercise of such a right by vessels engaged in legitimate trade between Nassau and Halifax," for the natural route of such vessels is a direct one to Hatteras and then a direct course to Diamond Shoal Lighthouse, and from thence to Halifax, so that this route would not bring the vessels within four leagues of the American shore.[3]

[3] The note of the Secretary reads, in part, as follows:
"While existing nefarious practices might be largely stopped by appropriate precautionary measures with respect to the issuance of British registries to vessels engaged in smuggling and with respect to the issuance of clearance papers to such vessels, the situation with which the authorities of this Government are confronted has become so serious that this Government feels prompted to inquire whether your Govern-

The memory of the controversy of 1912 over the Russian laws, extending jurisdiction for twelve miles in customs and fisheries, was still fresh.[4] One is not surprised, therefore, to find that the British Government frowned upon this last proposal. The reply of that Government of October 13, 1922, expressed a sincere desire to coöperate in the prevention of any breaches of the law in the Bahamas or elsewhere in the British West Indies, and to that end it was said that the Governor of the Bahamas had already been requested "to see that no irregularities of any kind should be permitted in connection with vessels clearing from that colony, and that the formalities required in connection with such clearances should be most strictly enforced," and that instructions had been given to the local Registrars of Shipping "which will, it is anticipated, have the effect of preventing any future transfers of United States vessels to the British flag until a complete investigation of the circumstances can be made." It was added that it would be difficult to require the production of the certificate from the United States Shipping Board as a precedent to registration, as there

---

ment would be disposed to enter into a treaty for the purpose of checking the illegal practices in question. Such a treaty might contain reciprocal provisions authorizing the authorities of each Government to exercise a right of search of vessels of the other beyond the three-mile limit of territorial waters to the extent of twelve miles from the shore. It would appear that no inconvenience would be experienced as a result of the exercise of such a right by vessels engaged in legitimate trade between Nassau and Halifax. It is evidently natural for such vessels to take a direct route to Hatteras and then a direct course to Diamond Shoal Lighthouse and from thence to Halifax. Apparently this course brings vessels at no point within four leagues of the American shore. I shall be glad if you will bring the contents of this communication to the attention of your Government, which I have no doubt will appreciate the serious considerations which prompt the request that the matters therein presented receive earnest consideration at the earliest convenient time."

U. S. Press release, February 16, 1927.

For the rest of this communication, see p. 213, note 20, *supra*.

[4] P. 286, *supra*.

would be "great difficulties in the adoption on British territory of such a requirement, and it would be still more difficult to give such a requirement the force of law," but that instructions had been given to the effect that in cases of transfer "in which any possible doubt exists as to the *bona fides* of the parties of the transaction, the non-production of the Shipping Board certificate should be taken as a ground of suspicion, involving reference of the case to the Board of Trade in London for further directions." If, in spite of these precautions, it was said, a fictitious owner succeeded in securing a registry, the vessel would be proceeded against and forfeited under section 51 of the British Merchant Shipping Act of 1906.[5]

[5] On March 27, 1926, in an Aid Memoire, the British Ambassador notified the Secretary of State that His Majesty's Government had adopted the following administrative measures:

1. United States cutters may enter British territorial waters at Gun Cay, the Bahamas, and the islands contiguous thereto without strict compliance with the Admiralty regulations governing the visits of foreign armed vessels to British overseas ports, if the cutters will first call at Bimini to inform the Bahamas' Commissioner of their intentions, and if they will maintain a correct attitude, and not use their lights to the danger of navigation. This privilege is limited to a period of one year, at the end of which, the British Government is prepared to entertain a request for the continuance of the arrangement if the United States Government deems this necessary.

2. His Majesty's Government will call upon Registrars of Shipping in the West Indies to take special care to prevent transfers to the British flag of vessels intended for the smuggling trade, instructing them to make the most searching inquiries before permitting any vessel to be placed on the British registry and to refuse to register a vessel unless they are completely satisfied as to the bona fides of the application.

3. His Majesty's Government are prepared "to take administrative action to prosecute masters for infraction of the Customs Act when reasonable grounds of suspicion are available to believe them guilty of making false declarations in regard to their destinations." Liquor smugglers will be removed from the British registry upon production by the United States authorities "of reasonably good evidence that the vessel concerned is really owned or controlled in America."

The United States Government on April 26 expressed its appreciation of this offer of coöperation, and it accepted an invitation by the British Government to send representatives to London to discuss the situation, in order that a fuller understanding might be arrived at. *U. S. Press release,* May 4, 1926.

In regard to the second point raised in the American note, it was said that more difficulty was felt. His Majesty's Government, ". . . feel, however, more difficulty in accepting the proposal that a treaty should be made authorizing the authorities of each government to exercise a right of search of vessels of the other beyond the three mile limit of territorial waters up to a distance of twelve miles from the shore. His Majesty's Government have consistently opposed any extension of the limit of territorial waters such as ·that now suggested.[6] They feel that the outbreak of smuggling which has led to the proposal cannot be regarded as a permanent condition, but as one which will, no doubt, be suppressed by the United States authorities within the not distant future." While a desire was expressed of assisting the United States in the suppression of this traffic, it was said that the British Government "do not feel that they can properly acquiesce, in order to meet a temporary emergency, in the abandonment of a principle to which they attach great importance."[7]

[6] The British Government again overlooked the distinction between "territorial waters" and a limited jurisdiction in the marginal seas over smuggling vessels. The note of the United States Government had not suggested an extension of territorial waters. It had only put forward the idea of the exercise of a limited authority to search certain craft "beyond the 3-mile limit of territorial waters."

[7] The following is the text of the British note:

". . . I am now directed to inform you that His Majesty's Government have naturally been desirous of preventing, by every means within their power, any breaches of the law in the Bahamas or elsewhere in the British West Indies by persons engaged in illicit trade with the United States and the proposals made by the United States Government with this object have received the most sympathetic consideration. With the object of preventing the development of illegal practices in connection with this traffic instructions had, in fact, some months before the receipt of the representations made by the United States Government, been sent to the Governor of the Bahamas, who was at that time requested to see that no irregularities of any kind should be permitted in connection with vessels clearing from that colony, and that the formalities required in connection with such clearances should be most strictly enforced. Instructions have also been given to the local Registrars of Shipping which will, it is anticipated, have the effect of

As pointed out above, it had not been long since the controversy in 1912 over the Russian revenue and fishery laws, extending jurisdiction generally for a distance of

preventing any future transfers of United States vessels to the British flag until a complete investigation of the circumstances can be made. Investigations, which it is hoped will shortly be concluded, are being made into the position and proceedings of the vessels, a list of which was enclosed in your note of June 26th.

"In dealing with the precautions to be taken to control transfers from the United States to the British flag, the suggestion that, in such cases, the local Registrar of Shipping should require the production of a certificate from the United States Shipping Board has been carefully examined. It has been found that there would be great difficulties in the adoption on British territory of such a requirement, and it would be still more difficult to give such a requirement the force of law. With a view, however, to meeting the wishes of the United States Government on this point as far as is practicable, instructions have been given to the Registrar of Shipping at Nassau to the effect that, in transfer cases in which any possible doubt exists as to the *bona fides* of the parties to the transaction, the non-production of the Shipping Board certificate should be taken as a ground of suspicion, involving reference of the case to the Board of Trade in London for further directions. The delay necessitated by this procedure would, it is hoped, be in itself sufficient to reduce to a minimum the danger of transfers being successfully effected in improper cases. It may be added that if, in spite of the precautions taken, a fictitious owner secures registry and there is reason to believe that his title is open to question, an enquiry may be instituted under Section 51 of the Merchant Shipping Act, 1906, and if, as a result of these proceedings, it becomes clear that the transaction was fraudulent, the ship is subject to forfeiture. Proceedings under this section of the act had in fact already been instituted in some cases, and the possibility of instituting similar proceedings in the case of some of the vessels referred to in the note from the State Department is being examined.

"His Majesty's Government had thus taken steps even before the receipt of representations from the United States Government to prevent the practices, to which attention has now been drawn. They have now, as already indicated, issued supplementary instructions in the matter, and hope that the measures taken will prove successful in preventing any breaches of the local law. They feel, however, more difficulty in accepting the proposal that a treaty should be made authorizing the authorities of each government to exercise a right of search of vessels of the other beyond the three-mile limit of territorial waters up to a distance of twelve miles from the shore. His Majesty's Government have consistently opposed any extension of the limit of territorial waters such as that now suggested. They feel that the outbreak of smuggling which has led to the proposal can not be regarded as a permanent condition, but as one which will no doubt be suppressed

twelve miles; the British Government, therefore, was reluctant to enter into such a treaty that named the same distance. Its reluctance, however, was not based on any objection to the seizure by the United States of her smuggling vessels beyond three miles from the shore, as is evidenced by her later agreement not to object to such seizures far beyond that distance, even beyond twelve miles in many cases, namely, for the distance that the rum-vessel could make in an hour's sailing, or, if the cargo was to be sent ashore by means of another vessel, as far as such other vessel could make in an hour's sailing. It, thus, objected not to the principle proposed by the United States' note, which would have authorized seizures only within twelve miles from the shore, but to specifying, *in miles,* a wider zone for the purpose under consideration, than the one she wished to preserve for other purposes. In other words, it did not object to seizures beyond three miles from the shore, so long as no definite distance were named in which the authority should be exercised. It was, thus, willing to permit the exercise of this authority for a considerable distance beyond what it conceived to be "territorial waters," but it was not willing to agree to a fixed distance, or a zone measured *in miles.* This was because it felt that the jeopardy to the "3-mile limit,"

---

by the United States authorities within the not distant future. While, therefore, they are desirous of assisting the United States Government to the best of their ability in the suppression of the traffic and in the prevention of the abuse of the British flag by those engaged in it, they do not feel that they can properly acquiesce, in order to meet a temporary emergency, in the abandonment of a principle to which they attach great importance.

"In communicating the above to you I am directed to add that while His Majesty's Government are, as already indicated, unable to acquiesce in the proposed treaty for the extension of territorial waters, they are nevertheless most desirous of taking any steps within their power to prevent any infractions of the local law by persons engaged in liquor smuggling."

U. S. Press release, February 16, 1927.

in whose maintenance it was especially interested for
some purposes, lay in permitting seizures of smugglers
within a limit defined in *miles*,[8] for if such a *limit* should
be fixed for one purpose, it might be claimed for other
purposes by some other power.

A decision by the Supreme Court of the United States
at this time had the effect of placing the United States
Government in an advantageous position in the subsequent negotiations of the treaty which it was urging.   In
the case of *Cunard* v. *Mellon*,[9] it was held that under the
National Prohibition Act foreign vessels are not permitted
to bring liquors into the United States or its "territorial
waters," even if they are kept under seal and are not
intended for delivery in the United States. This decision
threatened to injure foreign shipping, and it became a
subject of correspondence by the Governments of Italy,
Belgium, the Netherlands, Norway, Portugal, Sweden,
Denmark, and Great Britain. The general tenor of this
correspondence was to the effect that the strict enforcement of the prohibition laws against vessels in the
waters of the United States under the ruling of *Cunard*
v. *Mellon,* would be in violation of international "practice" and "comity," if not a principle of International
Law.[10]

[8] For a further discussion of this point, see p. 350, *infra.*

[9] (1922) 262 U. S. 100.

[10] On May 3, 1923, the Secretary of State wrote to the Chiefs of
Foreign Missions in Washington, as follows:

"The Secretary of State presents his compliments to Their Excellen-
cies and Messieurs the Chiefs of Missions, and has the honor to communicate to them the following notice issued by the Secretary of the
Treasury:

"To Shipping Everywhere:

"The Supreme Court of the United States in an opinion rendered
April 30 construing the National Prohibition Act holds that it is unlawful for any vessel, either foreign or domestic, to bring within the United
States or within the territorial waters thereof any liquors whatever
for beverage purposes. Treasury regulations are now being prepared for
carrying this decision into effect and will be promulgated at an early

The desire of the United States Government to break up the "rum-row" with the aid of far-reaching treaties, and the desire of foreign governments that their vessels be permitted to enter the ports and waters of the United States with alcoholic beverages under seal on board, presented an opportunity for a bargain, for which all parties were unquestionably eager.[11] Public sentiment in Great

---

date and become effective June 10, 1923. All shipping, both foreign and domestic will be subject to such regulations on and after that date without further notice."
U. S. Press release, February 20, 1927.

The Italian Government, in reply, drew the attention of the Department to "the serious inconveniences that might arise in connection with the enforcement of the decision." It was said that the "Italian Government emphasises the general principle of International Law and Comity according to which the exercise of the jurisdictional power by a Nation in its territorial waters finds an adequate limitation in the right of other Countries to the freedom of commerce and navigation." It was added that "such a limit is clearly indicated by the existing practice among Nations," according to which a country does not exercise jurisdiction over foreign vessels entering territorial waters except with reference to matters involving "questions of peace or dignity of the country or disturbing public order," and the presence, on Italian vessels, of a certain amount of alcoholic beverages could not affect the peace and dignity or the public order of the United States.

The Department replied that the matter was entirely within the competency of Congress and that it was a question of "the exercise of legislative discretion."

The Belgian Government also pointed out that the law would produce difficulties, as Belgian vessels were required to have alcoholic beverages on board for medicinal purposes and as beverage for the crew. It expressed the view that while a foreign ship in territorial waters is subject to the jurisdiction of that country, yet "it believes that such jurisdiction should not extend beyond restricting acts which might disturb public order. Upon this point, comity and practice of nations have seemed, so far, to agree."

The communications from the other complaining governments were similar to those from the Italian and Belgian Governments. The United States Government sent replies similar to the one sent to the Italian Government.
U. S. Press release, February 20, 1927.

[11] Secretary Hughes said in this connection:

"Again, foreign powers have complained of what they regard as a departure from international comity through the maintenance of the present restrictions of law under which their vessels are not permitted to enter our waters or call at our ports if they have cargoes of liquors

Britain against the decision in *Cunard* v. *Mellon* and the indignation in the United States over the conditions that existed off the coasts induced the representatives of both countries to renew their negotiations for a treaty in 1923, which had been begun in 1922. This time both governments were quite ready to cease their arguments in the interest of practical results. The United States Government was certainly prepared to agree that no penalty should attach to foreign vessels for entering its ports with liquors on board, if kept under seal, in exchange for the privilege of arresting foreign smuggling vessels farther out on the high seas than her statutes called for.

(2) *The Draft Treaty*

A draft treaty, as submitted to the British Government and some other governments in 1923, contained provisions permitting both parties to board each other's vessels within a distance of twelve geographical miles from the coast to make inquiry as to whether such vessels or the persons in control were engaged in any attempt,

---

on board, although these may be kept under seal and are not to be delivered within the territory of the United States. Nations who fully appreciate our authority, and our right to enforce our own policy, cannot understand such a restriction which interferes with their trade with countries other than our own. They cannot understand why a ship from a foreign port with a cargo consigned to another foreign port is unable even to traverse our waters, or to visit our ports, because the cargo on board, which is destined for other countries, is of the sort we do not wish for our own. In this situation there is the plainest opportunity for a fair agreement not in derogation of our principles but to aid in their proper enforcement—not only without the slightest departure from, but with a manifest increase in, the safeguards required for our protection against the introduction of intoxicating liquors.

"Accordingly, negotiations have been undertaken to reach an appropriate international agreement upon this subject and I am happy to say that such an agreement has been concluded with Great Britain today. There are other Powers which I believe are quite ready to act in a similar way. This will be a long step toward removing causes of irritation and it is precisely as we remove such causes that we shall really make progress in furthering the interests of peace." (1924) 18 *American Journal of International Law*, pp. 231, 234.

either with or without the coöperation of other vessels, or persons on board other vessels, to violate the laws of the contracting party making the inquiry, prohibiting or regulating the unlading near, or the importation of any articles into, its territory. The boarding officer was to be allowed to examine the manifest and to inquire as to the cargo and manifest; and if there was reason to believe that such vessels or persons on board, either with or without the coöperation of other vessels or persons on board the same, were engaged in the willful commission of acts which were a violation of the laws with respect to the unlading or importation of articles, search of the vessel was to be permitted with the aid of the master, and such vessels and their cargoes and/or persons, were to be seized and carried into port for adjudication and subjected to the imposition of the penalties provided by the municipal law. This section provided that this privilege would not be an attempt by the parties to extend, as between themselves, the limits of their respective territorial waters adjacent to the high seas. It was also provided that prohibited articles and articles destined for a foreign port might be brought into the territorial waters of the United States, under seal as sea stores, on condition that upon the vessel's arrival within twelve geographical miles of the coast, such articles should be placed under seal and kept under seal as long as the vessel was in such waters.[12]

This draft was taken under consideration by the British Government; while its reply is not available, its views are reflected in the American reply thereto of July 19. The American reply reiterated that it was not the pur-

---

[12] The Secretary of State, in forwarding this draft to the American legations for submission to the various governments, observed that certain maritime nations had sought to maintain as against other governments the privilege of visit and search, for the enforcement of their own laws, more than three miles from the shore.

pose of the Secretary of State, in submitting the draft treaty, "to propose an extension of the limits of territorial waters, and the draft proposal specifically negatived such an intention." It referred to Lord Curzon's opinion that "the theory of the international validity of the three-mile limit would be strengthened by the conclusion of a treaty making an exception for a special purpose," but that such a treaty "would weaken the principle because it would form a precedent, the following of which would ultimately deprive the principle of force," and in reply to this opinion, added that "It is not perceived that this would be the result as no Power would be under obligation to make any other agreements unless it saw fit to do so, or to treat the special agreement as a precedent except in a case precisely analogous, and there could be inserted in the special agreement any statement or qualification that might be deemed to be advisable to show that it was definitely limited to the particular situation in view."

Lord Curzon had been of the opinion that even if twelve miles were adopted in the treaty, certain cases might cause friction between the two countries, owing to the difficulty of determining with certainty the position of a vessel usually out of sight of land, at any rate on the Atlantic coast. The United States Government, in reply, stated that the proposed agreement would do much to reduce, if not wholly eliminate, "the cause of friction due to the present efforts to evade the laws of the United States."

It was pointed out also that the agreement would not interfere with British vessels engaged in legitimate commerce and bound for American ports, for such vessels would come not only within twelve miles, but within three miles of the coast and would, therefore, be subject to examination anyway. It was said that the proposed agreement would bear only upon those vessels which come within twelve miles, but hover beyond three miles from the shore, for the purpose of aiding in the smuggling of liquors and other prohibited articles into the territory of the United States, and that there would be no disposition on the part of the American authorities, and the agreement would not justify any attempt, to seize a British vessel except within the limits proposed, and only "when it was clear that the vessel concerned was directly involved in an attempt to introduce its illicit cargo into the territory of the United States."

Reference was again made to the conduct of vessels engaged as was the *Henry L. Marshall* and to the hope previously expressed that the British Government would interpose no obstacles in such cases to the enforcement of the laws of the United States. It was added that the proposed treaty, while not interfering with legitimate trade, would serve to "remove occasions for misunderstanding." [13]

[13] The text of this note reads as follows:

"The Secretary of State presents his compliments to the Chargé d'Affaires ad interim of Great Britain and acknowledges the receipt of the memorandum, under date of the fourteenth instant, expressing the views of His Majesty's Principal Secretary of State for Foreign Affairs, with respect to the proposed treaty relating to visit and search of vessels within twelve miles of the coasts of the parties, respectively, for the purpose of preventing the illegal introduction of articles into their territories, and also relating to the carriage, within territorial waters, of certain sealed stores and cargo destined for foreign ports.

"Preliminarily, it should be observed that a draft treaty was submitted informally, simply for the purpose of avoiding misunderstanding and of making a concrete suggestion which could form the basis of discussion. It should also be said that it was not the purpose of the Secretary of State to propose an extension of the limits of territorial waters, and the draft proposal specifically negatived such an intention.

"It is noted that Lord Curzon points out that the theory of the international validity of the three-mile limit would be strengthened by the conclusion of a treaty making an exception for a special purpose, but that he is of the opinion that such a treaty would weaken the principle because it would form a precedent, the following of which would ultimately deprive the principle of force. It is not perceived that this would be the result as no Power would be under obligation to make any other agreements unless it saw fit to do so, or to treat the special

The reply of the British Government of September 17 to this note referred to a statement of Mr. Haynes, the United States Prohibition Commissioner, to the effect

agreement as a precedent except in a case precisely analogous, and there could be inserted in the special agreement any statement or qualification that might be deemed to be advisable to show that it was definitely limited to the particular situation in view.

"In relation to Lord Curzon's further suggestion, it may be stated that while the proposed treaty could not be ratified until the Senate convenes, and while the Secretary of State is not in a position to give an assurance either with respect to the action of the Senate, or with regard to the prospect of securing from Congress an amendment to the Volstead Act in relation to ship liquor and cargo liquor destined for foreign ports, it is believed that the solution of the present difficulty through the making of a fair and reasonable agreement, such as is proposed, would be the most promising method of securing early action. Therefore, Mr. Hughes trusts that the suggestion will not be put aside upon the supposition that another course is equally feasible.

"With respect to Lord Curzon's suggestion that even if the twelve-mile limit were accepted, cases would inevitably occur liable to cause serious friction between the two countries owing to the difficulty of deciding with any certainty the position of a vessel usually out of sight of land, at any rate on the Atlantic coast, it is believed by this Government that the proposed special agreement would do much to reduce, if indeed it would not wholly eliminate, the causes of friction due to the present efforts to evade the laws of the United States. In this connection, it must be emphasized that the proposed agreement would not interfere with British vessels engaged in legitimate commerce and bound for American ports. Such vessels will necessarily come not only within twelve miles but within three miles of the American coast and will hence in any event be subject to examination by American authorities and will, of course, comply with the applicable laws of the United States. The proposed special agreement would bear only upon those vessels which come within twelve miles but hover off the three-mile limit for the purpose of aiding in the smuggling of intoxicating liquor, or other prohibited articles, into the territory of the United States.

"It is impossible for this Government not to take all proper and lawful measures to prevent this illicit traffic from being carried on. An illustration is afforded by the case of the schooner HENRY L. MARSHALL, the conduct of which recently came under the scrutiny of the United States Circuit Court of Appeals for the Second Circuit, as stated in the memorandum of the Secretary of State delivered to the British Embassy on the sixteenth instant. While it is understood that this vessel is not regarded as a British vessel, for the reason which His Majesty's Government has stated, reference may be made to the practice of the vessel as showing the conditions with which the American Government is required to deal. The vessel did not come within the three-mile limit, but she made her arrangements for the carriage of her

that the "moonshine-still" is the chief source of supply of illicit liquors in the country and that "the tales of wet waves sweeping in on our coasts" were largely fanciful, and were spread as propaganda to discredit law enforcement, as furnishing "additional hesitation in accepting proposals which . . . cannot, in Lord Curzon's opinion, fail to weaken the authority of the general rule of International Law, whereby three miles is regarded as the limit of territorial jurisdiction." It was reiterated that the Atlantic coast line, except that part between Port-

---

illicit cargo to the shore of the United States in violation of its laws, and, as the court found, while the unloading was begun outside the three-mile limit, it was continued within the territorial waters of the United States, and the vessel was engaged contrary to the laws of the United States in introducing her cargo of intoxicating liquors within the commerce of the United States.

"This Government has already expressed the hope that the British Government will interpose no obstacles in such cases to the enforcement of the laws of the United States, but it is believed that an appropriate agreement which would not injure bona fide trade but would facilitate the enforcement of the laws of the United States in preventing the smuggling of liquor would remove occasions for misunderstanding and eliminate the serious friction to which the Memorandum under consideration refers.

"It may confidently be asserted that there would be no disposition on the part of the American authorities, and the special agreement would not justify any attempt, to seize a British vessel, save within the limits proposed, and when it was clear that the vessel concerned was directly involved in an attempt to introduce its illicit cargo into the territory of the United States. British vessels bound for the ports of the United States would encounter no additional obstacle to their trade, and vessels destined for foreign ports, which happened to pass on legitimate errands within twelve miles of the American coast, would suffer no inconvenience, while such vessels as were engaged in the unlawful conduct above described would not be able to create difficulties between the two countries, much less serious friction, by attempts to secure immunity for their operations by invoking the protection of the British flag.

"Although the Government of the United States regards the proposed agreement as an appropriate setting forth of the proposal, it would cordially welcome the cooperation of the British Government in moulding the form of an arrangement which would reasonably serve a purpose which, it is firmly believed, may be found to be common to both countries."

U. S. Press release, February 16, 1927.

land, Maine, and the Bay of Fundy, is so low that it is not, as a rule, visible twelve miles out, and that the difficulty of deciding the exact position of the proposed new limit would, in consequence, be increased, and there would, therefore, be "a constant risk of disputes arising between the two countries whenever a British ship was boarded or arrested . . . on or near the new line."

The British note observed that "the ancient British Hovering Acts were modified in 1876 to bring them into harmony with the principles of international law,[14] and His Majesty's Government cannot admit that the municipal legislation of any country can override those principles."

It was observed that British legislation had been considered, with the view "to prohibiting the export of spirituous liquors to destinations adjacent to the United States except under license or to rendering illegal the discharge of such liquors at ports other than those to which they were originally consigned,"[15] but that such legislation was found to be impossible, and that even assuming that measures could be devised for stopping the export of liquors which might ultimately reach the United States, and that all other countries were prepared to take similar action, nevertheless His Majesty's Government still felt a hesitation in proposing such measures "so long as British ships are prevented from carrying liquor under seal in transit through United States waters." The hope was expressed that means could be found to modify the application of the prohibition law to British ships.

It was said, in conclusion, that "in view of the difficul-

[14] This statement begs the question. At any rate, British law still calls for jurisdiction over foreign vessels in some cases for a greater distance than three miles. See pp. 151, 152, and 154, *supra*.

[15] It was first said that no liquors were ever cleared directly from the United Kingdom to United States ports.

ties of the case His Majesty's Government could not agree to an extension of the three-mile limit, even for a limited purpose, until the matter has been submitted to the Imperial Conference, which will meet within a few weeks in London." [16]

[16] The full text of the British note reads:

"With reference to the note verbale which the Secretary of State addressed to me on July 19th last, I have the honour to inform you, by instruction of His Majesty's Principal Secretary of State for Foreign Affairs, that Lord Curzon has had under careful consideration, in consultation with the other Departments of His Majesty's Government concerned, Mr. Hughes's proposals for an extension of territorial jurisdiction in connection with the liquor traffic from the ordinary three-mile limit of territorial waters to a distance of twelve miles from the coast, as embodied in the draft treaty handed to me by the Secretary of State on June 11th last.

"The object of the United States Government in making these proposals is to secure the right to search and arrest ships from which spirituous liquors are sold just outside the present limit of territorial jurisdiction. The extent of this traffic seems, however, to His Majesty's Government to have been exaggerated, judging from the following statement published by Mr. Haynes, the United States Prohibition Commissioner in the 'New York Times' of July 18th last. . . .

"In face of this authoritative pronouncement Lord Curzon feels additional hesitation in accepting proposals which, with all due respect to Mr. Hughes, cannot, in Lord Curzon's opinion, fail to weaken the authority of the general rule of international law, whereby three miles is regarded as the limit of territorial jurisdiction. Moreover, the Atlantic coast line of the United States, except the small part between Portland (Maine) and the Bay of Fundy, is so low that it is not as a rule visible twelve miles out at sea; the difficulty of deciding the exact position of the proposed new limit would in consequence be much increased, and there would be a constant risk of disputes arising between the two countries whenever a British ship was boarded or arrested by the United States preventive service, on or near the new line. In this connection Lord Curzon would observe that the ancient British Hovering Acts were modified in 1876 to bring them into harmony with the principles of international law, and His Majesty's Government cannot admit that the municipal legislation of any country can override those principles.

"No spirituous liquors are cleared direct from the United Kingdom to United States ports and so far as British subjects are concerned, there is no violation of any law, British or international, in the sale of such liquors on the high seas to purchasers of any nationality; therefore there is no obligation upon His Majesty's Government to interfere with the prosecution of a perfectly legitimate trade. Nevertheless the whole question has been carefully examined with an earnest desire to afford the United States Government any proper assistance in the difficulties

The British Government reported to the Department on October 29 that the Imperial Conference had appointed a special committee to consider the two ques-

----

which they are encountering in the enforcement of the Volstead Act. In this spirit legislation was considered with a view to prohibiting the export of spirituous liquors to destinations adjacent to the United States except under license or to rendering illegal the discharge of such liquors at ports other than those to which they were originally consigned. It became apparent, however, that such legislation would necessitate and could indeed only be made effective by rationing supplies not merely to countries adjacent to the United States, but to all countries, for which purpose powers would be required similar to those exercised for the control of trade during the war. The United States Government will probably agree that His Majesty's Government could hardly be expected to revive such powers, seeing that the United States Government themselves (in March 1920) explained their inability to ratify the convention for the control of the arms traffic on the very ground that they were not prepared to revive the war regulations by which alone a private trade could be regulated.

"Assuming, however, that measures could be devised for stopping the export from the United Kingdom of spirituous liquors which might ultimately reach the United States and that all other countries were prepared to take similar action so that the traffic would not merely be diverted into other channels, His Majesty's Government would still feel great hesitation in proposing such measures to Parliament so long as British ships are prevented from carrying liquor under seal in transit through United States waters. As far as His Majesty's Government are aware, it has never been alleged that any liquor at all has made its way into the United States from the stores of British ships calling at United States ports, so that this restriction, besides constituting in effect an interference with the liberty of British ships on the high seas, appears to be entirely superfluous.

"His Majesty's Government do not deny the strictly legal right of the United States or any other country to impose its jurisdiction on all ships whether national or foreign within its territorial waters. His Majesty's Government themselves claim that right and it is even the case that some of the provisions of the British Merchant Shipping Acts are such that ships visiting ports in the United Kingdom must comply with them before entering and after leaving the jurisdiction. These provisions, however, relate solely to the safety and welfare of the ship, crew and passengers. Similar provisions exist in the legislation of the United States and other countries and they are generally recognized as reasonable.

"It is, however, equally well recognized that the circumstances of ships, travelling as they do from port to port in many different countries, are peculiar and that to subject them to all the different and often conflicting requirements of the various jurisdictions which they may enter, would create an impossible situation. Consequently, as a

tions between the two Governments, and stated that while the two Governments were in agreement as to the undesirability of altering the general rule whereby "territorial waters" extend only to three miles from low-water mark, it was hoped that on the conclusion of the Conference's consideration of the conditions now existing outside the territorial waters of the United States, His Majesty's Government would be in a position to make a definite proposal generally favorable to the United States in the suppression of the liquor traffic. It was said, further, however, that newspaper reports to the effect that the British Government had accepted, in principle, the proposal for establishing "a twelve-mile limit for the purpose of extending the right of search," were premature and inaccurate.[17]

matter of international comity and practice, the maritime Powers refrain from imposing their jurisdiction on foreign ships except for the purposes stated above, namely, the safety and welfare of the ships, crews and passengers. . . .

"In informing you of the above I am directed to express the earnest hope that means may be found to modify the present application of the Volstead Act to British ships, and thus to remedy what is, in effect, an unwarrantable interference with the domestic concerns of British ships on the high seas.

"I am to add in view of the difficulties of the case His Majesty's Government could not agree to an extension of the three-mile limit, even for a limited purpose, until the matter has been submitted to the Imperial Conference, which will meet within a few weeks in London." *U. S. Press release,* February 16, 1927.

[17] Viscount Grey of Fallodon, in reply to the King's speech on January 15 in the House of Lords, expressed delight over the approaching agreement with the United States relating to smuggling, because "the rum-running on the coast of the United States was something of which the Empire could not feel proud," and because "I believe in a separate agreement with the United States to waive for a certain purpose the three-mile limit, provided it was—and on this I should like the noble Marquess to inform us—on the distinct understanding that the United States is going to be as firm as we are in upholding as a part of International Law the three-mile limit except where nations have voluntarily agreed for a special purpose to depart from it." He added that such a "departure for this purpose from the three-mile limit is not going to weaken the general doctrine of International Law, but is going to strengthen it by giving solidarity between ourselves and the United

(3) *The Treaty*

The treaty, as finally concluded,[18] recited that the parties had agreed upon the treaty from a desire "of avoiding any difficulties which might arise between them in connection with the laws in force in the United States on the subject of alcoholic beverages."

Article I provides that, "The High Contracting Parties declare that it is their firm intention to uphold the principle that 3 marine miles extending from the coastline outwards and measured from low-water mark constitute the proper limits of territorial waters."

This article simply purports to define the extent of "territorial waters." The negotiations leading up to the treaty show that this article was inserted in order to meet the fear of the British Government that an agreement not to object to the seizure of smuggling vessels flying her flag beyond three miles from the shore, without more, might be interpreted as an abandonment of its contention that three miles is the limit of territorial waters.

By Article II, the British Government agrees not to object to the boarding and searching of vessels flying its flag "outside the limits of territorial waters," but not at

---

States for upholding the doctrine of International Law for the nations in general."

The Secretary of State for Foreign Affairs, the Marquess Curzon of Kedleston, in reply, said that when the Dominion Premiers came over, the point was brought up that "we should not in any way jeopardize or qualify the fundamental principle of International Law and of British policy, namely, the three-mile limit of territorial waters. On that point we found the United States government entirely prepared to meet us, and not only to agree to our enunciation of that principle, but to enunciate it themselves. And when the treaty comes before your Lordships' House you will find that it contains a declaration in which that principle is reaffirmed by both parties to the treaty." *Parliamentary Debates* (Lords) (Hansard), 1924, vol. 56, cols. 24 and 38. See, also, ibid. (1923), vol. 54, cols. 727, 728.

[18] 43 *Stat. at Large*, Part 2, p. 1761; U. S. *Treaty Series* No. 685. It was consented to by the Senate on March 13, 1924, by a vote of 61 "yeas" and 7 "nays," and 28 "not voting." *Cong. Record*, 68 Cong., 1st Sess., Part IV, p. 4084. It came into force on May 22, 1924.

a greater distance from the coast than can be "traversed in one hour" by the "vessel suspected of endeavoring to commit the offense," except in cases where the cargo (liquor) is intended to be conveyed to the shore by a vessel other than the one boarded and searched, in which event, the distance from the shore is determined by the speed of such other vessel.

The vessel may be boarded in order to address inquiries to those on board and to make an examination of the ship's papers for the purpose of ascertaining whether such vessels or those on board "are endeavoring to import or have imported alcoholic beverages into the United States" in violation of the law. When such inquiries and examination show "a reasonable ground for suspicion" a search may be instituted, and if there is "reasonable cause for belief" that the vessel has committed, is committing or attempting to commit an offense against the laws of the United States prohibiting the importation of alcoholic beverages, it may be seized and taken into a port for adjudication in accordance with such laws.[19]

[19] Article II reads:

"(1) His Britannic Majesty agrees that he will raise no objection to the boarding of private vessels under the British flag outside the limits of territorial waters by the authorities of the United States, its territories or possessions in order that enquiries may be addressed to those on board and an examination be made of the ship's papers for the purpose of ascertaining whether the vessel or those on board are endeavoring to import or have imported alcoholic beverages into the United States, its territories or possessions in violation of the laws there in force. When such enquiries and examination show a reasonable ground for suspicion, a search of the vessel may be instituted.

"(2) If there is reasonable cause for belief that the vessel has committed or is committing or attempting to commit an offense against the laws of the United States, its territories or possessions prohibiting the importation of alcoholic beverages, the vessel may be seized and taken into a port of the United States, its territories or possessions for adjudication in accordance with such laws.

"(3) The rights conferred by this article shall not be exercised at a greater distance from the coast of the United States, its territories or possessions than can be traversed in one hour by the vessel sus-

Article III provides that no penalty or forfeiture under the laws of the United States "shall be applicable or attach to alcoholic liquors or to vessels or persons by reason of the carriage of such liquors," when such liquors are listed as sea stores or cargo destined for a port foreign to the United States, on board British vessels, voyaging to and from United States ports or passing through the "territorial waters" thereof, and such carriage "shall be as now provided by law with respect to the transit of such liquors through the Panama Canal," provided they are kept under seal continuously while the vessel remains within territorial waters and no part of them is unladen within the United States.[20]

---

pected of endeavoring to commit the offense. In cases, however, in which the liquor is intended to be conveyed to the United States, its territories or possessions by a vessel other than the one boarded and searched, it shall be the speed of such other vessel and not the speed of the vessel boarded, which shall determine the distance from the coast at which the right under this article can be exercised."

[20] Article III reads:

"No penalty or forfeiture under the laws of the United States shall be applicable or attach to alcoholic liquors or to vessels or persons by reason of the carriage of such liquors, when such liquors are listed as sea stores or cargo destined for a port foreign to the United States, its territories or possessions on board British vessels voyaging to or from ports of the United States, or its territories or possessions or passing through the territorial waters thereof, and such carriage shall be as now provided by law with respect to the transit of such liquors through the Panama Canal, provided that such liquors shall be kept under seal continuously while the vessel on which they are carried remains within said territorial waters and that no part of such liquors shall at any time or place be unladen within the United States, its territories or possessions."

Treasury Decisions, vol. 26, 1924, No. 3601, contains the following regulations:

"The following regulations governing operations under the foregoing Treaty, and particularly under Article III thereof, are issued, effective forthwith, and will apply to all vessels, foreign and domestic, which now have, or may hereafter have, rights or duties under said Treaty or other treaties of a like nature which may hereafter be negotiated.

"Paragraph 1. *Present Regulations.* Article XVII of Regulations 60 (revised), relating to liquors on vessels, shall, except as modified by the foregoing Treaty, or by these regulations, remain in full force and effect, and no liquor may be used for medicinal or other purposes on board any vessels while in the territorial waters of the United

Article IV makes provision for the reference of claims by a British vessel for compensation, if it has suffered loss or injury through "the improper or unreasonable exercise of the rights conferred by Article II of this Treaty or on the ground that it has not been given the benefit of Article III." The claim is first to be referred for the joint consideration of two persons, one of whom shall be nominated by each of the High Contracting Parties.

States, except such as is required and held under a certificate of medicinal need, Form 1539, or other permit or right provided by law or regulations."

[Territorial waters, according to Article XVII, sec. 1700 of *Regulations 60, Revised*, extend to three miles.]

"Par. 2. *Sea-stores.* Sea-stores liquors, except such as are duly authorized for nonbeverage purposes on a vessel, which are carried by any vessel having a treaty or other lawful right to carry the same in the territorial waters of the United States, shall be regarded as not subject to the penalties of the national prohibition act if said vessel provides a safe and secure room or place in which such liquors are securely locked by the master, as defined in section 1704 of Regulation 60 (revised), during the continuous period while such vessel is within the territorial waters of the United States, or within the distance from the coast of the United States, its territories or possessions (except the Philippine Islands and the Panama Canal and the Panama Railroad, to which territories and possessions the above Treaty does not apply), which can be traversed in one hour by such vessel, or other vessel as provided in Article II (3), of the Treaty. The room or place so provided shall be devoted continuously to the storage and safekeeping of such liquors while said vessel remains in said waters and shall not be used for the storage of other articles, merchandise, or stores to which access is required while said vessel is in said waters. Such room or place may be unlocked only in the presence of an officer of the customs service of the United States or by the written order and consent of the customs authorities. Such room or place will be sealed by customs authorities as soon as may conveniently be done by such authorities and will be kept under seal continuously thereafter while the vessel on which such liquors are carried remains within such waters."

Paragraph 2 of *Treasury Decisions*, vol. 26, 1924, No. 3613, confines the application of this paragraph to the "period" when the vessel is in "territorial waters."

Paragraph 3 of *Treasury Decisions*, vol. 26, 1924, No. 3601, exempts liquors carried as cargo destined for a port foreign to the United States, when properly sealed, and

Paragraph 4 provides for the seizure of liquors for violations of the foregoing regulations, in accordance with secs. 1770, 1771, and 1772 of Regulations 60, Revised, sec. 598 of the *Tariff Act* of 1922, and other laws.

Effect is to be given to the "recommendations contained in any such joint report." But if no joint report can be agreed upon, the claim is to be referred to the "Claims Commission established under the provisions of the Agreement for the Settlement of Outstanding Pecuniary Claims signed at Washington the 18th August, 1910...." [21]

The treaty preserves the idea of "territorial waters," and, at the same time, authorizes the seizure and condemnation of smuggling vessels far beyond such waters. It clearly draws the distinction between the "limits of

[21] Article IV reads:

"Any claim by a British vessel for compensation on the grounds that it has suffered loss or injury through the improper or unreasonable exercise of the rights conferred by Article II of this Treaty or on the ground that it has not been given the benefit of Article III shall be referred for the joint consideration of two persons, one of whom shall be nominated by each of the High Contracting Parties.

"Effect shall be given to the recommendations contained in any such joint report. If no joint report can be agreed upon, the claim shall be referred to the Claims Commission established under the provisions of the Agreement for the Settlement of Outstanding Pecuniary Claims signed at Washington the 18th August, 1910, but the claim shall not, before submission to the tribunal, require to be included in a schedule of claims confirmed in the manner therein provided."

Article V reads:

"This Treaty shall be subject to ratification and shall remain in force for a period of one year from the date of the exchange of ratifications.

"Three months before the expiration of the said period of one year, either of the High Contracting Parties may give notice of its desire to propose modifications in the terms of the Treaty.

"If such modifications have not been agreed upon before the expiration of the term of one year mentioned above, the Treaty shall lapse.

"If no notice is given on either side of the desire to propose modifications, the Treaty shall remain in force for another year, and so on automatically, but subject always in respect of each such period of a year to the right on either side to propose as provided above three months before its expiration modifications in the Treaty, and to the provision that if such modifications are not agreed upon before the close of the period of one year, the Treaty shall lapse."

Article VI reads, in part, as follows:

"In the event that either of the High Contracting Parties shall be prevented either by judicial decision or legislative action from giving full effect to the provisions of the present Treaty the said Treaty shall automatically lapse, and, on such lapse or whenever this Treaty shall cease to be in force, each High Contracting Party shall enjoy all the

territorial waters" and jurisdiction for revenue purposes beyond such waters. It, thus, embodies a principle for which the United States Government has contended on many occasions. The willingness of the British Government to enter into this treaty would indicate that its objection to the seizure of its smuggling vessels beyond three miles from the shore did not rest upon any of the theories that are sometimes advanced, such as "sovereignty," "freedom of the seas," or "territorial waters," but upon the fear that the exercise of a wider jurisdiction for this special purpose might lead to a claim by the littoral state or states to a zone of "territorial waters" coextensive with the limits to which the special jurisdiction is exercised, in which event valuable fishing and other rights would be seriously affected.[22] By preserving such rights by Article I, by fixing the limit of "territorial waters" at three miles, it was not concerned about the seizure of smuggling craft beyond such waters. Its hesitancy in entering into the treaty was due to a failure to conceive this distinction between the idea of "territorial waters" and a limited jurisdiction beyond them in certain special cases, especially for revenue purposes,[23] but by preserving the idea of "territorial waters" in the treaty, and by agreeing not to object to the seizure of smuggling vessels beyond such waters, it acknowledged this distinc-

---

rights which it would have possessed had this Treaty not been concluded."

This article was inspired by the fear on the part of the British Government that the Federal Courts might hold that Art. III is unconstitutional. When the treaty was under discussion in the House of Representatives, Mr. Tucker declared that it was an amendment to the Volstead Act, without the action, or sanction of Congress, and that it was a modification and repeal of that law "by the substitution of Great Britain for the House of Representatives." *Cong. Record,* 68 Congress, 1st Session, Part 7, p. 6723. See p. 359, *infra,* for cases holding the treaty constitutional.

[22] See pp. 300 and 145, note (119), *supra,* for a fuller discussion of this point.

[23] This distinction is brought out in *The Times* (London) of June 15, 1923 (14f), and September 20, 1923 (10c).

tion in practice, if not in theory. The views of the two Governments, as expressed in the treaty, were in accord on this point, the only difference being that the British Government objected to fixing a distance defined *in miles* for the exercise of a jurisdiction which they both agreed might be exercised beyond what they conceived to be the limit of "territorial waters." The one point of departure is found in the fact that the United States Government took the position that these seizures might be made under her customs laws, irrespective of treaty, without the contravention of International Law, while the British Government maintained that a treaty was necessary.

§ 71. Treaties with Germany, the Netherlands, Cuba, and Panama

Practically identical treaties have been entered into with the following countries:

Germany, ratification exchanged, August 11, 1924;[24]
The Netherlands, "   "   April 8, 1925;[25]
Cuba,   "   "   June 18, 1926;[26]
Panama,   "   "   January 19, 1925.[27]

Article I of the treaty with Great Britain, in which the parties declare that it is their firm intention to uphold the principle that three marine miles constitute the proper limits of territorial waters, and Article II, fixing the hour's sailing as the distance in which search and seizure may be made, are both incorporated in corresponding articles in these treaties.[28] These countries, thus, agree that

[24] U. S. *Treaty Series*, No. 694; 43 *Stat. at Large*, Part 2, p. 1815.
[25] Ibid., No. 712; 44 *Stat. at Large*, Part 3, p. 2013.
[26] Ibid., No. 738; 44 *Stat. at Large*, Part 3, p. 2395.
[27] Ibid., No. 702; 43 *Stat. at Large*, Part 2, p. 1875.
[28] Under Article IV, claims growing out of the "unreasonable exercise of the rights conferred by Article II" are to be referred to the Permanent Court of Arbitration at The Hague, if no joint report can be agreed upon by the two persons nominated by the Parties. This change was due to the fact that no Claims Commission had been set up with these Powers as with Great Britain.

three miles is the proper limit of "territorial waters," but agree that the customs laws of the United States may be enforced at a greater distance from the shore.[29]

These treaties did not grow out of a controversy over seizures under the United States' customs laws. A Cuban vessel had been seized more than three miles out,[30] but the Cuban Government raised no objection.

§ 72. Treaties with Italy, Spain, France, Sweden, Norway, Denmark, and Belgium

Conventions with these Powers were entered into as follows:

Italy, ratification exchanged,	Octover 22, 1924;[31]
Sweden, " "	August 18, 1924;[32]
Norway, " "	July 2, 1924;[33]
Denmark, " "	July 25, 1924;[34]
Spain, " "	November 17, 1926;[35]
France, " "	March 12, 1927;[36]
Belgium, " "	January 11, 1928.[36a]

In the treaties with The Netherlands and Cuba, it is provided by an Exchange of Notes that in the event of the adhesion by the United States to the Protocol of December 16, 1920, under which the Permanent Court of International Justice was created at The Hague, the Government of the United States will not be averse to considering a modification of the treaties, or making separate treaty agreements, providing that claims as mentioned in Article IV shall be referred to such court instead of the Permanent Court of Arbitration. The Cuban treaty provides that in case Cuban vessels are seized under the provisions of Article II, a notification thereof shall be promptly transmitted to the diplomatic representatives of Cuba at Washington.

[29] Article I now appearing in the treaty with Italy and other powers (p. 354, *infra*), was submitted to Germany and the Netherlands, as an alternative to Article I as incorporated in the treaty with Great Britain, in the extent that these countries refused to accept the article as it appears in the latter treaty.

[30] See *U. S.* v. *Bengochea*, p. 226, *supra*.

[31] U. S. *Treaty Series*, No. 702; 43 *Stat. at Large*, Part 2, p. 1844.

[32] Ibid.,   No. 698;   "   "   "   "   p. 1830.

[33] Ibid.,   No. 689;   "   "   "   "   p. 1772.

[34] Ibid.,   No. 693;   "   "   "   "   p. 1809.

[35] Ibid.,   No. 749; 44 *Stat. at Large*, Part 3, p. 2465.

[36] Ibid.,   No. 755.

[36a] Ibid.,   No. 759.

(1) *Terms of the Treaties*

These conventions are in one respect radically different from those with Great Britain and the other powers already considered. Italy, Sweden, Norway, Denmark, Spain, France, and Belgium, have never accepted the so-called "three-mile limit" for all purposes, at least; and they naturally refused to sign a treaty that would pledge them to uphold that distance as the limit of their torial jurisdiction."

Article I reads:

"The High Contracting Parties respectively retain their rights and claims, without prejudice by reason of this agreement, with respect to the extent of their territorial jurisdiction."

In other respects, these conventions are essentially the same as those already considered. Seizures are permitted within the hour's sailing.

(2) *Negotiations of the Treaties*

The treaty as entered into with Great Britain, was submitted to Denmark, Italy, Sweden, Norway, France, Belgium, and Spain,[37] along with the article just quoted, as an alternative provision, with the statement that the Department preferred the provision contained in Article I of the treaty with Great Britain, but that it was willing to agree to the alternative provision if it was insisted upon.

Italy refused to assent to Article I of the treaty with Great Britain, and insisted upon Article I as it now appears in the treaty with that country.

The Swedish Government desired to omit Article I altogether, but if it were not omitted it wish to have inserted a provision to the effect that the treaty should not be considered as establishing a precedent with regard

[37] It was submitted in that form to Japan, also, but no treaty has been concluded with that country.

to the territorial limits hitherto upheld by the contracting parties. It desired reciprocal rights in regard to boarding smuggling vessels outside the limits of territorial waters, as it felt that such rights might prove to be of importance in the event Sweden should wish to make similar treaties with other countries. The Department refused to omit Article I, but reaffirmed its willingness to accept the alternative as finally agreed upon. It refused to accept the other suggestions put forward by the Swedish Government.

The treaty with Great Britain was submitted to Spain. The Spanish Government offered the proposal that the treaty should provide that the proper limits of the territorial waters of the two countries should continue to be those as determined by their legislation. It objected to Article I of the draft submitted in 1923, authorizing the boarding of vessels for twelve geographical miles in order to institute search,[38] because, it was said, a nation has exclusive sovereignty over its own vessels on the high seas, but it expressed itself as being willing to approve, as an alternative, the one-hour's sailing clause, as adopted in the treaty with Great Britain. The Department refused to accept the first proposal, but reiterated that it would accept the alternative, as finally adopted in Article I of the treaty with this country.

Both types of treaties were submitted to the French and Belgium Governments, which refused to accept Article I of the treaty with Great Britain.

A copy of the treaty with Great Britain was submitted to the Norwegian Government, which requested reciprocal rights of search of smuggling vessels, as did Sweden, but the United States again refused to accede to this request. This Government expressed a preference for a fixed distance from the coast within which the boarding of vessels

[38] P. 336, *supra*.

might take place, preferably ten nautical miles, which is the distance established by Norwegian law for the police activities of the customs authorities, instead of the hour's sailing. The United States rejected this proposal, and the Norwegian Government accepted Article I as it now stands in the treaty with that country.

§ 73. The Significance of the Treaties

Thus, only five out of these twelve countries would agree to stipulate that it was their "intention to uphold the principle that 3 marine miles . . . constitute the proper limits of territorial waters," while all of them agreed that the United States should not be confined to so narrow a "limit" in the enforcement of certain of its prohibition and customs laws. The positions of the governments as shown in the negotiations leading up to the treaties, and the terms of the treaties themselves, render it difficult to conclude that any principle of International Law defining the extent of "territorial waters" has been established, but they point to the conclusion that the subject is in a condition of confusion. In view of the historic practice of nations, it is submitted that the seizures of smuggling vessels made by the United States under her hovering laws were not inconsistent with any existing principle of International Law, and that these treaties were not, therefore, necessary in so far as these laws covered the ground, though they are helpful in permitting seizures at greater distances than is provided in such laws. The treaties are helpful, furthermore, in that they remove all possible friction and eliminate the likelihood of protest by any Government not sharing the view just expressed. They illustrate the point just made, that when this difficult question arises among nations, its solution is not found in some fixed principle of International Law, but in an adjustment of some sort—an adjustment that will assist a state in eliminating an evil that frequently appears off its coasts. These adjustments are made necessary not because a nation especially opposes the seizure of its smuggling vessels beyond the distance which it conceives to be the proper limits of territorial waters, but because it wishes to safeguard other interests against invasion beyond such limits. It seems desirable that future legislation—national or international—should recognize the principle embodied in these treaties, and that whatever limits, if any, are eventually agreed upon for other purposes, nations will be allowed the jurisdiction reasonably necessary to clear their coasts of smugglers.

It should be noted that the treaties are silent on the question of how far from the shore legislation of the United States may be enforced against the vessels of the treaty powers; this would seem to be left to the United States. The foreign governments only agree not to raise objection to the search and seizure of their vessels within the distance named in the treaties, when such vessels have violated, are violating, or are attempting to violate certain laws of the United States. There seems to be no reason why Congress may not legislate for a greater distance than four leagues. This new legislation could be framed to conform to Article II (3) of the treaties without disturbing the present four-league statutes, which would remain in force for vessels of non-treaty states,[39] and those of treaty-states when the offense is committed within four leagues from the shore, but at a distance from the shore which the vessel boarded or the one intending to carry its cargo ashore can not make in an hour's steaming.

[39] For a discussion of a bill introduced by Senator Goff, see Jessup, *The Law of Territorial Waters and Maritime Jurisdiction* (1927), p. 313, et seq.

The Solicitor General, Mr. William D. Mitchell, is of the opinion that such legislation would not meet with objection by the treaty powers. *Treasury Decisions,* 1925, vol. 49, No. 41613, p. 937.

§ 74. Practical Effects of the Treaties

The Treaties have proved to be very efficacious in wiping out smuggling from sea. According to the annual reports of the Coast Guard for 1925 and 1926, the conditions off the coast are greatly improved. The notorious rum-row, formerly lying off the entrance to New York and off Long Island and New Jersey, has been scattered. While some vessels were still found hovering in 1925, they appeared only "desultorily," and were continuously picketed by Coast Guard patrol boats. From April, 1922, to June 30, 1925, 213,802 cases of liquors were seized, and "vast quantities" were dumped overboard during chase, and there were 734 instances of seizures of narcotics. The new Coast Guard vessels, it is reported, had enabled the service to compete with the fast smuggling craft. Attention was called to the fact that the 10,000 miles of coast line offer many landing places for crafty rum-runners, who are familiar with the shore line and are among the best of boatmen.[40]

The report of 1926 notes that the menace of the rum-row in its old form "has been effectively dissipated" by the Coast Guard, though foreign ships were still appearing off certain sections of the seaboard in "varying numbers," without any fixed plan, watching for an opportunity to run the Coast Guard blockade, or to serve the small-boat customer from the shore. Picketing was continued to prevent this.[41] Twelve hundred and twenty-three

[40] *Annual Report of the United States Coast Guard*, 1925, pp. 11-14.

[41] *The Times* (London), of May 9, 1925, reported that the Federal Government was making a most determined effort to enforce prohibition. Off New York, for 100 miles along the coast, it was maintaining a virtual blockade of the so-called "Scotch Armada," the new name for the rum fleet. Every rum vessel was surrounded by government vessels, so that in three days not a drop had reached the shore. Seaplanes were being used in patrolling, it was said.

For an account of the smuggling that went on across the Canadian border, see *The Times* (London), June 7, 1924.

seizures had been made, and much "dumping" had taken place.[42]

The annual report of the Attorney General of 1925 states that the effect of the treaties had been to move the so-called "rum-row" farther out from the shore line to a position where the smugglers believed they were beyond the authority of the American Coast Guard vessels. The judgment of the officers had not always been good, but they usually kept themselves far enough out to sea to raise seriously disputed questions of fact as to their being within the one hour's run from shore.[43] The report of 1926 stated that the treaties had resulted in moving foreign vessels out from the coast "considerably farther than 12 miles." In 1926, foreign ships were seized as follows: British, 35; Honduran, 3; French, 3; Nicaraguan, 1; Dominican, 1; while 849 American vessels had been seized. Some of the cases against these vessels had been dismissed, because of the interpretation placed upon the treaties by some of the Federal Courts.[44]

§ 75. Court Decisions under the Treaties

(1) *Constitutionality of the Treaties*

Milliken v. *Stone*[45] was a suit to enjoin the enforcement of Article III of the treaty permitting British vessels to bring liquors into port under seal, on the ground that the treaty was, in that regard, repugnant to the Eighteenth Amendment of the Constitution of the United States, which forbade such transportation. It was held

[42] *Annual Report of the United States Coast Guard*, 1926, p. 13.
[43] *Annual Report of the United States Attorney General*, 1925, p. 42.
[44] Ibid., 1926, p. 56.
[45] (1927) 16 Fed. (2d) 981 (C. C. A., 2d Cir.). See, also, *The Frances Louise* (1924) 1 Fed. (2d) 1004, and *The Pictonian* (1924) 3 Fed. (2d) 145. The question of the constitutionality of the treaties has not been discussed very much by the courts; they seem to assume that they are constitutional.

that no relief by injunction could be granted, except to protect property rights against irremediable injuries, and no such rights were alleged.

(2) *The Four-League Statutes Survive the Treaties*

The treaties do not have "the effect of abrogating pro tanto the statute providing for search and seizure within the 12-mile limit," for it was not their object to restrict the rights of the United States, but to enable the United States better to police its seaboard; so that if a foreign vessel is seized 12¾ or 13 miles from the shore, beyond an hour's sailing distance, after pursuit is begun within 12 miles under section 581 of the *Tariff Act* of 1922, the treaty is not violated.[46]   A fortiori, a seizure may be made *within* 12 miles under that Act at a point beyond an hour's sailing from the shore.

(3) *Offenses for Which Seizures May be Made. Persons on Board and the Cargo, as Well as the Vessel Within the Operation of the Treaty*

United States v. *Ford.*[47]   This was an indictment for carrying on a continuous conspiracy at the Bay of San Francisco, contrary to section 37 of the *Criminal Code*, to violate the *National Prohibition Act*, the *Tariff Act* of 1922, and the terms of the treaty with Great Britain, by introducing into and transporting in the United States intoxicating liquors.   The other acts charged were the loading at Vancouver of 12,000 cases of liquor on the *Quadra*, a British vessel officially destined to La Libertad, the vessel's proceeding to a point less than twelve miles from the Farallon Islands off San Francisco, a distance

----

[46] *The Vinces* (1927) 20 Fed. (2d) 164. For a full statement of the facts of this case, see p. 238, *supra*.

[47] (1927) 47 Sup. Ct. Rep. 531.

which could be traversed in less than an hour by the *Quadra* and by certain motorboats, including the *903-B*, the *C-55*, the *Marconi,* the *California,* and the *Ocean Queen,* into which the liquor was delivered from the *Quadra* and imported to the United States. It was charged that liquor was landed by the defendants from the *Quadra* according to this plan. The *Quadra* was seized 5.17 nautical miles from the islands mentioned, while a motorboat that had transported some of the liquors could make 6.6 miles an hour. The defendants were the officers or crew on the *C-55* and the *Quadra* and certain persons on land. The captains of the *Quadra* and other vessels similarly employed, while hovering near the Farallones, were constantly in touch with the other defendants at San Francisco, and were, to some extent, under their orders and directions. The *Quadra* was supplied with fuel oil from the shore, pursuant to prearrangement. These vessels never went to their pretended destinations, but sailed up and down near the coast, receiving supplies from and delivering liquors to the small boats, which were landed at Oakland Creek in San Francisco. The defendants were convicted in the lower Federal Court,[48] and this conviction was affirmed by the Circuit Court of Appeals.[49] The case was carried to the Supreme Court by writ of certiorari.

On motion to suppress evidence based on the contention that the court had no jurisdiction over the defendants because the seizure was wrongful, since it was made "beyond the reach of the laws of the United States," and the officers and crew were British subjects, the Circuit Court of Appeals held:

[48] (1925) 3 Fed. (2d) 643 (D. C. S. D. Calif., Partridge, Dist. Judge).
[49] (1926) 10 Fed. (2d) 339 (C. C. A., 9th Cir., McCamant, Cir. Judge).

1. It was sufficient that the defendants were before the court, and that the jurisdiction was not impaired by the manner in which they were brought before it; [50]

2. The seizure was made within the terms of Art. II (3) of the treaty, for the vessel carrying the liquors ashore could make the distance from the *Quadra* to the shore in an hour; [51]

3. The speed of the receiving vessel is to be measured when the vessel is light and not when laden with her cargo.

On point 3, the Supreme Court held that the motion below to exclude and suppress the evidence of the ship and cargo on the ground that the seizure was unlawful for the reason advanced by defendants, was properly denied, for the question of the evidential weight of the test of the vessel's speed was for the judgment of the trial court. This court held that the treaty does not operate solely against the smuggling vessel as defendants contended, but against the liquor cargo and the persons on board, as well.[52]

4. It was contended by the defendants that the treaty contemplates seizures only for the offense of importing or attempting to import liquor illegally, and not for a conspiracy to do so. It was held by the Supreme Court

[50] The court said that this seizure could have been made under section 586 of the *Tariff Act* of 1922. It was also held that the crimes charged were committed on the American vessel receiving the cargo, that the defendants assisted in this crime, and were, therefore, principals, and since the crimes were committed partly in one place and partly in another, the venue could be laid in either place.

[51] See *Woitte* v. *United States* (1927) 19 Fed. (2d) 506, where, in an indictment for a conspiracy to violate the *Tariff Act* of 1922 it was held on motion to suppress the evidence that a foreign vessel may be seized sixteen miles from shore, even though it can not make that distance in an hour's sailing, if the launch intended to be used in transporting the liquors to the shore can make the distance in an hour.

[52] See accord, Solicitor General of the United States, *Treasury Decisions* (1926), vol. 49, p. 937, No. 41613, and *United States v. Henning* (1925) 7 Fed. (2d) 488, 490.

that, taking into consideration the friendly purpose of both countries, as evidenced in the preamble (which expressed a desire of avoiding any difficulties which might arise between them in connection with the laws in force in the United States, on the subject of alcoholic beverages) and the fact that no particular laws were referred to by title or date in the treaty, but only the purpose and effect of such laws, the parties to the treaty intended that the treaty should apply to persons taken under the treaty and proved to have violated *any* law of the United States by which the importation of liquor is intended to be stopped through forfeiture or punishment, which would include the *National Prohibition Act*, the *Tariff Act* of 1922, section 593 (b),[53] and section 37 of the *Criminal Code*,[54] which penalizes a conspiracy to violate these laws. It was said by the court that the overt acts of the conspiracy charged in this case include an actual importation, and it would, therefore, be absurd to hold that the conspiracy set forth does not come within the scope of the treaty, and that any law, the enforcement of and punishment for which will specifically prevent smuggling of liquor, should be regarded as embraced by the treaty.

5. On the question of conspiracy, the defendants contended that since they were corporally outside the United States during the alleged conspiracy, they could not commit an offense against the United States. The Supreme Court held that the conduct of the defendants constituted the offense of conspiracy to violate the laws of the United States, whether they were in the United States or not. The conspiracy was continually in operation between the defendants in the United States and those on the high seas, and some of the overt acts complained of took effect and were completed within the United States. Jurisdiction exists to try one who is a conspirator, whether the

[53] P. 243, *supra*. [54] P. 246, *supra*.

conspiracy is in whole or in part carried on in the country whose laws are conspired against.[55]

(4) *Seizures within an Hour's Sailing*

It has been held by most courts that seizures must be made within an hour's sailing, unless the vessel, having been within that distance, is pursued beyond it, in which event, it may be seized when overtaken.

It is not necessary for the liquor-laden vessel to come within three miles of the shore before a seizure may be made under the treaty; the treaty applies when the vessel is endeavoring to import liquors, or when there is reasonable cause for belief that the vessel is committing or attempting to commit an offense against the laws of the United States, so that the seizure may be made under the *Tariff Act* of 1922 when the vessel comes within twelve miles of the shore, and under the treaty, when it comes within an hour's sailing of the shore, when there is the intention to land the liquor either by herself or by means of small boats.[56]

Unless the vessel has come within the hour's sailing and has escaped beyond it, it may not be taken beyond the hour's sailing.[57]

[55] See, Wharton, *Criminal Law* (1912) (11th ed. by J. M. Kerr), sections 324, 330, and 341. See, also, *Woitte* v. *United States* (1927) 19 Fed. (2d) 507.

The Supreme Court held that that part of the indictment charging a conspiracy to violate the treaty (for which the defendants attacked the validity of the indictment, since the treaty creates no offense against the laws of the United States), may be rejected as surplusage, without affecting the validity of the indictment, and that the indictment is not bad for duplicity, for the charge is unitary in relating to one continuous conspiracy, although in proof of it different circumstances constituting it and overt acts in pursuance of it are disclosed.

[56] *The Vinces* (1927), 20 Fed. (2d) 164. See p. 238, *supra,* for a statement of the facts of this case.

[57] Unless, of course, it is within four leagues of the shore, for it may be seized within that distance, even if it has not a speed of twelve miles. See p. 360, *supra.*

The Frances Louise,[58] a British vessel, had been seized 16½ miles out by customs officers (from which point she had, from time to time, delivered liquors to small boats not her own, and over which she had no control and which carried it ashore), who were under the impression that a motorboat to which she had delivered liquor could make that distance in an hour, and that, therefore, the seizure was within the terms of Art. II (3) of the treaty. When it was learned that the motorboat was incapable of such speed, the Government abandoned its contention that the seizure was made within the terms of the treaty, but it contended that as "the schooner was 'trading with the shore' " (that is, delivering liquor to small boats which put out from and returned to the shore) she was "subject to seizure and forfeiture under the general principles of international law; and that the treaty does not cut down this general right of seizure." The court rejected this contention, and dismissed the libel on the ground that "the whole situation is covered by the treaty," and that a vessel is not "amenable to seizure as long as she keeps to the high seas, except as provided in the treaty."

The Panama[59] is contra on this point. A British schooner was seized 12.1 miles from the shore, which distance she was incapable of making in an hour.[60] The claimant of the vessel contended, therefore, that the seizure was unlawful, because made outside the statutory twelve-mile and the treaty-limits. Forfeiture was decreed, however, on the ground that the "right of the executive to seize and search for violations of our laws is not limited by any particular distance from the shore. Nor do I think

[58] (1924) 1 Fed. (2d) 1004 (D. C. D. Mass., Morton, Dist. Judge).

[59] (1925) 6 Fed. (2d) 326 (D. C. S. D. Texas, Hutchinson, Dist. Judge).

[60] The court held that the vessal had, five days before seizure, violated the laws of the United States by unlading and by making actual contact with the shore by means of small boats. See p. 241, *supra,* for a fuller discussion of this case.

the treaty changes this right. It merely expresses a diplomatic agreement in advance to the doing of those things which the United States already had authority to do, subject only to political accountability to foreign nations whose bottoms were searched. . . .'"

In *United States* v. *Ferris*,[61] a Panaman vessel, the *Federalship,* was seized 270 miles from the shore, and the crew were indicted for a conspiracy to violate the *National Prohibition Act* and the *Tariff Act* of 1922. Pleas to the jurisdiction of the court were sustained on the ground that the seizure was "sheer aggression and trespass . . . contrary to the treaty, . . . and cannot be the basis of any proceeding adverse to defendants." The court said that the treaty is the only law authorizing seizure of Panaman vessels, and by becoming a party to the treaty the United States "abandons all claim of right exceeding it, and promises to comply with it."

If a foreign vessel comes within an hour's sailing distance of the coast, and escapes beyond it, however, it may be pursued and seized under the treaty. Such a vessel is under a duty to stop and submit to examination when it comes within the distance designated in the treaty, and if it does not do so, "the United States has the right to compel her to stop, and in pursuance of this undoubted right may pursue her and enforce it, even though the offending vessel escape beyond the hour's sailing distance of the coast."[62]

(5) *Distance from the Shore within Which the Offense Must be Committed*

Before the treaties came into force, Congress had authorized the seizure of all vessels within four leagues

---

[61] (1927) 19 Fed. (2d) 925 (D. C. N. D. Calif.). See p. 324, *supra.*
[62] *The Vinces* (1927), 20 Fed. (2d) 164. See p. 238, *supra,* for a statement of the facts of this case.

of the shore that had committed certain offenses within that distance. Now that the treaties authorize a seizure in many cases beyond four leagues, the question arises if the act complained of must still have been committed within four leagues, in spite of the extension of the distance within which seizures may be made. The courts have answered this question in the affirmative and have held that the treaties do not enact new criminal legislation and that it is necessary to show in an indictment, or in a forfeiture proceeding, not only that the seizure was made within Art. II (3) of the treaties, but also that some act or acts were committed in violation of some law of Congress within the distance specified in such law.

In *The Over the Top*,[63] a British vessel had sold liquors nineteen miles from shore, which was within an hour's sailing by the purchasing vessel, a government vessel in disguise. The court held that this was not an offense against the laws of the United States, and the seizure was illegal, for Congress had legislated for four leagues only, and that in this respect the treaty was not "self-executing," but that its only effect was to fix a new distance within which seizures might be made.

In *The Sagatind*,[64] a Norwegian vessel was seized twenty miles from land, where she had unladed liquors to a Canadian vessel, the *Diamantina*, which intended to peddle the liquors along the coast. There was no evidence that the latter vessel ever landed any of her cargo in the United States. Neither vessel could make over ten knots an hour. The Circuit Court of Appeals held that no offense had been committed in violation of sections 585 and 586 of the *Tariff Act* of 1922, since the *Sagatind* had not physically arrived within any collection district

[63] (1925) 5 Fed. (2d) 838 (D. C. D. Conn., Thomas, Dist. Judge).

[64] (1926) 11 Fed. (2d) 673 (C. C. A., 2d Cir., Hough, Cir. Judge). For the reports of the case in the District Court, see (1925) 4 Fed. (2d) 928 (Augustus N. Hand, Dist. Judge), and 8 Fed. (2d) 788.

or within four leagues of the coast, and that section 26, title II of the *National Prohibition Act* could not be invoked for the vessel's forfeiture, for the person in charge of the vessel must first have been convicted.[65] The court held that any act to be punishable must be committed within the terms of the statute, namely, within four leagues of the coast, and that when seizures are made under the treaties, it is necessary to allege and prove: 1st, the place of seizure, to determine whether or not it was made within the terms of the treaty, and 2d, facts which show a cause of action under the laws of the United States.[66]

In *The Majorie E. Bachman*,[67] it was held that the sale of liquors made 12.1 miles from shore by a foreign vessel, was not an offense against the laws of the United States, for a vessel is not constructively within twelve miles of the shore simply because she trades with boats from the shore, or because her general movements are controlled by a person on the shore, who communicates with her from time to time; but it was said, by way of dictum, that if in addition to these two facts she were *provisioned* from the

[65] See p. 218, note, *supra*.

[66] *The Pictonian*, (1927) 20 Fed. (2d) 353, (C. C. A., 2d Cir.), accord, reversing 3 Fed. (2d) 145. The Norwegian Government was under the impression that the *Sagatind* was seized twenty-two miles from the shore and notified the Department of State that if that were the case, it was seized in contravention of the treaty, and that claim was reserved under Art. IV of the treaty. It was added that the authority of the United States to seize and take into port Norwegian vessels is determined and limited by the treaty. The Department replied that questions of fact would be cleared up at the trial of the case.

According to the Solicitor General of the United States, an application for certiorari to the Supreme Court was not made in the *Sagatind* and *Diamantina* cases, because there was some doubt as to their being seized under the terms of the treaty, and because the effect of the treaties is not, in his opinion, to extend the limits within which the penal laws of the United States regarding the importation of liquor formerly applied. *Treasury Decisions* (1926), vol. 49, p. 937, No. 41,613.

[67] (1925) 4 Fed. (2d) 405 (D. C. D. Mass., Morton, Dist. Judge). Appeal dismissed, 270 U. S. 666, 667. For a statement of the facts in this case, see p. 373, *infra*.

shore, she would be "in such close contact with the shore as to be subject to our municipal law."

In *United States* v. *Archer,*[68] a British schooner was seized twenty-four miles out; in an indictment against the crew, it was charged that they aided in the possession, transportation and importation of liquors, and had formed a conspiracy to possess, sell, transport and deliver liquors at the point of seizure and at the Bahama Islands.   The indictment was held demurrable on the ground that there was no allegation of an unlading within twelve miles of the coast, or that the defendants had agreed to do anything within the territorial waters of the United States or within twelve miles of the shore.[69]   It seems from the language of the court that an agreement to have sold or delivered liquors within twelve miles of the shore would have been held to be a punishable offense.

In *Hennings* v. *United States,*[70] the British schooner *Frances E.* was taken 8.4 miles west of Sea Horse Bell Buoy, off the coast of Florida, or 16 or 17 nautical miles from the nearest land, which was a small key, and over 20 miles from the shore.   She could not make over 12 knots an hour; there were no speed boats in the vicinity, and it was not shown that she had made contact with the shore or that any sales or deliveries of liquors had been made from her.   Plaintiff in error, the master, was convicted in the lower court of possessing, transporting, and importing liquors in violation of the *National Prohibition Act.*   The Government contended that the treaty is self-executing and has the force and effect of a statute, extends

[68] (1926) 12 Fed. (2d) 137 (D. C. S. D. Alabama, Ervin, Dist. Judge).

[69] Compare *United States* v. *Ford,* p. 360, *supra.*

It was said, also, that there was no violation of the *National Prohibition Act,* for that Act, under the decision of *Cunard* v. *Mellon,* 262 U. S. 100, applies only for a marine league, and there was no conspiracy to do anything within that distance.

[70] (1926) 13 Fed. (2d) 74 (C. C. A., 5th Cir.), reversing 7 Fed. (2d) 488.

the territorial waters within its terms, and that, therefore, the criminal laws of the United States dealing with liquor are in force in said territory. It was held by the Circuit Court of Appeals that the treaty has not this effect; the contracting Powers had no intention of extending the criminal laws beyond three miles from the shore, and the statutes dealing with offenses within twelve miles of the shore are not in point.[71]

Should the Supreme Court sustain the view held by the Circuit Courts of Appeals, the treaties, however, are helpful, in that vessels may be seized beyond four leagues from the shore (i.e., within the hour's sailing), without further legislation, when such vessels have violated the laws within four leagues and then moved farther out to sea; for by Article II (2) of the treaty, if there is reason to believe that the vessel "has committed or is committing or attempting to commit an offense against the laws of the United States ... the vessel may be seized and taken into port ... for adjudication in accordance with such laws," and may be boarded within the hour's sailing in order to ascertain "whether the vessel or those on board

---

[71] The Solicitor General holds that they are not "self-executing." *Treasury Decisions* (1926), vol. 49, p. 937, No. 41,613.

The *Annual Report of the Attorney General for 1926* (Dec. 6) says that many cases had been dismissed because of the holding that the treaties are not "self-executing," and that further legislation will be required before the treaties are of substantial value; for, as his report of 1925 (p. 42) says, if the Coast Guard is restricted in its operation to twelve miles, the force of its operations against the rum-row will be largely nullified. See pp. 46-47 for some problems that arise from the peculiarities of the American coast, and some suggested changes in the law.

This question presents a problem of American Constitutional Law which is outside the scope of this treatise. The following references are given as helpful for one who wishes to pursue the subject further:

26 *Columbia Law Rev.*, p. 859.

Two articles by Dickinson, Edwin D., 20 *American Journal of International Law*, pp. 111 and 444.

Jessup, *The Law of Territorial Waters and Maritime Jurisdiction* (1927), p. 300, et seq.

Hearings on House Resolution No. 174, 68th Congress, 1st Sess., February 20 and March 7, 1924.

are endeavoring to import or have imported alcoholic beverages into the United States . . . in violation of the laws there in force." [72]

It does not follow from these decisions, however, that a vessel must always be or have been physically present within four leagues of the shore before it can violate some law of the United States, for there are cases in which its conduct beyond twelve miles from the shore might be construed to constitute a violation or an attempted violation of some law pertaining to the illicit importation of merchandise. This is a question of municipal law, and involves the construction of the law or laws under which proceedings are brought. A clear case would be presented, it seems, if a foreign vessel stands beyond twelve miles from the shore and sends its illicit cargo ashore by means of its own small boats or boats sent out from the shore under its control; [73] or if it is attempting beyond that distance to get it ashore, it could be seized and proceeded against for an attempted violation of the laws against fraudulent introduction of merchandise into the United States. Or if the persons on board conspire beyond that distance to introduce liquors into the United States in violation of some law or laws, an indictment for conspiracy could be brought. [74] There would seem to be no difficulty in such cases, and other cases which occur to one, as long as the *seizure* is made within the terms of the treaty.

(6) *Method of Computing the Hour's Sailing*

It was held in *Hennings* v. *United States*, [75] (the *Frances E.*) that it is not necessary to prove that the distance from the shore to the place of boarding may be

[72] See *The Pictonian*, (1924) 3 Fed. (2d) 145.
[73] See pp. 217 and 222, *supra*.
[74] See *United States* v. *Ford*, p. 360, *supra*.
[75] (1925) 7 Fed. (2d) 488. For a statement of the facts of this case, see p. 369, *supra*.

made in an hour by any particular vessel in which it is intended to convey liquors from the vessel boarded and seized, but that it is sufficient to prove the speed of boats that ordinarily go out to the vicinity where the vessel boarded stands, for the purpose of determining whether she was seized within the hour's sailing.[76] There was no evidence in this case that any particular boat had been out to the *Frances E.* from the shore, but it was shown that the boats that ordinarily went out to the rum ships were fast and could make the distance in an hour's time.

This case held, also, that the distance named in the treaty is to be measured from the *coast*, and not from a beacon built on a shallow reef, which is wholly under water.[77]

It was held in *United States* v. *Ford*,[78] that in determining whether the distance may be made in an hour's sailing by the vessel in which it is intended to convey the liquors to the shore, the speed of such vessel is to be measured when it is light and not after she has taken on her cargo.[79]

(7) *Kind of Vessel Contemplated by the Treaty*

It has been held that if revenue officers in disguise make a purchase of liquor, and base their jurisdiction to seize upon such purchase, they must use the vessel

[76] This point was not discussed on appeal by the Circuit Court of Appeals, as the case was reversed on another ground. According to the Solicitor General (*Treasury Decisions,* 1926, vol. 49, p. 937, No. 41,613) and *Ford* v. *United States* (p. 360, *supra*), the British Government registered objection to this method of measuring the distance named in the treaty.

[77] This point was not discussed on appeal by the Circuit Court of Appeals.

[78] P. 360, *supra*.

[79] In *The Over The Top* (p. 367, *supra*) it was said that the speed is to be measured when the receiving vessel is laden with her cargo; but the court's remarks are obliter dictum, since it was found that no law had been violated. The language of the court on this point, however, is very strong.

similar in speed to vessels commercially used for such purpose. In *The Majorie E. Bachman*,[80] revenue officers went out in a sea sled capable of 35 or 40 miles an hour, with a disguised crew, and purchased liquors from a Canadian vessel 12.1 miles out, where she was seized, some of which liquor they later threw overboard, while some was carried to Boston. The officers of the sea sled represented to the officers of the *Bachman* that the sled had a speed of only 15 miles an hour. The court said that this procedure was a "mere entrapment" not contemplated by the treaty, and that if an alleged right of seizure is based upon such a transaction, the officers must use a vessel "similar in speed to those commercially used for such purposes or to those with which the foreign vessel has heretofore been dealing, neither of which is true in this case."[81]

Since the court found, however, that no law had been violated by the transaction 12.1 miles from the shore, the finding as to the kind of vessel contemplated by the treaty was unnecessary for the decision of the case.[82]

§ 76. Treaties Between Other Powers

On August 19, 1925, the Governments of Germany, Denmark, Estonia, Finland, Latvia, Lithuania, Norway, Poland, the Free City of Danzig, Sweden, and the Union of the Soviet Socialist Republics entered into a convention for the suppression of contraband trade in alcoholic liquors, Article 9 of which is similar to certain provisions

[80] P. 368, *supra*.

[81] A government-owned sea sled was used, also, in the case of *The Over The Top* (p. 367, *supra*); while the court did not discuss at length the point made by respondents that such procedure was an "entrapment," it said that there was "much merit in the defense," taken in connection with other considerations discussed.

[82] For an interesting discussion of some problems connected with these treaties, see an article by Dickinson, Edwin D., 20 *American Journal of International Law*, p. 111.

of the liquor treaties just considered.[83]   It is provided
that the Parties to the agreement shall not object to the
application within an area of twelve marine miles from
the coast or from the exterior limit of archipelagos, of
each other's laws to vessels obviously engaged in smuggling. If a vessel, suspected of being engaged in smuggling, is found inside this area, and if she escapes outside,
the authorities of the littoral state have the power of
pursuing her on the high seas and of enforcing, in regard
to her, the same laws that would apply within the twelve
mile zone.[84]

The above provisions are adopted without any
prejudice to the individual positions of the contracting
parties in regard to the legal principles governing territorial and customs zones.

This convention, thus, embodies the same principles
adopted in certain of the liquor treaties with the United
States; the essential difference is that it adopts twelve
miles instead of the hour's sailing.[85]

[83] This Article reads:

"Les Parties contractantes á'engagent à ne faire aucune objection à
ce que chacune d'entres elles applique, dans une zone s'étendant
jusqu'à douze milles marins de la côte ou de la limite exterieure des
archipels, ses lois aux navires qui se livrent manifestement à la contrebande.

"Si un navire soupçonné de se livrer à la contrebande est rencontré
dans la zone élargie nommée ci-dessus et qu'il s'échappe hors de cette
zone, les autorités du pays dont relève cette zone pourront le poursuivre
aussi au delà de cette zone dans la mer ouverte et user envers lui des
mêmes droits que s'il avait été saisi à l'intérieur de la zone.

"Ces dispositions son adoptées sans préjudice de la position prise par
chacune des Parties contractantes vis à vis des principes juridiques
régissant les zones territoriales et douanières." *League of Nations
Treaty Series,* vol. 42, p. 73.

[84] See *The Vinces,* p. 364, *infra,* which interprets the treaties with the
United States as giving this power. It is sometimes spoken of as the
doctrine of "hot pursuit."

[85] See, also, 9 *Stat. at Large,* p. 926, for a treaty between the United
States and Mexico (1848), and 73 *Brit. and Forn. State Papers,* p. 711,
for a treaty between England and Mexico, both adopting three leagues
for the limit of jurisdiction for customs purposes and prevention of
smuggling. Other such treaties between Mexico and Germany, and
Sweden and Norway, France, Salvador, and China, are referred to in
Crocker, *The Extent of the Marginal Sea,* pp. 604-5.

PART V

CONCLUSIONS

§ 77. Distinction Between General Jurisdiction in the Marginal Seas and a Wider Special Jurisdiction for Customs Purposes

(1) *In Treaties, Diplomatic Correspondence, and Municipal Laws*

In the discussions of the English and American law, diplomatic correspondence, and treaties, the distinction between the general jurisdiction of a state over a narrow strip of water near its coast and a wider special jurisdiction to protect its fiscal interests has been repeatedly pointed out. The so-called hovering laws have existed in the codes of most maritime states, including England and the United States, for many years, and they have been maintained as distinct from the so-called zone of sovereignty or territorial waters near the coast.[1]

[1] For some very interesting dicta to this effect, see:
Regina v. Keyn (1876), L. R. 2 Exch. Div. 63, opinions of Phillimore and Cockburn;
The Annapolis (1861), Lushington 410;
Le Louis (1817), 2 Dodson's Admiralty 121;
Manchester v. Mass. (1891), 139 U. S. 240;
The Ship North v. The King (1906), 37 Sup. Ct. of Canada 385.
See, also:
Balch, *Proceedings of the Society of International Law,* 1912, p. 132;
Borchard, ibid., p. 141;
Philip Marshall Brown, ibid., 1923, pp. 17 and 19. See, also, the memorandum prepared by the Royal Norwegian Committee of Nov. 7, 1924, on *The Principal Facts Concerning Norwegian Territorial Waters,* p. 51.
This distinction is made by the British and United States representatives in the discussions before the Arbitral Tribunal in the Behring Sea

375

(2) *In Draft Conventions*

Most of the draft conventions adopted by International
Law associations and societies make provision for the
enforcement of customs regulations beyond the zone of
"territorial waters" or "sovereignty." No distance is
fixed in some of these Drafts to which this jurisdiction
may be exercised. The Draft of the International Law
Association, adopted at Stockholm in 1924,[2] provides for
jurisdiction over "territorial waters" for three marine
miles for the purpose of maintaining the laws of the
littoral state and of securing the full use of the seas, and
for jurisdiction beyond these waters for the purpose of
supervising and controlling their sanitary and customs
regulations. The Draft of the Institute of International
Law, adopted in 1927,[3] provides for a zone of six marine
miles for the "territorial sea," and a supplementary zone
of six miles for the enforcement of laws and regulations
relating to the security, neutrality, police, sanitation and
customs. The Draft of the American Institute of International Law [4] leaves the extent of the "territorial sea"
blank, and it provides that the American Republics may

Arbitration in 1893. The United States representative said that while
the precise limit of jurisdiction had not been settled, yet no nation
that had become a party to a treaty fixing three miles or cannon-shot
as the limit, had ever agreed to surrender the right of self-defense
beyond that distance, citing the hovering laws among others *Argument* of the United States, pp. 144, 149 and the *Case* of the United
States, pp. 229, 231. The British representative said that while these
laws have been acquiesced in by the United States and Great Britain,
yet they do not extend the limit of territorial waters or assert any
general claim of dominion beyond such waters. *Argument* of the British
Government, pp. 12, 15; Moore, *Int. Arb.*, vol. I, pp. 892-3 and 903.

[2] *Report of the 33d Conference of the International Law Association*,
p. 262. The Draft adopted by this Association at Vienna in 1926, however, makes no provision for this extended jurisdiction. See the report
of the 34th Conference, p. 101.

[3] *Annuaire de L'Institut de Droit International* (1927), vol. 33 (I),
p. 99. See, also, ibid., vol. 13, p. 328, for draft of the Institute of 1894.

[4] Supp. *American Journal of International Law*, vol. 20, p. 318,
Projects Nos. 10 and 12.

extend their jurisdiction beyond this sea for an additional distance, which is, likewise, left blank, for reasons of safety and in order to assure the observance of sanitary and customs regulations. The Amended Draft Convention of 1927 [5] prepared by a Sub-Committee of the Committee of Experts appointed by the Council of the League of Nations provides for a "coastal sea" of three marine miles, and for the exercise of "administrative rights" beyond that distance.

(3) *Views of Writers*

This distinction is pointed out by many of the best writers, including Halleck,[6] Creasy,[7] Sir Henry Maine,[8] Kent,[9] Wheaton,[10] Woolsey,[11] Taylor,[12] Foulke,[13] Hyde,[14] George Grafton Wilson,[15] Philip Marshall Brown,[16] Wharton,[17] Fulton,[18] Oppenheim, Piggott, and Westlake.

Oppenheim,[19] after noting that no unanimity exists as to the breadth of the territorial waters, says that "the zone of the open sea over which a littoral state extends

[5] *League of Nations Documents* C. 44. M. 21. 1926. V, p. 47. This draft is considered more fully in another connection. See p. 385, *infra*.

[6] *International Law* (4th ed. by Sir G. Sherston Baker, Bt. and Maurice M. Drucquer) (1908), p. 167, et seq.

[7] *First Platform of International Law* (1876), p. 239.

[8] *International Law* (1894), p. 78.

[9] *Commentaries on American Law* (1826), vol. I, p. 25.

[10] *Elements of International Law* (8th ed. by Richard Henry Dana Jr.) (1866), sec. 177, p. 255. Mr. Dana, the editor, takes a different view.

[11] *Introduction to the study of International Law* (1891), pp. 67 and 365.

[12] *A Treatise on International Law* (1901), p. 293.

[13] *A Treatise on International Law* (1920), vol. I, p. 376.

[14] *International Law, Chiefly as Interpreted and Applied by the United States*, vol. I, pp. 251, 257, and 323.

[15] *Handbook of International Law* (2d ed.) (1927), p. 88.

[16] 17 *American Journal of International Law*, p. 93, and *Proceedings of the American Society of International Law*, 1923, p. 15.

[17] *A Digest of International Law*, vol. I, sec. 32, p. 114.

[18] *The Sovereignty of the Sea* (1911), pp. 593-5, 603, and 664.

[19] *International Law* (3d ed. By Ronald F. Roxburgh) (1924), vol. I, p. 340.

the operation of its revenue and sanitary laws" is not to be confounded with the "territorial maritime belt." He notes that Great Britain and the United States, as well as other states, possess revenue and sanitary laws which impose certain duties not only on their own but also on such foreign vessels bound for one of their ports as are approaching, but not yet within their territorial maritime belt, and adds that since these laws have been in existence for more than a hundred years, and have not been opposed by other states, "a customary rule of the law of nations" may be said to exist, which allows littoral states in the interest of their revenue and sanitary laws to impose certain duties on such foreign vessels bound for their ports as are approaching, although not yet within their territorial maritime belt.

Piggott [20] approaches the question by asking ". . . whether a State may, for a particular purpose, create an area outside its territorial waters within which it may declare certain acts to be offences, even when committed by foreign vessels: such vessels being liable to chase on to the high seas and to seizure. . . ." He adds that the contention that a hovering act is unsound in principle because it applies to an area outside the territorial waters of the state, is equivalent to saying that the limit of jurisdiction of a state seaward is the same for all purposes, which begs the question under discussion. He concludes that the hovering acts are "sound in principle, and warranted by the law of nations, so long as the essential conditions are fulfilled, that the provisions of the law, and the distance to which they operate seaward, are reasonable."

Westlake [21] says that the jurisdiction taken under the hovering laws is justified on the ground of self-defense,

---

[20] *Nationality*, Part II, p. 49, et seq. See, also, Part I, pp. 31-40.
[21] *International Law* (2d ed.) (1910), vol. I, p. 175.

and that if the foreign vessel interfered with is on its way to effect, or is actually engaged in facilitating for others, an illicit landing on the coast, it would be difficult to distinguish her case from that of the *Virginius*, in which the Spanish authorities seized an American vessel on the high seas, engaged in carrying arms to the insurgents in Cuba.[22]

Some writers maintain, however, that these laws, while they have been in force for many years, and have been enforced in judicial proceedings, have no foundation in strict right or law, but that they may be enforced only as a matter of "comity," "acquiescence," "permissive jurisdiction," or "consent."[23] The reason advanced by these writers in support of their views is that a nation has no jurisdiction beyond "territorial waters," and that, therefore, a seizure made beyond such waters under the hovering laws is a violation of International Law. This amounts to advancing, as a reason for the rule which they advocate, the rule itself. As Piggott says, it is an interesting example of begging the question, for it assumes the answer to the problem. It assumes that the limit of jurisdiction seaward is the same for all purposes, and it has been shown that such is not the case. Such an assumption overlooks the actual practice and usage of nations in protecting their fiscal interests.[24]

[22] See Moore, *Digest of International Law*, vol. II, pp. 895, 980, for the case of the *Virginius*.

[23] See, for example:

Twiss, *The Law of Nations Considered as Independent Political Communities* (new ed., 1884), p. 309.

Hall, W. E., *A Treatise on the Foreign Powers and Jurisdiction of the British Crown* (1894), p. 243, sec. 108.

Phillimore, *Commentaries Upon International Law* (3d ed.) (1879), p. 274, et seq.

Holland, *Studies in International Law* (1898), p. 182.

Pitt-Cobbett, *Leading Cases on International Law* (4th ed. by Hugh H. L. Bellot) (1922), vol. I, p. 136, et seq.

Lawrence, *The Principles of International Law* (3d ed. revised 1900), p. 176.

[24] For the views of some of the Continental writers, see the following:
De Lapradelle, "The Right of the State over the Territorial Sea"

§ 78. The Hovering Laws and the Freedom of the Seas

It is submitted that the distinction pointed out in the previous section is a logical one; and that, as Oppenheim says, in view of the practice of nations in enforcing their revenue laws beyond the zone of "territorial waters," or sovereignty, a customary rule of the law of nations may be said to exist which permits a state to take jurisdiction, under such laws, over foreign vessels beyond such waters.

The attempt to test the soundness of this legislation from the standpoint of International Law by approaching it through the theory of "sovereignty," "territorial waters," or the "freedom of the seas," has led to confusion on the part of some writers and several governments. It is sometimes argued that the enforcement of these laws is a violation of International Law, because a state may exercise or possesses sovereignty, sovereign rights, or territorial dominion only over a narrow zone of water near its shore, upon the width of which there is no agreement,[25] and that action taken beyond such zone is a violation of the freedom of the seas.[26] As pointed out,

---

(1898), *Revue Générale de Droit International Public,* vol. V, pp. 264 and 309.

Latour, *La Mer Territoriale au Point de Vue Théorique et Pratique* (1889).

Martens, F., "Le Tribunal d'Arbitrage de Paris et la Mer Territoriale," *Revue Générale de Droit International Public,* vol. I, 1894.

Nuger, *Les Droits de l'Etat sur la Mer Territoriale* (1887).

Raestad, *La Mer Territoriale* (1913).

Schücking, *Das Kustermeer im Internationalen Rechte* (1897).

Visser, *De Territoriale Zee* (1894).

Villeneuve, *De la Détermination de la Ligne Séparative des Eaux Nationales et de la Mer Territoriale* (1894).

[25] The claims of the states vary from 3 to 12 miles, but there is universal agreement upon 3 miles as the minimum.

[26] The underlying reason why some governments object to this special jurisdiction is the fear that it may be the basis for claiming jurisdiction beyond such waters for the protection of other interests, such as the fisheries. See p. 300, *supra.*

however, this legislation has existed and has been enforced both before and after there was any attempt to fix the limits of territorial waters or sovereignty, or dominion, and that it has arisen from considerations that bear no relation to the conception of a zone of general jurisdiction, or dominion in the marginal seas.

It is submitted that the real basis for this special jurisdiction and the test of its soundness from the standpoint of International Law is found in the theory of interests. The facts of life—the needs of nations—must be considered in this connection. The state clearly must exercise jurisdiction in the waters adjacent to its coasts for the purpose of protecting its various interests; one such interest is in its revenue, which is protected by jurisdiction taken under the hovering laws over illicit trade from the sea. This legislation unquestionably serves and has always served a purpose highly useful, from many standpoints, in the life of the individual state that has enforced it. It should be asked, then, if any interest of the flag state or of the community of nations is violated by the enforcement of the hovering laws against foreign smuggling craft beyond the zone of the so-called "territorial waters," or "sovereignty." In other words, what interest, if any, of the flag state or the community of nations is there to be balanced against the interest of the individual state secured by such laws?

In order to answer this question, the objects sought to be accomplished by these laws must be considered. It must be borne in mind that these laws have no application to a vessel engaged upon some lawful enterprise; they are levelled at smuggling vessels. They do not interfere with the so-called "right of innocent passage." Legitimate commerce does not, therefore, suffer from them. They reveal no intention on the part of the legislator to claim for the littoral state dominion, or a zone of "sovereignty" or "territorial waters" for the distance to which they apply. The foreign fishing vessel is not excluded by these laws, and they are silent on the question of neutrality. Their sole design is the protection of the revenue by the prevention of the clandestine importation of dutiable merchandise or merchandise which a nation has decided to exclude altogether. They, thus, assert no general jurisdiction over all vessels. They have simply followed in the tracks of an evil which has been a serious menace to England, the United States, and many other countries. They have been enacted and re-enacted by some countries, which, by judicial decision, treaty, or legislation, have adopted narrower limits for the protection of other interests.

What interest, if any, is there to be weighed against this tangible interest of the littoral state in protecting its revenue and in maintaining law and order near its coasts? As just pointed out, an objection to the hovering laws is sometimes said to be found in the doctrine of the "freedom of the seas"; it is argued that that doctrine inhibits the littoral state from interfering with the activities of foreign vessels hovering an inch beyond the zone of the so-called "territorial waters," or sovereignty, however suspicious or threatening the conduct of such vessels may be, or even if they are engaged in or are attempting to engage in a violation of the laws of such state. This reasoning begs the question.

That doctrine does not leave the seas free to foreign vessels for all purposes. Pirates carrying the flag of any country may be seized by any nation anywhere on the high seas and tried by the courts of that nation. During times of war, neutral vessels may, under certain circumstances, be visited and searched by the armed vessels of belligerents anywhere on the high seas. During the late war, neutral vessels were excluded from or controlled within wide "defensive areas," often embracing whole seas.[27] Governments have raised objections to hostile engagements by belligerent war vessels and to target practice near enough to their shore so as to endanger lives and property on the shore, but beyond the zone which they claim as "territorial waters."[28] The British Government, the strongest defender of the so-called "three-mile limit" for all purposes, admits that the seas are not free to merchant vessels whose crew, small boats, or equipment enter that limit for unlawful purposes.[29] That Government, also, penalizes certain conduct on the high seas, if the offending person or vessel afterwards comes within that distance from the shore.[30] Foreign vessels which violate the laws of a State within its waters may be pursued and taken anywhere on the high seas, short, of course, of the waters of another State, under the so-called doctrine of "hot pursuit."[31]

The interference with vessels in these cases is not considered a violation of the freedom of the seas. If the exercise of jurisdiction on the high seas in these cases is permitted to a State without doing violence to that principle, certainly there is little to be said in favor of invoking it on behalf of the vessel hovering in the vicinity of the coast for the purpose of smuggling, or actually engaged in it; for it is difficult to understand how the seizure of such vessel is any more of a violation of the freedom of the seas than the action taken in the cases enumerated. That principle, it is submitted, does not protect the smuggler, but it forbids the claim, generally, to jurisdiction on the high seas; that is, a claim to juris-

[27] See pp. 394, note (51), and 397, note (59), *infra*.

[28] See pp. 397, note (59), 398, note (62), and 388, note (43), *infra*.

[29] See p. 311, *supra*.

[30] See p. 121, *supra*.

[31] See Piggott, *Nationality*, Part II, p. 35, et seq.; *The Ship North* v. *The King* (1906), 37 Sup. Ct. of Canada, 385; *L'Abandance*, p. 134, *supra*; *The Mousmée*, p. 322, *supra*.

diction which might result in the interference with or
annoyance to innocent trade or commerce, or an unwarranted encroachment upon the economic interests of
foreign powers. It developed out of the general demand
that such interests as these be protected, and when it is
invoked, the interest sought to be protected must be
shown. The smuggler can show no such interest. This
principle, therefore, has no application in this connection.
There are, therefore, no interests of the flag state or any
interest of the community of States to be balanced against
the interests of the littoral state, secured by the hovering
laws. These laws would, thus, seem to be sound in
principle.

§ 79. Possibility of International Legislation

(1) *Practice of Nations under Municipal Laws and Treaties*

It is believed that a general agreement could be reached
upon a convention providing for the protection of the
fiscal interests of a State beyond the zone of the so-called
"territorial waters," or "sovereignty."

First, the municipal laws and regulations of most
maritime powers have taken this jurisdiction for many
years.

Second, many treaties have made provision for such
jurisdiction. The recent rum treaties between the United
States and Great Britain,[32] Germany, the Netherlands,
Cuba, Panama,[33] and Italy, Sweden, Denmark, Norway,
Belgium, Spain, and France [34] provide for seizures, by the
United States, within the distance from the shore that the
offending vessels can make in an hour's sailing, while

[32] P. 346, *supra.*
[33] P. 352, *supra.*
[34] P. 353, *supra.*

separate provisions are inserted as to the extent of "territorial waters," or "territorial jurisdiction." Seizures have been made under these treaties for many miles beyond the widest limit claimed by any nation for its territorial waters.[35] The convention of 1925 between Germany, Denmark, Estonia, Finland, Latvia, Lithuania, Norway, Poland, the Free City of Danzig, Sweden, and the Union of the Soviet Socialist Republics [36] provides that the parties shall not object to the application of each other's laws to vessels engaged in smuggling, within twelve marine miles from the shore or from the exterior limit of archipelagos.[37]

(2) *Replies of Governments to Questionnaire on Territorial Waters Prepared by Committee of Experts for the Progressive Codification of International Law*

Third, many of the governments have recently expressed themselves as being in favor of this jurisdiction, in connection with their replies to a questionnaire on territorial waters sent to them by the Committee of Experts for the Progressive Codification of International Law, appointed by the Council of the League of Nations. This Committee, appointed in execution of the Assembly's resolution of September 22, 1924, was required, under its terms of reference, to prepare a provisional list of the subjects of international law whose regulation by international agreement would seem to be "most desirable and realisable at the present moment," and after the communication of the list by the Secretariat to the Governments of States, whether members of the League or not, for their opinions, to examine the replies received,

[35] P. 365, et seq., *supra.*

[36] P. 373, *supra.*

[37] P. 374, note (85), *supra,* for similar treaties between Mexico and several countries.

and to report to the Council on the questions which are "sufficiently ripe and on the procedure which might be followed with a view to preparing eventually for conferences for their solution." The Committee decided to include in its list the question of whether there are "problems connected with the law of the territorial sea, considered in its various aspects, which might find their solution by way of conventions, and, if so, what these problems are and what solutions should be given to them, and, in particular, what should be the rights of jurisdiction of a state over foreign commercial ships within its territorial waters or in its ports."

On January 29, 1926, there was communicated to the Council, the Members of the League, and other Governments, a report on territorial waters prepared by a Sub-Committee of the Committee of Experts, consisting of M. Schücking, as Rapporteur, M. de Magalhaes, and Mr. Wickersham; this report comprises a memorandum by M. Schücking, to which is appended a draft of a Convention, observations by M. Magalhaes and Mr. Wickersham, and finally a text of the draft Convention amended by M. Schücking in consequence of the discussion in the Committee of Experts.[38]

Article I of the Amended Draft, in defining the "character and extent of the rights of the riparian State," provides that the State "possesses sovereign rights over the zone which washes its coast, in so far as, under general international law, the rights of common user of the international community or the special rights of any State do not interfere with such sovereign rights," and that such "sovereign rights shall include rights over the air above the said sea and the soil and subsoil beneath it." Article II, in defining the extent of the rights of the riparian

---

[38] *League of Nations Documents* C. 44. M. 21. 1926. V.

State, provides that the "zone of the coastal sea shall extend for three marine miles (60 to the degree of latitude) from low-water mark along the whole of the coast," and that beyond "the zone of sovereignty, States may exercise administrative rights on the ground either of custom or of vital necessity. There are included the rights of jurisdiction necessary for their protection. Outside the zone of sovereignty no right of exclusive economic enjoyment may be exercised." "Exclusive rights to fisheries" were left to "existing practice and conventions." [39]

While the replies of the governments, studied in connection with the recent negotiations of the liquor treaties between the United States and several other countries,[40] emphasise the fact that there is no uniformity of opinion or practice in regard to the extent of territorial waters,[41] they show that under the practice and laws of most nations, jurisdiction for customs purposes has been and is exercised far beyond such waters.

France, Italy, the Netherlands, and Poland replied that they consider that the regulation of the question of territorial waters is impossible or difficult, because of the divergent views and requirements of the various States and because of the failure of past efforts to regulate it.[42] No reference was made to any specific article of the Amended Draft. France exercises customs jurisdiction for

[39] Ibid., p. 47.

[40] Pp. 326 and 354, et seq., *supra*.

[41] The statement of many writers to the contrary is without justification. See 23 *Columbia Law Rev.*, pp. 472-6, N. W. C., 1904, pp. 130-141, and 1913, pp. 11-34, an article by Quincy Wright, 7 *Minn. Law Rev.*, pp. 28, 36, Hall, *A Treatise on International Law* (8th ed. by A. Pearce Higgins, 1924), p. 190, et seq., Crocker, *The Extent of the Marginal Sea* (1919), pp. 509-695, and Fulton, *The Sovereignty of the Sea* (1911). Attention is called to the wide variety of limits in the memorandum of M. Schücking and the observations of M. Magalhaes and Mr. Wickersham, of the report.

[42] *League of Nations Documents* C. 196. M. 70. 1927. V, pp. 165, 170, 180, and 186.

four leagues under her municipal laws,[43] and Italy for ten, and in some cases five kilometers.[44]

Norway, Sweden, and Portugal replied [45] that they are unable to sign a convention that fixes three miles as the extent of the coastal sea, and they base this refusal upon their laws and long-established usage in exercising jurisdiction for customs and other purposes beyond that distance, and upon their local economic necessities. They object to a uniform line for all countries, for, in their opinions, due consideration should be given to the various characteristics of the different coasts and to the question of maintaining for the coastal populations the exclusive privilege of exploiting the economic wealth in the marginal waters.

The Norwegian reply states that according to Norwegian opinion and practice, Norway "possesses full sovereignty within the limits of her territorial sea," and for ten marine miles beyond these limits, its customs laws are applied to foreigners, and that "from time immemorial" the Norwegian Government has claimed for her "territorial sea a breadth which has never been less than one geographical league (one-fifteenth of an equatorial degree, or 7,420 meters)," that this limit, which has been maintained for nearly 200 years, was not an

[43] Law of 4 Germinal Year II (March 24, 1794), Art. 1, 2, 3, and 7, Title II, L. R. D. t. I, p. 495. Law of March 27, 1817, Regarding Customs, B. L. 7th S. Bull. 147, No. 1900, arts. 13 and 15. France takes jurisdiction beyond three miles for purposes of neutrality. See U. S. *Diplomatic Correspondence*, 1864, Part III, pp. 104, 121; *Journal Officiel* of June 14, 1913, p. 5097, and N. W. C., 1913, p. 23.

[44] Customs Law of January 26, 1896, c. II, No. 20, Art. 24, p. 13.

Italy claims six miles as the extent of her territorial waters as regards neutrality. *Gazetta Ufficiale*, August 10, 1914, No. 190. And she prohibits the sojourn of merchant vessels within ten miles of her coast when the national defense requires it. Ibid., of June 27, 1912, No. 151.

The Netherlands claim only three miles for purposes of neutrality. U. S. *Forn. Rel.*, 1904, p. 27; N. W. C., 1916, p. 61.

[45] *League of Nations Documents* C. 196. M. 70. 1927. V, pp. 172, 230, and 188.

extension, but a restriction of the area over which Norway had exercised sovereignty.[46]   It was observed that this restriction to one geographical league was inspired in the beginning solely by "considerations of neutrality, though it gradually came to be applied to fisheries," and that the "considerable interests which are bound up with this limit also preclude its abandonment in the future." [47]

The Swedish Government replied that Article I of the Amended Draft is "quite in keeping with Swedish opinion"; but as to Article II, it was pointed out that for "over a century the territorial waters of Sweden have been regarded as extending for a distance of four sea miles from the coast," [48] and that such a claim is not a departure

[46] Reference was also made to the Convention of 1925, of which Norway is a party, adopting 12 miles for the suppression of smuggling. See p. 373, *supra*.

[47] The Norwegian Government, it was said further, is of the opinion that it would be "unreasonable to fix a definite zone of sovereinty if, in accordance with the suggestions of the revised Draft, this could only be achieved by avoiding the discussion not only of all questions of neutrality but even of fishery," for if these questions are "left on one side, it is rather difficult to see what need would remain for fixing a limit by a general international convention or what arguments could be adduced in its favor," and a failure "to examine or discuss considerations connected with fisheries when an attempt is made to fix a normal rule for the extent of the territorial sea would . . . be an intrinsically erroneous procedure and would constitute a social injustice for a country like Norway by fixing a rule without regard for the vital interests of the State and its coastal population."   It was added that for Norway to agree to the proposed Convention, it would be necessary so to draft Article II of the Amended Draft that "as regards the extent and delimitation of the zone of sovereignty itself, it should . . . take into proper account a peculiar *de facto* situation which has been consecrated by continuous and century-old usage," for ". . . it would be neither natural nor reasonable to fix an identical limit of territorial waters for all coasts without taking into account the various characteristics of the latter and without making due allowance for the varying importance, from the point of view of national economy and the very existence of the inhabitants, of the question of maintaining for the coastal population an exclusive right to exploit the economic wealth of the territorial sea."

[48] The Swedish Legation at Washington notified this fact to the Secretary of State on March 5, 1915, N. W. C. 1918, p. 153.   By a Royal Order of December 20, 1912, all acts of hostilities, including capture

from "present-day international usage." The "present Swedish four-mile limit" was mentioned for the first time in the "Instructions" to the Commander of the Fleet in 1779, and shortly after that date it was "embodied in various official texts regarding neutrality, pilotage, Customs and fishery"; and the Customs Regulation of 1904, which is still in force, "contains provisions to the effect that Swedish territorial waters shall extend for four sea miles from the coast"; and a similar Ordinance of 1871 fixes the same distance on the west coast for fisheries. It was said that "a considerable number of interests are bound up with the maintenance of this limit," and that it would be particularly desirable, in fixing the extent of the zone of sovereignty, to take into account "rights in favor of which an uninterrupted usage for centuries can be invoked."

Portugal replied that the Amended Draft should be framed so as to allow the States "sovereign rights over the maritime zone which washes their coasts, over the air above that zone and the soil and subsoil beneath it," and that this zone should extend to 12 marine miles (60 to the degree of latitude) from low-water mark; and beyond this zone, States should be allowed to occupy the sea for the establishment of constructions for bases for non-military aircraft, wireless, and submarine cable stations, lighthouses, scientific research, and assisting the victims of shipwreck. "Portugal," the reply continues, "is unable to forego a very much wider limit to her territorial waters than three miles, since it is absolutely necessary for her to preserve the species of fish which inhabit

---

and right of search, were forbidden in territorial waters. Ibid., p. 150. Submarines were forbidden in 1916 to navigate or lie in Swedish territorial waters within 3 nautical minutes (5,556 meters). Ibid., 1917, p. 215. See p. 393, note (51), *infra*, for a Swedish protest against the seizure, by a German vessel, of a prize between the 3 and 4-mile lines off the Swedish coast.

her waters, these fisheries contributing largely towards the feeding of her population and the employment of her industries.[49]   If these species become rare or disappear, Portugal's economic crisis, which is already acute, will be considerably aggravated."   This claim of Portugal, it is said, is not a special case, for "this extended limit" has become an established usage in Portugal and in other countries.   It was added that if the extension of twelve miles is impossible, a minimum of six miles should be chosen, and that States should have "the right, in order to satisfy their vital needs or those of their defence, to exercise administrative rights over a further zone of six miles beyond the zone of their sovereignty."

The replies of Egypt, Estonia, Finland, Germany, Greece, Spain, and Cuba [50] indicate that they would probably be willing to accept three marine miles as the extent of the coastal sea, over which the State possesses sovereign rights, with jurisdiction to exercise certain administrative rights, however, beyond that distance.   Some of these Governments, however, prefer to define administrative rights, and to designate a distance within which they may be exercised.

The Egyptian Government replied that "from a legal point of view," it has no hesitancy in accepting the distance of three miles, with the reservations laid down in Article II of the Amended Draft, for the extent of Egyptian "territorial waters" was fixed at that distance by the Decree—Law of April 21, 1926, as regards fishing and

[49] By a law of October 26, 1909, foreign vessels are prohibited from fishing within three nautical miles of the shore. *Brit. and Forn. State Papers*, vol. 102, p. 788. By a law of June 5, 1914, however, the limit of Portuguese territorial waters, especially for fishing purposes, was defined, as regards foreign fishermen, by the line which, for similar purposes, has been adopted by the legislation of the country of which the fishermen claim nationality. Hertslet, *Commercial Treaties* (1922), vol. 28, p. 1040.

[50] *League of Nations Documents* C. 196. M. 70. 1927. V, pp. 257, 157, 162, 129, 166, 153, and 148.

sponge-fishing, except in the Bay of El-Arab, the whole of which is included in the territorial sea, while the extent of "the Customs surveillance zone is at present ten kilometers," and according to Article II of the Amended Draft, States may exercise administrative rights beyond the zone of sovereignty. It was said that the expression "administrative rights" is somewhat vague, and that it should be made clear beyond any doubt that it covers at least customs supervision.

Estonia replied that the Amended Draft "appears . . . to be deserving of Estonia's adhesion." It was suggested, however, that "a precise definition" of the zone in which States may exercise administrative rights should be given, and that it would be "preferable to try to reach an agreement . . . on the basis of the farthest line up to which any particular State has hitherto exercised a special right." It was proposed that this limit should be fixed at twelve miles, "which from the Customs point of view corresponds to the laws at present in force in Estonia."

The Finnish Government replied that Finland and many other countries consider the prevention of the illicit importation of alcoholic beverages from sea as a matter of great importance in connection with regulating the question of territorial waters, and that such prevention requires "rules of conduct universally observed and measures of supervision and repression taken by common agreement." For practical reasons, it was observed that it seems "essential to admit the possibility of several maritime zones of diverse legal character," but whether the "designation 'territorial waters' should be reserved for the zone 'within which the powers of the coastal State are most complete,' or whether it should be used to indicate all zones, which, owing to a particular interest or a special function or competence have a different legal character from the 'open sea' ('free sea')," is of secondary importance, though it is necessary to distinguish between "territorial waters proper, which constitute a sort of annex to the dry land, and which are consequently considered as subject to the sovereignty of the coastal State, and the outer zones in which the State can only exercise strictly limited functions," and to which "sovereignty" cannot be applied. "On these conditions," it was said that "the zone of three nautical miles may usefully be recognized as the 'zone of sovereignty' provided no exceptions to this rule are admitted other than those already stipulated in the preliminary draft," while "the extent of the other zones depends on special circumstances."

Germany replied that she favored three nautical miles as the extent of the territorial sea, beyond which administrative zones may be established in which a country may exercise customs control and supervise shipping, but that it would seem necessary to "define the grounds on which such administrative zones may be demanded, and the extent of the zones, instead of making the exercise of administrative rights depend, in a general fashion, on custom or an essential need." Supervisory services intended "to protect navigation, such as pilotage or buoyage services, or services for the clearing of obstacles," should be demanded by the State, and they should be permitted to operate outside the administrative zone "to the same extent as heretofore." It was added that it would be desirable to state expressly that in future, apart from existing customs and conventions, fishery rights may not extend beyond three nautical miles.[51]

[51] In *The Elida* (Entscheidungen des Oberpreisengerichts, vol. 9; 10 *American Journal of International Law*, p. 918), the German prize court held that an enemy vessel taken between three and four miles off the coast of Sweden was a good prize. The Swedish Government protested against this seizure as having been made in her territorial waters.

Under German Prize Regulations of September 30, 1909, the right of capture was not to be exercised within territorial waters, i.e., within 3

The Greek Government considered that the question "whether the territorial sea does or does not form part of the territory of the State seems to be a purely doctrinal point on which it would be difficult to reach an agreement in view of the divergent opinions held by various jurisconsults," and that it would be preferable "merely to define as clearly as possible the rights and duties of the riparian State within the limits of its territorial waters." It was added that Greece adopts a zone of three miles as regards the extent of the territorial sea, and that while this zone should be extended for the exercise of "rights arising out of security and Customs and health supervision," a maximum limit should be fixed for their exercise; a zone of ten miles is suggested. A limit also should be fixed for the exercise of fishery rights, and the distance of six miles suggested by the 1898 Fishery Congress is proposed.[52]

The Spanish Goverment observed that Article II of the Amended Draft, fixing the area of the territorial sea at three marine miles, is "contrary to Spanish law," which has adopted "the unwritten principle that territorial waters shall extend for six miles (or 11,111 meters) from the extreme seaward limit of the coast-line or from low-water mark." This rule has been derogated from only once by the Royal Decree of November 23, 1914, which

---

nautical miles from the coast line at low-water. *Brit. and Forn. State Papers,* vol. 108, p. 832.

By a proclamation of February 4, 1915, the waters surrounding Great Britain and Ireland, including the English Channel, were declared to be "war zone," in which any neutral ship was declared to be exposed to danger. N. W. C., 1917, p. 106. On March 23, 1917, the German Ambassador notified the American Secretary of State that foreign governments had been informed that in the Northern Arctic Ocean east of the 24th degree of eastern longitude and south of the 75th degree of north latitude, with the exception of Norwegian territorial waters, all ocean traffic would be opposed with arms. Ibid., p. 115.

[52] In 1914, Greece fixed six marine miles as the extent of her neutral zone. *Brit. and Forn. State Papers,* vol. 108, p. 821.

laid down that "for the purpose of Spain's neutrality in the European war, neutral Spanish waters shall be those included between the water line and an imaginary line drawn parallel to the latter three miles out at sea." [53] Attention was called to the recent "rum treaties" between the United States and several European powers, by which "the normal limit of the territorial sea has been fixed at three miles," [54] and it was added that "this proposal might therefore be accepted as a general and final solution of the much discussed problem of the territorial sea, and it is a solution that merits the consideration of the Spanish Government." [55]

The Cuban Government replied that there would be "no difficulty . . . in principle, in preparing a convention on territorial waters," though "the special usages and requirements of America must, of course, be taken into account." As to the final sentence of Article II, it was said that provision should be made for "rights of eco-

[53] The Spanish Minister of State notified the Embassy of the United States on February 28, 1924, that after the disappearance of the causes that brought about this Decree, in which Spain accepted provisionally until the termination of the war and only as regards neutrality a reduction of her territorial waters to three miles, its jurisdiction over such waters extended to six miles, in conformity with the usual Spanish practice. Under a Royal Decree of June 20, 1852, relating to jurisdiction to suppress smuggling, the crime of contraband is constituted by the running of vessels of less than a certain tonnage, carrying prohibited goods, into an unauthorized port, or bay, inlet, or cove, and by their sailing within two leagues along the coast in the vicinity of such places. *Coleccion Legislativa de España* (1852), vol. 56, p. 194, Art. 18, par. 10. See, also, the memorandum of M. Schücking, p. 7.

For diplomatic discussions in regard to Spain's claim of six miles for all purposes, see pp. 257 and 265, *supra*.

[54] These treaties do not fix the limit at three miles, but the parties declare that it is their "firm intention to uphold the principle that three marine miles . . . constitute the proper limits of territorial waters." See pp. 346 and 352, *supra*.

[55] The reply seems to indicate that since the Spanish law takes jurisdiction for six miles as regards fisheries, neutrality, and customs, and since, under the Amended Draft, the protection of these interests is not confined to the three-mile zone of sovereignty, the Spanish Government is willing to agree to three miles as the extent of the "coastal sea."

nomic jurisdiction which have their source and origin in the coast or territorial sea" and which "are often exercised far beyond the zone of sovereignty."

Roumania and Brazil favor only one zone for all purposes.

In the opinion of the Roumanian Government,[56] the nature of the right in the "territorial sea" is that of "sovereignty," and that only one zone should be provided for, which it would fix at "three nautical miles," though it recognizes that it has been fixed at various distances by the different States. It considers that the rights whose exercise is permitted under Article II beyond the zone of coastal waters are vaguely designated, for almost any right may be regarded as "an administrative right or as being of vital necessity."

The Brazilian Government replied[57] that it would be highly desirable to fix a zone of the "jurisdictional sea by international agreement in such a way that states might, without conflict of sovereignty, supervise and police this area for the maintenance of order, the punishment of crime, the regulation of fishing, the prevention of contraband and the establishment of such general rules as may be deemed necessary for navigation and commerce, without prejudice to the rights of international trade." This Government would extend the breadth of the territorial sea beyond three miles, and, thus, avoid the necessity of admitting that a State may "exercise administrative rights outside its territorial waters."[58]

The Governments of the British Empire, Denmark, India, the Irish Free State, Japan, and New Zealand

---

[56] *League of Nations Documents* C. 196. M. 70. 1927. V, p. 198.

[57] Ibid., p. 143.

[58] In 1914, the Brazilian Government issued rules of neutrality, by which it was declared that any act of war, including capture, in "territorial waters," constitutes a violation of the sovereignty of the Republic. N. W. C., 1916, p. 10.

consider the Amended Draft a useful basis for discussion;
no reference is made to Articles I and II.[59]

The reply of Denmark stated that the Minister of

[59] *League of Nations Documents* C. 196. M. 70. 1927. V, pp. 145, 150,
168, 170, 171, and 260.

See pp. 1 to 162, *supra,* for the development of the English hovering
laws, which have taken jurisdiction for various distances ranging from
one to one hundred leagues, at different periods of history.

In 1864, the British Government expressed the opinion that vessels
engaged in hostilities should not fire towards a neutral shore at a less
distance than that which would insure shot not falling in neutral waters
or territory. Mr. Seward to the British Minister, U. S. *Dip. Correspondence,* 1864, Part 2, p. 708.

The preamble to the *British Territorial Waters Jurisdiction Act,* 1878,
41-42 Vict., c. 73, p. 579, which is now in force, declares that "the rightful jurisdiction of Her Majesty, . . . extends and has always extended
over the open sea adjacent to the coasts of the United Kingdom and
of all other parts of Her Majesty's dominions, to such a distance as is
necessary for the defence and security of such dominions." Lord
Halsbury, who passed this bill through the House of Commons, remarked in 1895 that the Act took care to avoid any measurement, but
that the distance was left at such limit as was "necessary for the defence
of the Realm," and then the exact limit was given for the particular
purpose in view, namely, jurisdiction was given the Admiralty over
any offense committed on board or by means of a foreign vessel within
territorial waters, and for the purposes of the Act, such waters were
declared to extend one marine league. *Parl. Debates,* 1895, 4th series,
vol. 33, col. 504. See, also, ibid., for the remarks of the Lord Chancellor.

This discussion arose in connection with the *Sea Fisheries Regulation
(Scotland) Bill,* passed in 1895, clause 10 of which gave the Fishery
Board power to prohibit certain kinds of fishing for thirteen miles off
certain parts of the Scottish coast.

During the late war, the British Prize courts held that enemy vessels
taken beyond three miles from neutral coasts were good prizes. See,
for example, *The Bangor* (1916), Probate 181; *The Dusseldorf* (1919),
ibid., p. 245; *The Valeria* (1920), ibid., p. 81. For an excellent discussion of these cases, see Colombos, C. John, *A Treatise on the Law of
Prize* (1926). According to J. A. Hall, Lecturer on International Law
to Admiral's Secretaries Course, Portsmouth, however, during the same
war, the British Government instructed British warships "to respect the
six miles claimed by Italy," but that this was an act of courtesy and
is not to be regarded as accepting a principle. *The Law of Naval
Warfare* (1921), p. 130.

See N. W. C. 1917, p. 133, for a notification by the British Government that large mined areas in the North Sea would be rendered dangerous to all shipping by operations against her enemies, and should,
therefore, be avoided.

Finance had raised the question of "the possibility, under special conventions for the suppression of contraband and alcoholic substances, of extending the area of territorial waters."

The Japanese Government added that it could not approve the Amended Draft in certain points, though those points were not named.

The replies of Venezuela, Salvador, and the Kingdom of the Serbs, Croats, and Slovenes [60] do not refer specially to the Amended Draft, but state that the regulation, or codification of the question is desirable or ripe for consideration. The United States Government replied [61] that an arrangement on the general subject would be desirable, and that there would be no insuperable obstacles to the concluding of such an arrangement, but that it was not prepared to state if it would be desirable or possible to regulate all points until it had had an opportunity to make a more extensive study of them. [62]

Among the Governments whose replies had not been received on April 2, 1927, when the Committee reported to the Council on the questions which appear ripe for

[60] *League of Nations Documents* C. 196. M. 70. 1927. V, p. 225.

[61] Ibid., 160.

[62] For the customs laws of the United States, taking jurisdiction for four leagues, see p. 228, et seq., *supra.*

In 1886, the Secretary of State wrote the Secretary of the Treasury that in target practice or warfare, when projectiles might fall on neutral land, vessels should move farther from land than cannon range, as was insisted by France in 1864, in the *Kearsage-Alabama* incident. It was also said that the State, "on the principle of self-defence," might "pursue and punish marauders on the sea to the very extent to which their guns would carry their shot; and that each sovereign has jurisdiction over crimes committed by them through such shot, although at the time of their shooting, they were beyond three miles from the shore." 160 *MS. Dom. Let.*, p. 352. This discussion arose over the fisheries question.

The U. S. Naval War Code of 1900 provides that the territorial waters of a State extend to the distance of a marine league from low-water mark. N.W.C., 1903, p. 18.

See p. 375, note (1), *supra,* for the view of the representative of the United States before the Behring Sea Arbitration in 1893.

international regulation, are Argentine, Chili, Ecuador, Uruguay, and Guatemala. Argentine and Chili take jurisdiction for four leagues for customs purposes,[63] and Ecuador claims the same distance as the extent of her territorial waters.[64]

Austria and Switzerland, not being maritime powers, refrained from expressing opinions, and Turkey replied that it desired only to "follow the course of the work"

[63] Article 2374 of the Civil Code of Argentina provides that the public property of the general State or of the individual states includes the seas adjacent to the territory of the Republic to a distance of one marine league, measured from the lowest tide line, but the right of police in matters pertaining to the security of the country and the observance of the fiscal laws extends to a distance of four marine leagues measured in the same manner. Under the declaration of neutrality of August 5, 1914, it was declared that "the rules of law and the manner of procedure set forth in the Convention relative to the rights and duties of neutral powers signed at The Hague October 18, 1907," would be followed. N.W.C., 1916, p. 9.

Article 593 of the Civil Code of Chili of December 14, 1855, provides that the adjacent sea for a distance of one marine league, measured from the low-water mark line, is territorial sea and belongs to the national domain, but that the right of police in matters pertaining to the security of the country and the observation of the fiscal laws extends to the distance of four marine leagues measured in the same manner.

On November 5, 1914, a zone of three marine miles, measured in the same way, was fixed as "the jurisdictional or neutral sea" for the "safeguarding of the rights and the accomplishments of the duties relative to . . . neutrality . . . ." N.W.C., 1916, p. 19.

[64] By a Decree of Ecuador of November 19, 1914, relating to neutrality during the late war, every vessel found sailing in Ecuadorian territorial waters, which, according to Article 582 of the Civil Code, extend for four naval leagues of 5,555 meters each from the shore, was subjected to inspection of papers; warships were forbidden to make preparations for warlike operations or exercise vigilance over enemy vessels, and merchant vessels were prohibited from using their wireless telegraph in such waters. *Brit. and Forn. State Papers,* vol. 108, p. 818.

By a Presidential Decree of August 7, 1914, it was declared that in case of war, when Uruguay is a neutral, territorial waters are to be considered to extend to a distance of five miles from the coast, in accordance with the principle established by the treaty of Montevideo (Penal Law, Article 12) and the principles generally accepted in such matters. Belligerent ships were forbidden to remain in territorial waters for over 72 hours. *Brit. and Forn. State Papers,* vol. 108, p. 856; N.W.C., 1916, p. 106.

of codification.[65] Czechoslovakia replied [66] that it had no
direct or immediate interest in the solution of the questions because it was not a marine power, but that it had
a general interest from its desire to see international relations regulated.[67]

(3) *Procedure*

These replies of the Governments, together with the
treaties and municipal laws and regulations of the various
maritime states, indicate, as already noted, that, while
considerable difficulty would be encountered in securing
a general agreement upon the extent of territorial waters
or a zone of sovereignty, practically all the nations are
prepared to agree that jurisdiction may be taken beyond
these waters for the purpose of securing the fiscal interests of the state, as well as certain other interests.[68]

[65] *League of Nations Documents* C. 196. M. 70. 1927. V, pp. 137,
240, and 260.

[66] Ibid., p. 253.

[67] It was suggested that the questions of territorial waters, piracy,
and exploration of the products of the sea should be undertaken from
"a more general point of view" and dealt with in a general convention,
"a sort of Convention on Maritime Laws and Usages."

[68] These observations are pertinent as suggesting a new approach to
the solution of the general question of territorial waters. Since the
nations are prepared to come to an agreement upon certain phases of
the question, it would seem that an endeavor should be made to find
separate solutions of the various interests, such as fisheries, neutrality,
and revenue, as distinct problems. This would, of course, require
extensive investigation and research. The usual method of approaching
the question by fixing in miles, at the outset, a uniform zone of
"territorial waters," "sovereignty," or "sovereign rights," offers many
difficulties. In the first place, this is the phase of the question upon
which an agreement could probably not be secured. In the second
place, there seems to be no reason why "territorial waters," "sovereign
rights," or "sovereignty" should be employed to define the status
of the waters near the coast. The relationship of the State to this strip
is certainly not the same relationship that it bears to its land, or
territory; it is a special relationship, for the State is only interested in
securing to itself certain advantages, or interests in these waters, and
the State has only jurisdiction, or power, to legislate for the special
purpose of securing these advantages, or interests, and this power, or
jurisdiction, is not as broad as it is on land. Furthermore, the obliga-

Whether this special jurisdiction should be dealt with in a separate convention or in a general convention on territorial waters is a question of procedure. If it is dealt with in a separate convention, embodying some such provisions as are found in the rum treaties between the United States and other powers or the Baltic Convention of 1925 for the suppression of contraband liquors, it is believed that most States will adhere to it. If it is dealt with in a general convention, the convention should be so drawn as to permit a State to accede to the provisions relating to this special jurisdiction, in case it should refuse to accede to other provisions of the convention. In either case, at least this phase of the more general question of territorial waters would be definitely disposed of.

tions of a State within the adjacent waters are not as broad as its obligations on land. These considerations point to the fact that this relationship is not one of sovereignty or territory.

LIST OF STATUTES

ENGLISH

ENGLISH—Continued

AMERICAN

AMERICAN—*Continued*